Haunted Heart

# A BIOGRAPHY OF
## SUSANNAH MCCORKLE

*by Linda Dahl*

THE UNIVERSITY OF MICHIGAN PRESS

*Ann Arbor*

First paperback edition 2008
Copyright © 2006 by Linda Dahl
All rights reserved
Published in the United States of America by
The University of Michigan Press
Manufactured in the United States of America
⊗ Printed on acid-free paper

2011   2010   2009   2008       5   4   3   2

*A CIP catalog record for this book is available from the British Library.*

Library of Congress Cataloging-in-Publication Data

Dahl, Linda, 1949–
    Haunted heart : a biography of Susannah McCorkle / by Linda Dahl.
        p.      cm.
    Includes bibliographical references and discography.
    ISBN-13: 978-0-472-11564-8 (cloth : alk. paper)
    ISBN-10: 0-472-11564-2 (cloth : alk. paper)
        1. McCorkle, Susannah.    2. Singers—United States—Biography.
    I. Title.
    ML420.M34118D34      2006
    782.42165092—dc22                                                    2006008016

ISBN-13: 978-0-472-03273-0 (pbk. : alk. paper)
ISBN-10: 0-472-03273-9 (pbk. : alk paper)
                                            0

Frontispiece: Susannah in a signature sparkly dress at her anchor gig,
the Oak Room at the Algonquin Hotel, in the late nineties, with Steve Gilmore
on bass (and Allen Farnham on piano, not shown). (Photo by Carlos Spaventa)
Cover photograph: Rahav Segev/Photopass.com © 1999-2006; Susannah McCorkle
performing at The Algonquin Oak Room, June 25, 1999.

# Contents

Thank God for the singers
who follow in the path of Mabel Mercer.
Susannah McCorkle is in the forefront.

—Tony Bennett,
liner notes to *Dream,* 1986

# *Acknowledgments*

In a very real sense, writing a biography is a collaborative effort, and many people helped me with *Haunted Heart*. (A beautiful ballad written in 1938 by Arthur Schwartz, with lyrics by Howard Dietz, "Haunted Heart" was an ideal song for Susannah McCorkle, a deeply romantic song shimmering with regret for lost love.[1]) Susannah McCorkle was a complex woman, inspiring in others complex responses and deep emotions. Almost everyone who knew her—her small number of intimates, her circles of friends and acquaintances and musical partners—gave willingly of their time and memories. It cannot have been easy to talk about this gifted romantic who had but recently, and tragically, died.

I wish to thank especially journalist Thea Lurie, Susannah's close friend of many years, for sharing her memories of Susannah, as well as many letters, Susannah's memoir in progress, and other writings and photographs. Pianist Keith Ingham, Susannah's second husband and her first longtime musical partner, was unflinchingly honest about both their musical and personal relationship during Susannah's first years as a jazz singer in London in the 1970s and then in New York into the early 1980s. Susannah's third husband, journalist Dan DiNicola, opened his home (once also Susannah's) in Schenectady and gave me many hours of his time, as did his sons Roy and Jeff and their families. Thea, Keith, and Dan led me to other valuable sources—Susannah's friends, lovers, professional associates, therapists, and fellow performers. In Berkeley, Susannah's mother, the late Mimi McCorkle, invited me into her home for a long weekend of talk and allowed me free access to files containing a lifetime's worth of memorabilia about the McCorkles, the Savages, and the Manchesters, Susannah's forebears, and decades of letters saved from Susannah. Susannah's younger sister Maggie was likewise generous in her sharing. Roy Schecter, who followed Susannah's career in New York, gave me copies of audio- and videotapes from many live performances, club dates, radio broadcasts, and television appearances in the 1980s and 1990s and many helpful factual and critical tips. Writer Rex Reed, who knew Susannah for more than a quarter-century, shared a long November afternoon with me by a crackling fire in his country farmhouse. The composer, pianist, and singer Sir Richard Rodney Bennett, who also went way back with Susannah, offered his own brand of insight over a long lunch. And writer Jim Gavin, who befriended Susannah in the 1990s, met with me in his cozy New York flat, and lent me more tapes of Susannah in performance. Susannah's friends Ellen Bollinger and Diane Feldman, Gary Gates and David Alpern, and one-time Algonquin Oak Room manager Arthur Pomposello met with me at other tables, other lunches. Jackie and Hubert Osteen, connoisseurs of singers who befriended Susannah when she was a beloved regular performer at the Algonquin, opened their hearts and their lovely South Carolina home to me, as did Susannah's very close friend, the talented performer Mark Nadler, in Riverdale. Brad Kay and Eric Olson were particularly insightful about Susannah's personality. Her biofeedback therapist, Stephen Kahan, who was, with Thea Lurie, Susannah's closest confidant at the end of her life, shared openly with me about the difficult last months of her life.

I had dozens of other insightful conversations with many generous people, including detractors, whose criticisms provided a healthy counterweight. Susannah McCorkle knew so many talented people. To all of them, I owe a debt of gratitude. Each knows what Susannah meant to them, and they to her. Thank you all. It was a pleasure to meet you.

In *Haunted Heart,* I have quoted from those conversations, sometimes extensively, often in brief. I would like to acknowledge and thank each person for these remembrances. If I have left anyone out, I apologize for the inadvertent omission. In alphabetical order, they are

David Alpern, Frances Bendixson, Richard Rodney Bennett,
Paul and Julie Ben-Susan, Pam Berlin, Ellen Mullins Bollinger,
Joe Boughton, Kathrin Brigl, Lana Cantrell, Jon Carroll, John
Chilton, Michael Colby, Paul Conley, Dick Corten, Robert
Cushman, Francis Davis, Lee Davis, Rich DeRosa, Anne
DiNicola, Dan DiNicola, Jeff DiNicola, Holly DiNicola,
Kim DiNicola, Roy DiNicola, Dr. Ronald Dushkin, Chris Ellis,

Digby Fairweather, Allen Farnham, Diane Mich Feldman, Linda Fennimore, David Finck, Angela Forti-Lewis, Carol Fredette, Will Friedwald, Lynn Gambles, Gary Gates, Phyllis Gates, Jim Gavin, Steve Gilmore, Josiah Gluck, Art Goldberg, Jane Goldberg, Dick Golden, Peter Haas, David Hadju, Dr. Robert Harman, Gail Hochman, Tim Horner, Keith Ingham, Bob Jones, Stephen Kahan, Brad Kay, Robert Kimball, Peter Keepnews, Amos Korn, Barbara Lea, Andy Lipman, David Lubarsky, Tom Luddy, Thea Lurie, Christine MacDonald, Dr. Christine Macmillan, Donna Marshall, Nancy McGraw, Barbara McGurn, Rick McKay, Marian McPartland, Susan Monserud, Daniel Moran, Dan Morgenstern, Bill Moring, Mark Nadler, Dick Oatts, Karen Oberlin, Eric Olson, Hubert Osteen, Jackie Osteen, Ken Peplowski, Diana Lang Philips, Nick Philips, Ken Pitt, Arthur Pomposello, Lisa Dawn Popa, Rex Reed, Phyllis Rosser, Lorraine Ruggieri, Roy Schecter, Siegfried Schmidt-Joos, Daryl Sherman, Joel L. Siegel, Barbara Singer, Theodora Skipitares, Carol Sloane, Donald Smith, Sean Smith, Jose Carlos Solimeo, Janet Sommer, Ric Sonder, Carlos Spaventa, Richard Sudhalter, K. T. Sullivan, Roberta Todras, Pat White.

Although a writer always needs a room of her own, she also needs a lot of support. I'd like to thank Peggy Day for her helpful legal advice and Matthew Budman for fine-tuning the manuscript. I am, as ever, deeply grateful to Susan Zeckendorf, my friend and literary agent, and especially to my family for their patient encouragement and good humor while I "ran another marathon." Thanks, Katrina, thanks Tim. Lastly I want to thank A. J. Vogl, editor extraordinaire, who never lets the fact that we're married interfere with his red pencil, and Chris Hebert, my editor at the University of Michigan Press, for having faith in this book and giving it a home. The final responsibility for *Haunted Heart* is, of course, my own.

# Skylark

The truth is rarely pure and never simple.
—Oscar Wilde

So she took this really interesting right turn and
reinvented herself.
—Jon Carroll

It was a warm June afternoon in the year 2001 when I entered the back of St. Peter's, New York's "jazz church," in midtown Manhattan, for a memorial service in tribute to Susannah McCorkle. The pews were filled to capacity. It was only a month after her unexpected death, and emotions were still raw. I hadn't known Susannah personally, but I knew her music and I knew she was a presence on the jazz scene, in both clubs and cabaret rooms. She had seemed to burst out of nowhere when she arrived in New York in the late 1970s, an unabashedly romantic vocalist who chose songs from the so-called Great American Songbook, by Irving Berlin, Cole Porter, the Gershwins, and from slightly lesser-known lights such as Johnny Mercer, way before most other singers of her generation "discovered" this material. But Susannah was not interested in nostalgia for its own sake. She avidly collected new songs as well, by more contemporary songwriters such as Dave Frishberg, Blossom Dearie, and Rupert Holmes. Few people in New York knew then that she had already been singing for a number of years in England, where she won admiration and several awards for her first records. New York was, of course, a tougher proving ground, but there was a lot of buzz about her in the jazz community. She had a magnificent figure, an actress's chameleon beauty, and a brilliant way of putting over a lyric. Even as she toiled for gigs and reviews and recordings, Susannah soon won a raft of impressive admirers to her singing style: fellow singers like

Joe Williams and Tony Bennett and composers like Alec Wilder, Harry Warren, and Yip Harburg. Says club owner Amos Korn, who ran the noted jazz club Gulliver's for many years, "More than any other singer I've ever heard, she had a narrative ability."

All these years later, I discovered that Susannah and I had had certain things in common. We'd fallen in love with jazz in the same year, 1969. We had made the move to New York about the same time, where we'd paid our artist dues in cramped apartments in questionable neighborhoods. We had hung out at some of the same jazz clubs. We had even supported ourselves the same way—as translators—and each of us had learned Portuguese after we heard bossa nova. And one more thing. We had both had difficult battles with our dark side. The more I heard Susannah in the last part of the last century, the more I liked what I heard: a velvety, deeply sensitive voice, great phrasing, a writer's sense of the arc of the story in the song. It was no surprise to learn that Susannah was a gifted linguist and a writer before she became a singer. At the University of California at Berkeley in the 1960s, her prize-winning short stories and social satire in the college humor magazine led admirers to predict she'd become the next Dorothy Parker or Alice Adams. In her twenties, she won an O. Henry Award, and in her thirties, fellowships to MacDowell and Yaddo, the prestigious artists' colonies. And she continued to write—song lyrics, stories, articles, a memoir—all her life. But in her early twenties, Susannah's life took a 180-degree turn. She was living in Paris then. One day, she visited an American friend who wanted to become a professional singer. She put on a Billie Holiday record for Susannah to hear, and that was it. Susannah, not the friend, became the jazz singer.

In the 1970s, few female singers were singing many of the standards from the American songbook. Stars like Sarah Vaughan and Carmen McRae and Tony Bennett and Ella Fitzgerald did, but even they were pressured to "branch out" and sing pop tunes as well. Other vocalists like Teddi King, Irene Kral, Jackie Cain (of Jackie & Roy), Barbara Lea, Lorez Alexandria, Shirley Horn, and Carol Sloane also sang standards, but to smaller audiences. Among the baby-boomers, Susannah's generation, a few singers like Daryl Sherman and Carol Fredette kept the tradition alive, but the old songs were not "in" again yet, and many of the younger singers either ignored them, or were ignorant of them. Still other singers opted for experimentation, for stretching the possibilities of scat singing—"blowing" like a horn, bending the voice wordlessly as an improvising instrument. But Susannah didn't scat and wasn't cutting-edge in her message, like Betty Carter and Abbey Lincoln and Sheila Jordan in their very individual ways. These things counted against her, limiting her audience and the club work she got. Nevertheless, Susannah was growing her own audience all the while, particularly as her own generation matured. She was not, however, easy to categorize. Many cabaret folk thought she was jazz, and a lot of jazz lovers thought she was cabaret—and if the twain does meet, it seldom develops into a meaningful relationship.

By the nineties, Susannah, who seemed to defy middle age without resorting to artificial aids, had worked hard on her image and it paid off: Onstage she was more chic, slimmer and toned. And many thought she was a better singer than ever. She had a loyal and literate following who loved her reclamation of forgotten, even lost tunes. She unearthed new-old lyrics, as in the rarely heard second chorus of "It Never Entered My Mind": "Once you said in your funny lingo / I'd play bingo every night / and never get the numbers right" and did the same for "Let's Do It (Let's Fall in Love)." She was also a bull's-eye re-interpreter, turning "If I Only Had a Heart" from a chipper ditty into a lament, making "Let's Face the Music and Dance" into a moody bossa nova, transforming the razzle-dazzle of "There's No Business Like Show Business" into a mournful plaint, explaining that Irving Berlin had probably written the song to "urge himself up out of one of his many stretches of despair." She turned "Thanks for the Memory," a jauntily wistful Bob Hope–Shirley Ross anthem, into a darkly bittersweet farewell. The heartbreak in her voice was genuine, and there were often real tears in Susannah's eyes when she sang. She was known to cry when a song fit a poignant occasion—a friend's pending divorce, her parents' wedding anniversary.

Her fans have their favorites, of course. Critic Rex Reed's was "Me and the Blues," a song from the out-of-print collection of Harry Warren songs on her very first solo album. He said, "She sung it pure and straight and sad: 'I'm going down to the river . . .'" Bob Jones, a popular radio host in the seventies and eighties, was crazy about another Harry Warren song, "A Quarter to Nine," and Dan DiNicola, her former husband, loved her version of Irving Berlin's "Waiting at the End of the Road." But the song that became most closely associated with her was Brazilian Antonio Carlos Jobim's "Os Aguas de Março," "The Waters of March" in English, a meditative song celebrating the end of winter and the coming of spring—of new life. For Susannah, there was a deeply personal subtext in the song. If some of her audience sensed this, no one knew just how cold was the winter of her depression, how deeply she longed for the "spring" of hope.

Her struggle to realize herself was professional as well as personal. Though she called herself a jazz singer at times, she was more apt to describe herself as a pop-jazz singer, a jazz-pop singer, or an interpretive singer. Toward the end of her life, she told an interviewer rather wearily that she was "a singer of standards with a jazz backing. And I have always surrounded myself with good jazz musicians." One thing she was not, she declared, was a cabaret singer. Not for her was what she decried as the controlled, packaged emotion of that genre—its "preciousness," as she termed it; after all, she'd been inspired to sing by no less than Billie Holiday, the masterful, swinging distiller of the emotional moment, the honest "now." Paradoxically, however, as much as she lauded jazz, Susannah exerted as much control over every element of her performance as a cabaret veteran. Added to which, her most prized performances took place at the Oak Room of the Algonquin Hotel, the ultimate cabaret room. It will come as no surprise, then, that jazz musicians and the jazz community as a whole are divided about the success of Susannah's venture as a jazz-based singer.

On that June day in the jazz church when so many had gathered to remember Susannah, grief was heavy in the air; an undercurrent of sorrow and a sense of betrayal further weighted the atmosphere. Suicide was the invisible elephant in the airy sanctuary. That Susannah had died by her own hand was a catastrophe, a great shock. When she was alive, Susannah did not hide from her intimates that she had her ups and downs, her disappointments and lost loves. She'd survived cancer, divorce, all kinds of career disappointments along with the prizes and the good reviews. But Susannah had a way of celebrating life as only a survivor can savor it. She'd fashioned her vocal programs in later years around the lessons life had taught her. Her friends all mention the glow she had, her lighthearted, funny side, her fast mind. She was known as a healthy, disciplined woman. She wasn't into drugs and she drank alcohol moderately; she ate health food, never smoked; she exercised regularly and dieted religiously for decades. She had an old-fashioned sense of high style, a lacquered presence with her public. But she had ended it all in the middle of one terrible night by jumping out the high window of her Manhattan apartment, shattering the smooth, put-together persona with that final tragic action.

As I listened to her friends and family pay tribute to Susannah, I sensed that the explanation for Susannah McCorkle's suicide would not be a straightforward one. There was a complexity about her life, layer upon layer enfolding and defining yet at the same time obscuring her, that I found compelling. Susannah, it seemed, kept friends and lovers in careful compartments, kept aspects of her life and work from ever touching.

Whatever her success—the good reviews, the two dozen CDs to her name, her annual sinecures at the Algonquin—Susannah inevitably won greater attention with her death than she had in life. And with the attention came the scrutiny, all the questions. Who was this woman of such disparate parts? How had it happened that her accomplishments, her triumphs, her grit, had not saved her from such a tragic end? How could this gifted singer who was at the top of her game have decided to throw herself out of her 16th-floor window in the dead of night? For me, Susannah's complex life, her art, and her tragic ending begged to be written about.

In retrospect, as I learned more about Susannah's childhood and about the bipolar disorder that ran like a terrible red thread through her family, it became clear that hers was a preordained death, that it was probably unavoidable. Not even her therapists understood how far she had descended. For among Susannah's many gifts was a talent not just for a convincing performance but for cloaking her panic and despair. Almost all of the time. There were clues, of course, about her tumultuous internal struggles. But they were not easy to find. Said one of her last lovers, Daniel Moran, "Her public image was terribly impor-tant to her—every bit of that image. And it was all different from the private. Her emotional self wasn't sane—it was unpredictable and bizarre." Concurs Rex Reed, who knew Susannah for several decades, "Susannah was really two people. One was brave, courageous, self-made, brilliant, who slaved for perfection. The other Susannah was a recluse who resorted to e-mailing her friends because she was so depressed she didn't feel worthy of their loyalty and love."

By the spring of 2001, it seemed on the surface that Susannah was moving into a new chapter in her career. After several rewarding expe-riences, she was thinking seriously about embarking on a career as a music therapist. She was nearly done completing a memoir about her coming of age after leaving America to live in Mexico City and then Paris and Rome and London in the late 1960s and 1970s; the time when she had discovered her true vocation as a jazz singer. That spring, there were other good things in Susannah's life. She had had a bout with breast cancer ten years before; now she was declared cancer-free. She had a small but affordable apartment in Manhattan, some savings, and a network of good friends and admirers. She was still attractive and chic. Yet from Susannah's point of view, things were falling apart utterly. In the spring of 2001, she lost her contract with her recording company, her best gig at the Oak Room in the Algonquin Hotel was canceled, she fought with her mother, she was struggling with menopause. Above all, she was no longer taking any prescription medication to treat her bipolar disorder and she was not singing. Which was worse? Without medication, she could not climb out of a worsening depression. But without singing, "Skylark"—her internet moniker, her secret name—seemed to lose her connection to the world. She couldn't even bear, she wrote, to listen to music anymore.

Famously well-mannered with the outside world, Susannah kept the white gloves on to the end. Before she enacted her dreadful decision to jump, she made sure that, true to form, all would be neat and tidy. Her apartment was clean, files put away and organized, cats fed, plants watered. For weeks, she had been making a disguised farewell by letter, phone, and e-mail to her friends. She had legalized her will and paid her bills and returned her library books. She even wrote a letter to return an advance against a future performance at a midwestern college later in the year. But she did not open the new prescription of antidepressants she'd just picked up at the pharmacy. She left the sealed bottle in her medicine cabinet.

*Haunted Heart* is about the hidden pathways of Susannah's inner struggles, the twists and turns of her nature that mixed sunshine and shadow to such a confounding degree. It is about the triumphs and accomplishments of an extremely smart, extremely sensitive artist who earned her place among a small and select group of singers who make art out of popular music. It is about an incurable romantic who had three divorces and a string of failed love affairs. Above all, it is about an artist who worked with incredible intensity, tenacity, and intelligence to develop her own voice. She was a combination of Dorothy Parker and Doris Day, Sylvia Plath and Sylvia Sims, a fascinating blend of toughness and innocence, chiseled wit and girlish wonder. She married romantic lyricism to a modern, edgy sophistication. Above all, Susannah found the emotional core of so many lovely songs. The fall she took not only shattered Susannah literally, but also shattered the illusions of those who knew her, who never knew the extent of her demons. The odds she was up against became apparent only after her death.

# 1946–1963

# Careless Love

I think my mom decided from the start to be her own person and hang the rest. My parents didn't want to think of themselves as responsible adults, much less parents.
—Maggie McCorkle

One could say of Susannah McCorkle that she was a girl who seemed to have everything. Brains—she was a prize-winning short-story writer, an accomplished linguist, and an exquisite interpreter of the lyrics to a song. Beauty, the kind that radiates from within, and the kind that can be cultivated and tweaked and managed, so that even at the end of her life, she could cut a stunning figure. Talent—she had not only an eye for great songs but a voice that brought them to life. And true grit—how many 23-year-olds, without musical training, would aspire to emulate Billie Holiday, and then come close to realizing that dream? How many would persist?

What she lacked was faith in herself, the confidence that carries one from the last defeat to the next victory. But this was not ordinary failure of nerve: It was something deeper and more disturbing.

As much as anything, Susannah's is a story about family. To the end of her days, she was linked to a family that at its best was equivocally supportive and at its worst brought her down. It was not only the lack of the ballast of unconditional love that tore her apart—it was family disease. Susannah, said her second husband Keith Ingham, once told him that depression had been a problem for family members as long as she could remember. "Depression and then she thought her mother was an alcoholic and her father and older sister were manic depressives," he adds. "She said she felt she got off lucky with 'just' depression!" Characteristically, she thus managed to disarm and to downplay the seriousness of her own pain. And pain it was. Not simply the blues. It was what she called "the black black blues," when the glass was not only half-empty but seen through darkly.

Susannah's story really starts with her parents, Tom and Margery.

Tom and Margery—everybody called her Mimi—McCorkle were a stunning young couple. "People did say we looked rather like Scott and Zelda," Mimi admitted in an interview not long before she died, still fashionable, still dieting, still sharp of wit. Tom—Homer Thomas McCorkle, Jr.—was tall and dark and thinly handsome in a nervy, Gregory Peck way. Mimi Manchester was small and slim and pixieish. She was a clothes horse, an accomplished seamstress who made copies of couture designs and peroxided her hair like the glamorous Hollywood stars of her day, the 1930s and 1940s. "Mimi always believed all the men were in love with her," commented her youngest daughter, Maggie. Many of them were. But it was Tom who won her. She and Tom met on the campus of the University of California at Berkeley in the middle of the Great Depression. Tom was poor and intellectual and ambitious, but he had a fun-loving, frivolous side too. Like Mimi, he loved acting and met his future wife, the "catch" of Cal, the prettiest girl on campus, at an amateur theater group. For both of them, it was first love, and last.

They came from different worlds. Mimi was a Savage and a Manchester, with a thin (but tough) American veneer of recently acquired money, privilege, impressive houses. It had taken her forebears two generations to make the jump from pioneer to privilege. Great-grand-father Savage had come to California during the Gold Rush and ended up as a small mine owner; his son Philip Savage was a farmer in the town of Darby near Fresno, whose wife Flora Lizette bore twelve children (several died in infancy). It is the women of the Savage and Manchester families who stand out. Flora, between childbearing and farming, wrote a memoir she called *A Homespun Saga of California* and became an active member of the WCTU—the Women's Christian Temperance Union—after she left the farm and settled in Berkeley in the late 1890s.

Her daughter, Genevieve "Gevie" Savage (Mimi's mother and Susannah's grandmother), was just as impressive. Born in the 1880s, she was expected to take care of the stream of younger siblings who followed her on the farm. It was a rough-and-ready kind of life: "She told me how they would put the animals on one side of the kitchen, and the kids on the other to play," recalled Mimi. But after the family resettled in Berkeley, Gevie achieved not one but two higher degrees at the newly formed and excellent university, which offered free tuition. Then Gevie determined to start her own prep school, with financial backing from her brother Phil, a successful businessman. The A-to-Zed School, at 3037 Telegraph Avenue in Berkeley, prepared students for Cal's rigorous entrance exams. Among the students who took "cramming" courses to prepare for college during the school's tenure from 1912 to 1951 were William Randolph Hearst's sons William Jr. and George.

Gevie married well. George Peabody ("G.P.") Manchester published trade magazines about jewelry, clothing and shoes in thriving San Francisco. A newspaper article in the twenties described the couple as "prominent educators," but it was really Gevie, said Mimi, who ran the school. "When my mother became so successful with the school, she gave Dad half, because she was doing better than he was. And boy, she had a time with my father, G.P. He was physically abusive and he had a bad temper. By my birth—I was the youngest of three, 10 years younger than my brother Robin and sister Dorothy—he was somewhat broken in. Still, he was fierce." Robin became estranged from G.P. after loud arguments and left home for good when Mimi was fairly little. Mimi seems to have inherited her father's temper. When she was a grown, married woman and the mother of two young daughters, Katie and Susie, Mimi had to live at her parents' home in Palm Springs for a year, while Tom, an anthropologist, did fieldwork in the jungles of Venezuela. Susie remembered regular shouting matches between Gevie and Mimi, after which Mimi would storm off in her jalopy.

In 1912, G.P. and Gevie built a large wooden house in the newly fashionable arts-and-crafts style. The house peers over a canyon on Shasta Road in the dramatic Berkeley Hills neighborhood close to the university. Four years later, Mimi was born there and would live there, off and on, for much of her life. The all-wood house first escaped the fires of 1923 that destroyed so many Berkeley structures, and was added onto later in the decade. It was a fun, flush time, Mimi remembered: The family had the large sum of a thousand dollars a month to live on, and she had a generous allowance, which she spent on clothes, often designing and sewing them. There were other houses too, a commodious cabin in the north and a place in Palm Springs, where the dry air helped Gevie's chronic bronchitis.

Then came 1929. "I was 12 when the crash came," Mimi remembered. "We were in Palm Springs. We had to go back home." Yet if the depression meant stricter economies for the Manchesters—there were far fewer students at A-to-Zed—there was no real deprivation. They held onto their properties and, after the worst of the economic downturn, even remodeled their arts-and-crafts house again.

In Berkeley Hills, all of the views were good, some breathtaking. It was fashionable, though, not to seem to have money—and it was thought vulgar to flaunt it. This was a neighborhood of raffish and bookish privilege, an aerie where professors and artists commingled. The physicist J. Robert Oppenheimer, the "father" of the atomic bomb, was perhaps the Manchesters' most famous neighbor, but not the only one.

From such a place, Mimi sailed forth to college at Cal-Berkeley in 1934, a bicycle ride away. A college education was a given in the Manchester family, though Mimi was never a brain. She was much attracted to playing in revues and skits and the more droll kinds of theater. But the college had no official drama department yet and Mimi thought she would become a teacher. "She was what Susannah called a 'campus cutie' type—you know, the most popular cheerleader kind," explains pianist Keith Ingham. "She thought her mother was an airhead. And she despised Mimi for that."

Though Tom McCorkle was also good-looking and fun-loving, he was also very bright and very ambitious. The McCorkles had a proud lineage, tracing their name back to the ninth century, when a Torquill was awarded a "Mc" after helping the Scottish king defeat invading Picts and Vikings. In the 1700s, McTorquills were now McCorkles who landed in America, settling first in the hills of Tennessee, where indeed Tom was born in 1912. But where the Savages and Manchesters rose quickly to wealth and its accoutrements, the McCorkles were struggling farmers. Tom's father Homer was a skilled laborer who sought to make a living as a jewelry repairman, but he found it a struggle. His wife, Helen, took in sewing to help out. She also wanted better for her three sons and pushed hard for education, as the farming Savages had done. As the McCorkles moved around, from Texas to various towns in agricultural California, they at last settled in the town of Hemet. From there, Helen saw that each of her sons became something: Tom would become a college professor, Horace a surgeon, Cason a businessman.

There was trouble in the McCorkle family, hints of the manic depression that was to bedevil Tom and his children in an unfinished memoir he wrote late in life. In this memoir, he wrote that both Homer and Helen suffered from "low moods," and he wondered if that was why his father, a talented if itinerant mechanic, always took the least stressful jobs. As for Helen, Tom recalled times when he was a boy that his mother would lie on the floor with a wet towel over her face for hours during the hot summer months. Tom understood this to be her way of coping. Years later, when Helen came down with cancer as an elderly woman and had to be hospitalized, his father, wrote Tom, "went into shock and stopped eating and functioning normally."

Yet by the time Tom and Mimi met in the mid-1930s at the Drama Club at Cal, the world must have seemed to lie at his fingertips. Tom was an excellent student and loved the university, and he was drop-dead handsome. Mimi was a catch, a vivacious, glamorous girl who must have seemed to have come from another world. Theirs was a fairy-tale romance, both competing with rivals, having hilarious good times drinking and smoking at the beer bashes on campus, acting out scripts for the Mask and Dagger Revue, including farces Tom delighted in writing, like *One Foot Off the Gutter,* with an urchin star part for Mimi. Gregory Peck, who joined the Drama Club a year or two after Tom and Mimi, recalled the drama "eccentrics at Cal," especially Professor Edwin Duerr, the group's director, whom Peck described as a man "with wisps of hair under his tweed hat and thick glasses." "They were careless people . . . they smashed up things and creatures and then retreated back into their money or their vast carelessness, or whatever it was that kept them together." So wrote F. Scott Fitzgerald about Tom and Daisy Buchanan in *The Great Gatsby;* he might have been writing about Tom and Mimi. They loved acting, the costumes, the "hoe-downs" with their friends featuring beer and "weenies." Flirtations with admirers were all part of the fun. "I don't know if I was a good girl or a bad girl," Mimi would confide at the end of her life.

They had a splendid wedding, right after Mimi graduated from Cal, in 1938. She was 20, and Tom was 26, still in school, working toward his master's degree. The ceremony was held at the Shasta Road house, an August wedding in the grand style. All the San Francisco and Berkeley papers covered the event, or, rather, the *Manchester* part of it—there was no mention at all of the McCorkles beyond the name and photograph of the groom himself, although presumably his parents and brothers were there. Miss Manchester's heirloom silk wedding gown was described, the trailing silk and embroidered veil first worn by Grandmother Flora Savage at her wedding. There were six brides-maids and a hundred guests to supper, after which, said the papers, the newlyweds planned to "motor" through the Canadian Northwest, stopping at the Manchesters' summer home in Mendocino County near Fort Bragg. (Kurt Russell and Goldie Hawn later bought this "cabin.")

Afterward, Gevie and G.P. bought Tom and Mimi a small house to start their married life. When the very next year the Manchesters decided to move full-time to Palm Springs, the young couple gratefully accepted the offer of free room and board at the otherwise empty Shasta Road house, selling their cramped little cottage. With no overhead, their financial obligations eased up—a good thing, as Tom had years of school ahead, intending to get his doctorate in anthropology, with a spe-ciality in the cutting-edge field of medical anthropology, which meant a load of additional coursework. He was influenced in his decision by his brother-in-law, anthropologist Ralph Beals, who had married Mimi's older sister Dorothy. Beals was already successful—he would write a standard text used in anthropology courses around the country. But Tom, who loved fieldwork far more than the classroom, showed every sign of becoming a star in his own right.

Given the example of her own mother, Gevie Manchester, as a suc-cessful businesswoman, one might have expected that Mimi would have greater ambitions than simply to play wife and mother. She did not—at first—though, being Mimi, there was a somewhat bohemian edge to the way she played those roles. "When I got out of college, the only way I saw myself was married with the little home, dining with friends and having large parties," she explained decades later in a letter to Susan. Tom, she explained, was "against" her working—unless it involved a career: She should do nothing "beneath" her. So there she was, only 20, a married woman with no real plan for herself. Though Tom did work part-time, his income was insufficient to support the couple as he proceeded through graduate school. And while G.P. and Gevie sent occasional checks to "help out," Mimi felt that, despite his disapproval, she had to do something to add to the family income. At first, she worked at her mother's A-to-Zed School, teaching seemingly anything that was needed. "English, history, math, folk dancing, Ger-man, French," recalled Mimi. "I got a hundred dollars a month. And my mother gave Tom a job for one semester teaching, but he couldn't stand it. He quit and began managing a warehouse for a shipping company in Albany, nearby." In 1941, the school closed; it reopened after the war, but not for long. Meanwhile, Mimi found a new job working on the Cal campus as a secretary for an athletic group. "They asked Tom and me to write a skit for them, which turned out to be a fashion show where they marched around and showed off in women's clothes. That was fun."

Fun: They both loved it, loved to throw good-time parties for the circle of graduate students and their wives they knew in the big house. Dancing, parties, skits—all lubricated with plenty of booze. And no children to tie them down. It was going to be a wild ride, though, in Susannah's view, given the strain of mental imbalance and problem drinking on the marriage. Tom saw things very differently. After he'd been married more than half a century, he wrote in 1989, "A psychiatrist once remarked that he didn't see how we got along with each other. I think the fact is that we get along because we *entertain* each other." Being amused was very important for both parties to the marriage.

Greatly amusing was the first of many trips to Mexico, in the summer of 1940, for Tom's fieldwork in anthropology. Uruapán, in Michoacán, Mexico, was and is a good-sized small city. Tom worked at first as a field assistant doing ethnographic research on the Tarascan Indians of the region, along with his social anthropologist brother-in-law. He was in his element, never happier than off among an Indian tribe, combining intellectual and physical labor. There were plenty of dances, fiestas, and dinners to keep Mimi happy as well, and she entertained herself by making what she called "copies of movie stars' clothes" and curtains with Mexican fabric and fixing up their adobe house.

When the United States entered World War II, the field trips came to a halt. Tom's poor eyesight kept him out of the army, but he was given a war-related job as a supervisor at the warehouse on the docks where he'd worked as a clerk in graduate school. "His union there loved him," recalled Mimi, "and they let him change his hours so he could work on his Ph.D., though that wasn't supposed to be done."

In the middle of the war, in February 1943, Tom and Mimi's first child was born, a pretty blonde girl they named Katherine and always called Katie. Cute as a little doll, Katie was a source of great satisfaction and pride to Mimi. She would become a child model, a homecoming queen runner-up, and just as important, said Mimi, an amusing child. "But only as a little girl," her mother added. When little Susan, always called Susie or Suzy, was born three years later on January 1, 1946, she was also a cute blonde baby—but not as pretty (said her mother) and emphatically not amusing, a fussy child who cried constantly and was always hungry, her mother remembered. The third child, Marjory (Maggie), born eight years later in 1954, recalls a remark her mother made that devastated Susan. "My mother tended to be very blunt and told Susan that she hadn't really wanted that second child," says Maggie. "Some children would get over that, but Susan was not the kind to get over things. She was a drama queen. She was always very oversensitive." But perhaps worse than being told that she was produced as a playmate for her older sister was the job of being little sis.

The big house in Berkeley was designed so that the parents slept in a separate area from the children. Of course, the late forties and fifties was an era of far different customs and attitudes towards child-rearing generally, and the notion of a child-centered family was a mostly foreign one. Children were expected to amuse themselves, to play with whoever was nearby, and to follow along with grown-ups' plans. Katie and Susie, in their mother's phrase, "had to learn how to cope with each other." That siblings squabble is routine, but it was both the intensity and meanness of those fights that seared Susan's memory, and several times brought neighbors over to intervene. She remembered how when she laughed at Katie for having trouble starting the lawnmower (one of her chores), Katie flew into a frenzy and held her down, whipping her back with the cord of the starter until Susan's screams finally brought neighbors. Or the time during a game of cowboys and Indians that Katie left Susan bound to a tree, sobbing and calling for her mother. The younger sister was afraid of the elder. "She would abandon me, or make me think she would, at the movies." Susan remembered many such incidents, mostly out of sight and sound of parents or neighbors, in the house: a furious Katie bending back her fingers until they almost broke, teasing her into sobs in her bedroom.

Where was Mimi? She did discipline both girls, presumably modeling the punishment on what had been meted out to her. When Katie threatened to run away and then made good on the threat, Mimi recalled "lightly tying her up to restrain her, which was done to me when I was little. But it had no impact. Nothing worked. She'd cut things up for no reason, she wouldn't come home from school. She was always mean." When Susan as a toddler misbehaved, Mimi used the same tactics: She was tied to a chair, her mother sitting nearby, ignoring her sobs as she sewed, her mother's face, said her daughter, "contorted with rage" when the little girl then soiled her pants. "Mimi rode her back endlessly," commented a neighbor.[1]

They squabbled constantly, these two little girls. And they were chalk and cheese: Katie, full of restless energy, angry mischief, liked to play with trains and wear trousers and climb trees, while Susan loved her little dresses, her family of dolls, and sitting quietly to write stories from the time she was old enough to shape words with a pencil. During Tom and Mimi's frequent parties, the girls, left to their own devices, wandered in and out of the living room or the backyard observing the grown-ups at play. Susan did love the laughter, the good loud fun of the early hours, the pounding of dancing feet above her head that lulled her to sleep eventually. Both her parents had a sense of humor, of the absurd, which she credited as an adult as "the saving grace of my wacko family."

At the end of her life, looking back on those years, Mimi asserted, "It seems to me that the children examined our doings too closely. As little kids, they felt we were wrong—smoking cigarettes, and we drank a lot at parties. They spent a lot of time and thought trying to make us act in a better way."

Susan both adored her mother and feared her. "When she got mad," said another neighbor, Lee Davis—a swing-era clarinetist—"she'd run away to our house. We would let her talk it out, and I'd draw little pictures to amuse her."

Little Susan—everyone called her Susie then—became known as the family storyteller and liked to perform. "When we were driving in the car, she'd tell us funny stories and we listened carefully," said her mother. "We were amused and enchanted. She always liked to put on a show." Receiving her first transistor radio, a little red plastic concoction (later replaced by a sleeker turquoise and cream model) was a momentous event. Susie made her first intimate connection to the pleasures of music as a little girl listening to her radio in bed after lights out: "I remember lying awake long past my bedtime with my crackly little radio turned as low as possible so my parents wouldn't hear. I always had favorite songs, and I tried hard to learn the words so I could sing along and be part of the music. I learned at any early age to concentrate, listen carefully, and picture things in my mind that I couldn't see with my eyes."[2]

If listening was heaven, performing was difficult. "Always she felt that everything should be perfect," said her mother. "She did a lot of worrying. If it wasn't 100 percent, she was crushed. As a little girl, even. Then she'd look gloomy, but she'd get over it by the next day." Susie also craved the glamorous sheen her mother had perfected. She spent hours watching Mimi dress and sit before her vanity table to apply her makeup and fix her hair, but she felt, even as a girl, hopelessly outclassed in the glamour department, lamenting "Mimi's fashionableness, her tinted glasses and picture hats and thick strapped sandals and gloves of different lengths and colors."

"Our house wasn't a very kid-focused place," comments Maggie, the youngest. "I think my parents were more interested in their own lives than in us." Mimi, not unnaturally, saw the situation very differently. She was always busy, she had jobs and had to run a household—having fun was her reward. When Katie and Susan were small, she offered childcare in her home and took in sewing jobs—"mostly hemming up dresses, and I sewed my girls' clothes too. Katie and Susie always had lovely outfits, billowy Christmas dresses, elaborate Halloween costumes. And I made them little colored panties with ruffles that fit so nicely."

A vision of halcyon days—yet Mimi suddenly adds, "I *never* thought that I *knew* Susan. Even when she was a little girl, barely talking, she had all kinds of ideas. She said to me, very serious, 'When I get to be grown up, I'll be bigger than you and you'll hear from me.' I replied, 'But you won't get to be bigger than me.' But she *did*." Their competitiveness would last a lifetime.

Tom, of course, was offstage a great deal of the time—it was the fifties. Kind and gentle as Susan remembered him to be when she was a little girl, he was also already emotionally distant. The door to his study door, she remembered, would be closed, his typewriter going "so fast it sounded like the whir of a sewing machine." At such times, his children saw him only to take him a sandwich, and then tiptoe out. When he was not at work or writing, he'd play cards or cribbage with the girls. And then he was gone again. The postwar decade was both a heady and troubling decade for Tom McCorkle. Though he'd started at Cal in the thirties, he still hadn't completed requirements for his doctorate by 1950, which encouraged his own inner demons. He had come to realize that he was not interested in academia per se, but in the excitement of doing research in the field, where he was not subject to staid rules and regulations. But with young children, he was under mounting pressure (including from Mimi) to get the brass ring of a full-time, permanent, tenure-track university job. Meanwhile, his dissertation fieldwork not nearly done, he kept working as a shipping clerk at the docks and found short-term jobs teaching anthropology. In 1949, he did research for the Federal Bureau of Reclamation, and in 1951, he was an instructor in Elementary Physical Anthropology at Cal. By all accounts, he was not cut out to be in the classroom. At any rate, it was his first and only job at his alma mater.

So Tom was in a bind: He needed research grants to undertake the extended fieldwork to complete his dissertation to get a good job, but he had to support his family also. When he finally landed a fellowship (from the Henry and Grace Doherty Foundation), he was euphoric: This would at last allow him to do a year's research in Venezuela on the island of Santa Margarita, and in the remote mountainous states of Sucre and Monaguas in northwestern Venezuela. "UC Anthropologist, Family Going to Venezuela Wilds" was the headline in the Berkeley newspaper in 1952. Tom exhibited his sly brand of humor with the reporter. The area, he said with a straight face, was inhabited by "former cannibals who he believed now confine themselves to tropical fruits, vegetables and four-legged animals." In fact, Tom was looking forward to introducing nine-year-old Katie and six-year-old Susie to the tropical rainforest.

But the trip turned out to be a fiasco for everyone in the family, a disaster that seems to be foreshadowed in the newspaper photo accompanying the article. It is a curious and—as it turns out—typical McCorkle pose: Each McCorkle is looking away from the camera—and from each other. Katie clutches the family Siamese cat, Susie holds "Country," her beloved doll, Mimi looks rather stunned, and Tom simply appears remote. Each seems to be in some private funk.

But at first, the venture was exciting and fun. They made their way from San Francisco to Venezuela on a freighter, landing in then-beautiful Caracas, set between the ocean and the Andes mountains. There they bought bulk provisions for the island of Santa Margarita, where they were going to live initially. They found a house there in the town of Palamar. Years later, Susie wrote to her father of the happy memories she had, in the glow of those first weeks in such an exotic place: "The walks we took along the sidewalk by the beach there. Lots of times you carried me on your shoulders and I could see very well all around me and felt so high."

Soon, though, the children sickened from the unfamiliar food and the water—fresh water was delivered from the mainland only one day a week, and everything was far more expensive than they'd planned, so that Tom's research grant, they soon realized, would not carry them through. Tom and Mimi quarreled. After two months, Mimi left with the children, going to stay with her parents in Palm Springs, where she got a job she loved working for the fashionable dressmaking shop Lanz. "She loved dressing up every day," recalled Susannah years later. "She met movie stars who shopped at the store—Zsa Zsa Gabor, Eartha Kitt."[3] Meanwhile, back in the jungle alone, Tom did his research. Though his grant was inadequate even for him on his own, he was determined to stay and lived like a peasant. Years later, after he'd had a severe breakdown, he wrote of how he'd been plagued in Venezuela by thoughts of suicide. Was this the first time? From then on, what Mimi always referred to as "Tom's disease," marked by extremes of mood and inability to cope with routine and regulation, became more and more troubling and evident.

Katie and Susie had new schools. Susie in the first grade was reading at the same level as Katie in the fourth, and Katie paid her back by bullying her as they waited for the school bus. Mimi argued with Gevie and went to parties to while away the year; Susie listened to the radio and watched her grandmother paint in her studio—and hugged her first large, shameful secret to herself. It was only years later, her mother recalled, that she finally told her parents about how she had been touched inside her underpants by a man in a hotel in Margarita. "Tom," said Mimi, "was amazed to hear her story. Susan said afterward he left the porch and disappeared."

Tom and Mimi mishandled another sexual assault a few years later, when Susie was at the edge of puberty, on one of their annual summer trips to Uruapán, according to Keith Ingham. Susie, rushed precociously into womanhood, was developing what would eventually become a Jayne Mansfield–sized chest (beyond "full figure" DD/EE sizes, she had to wear custom-made brassieres). But she was still a girl. When she managed to break away from a man she knew who grabbed and fondled her while she was walking around the Mexican town, she ran home and sobbed out the assault to her parents. Then came the double betrayal so often meted out to such young victims. Her parents did nothing. Or as she put it, they *decided not to do anything about it.* Why? Because, she went on, they were afraid that if they confronted the man, Tom's research would be jeopardized in the community due to the man's standing. Instead, she told Ingham, "they whisked me away, back to the States."

Though she both sensed and had proof of her father's aloofness, of his lack of support, as a girl Susie adored her father, who seemed to have played good cop to Mimi's bad cop. "She and Katie were in love with *him*," said Mimi at an advanced age. "But he wasn't with *them*." The girls' adolescence forced him to contend with their sexuality. Susie would later write of her mortification when Katie would remove her clothes and walk around the house while her father (and mother) tried to ignore her. As for Susie, she complained that once she became an adolescent, she was "invisible" to her father. In a story written in her twenties, she observed: "'I think it's fathers who make their daughters unsure of themselves in the first place, and we never really change,' I said, remembering how my father had seemed to forget that I existed the summer I got breasts and hips. I lost his interest that year, but suddenly I had all the other men in the world instead, starting with the sixteen-year-old boys. . . . After my first hot kiss I used to pass him in the hall without speaking or even smiling and wonder why he wouldn't let me feel pretty."[4]

Yet Tom doted on his children in his fashion. If Katie was wild and out of control, he loved her just the same, never gave up on her, though he was not a disciplinarian. Katie was his pretty wild rose. Susie—his "brown-eyed girl," his "Sooze," his "Suby," was his intellectual sparring partner, the "smart one." The baby, Maggie was the "sweetest," the one who wasn't difficult, a little doll for her much older sisters to play with. For his girls, Tom drew clever cartoons and children's stories and wrote limericks. His sweet letters to Susie were full of praise for her many accomplishments in school—she was always one of the top students in her class. And for the rest of his life he would be supportive financially, if erratically, sending her checks along with avuncular letters.

Back in the States after Tom's Venezuelan year, the McCorkles regrouped in Berkeley in 1953. Tom was re-energized. He wrote and published articles and bits of his dissertation in scholarly journals; the year before, he'd completed his doctoral dissertation, "Fajardo's People: Cultural Adjustment in Venezuela of the Guayueri People" (published as a book a decade later by the University of California).[5] Susie walked to the nearby Hillside Elementary School, but not for long—Tom took a job as an instructor in anthropology at U.C. Santa Barbara. It was one more move, another house, another set of strange faces in the classroom for Susie and Katie, with more to come.

In 1955, now 39, Tom McCorkle saw his family growing. Maggie was born, putting more pressure on him to find a "real" job. That year, it was pick up and move again, this time to Santa Clara. And then in 1956, the McCorkles moved once more, but this time they left California entirely for the heart of the Midwest: Iowa. It was no exaggeration when Susan said years later that, "I attended 14 different schools before I went to college." To these Berkeley bohemians, Iowa was the equivalent of an inhospitable foreign country—Siberia, say. But Tom had not been able to turn down such an attractive job offer: as assistant professor of preventive medicine and anthropology at the University of Iowa in Iowa City. There were abundant research possibilities and the added lure of the then-attractive salary of $28,000. After more than twenty years in school and a series of short-term research stints, it should have seemed like a dream job. But Tom and Mimi treated it like a hardship post. "We were there from 1956 to 1960," said Mimi. "Five bloody years, we called it. There were no bars for ladies in Iowa City!" she exclaimed in amazement.

Tom struggled with the demands of his job. "They had to keep very regular hours at the medical department. It was hateful," recalled Mimi indignantly. "I remember his boss, the chairman of the department, told me that Tom was crazy. He was angry at him because Tom provoked him, did mad-making things." Yet Tom did produce. He put out what he called a "little magazine" for the medical department and wrote about the Amish people in Iowa, and chiropractic—always a particular interest of his.[6] He also studied suicide, said Mimi, later mentioning with disconcerting casualness that Tom noticed how "sometimes the farmers carried ropes around in the back of their trucks in case they wanted to kill themselves."

The children had their new schools to adjust to yet again. In 1957, Susie started junior high school. She eagerly added French and German to her courses. "I loved the grammar, the conjugating of verbs—everything about every language," she said. In Uruapán, where the family continued to visit every summer, she'd listened with a keen but untutored ear to the Spanish conversations around her. "Very early, I heard my parents speaking Spanish to keep a secret from me," she said, "and I was fascinated by the idea that what sounded like gibberish to me made sense to them."[7] She decided to memorize an entire Spanish-

English dictionary, so she could eavesdrop on her parents as well as go shopping on her own. She had a prodigious memory.

Susan had been composing little stories and poems since she learned to write. A precocious talent, in 1957, at 11, she published her first story, an homage to Carolyn Keene, the pseudonymous author of the Nancy Drew series, in "Keen Carolyn and the Christmas Mystery." And the story was published not in a children's magazine but in the University of Iowa's literary magazine, *Parnassus*. At 13, another story of hers was accepted by *The American Girl* magazine (then a Girl Scout publication), with many more to follow. They were polished, well-constructed stories—and, as would always be the case, tended to be darkly autobiographical. "The Dog," though written at just 13, was a bleak snapshot of human cruelty and misery during a car ride to school, during which a careless teenage driver not only strikes the mangy old dog of a pathetic old man walking by on the road but is completely indifferent to it (while his rider notices, and takes to heart, everything). Or take "The Turning Point," also written at 13, a paper for her English class (she received an A+). The main character—a girl like Susan—has swapped parents with her cousin for a year. Her aunt-mother is cold, crabby, and uncaring—a view Susan had of her own mother. And her uncle is hardly ever around—again, like Tom. The unnamed main character (she rarely gave her protagonists names) is always alone. She walks home from school up a long hill to her aunt's home alone. She notices the other mothers who come down the hill to collect their children and says: "I always used to stand at the bottom of the hill and look up and wish she'd come down for me. But she didn't, not ever." In another scene, the girl opens a letter addressed to her aunt from her mother. It is full of criticism about the girl: She is sneaky, she lies a lot, she loves money more than anything. The turning point of the story is simply the wretched girl's realization of how poorly her mother and aunt think of her. It is a remarkable piece in its way. For Susan, writing was clearly a release, a way to work through a thick mass of turbulent emotions, to ponder the absorbing puzzle of identity, and, in time, to reinvent herself on the page.

At the end of her life, Susan fleshed out the memories of her childhood in a memoir that measured the awkward, painful, coltish period that is a rite of passage for so many young women, that breathless time when complexion and hormones and body shape are constant obsessions.[8] She wanted to be as beautiful and alluring as her mother, but she was lumpy and pimply even as Mimi continued to get blonder and remained svelte through rigorous dieting. "She said that even though they were living in genteel poverty, Tom saved up to buy Mimi a red convertible," her stepdaughter Anne recalls Susan telling her. "Because Mimi wanted to be the blonde with the convertible."

Mimi was prone to crash diets of black coffee and cigarettes and the Benzedrine "diet pills" that kept a lot of moms speeding at the time. And she was critical of her daughters' looks—especially, it seems, of her second daughter's. "Susan had kind of thick legs. And she had a hideous face—complexion, I mean," she later described her. Susie would stand in her mother's bedroom, watching her mother apply makeup, looking for clues at how to escape the "hideousness" of her condition. "Her long long ritual. The drawers full of carefully organized accessories—long gloves, short gloves, black gloves, white gloves, jewelry, makeup." At such times, she wrote, she wished she could be far, far away. She was already in the habit of taking money from her mother's purse to buy clothes; next, she began to stare at her jewelry, calculating its worth for her getaway. She was chilled, she added, when one afternoon her mother turned around, witch-like, and told her, "They wouldn't get you far."

This was the extent of her crimes, however. Still an outstanding student, she turned to school activities. When she was home, she spent most of the time in her room with the door locked, with her books, her journals, her radio.

Then the family moved again. Tom had found another promising job in 1960, as director and resident research anthropologist of the Division of Behavioral Science at the State Health Department in Harrisburg, Pennsylvania. New schools again: Katie a senior and Susie a freshman at John Harris High, a large, racially integrated school. They moved into a nice old stucco house in a middle-class neighborhood surrounded by green, rolling hills.

But Tom brought to the new job his by-now familiar inability to conform. "He wasn't allowed his freedom—he had to be there at eight and all that," said Mimi. Still, they stuck it out, for four years; during that time, Mimi became a substitute teacher at the high school.

In her senior yearbook, Susie McCorkle is a cute, smiling 17-year-old with a pageboy, wearing a cardigan sweater and a plaid pleated skirt. An utterly wholesome-looking girl with the résumé of a high-achieving young woman destined to succeed: active in the National Honor

Society, the French Club (she was president), the Senior Literary Society, and two school choirs. Nor was that all. Encouraged by her progressive parents to work for civil rights, she participated in a sit-in—or rather, a stand-in at a Harrisburg store where de facto segregation still existed.

But Susie's nice milkmaid looks masked her own growing turbulence, as for all in the family. There was her older sister. When Katie graduated, she left behind a reputation that embarrassed her younger sister—and intrigued her. When Tom and Mimi were out, Katie became known for her wild keg parties. Susie wanted to join in the partying but fled to the safety of her room to fantasize. She was envious but also repelled by Katie, who returned from a year abroad to study French in Grenoble in 1961–62, a graduation present from Mimi and Tom, and ended up getting pregnant. Mimi took Katie down to Mexico for an "operation"—this was long before *Roe v. Wade*—with the experience leaving both relatively unfazed.

By now Susie was as fully developed as her sister, tall and big-boned and well-proportioned, but she was terribly self-conscious and hated her looks, agonizing over her large nose and breasts and bad complexion, convinced she was fat. She wasn't helped by the critical, diet-conscious Mimi any more than she had been in the past. For a Junior League prom at 16, Mimi made Susie buy a dress secondhand from the Salvation Army store. True, it was a find, a beautiful, long dress, but it was secondhand. Then, when she was all ready, Susie remembered, she descended the stairs from her bedroom to the living room, where she waited for a comment from her mother. In vain—Mimi said nothing. When Susie asked her mother, "Do I look nice?" she later recalled, Mimi smacked her forehead, saying, "Oh! Do I have to give attention to you too now?!" and walked away.

In truth, Mimi had much to worry about. Besides Katie, there was Tom, whose emotional balance was increasingly wobbly. By 1963, he was no longer working, and while he looked for something suitable—only in California, both agreed—they pinched pennies (hence, presumably, the Salvation Army party dress), living on Mimi's salary as a substitute teacher at John Harris High.

Later, Susie was to write of the depression that glazed her high-school years, of whole summers spent doing nothing, getting up at eleven and going out to the pool all day, watching television at night. No real friendships, no boyfriends. At 16, she wasn't yet dating, and despite her accomplishments, she wasn't part of the "in" crowd. The community pool was the summertime focus of the pack of popular girls. Susie gamely showed up, laying her beach towel at the end of the line of "cheerleaders and drum majorettes," as she described them. And with her camera-ready memory, she remembered all their names decades later: "Sally Williams, Sharon Peoples, Barbara Lopinto, Karen Hochenberry, Janice Fenstermacher. They were nice enough, but I didn't really fit in and we all knew it. For so many years, all through junior high and high school, I was so lonely and felt like some sort of freak because I could never make myself accept the drum-majorette and Progress Saturday night dance kind of life that my 'friends' adored so much. . . . For awhile I thought I must be crazy. I used to want to be in love so much. I searched for attachments and was terrified of being alone, of having no one ask me out."[9] It was the mid-1960s, and in middle-class middle America, those who didn't fit in became invisible—or fell in with the "losers," the hoods, greasers, hippies, druggies. Or got pregnant.

Susie—who around the time she graduated from high school began to spell her name as the more sophisticated *Suzy*—had always loved to sing. The school choir taught her "to be confident about opening up your mouth and singing. I always liked old songs," she said, "but the only frame of reference I had was musical comedy. I used to lie on the floor listening to them and figuring out who was singing, why they were unhappy or happy. Chita Rivera's singing 'A Boy Like That' (from *West Side Story*) fascinated me much more than Carol Lawrence's beautiful soprano."[10] She typed lists of her favorite songs, Top Ten pop hits like "You Don't Have to Say You Love Me," "We'll Sing in the Sunshine," "The End of the World," along with favorites from her parents' Broadway cast albums—*Oklahoma!, Carnival, South Pacific.* There were a sprinkling of standards and other show tunes too: "It Might as Well Be Spring, "Baubles, Bangles and Beads," and "While We Were Young," an Alec Wilder tune with a lyric by William Engvick, a friend of Tom and Mimi's from Berkeley and their little theater days. (Almost twenty years later, she would sing a televised program of Wilder's music with a jazz orchestra.) Mimi, ever the theater lover, took the girls to local productions of the then-popular musicals and urged Suzy to try out for school plays. She did. She had a bit part in local summer stock after her junior year in 1962, in *L'il Abner.* And despite her physical awkwardness and introversion, for the annual high-school variety show in her senior year, she wore a white trench coat and red spiked heels, with a fog machine spewing mist around her while she belted out Gershwin's "A Foggy Day."

In the summer of 1963, after graduation, came a plum part in the musical *Bye, Bye, Birdie* (on the strength of the fog machine number?). "She played Rose, the girlfriend of the writer in the play," recalled Mimi of the role played on Broadway by Chita Rivera. "A good family friend, who did the music in that show, had her try out and then offered her the part." "I was the only alto who could act," explained Suzy, "the only high schooler, much too young." The women in the cast complained that she was awkward and amateurish, but she seemed to have caused all the males in the cast, straight and gay, to fall in love with her: She kept mash notes and admiring letters several wrote to her after she'd gone away to college. And she had her first platonic love affair, with Bob, an "older" man in his twenties she'd already known from her part-time job at a Harrisburg department store. It was puppy love on her part, a chaste affair full of kisses and sighs. But Bob carried a torch all the way to Nigeria, where he was stationed in the Peace Corps. "I haven't forgotten about a little blonde (and somewhat bleached in front) salesclerk who transformed into my Latin Beauty! God, Suzy, I really do miss you!" he wrote in 1963. "You came along and completely shattered my exterior. . . . I fell in love with you Suzy and I don't know what to do about it."

As she would nearly always do, Suzy wove Bob and the store—and above all, herself at 17—into a story. "Love in a Department Store" is about a nameless high-school girl (Miss X) working part-time as a sales clerk in the store who dazzles a repressed older (by four years) fellow worker (Mr. Y). Harrison's Store is the stage set, with scenes in menswear, ladies' lingerie, and shoes. It is a dreamy, twilight kind of place, removed from the unbearably trivial nature of "normal" life. We are, in Suzy's stories, in Susannah-land, the country of alienation, of running away, of starting over with a fresh identity or sense of self, a land where the characters long—sometimes desperately—for something or someone outside of themselves to come along and free them from their everydayness. In this youthful story, that "something" is love—romantic love. Mr. Y is handsome, the handsomest man at Harrison's Store, but he is not happy. He sees himself as a formerly fat man who does not even have the pleasure of overeating anymore. (This is pure, cleverly reshuffled autobiography: It is Suzy who is the obsessive overeater in reality. Mr. Y is her alter ego, "a fat man in a thin body. . . . *Being slender was his only defense against the world, but eating was still his only comfort. He had always thought that it was his layers of fat that kept him apart from all others. But now that he was slim and good-looking . . . he still felt lonely and isolated.*" But Mr. Y does change. He falls in love with Miss X, a precocious high-school student who works part-time in the store. Though not beautiful, she attracts him because she is different. When he discovers that she has just bought the most expensive luggage set in the store, he panics. "Where are you planning on going?" he asks. "Away, just away," she replies. "I belong in a place where people care more about things."

Mr. Y plunges into depression: "He reflected that hope was a habit, an addiction, like smoking. It gave a certain amount of momentary comfort, but the consequences of withdrawal were too painful to make it worthwhile in the long run." But the two are reunited: Running away from their old lives, they resolve to begin a new one together.

After her success in *Birdie,* Mimi urged Suzy to study acting at Cal, which by now had a bona fide theater department, and to try for a career on Broadway in musicals. Tuition was still free at Cal, and Suzy could even have free room and board if she cared to at the Shasta Road house, which had been willed to Mimi after Gevie's recent death. But Suzy wasn't interested in a musical career. "I was too thin-skinned, restless and not enough in love with the limelight. I just liked opening my mouth and singing."[11] But whatever Suzy intended to do with her life, she appeared to have a shiny bright future before her, everyone was certain. She had graduated with honors and awards (though not for "most musical"—little did they know), she had acquired a boyfriend and a clutch of male admirers from her starring role in *Birdie,* she had had stories published, and she had a plan, to study literature and languages and write.

Meanwhile, Tom finally found a job, "a step up" as he called it, as a senior social-science analyst for the Public Health Service's Dental Health Center in San Francisco. He and Mimi were wild to get back home. So the McCorkles headed back to California, to what seemed like sure success. They couldn't have been more mistaken.

# 1963 TO SUMMER 1966

# Susan Savage

Your family is a burning building. Get out.
  —Rose Segure, mental health professional, to Susan McCorkle

I was appalled to see the casual, throw-away attitude some of the
Berkeleyites like Mimi had, be it their children or inherited
property.
  —Letter from Ethel Hanson, neighbor, about Mimi McCorkle

"Sometimes—when I'm sitting in the Berkeley sunshine, or the San
Francisco fog, or the Oakland drizzle—I'll think about you," wrote
Suzy to her parents. She was 17, fresh out of high school, looking forward to college in the fall of 1963. "I'll remember all the selfish little
things I've done in these seventeen years, and be very much ashamed.
Maybe even cry a little. But then I'll think of some moment when I was
truly unselfish—helping at Maggie's birthday parties, or bringing you
breakfast in bed, or baking Tom an apple pie. And I'll realize that life
will still go on for me. . . . I can only try to be a better person, with all
my heart, with all my heart, with all my heart. Suzy." It was the kind of
letter she'd write all her life; the hyper-sensitivity of a teenager was
something she never outgrew, along with the need to do, to achieve, in
order to be "a better person."

She was determined to achieve all right—in her own way. At first, to
save money, she stayed in the big, dark family house on Shasta Road
and bicycled to the nearby U.C. Berkeley campus. But home was a
strange and unhappy place. Mimi and Tom and Maggie were there,
Tom busy with his new job, Mimi setting up the house while the marriage was showing increasing signs of strain. Added to which was trying to cope with Katie, who lived off-campus in what Suzy described as
"a squalid apartment with pet white rats running loose." Katie was also

28

in the process of flunking out of college (she would eventually graduate from nursing school, years later).

Part of Suzy's shyness and isolation her freshman year had to do with Katie. Arriving in September to the campus, she soon learned that people often mistook her for her sister, whom she then physically resembled. Katie, she found out, had a wild reputation, and people at school assumed Katie's little sister would be the same. Mimi, with her progressive attitudes, assumed—indeed, encouraged—her daughters to be grown-up about their sexual needs, pushing Suzy to be fitted for a birth-control device (no doubt fearing a repeat of Katie's pregnancy and subsequent "operation"). But Suzy shrank from such advice, repelled by her sister's behavior and timid about her own sexuality. Indeed, what she deeply craved then and forever after was romance to go with the sex. About her college years, she wrote, "I never went in for floral shirts, love beads, acid rock, sleeping around. . . . I hated going to parties where everybody smoked dope and lolled around, not talking. I wanted to go to parties to dance, meet a boy, and fall in love."[1]

Spurning both the late-stage beatnik black-clothes scruffy look or the aborning "flower child" look of flowing hair and "ethnic" clothing and bell-bottoms, Suzy cultivated the style of a proper young lady, her hair carefully styled, her dresses prim. Still, for many men she held a paradoxical allure. "She was a big woman, blond, with a generous nose, a million teeth, a bust so large she got used to men holding conversations with her chest," recalled Jon Carroll, a fellow student who became an editor for the campus satirical magazine, the *Pelican,* and is today a columnist for the *San Francisco Chronicle.* "She had big hands that were rarely still, a tiny speaking voice. . . . She looked like some casting director's idea of a barmaid. Inside, though, she was Sylvia Plath. If she had looked like Sylvia Plath, maybe people would have understood."[2] "She was fabulously attractive and did not think she was attractive. I often wondered if she were a prisoner of her own looks," Carroll concluded later. "We were knocked out by her great figure," adds Dick Corten, another of Suzy's editor friends on the *Pelican.*

Another admirer was Art Goldberg, in the circle of campus activists of the New Left in the mid-sixties (he contributed to *Ramparts* magazine, covering Black Panther Bobby Seale's trial in 1971, and became an activist lawyer). It was a time of great social upheaval, tapping into what writer W. J. Rorabaugh describes as "an undercurrent of deep anger, anxiety, frustration with modern life and the sense of powerlessness."[3] And Berkeley, Rorabaugh points out, was at the center of it—a place of friction between "those who clung to tradition" and "those anxious to make changes." In the midst of all this, Goldberg met Suzy at the campus hangout, called the Bear's Lair, where she had a part-time job dishing out ice cream and "weenies." "She was known as Suzy Ice Cream," recalls Goldberg. "I thought she was gorgeous. She was California strikingly beautiful. I was sort of a boyfriend. We went out during the political times there. She was not an activist but open to it." In July 1966, jailed for political activism, Goldberg wrote Suzy letters, but she kept him at an affectionate arm's-length. As indeed she held off everyone. Her naïveté led her into dangerous situations, as when she called Jon Carroll, who'd become an older-brother figure to her, in the middle of the night from a pay phone in an Oakland slum. "Come and get me," she implored; a rebuffed Latin American journalist had dumped her there. Carroll came, and not for the last time. "You're so much trouble," he told her. "But somehow being with you is like being in a movie."

Despite the free room and board at home, Suzy was eager to move out. In her sophomore year she moved into the first of the many modest student studios and bare-bones apartments in which she would live most of her life. She had no boyfriends, she wrote later, and few friends. Apart from the occasional roommate, she seemed to have had virtually no girlfriends until she met Theodora Skipitares, a theater costume-design major who would be her gold standard for colorful, gutsy female independence. At Berkeley in the mid-sixties, Skipitares did outrageous things that entranced Suzy: "She dressed up on holidays— a turkey at Thanksgiving, a rabbit at Easter—and strolled around the campus distributing candy to amused students." Her whimsical and sardonic take on life attracted Suzy, and it was mutual. They became confidantes before Skipitares left for graduate school at UCLA.

She still didn't fit in, not with the hail-fellow-well-met beer and cheap wine-drinking crowd, nor with the beats and just-emerging hippies who offered her pot, which she didn't like. Instead, she kept to herself most of the time, and her drug of choice was food. For once out from under the eagle eye of always-dieting Mimi, Suzy's overeating blossomed. Like a closet drinker, she ate for solace, but it wasn't just a few too many cookies. As she later told her mother, she did outrageous, addict-y things: Unable to wait for the pancakes she was frying to be cooked, she ate from the bowl of raw batter. She crouched in a supermarket aisle, eating an entire box of cookies, then paying for them at the checkout counter. With her weight ballooning, she turned to Mimi's diet pills to slim down. It became a cycle: She'd feel depressed and isolated and eat, feel even dumpier and more unattractive, diet hard and speed on dexies, then stop, crash, and eat some more. "All three of us girls felt mousy and unattractive and that we could never measure up to Mother," says Maggie. "And we all had an eating disorder, including our mother." The fear of fat pursued Suzy all her life. Yet it was largely a distorted perception on her part; she was indeed a bit *zaftig* then but basically a tall, generously framed, well-proportioned young woman.

Suzy found her college courses mostly a disappointment. Intent on a career as a writer, she had decided to major in comparative literature, but though she nailed mostly A's in her introductory courses in sociology, philosophy, and speech (and the required one semester of physical education), she seldom got A's in her lit courses—in fact, she received a lowly C her first term. Like many truly bright students, she floundered in the anonymous, lecture-hall classes the huge university offered. Her freshman year was lackluster as she soldiered on through the requirements (another C in Animal Biology in summer school). In her sophomore year, there were more A's than B's—and no C's. But still just a B in English.

Music—at least the kind of music offered at Cal—was no longer an interest, let alone a passion. She tried it, but she soon dropped out of the hundred-voice female Treble Clef choir and the smaller Choral Ensemble. There were "99 girls singing hymns and Rodgers and Hammerstein," she recalled later. "Suddenly Broadway musicals seemed very establishment and phony to me. Even Peggy Lee and Jo Stafford, though their music was of very good quality, seemed very creamy white and out of character with what I was going through. I went through the '60s thinking [it] was stupid and establishment and boring."[4] Motown was fine to dance to, but rock 'n' roll wasn't, and she spurned "the reedy voices and rudimentary melodies of folk music." There were jazz clubs in the Bay Area, but she wasn't part of the crowd that admired Coltrane's modalism and avant-garde "out" blowing. No one was playing the kind of jazz that would later attract her.

But she had begun to develop other interests and find other outlets for her creativity, as a writer. Suzy made her friends among the mostly male staff on the school humor magazine. The school literary magazine, the *Omnibus,* was not her style (she probably found it tiresome and pretentiously "literary"), nor was she a reporter type, which eliminated the *Daily Californian.* But the *Pelican,* or *Pelly,* as it was nicknamed, was just her style, a beloved institution for Cal satirists, cut-ups, and journalists in the making, the West Coast's answer to the *Harvard Lampoon.* The magazine had its own beautiful building on campus, a California-Japanese Maybeck structure with a double-sized statue in bronze of the California state bird in front, a whimsy donated by Packard car dealer Earle C. Anthony in 1957. Today, surrounded by an architectural hodgepodge of square, boxy teaching warehouses, the *Pelly* building houses the Graduate Student Assembly. But then it was raucous, a kind of alternative frat-house for its staff of eight to ten. An editor, Bob Wieder, reminisced that it was "hobby, obsession, dating service, crash pad, study hall, vice den, and hideaway. . . . We raised hell as we cranked out a humor magazine every six weeks or so. "But then-editors Dick Corten and Jon Carroll quickly admitted Suzy to the fold when she showed up freshman year, submissions in hand. With a platform for her special brand of biting wit, the demure and magnificently busted Suzy fit in. "Her social satire kind of astounded us," recalls Corten. "She was a mixture of shy and bold, and we didn't expect such a tough and searing perspective from her. She'd set up these little playlets, characterizing people very deftly." Jon Carroll wrote her a jocular mash note: "Suszie, Suzie, Susie, Suzy, or ?, the funniest woman in America and the best writer on the Pelican for as far back as I can remember. . . . I love you unashamedly."

She was quickly made an associate editor at the *Pelly,* playing a kind of Dorothy Parker role to Carroll's Robert Benchley and Corten's Donald Ogden Stewart. And like those restless, barbed writers of another turbulent time, the *Pelly* scribes "were not in revolt against society; they merely felt superior to it. Their point was that even if most people might pursue false values, they pursued good ones of their own."[5] It was in Suzy's nature to be a sly satirist, a subversive from within—if never one to storm the campus barricades. Her *Pelly* pieces skewered coeds and campus radicals equally, be they newly minted women's-libbers or free-speech agitators, marijuana-clouded hippies, or Southern Californians. For her *Pelly* nom de plume, Suzy dipped into her pioneer past and came up with the perfect "Susan Savage." It was her first large performance and not often sophomoric. And it was as Susan Savage that she became something of a celebrity on campus, said a

reviewer, for her "unbelievably accurate pictures of the campus scene
. . . cogent, relevant, timely, brilliant, etc."[6]

"Suzy awed *everybody* by her writing and her sharp wit," Dick
Corten stresses. "She was surrounded by competitive, highly prolific
male writers who'd preceded her. But her writing was so different from
theirs and strong on its own." In the yellowing old *Pelicans,* hardy survivors of frequent moves and much neglect, survivors even of a building's fire (now safely archived in the basement of Berkeley's Eshleman
Hall), the young writer's development can be traced, in articles that
vary from adolescent to brilliant. And what a savage bite this teenaged
writer has as well, with none of the *joie de vivre* that infused her later
public personality as a performer.

At 19, a junior, Susan Savage published some clearly autobiographical fiction. "The Physicists," subtitled with broad humor as "an episode
from the a-good-man-is-hard-to-find life of Susan Savage," presages
the bleakly acerbic fictional landscape she inhabited as a writer from
then on. Typically also is the bare-bones plot; psychology and atmosphere and implication are important, not the storyline per se. A protagonist (here called Susan!) picks up two men at a party, bringing
them back to her house, where she gives them food and listens to them
talk—about themselves, what else? Abruptly then, at the edge of some
kind of implied sexual event to which all three seem to have been moving, she angrily kicks them out into the night. (The only clue as to why
she does so is that the two have never talked either about, or to, *her.*) It
is a story that foretells how she'll experience—and write about—many
encounters to come.

Tom and Mimi had returned to Berkeley eagerly from Pennsylvania in
the summer of 1963. "But Tom's new job was another eight o'clock-in-
the-morning thing," said Mimi. "And he wasn't doing real anthropology. He hated it. It was too much for him." Miserable and feeling
trapped at age 52, he complained about the rigidity and rules, about the
"mistrust, double dealing, deception, and counterproductive actions" at
work. This litany was nothing new, but the *intensity* of his mistrust was.
Things were not much better at home. He and Mimi quarreled bitterly;
she was convinced he had betrayed her with a friend called Ann after
she caught them kissing at a party. In retaliation, she pushed apart their
twin beds in the bedroom. (Suzy later went into the bedroom and

pushed them back together, always referring later to the incident—dalliance or affair—as "Ann the hurricane who tore through our family.") Mimi had her own flirtations. "A.D.," one of those Berkeley neighbor ladies who so disliked her, wrote a letter in the 1980s to Jon Carroll, after he'd reported on Susannah's first Bay Area concert in his *San Francisco Chronicle* column. The letter charged Mimi with, among other things, sabotaging her late-bloomer daughter's occasional dates by competing for attention. Wrote A.D., "Suzie always was much too solemn and smart for that mother of hers, for which Mimi never forgave her. . . . When Suzie had boyfriends come around, Mimi would fly into a dither, dressing up in her favorite Lanz nothing, painting her batting eyelids her favorite baby blue, and swirling down to the door, which she opened to reveal some innocent boy. She would overwhelm this poor kid with her attentions, placing herself into direct competition with poor, depressed Suzie."

Despite job and personal problems, Tom was determinedly focused on his career, completing a major paper for presentation at a Dental Health Service convention, rewriting his dissertation into a book, and actively seeking new jobs in his field. But as 1964 led into 1965, Tom's wobbly emotional state took a sharp dip for the worse. His moods were wilder, and his behavior deteriorated. Suzy was terrified, all the more so because Mimi seemed so resolutely bent on denying what was happening. Tom, Suzy felt, had always been somewhat odd and remote, but now her father had taken to doing undeniably strange things, such as wearing his pajamas over a suit. And he mentioned plots: The family dog had informed him of a bomb planted in the yard, he told Mimi, and to Suzy, he said he heard voices telling him about coming disasters, voices emanating from the vacuum cleaner. Later, Tom would write about this awful period when filing for disability claims with his insurance company. He had felt, he wrote, that he was "going crazy," plain and simple, that he wanted the entire public health service "dismantled," that he was full of a blinding brilliance. In his extreme agitation during the early days of 1965, he sought out a psychiatrist, who prescribed the tranquilizer Mellaril. On the medication, he calmed down enough to complete his research project.

But not for long. By February, he was exhausted to the point of collapse and found himself crying uncontrollably in his office. He decided to take a week off, but he could not rest. He wrote that he began to have grandiose delusions of "doing something meaningful for the poor people. After a long period of prolonged disappointment," he added, "and trying to get out of the box, I was out." This was what he termed his "crack-up." Mimi didn't know what to do, where to turn, though she would afterwards downplay the gravity of his breakdown. "He became too jolly, that's all that was the matter," she said years later. But at the time she was desperate. Tom was hallucinating, raving. She called his surgeon brother Horace about finding a psychiatrist. "You're the problem," she said he told her. "He doesn't need a psychiatrist." At last Mimi dug out the name of the psychiatrist Tom had seen in 1964. But when she called, he said he was not available. (In a sad and eerie parallel, Susannah would be similarly turned away by her former psychiatrist when in a terrible mental state in the spring of 2001.) Tom, now paranoid, decided that the doctors were hiding from him under pseudonyms.

Finally, friends gave Mimi the name of a psychiatrist who would see Tom, and she drove her husband to his appointment at the U.S. Public Health Service Hospital in San Francisco, where Tom was hospitalized immediately. "I just never went back to my job," he wrote. He was in the hospital for about three months, part of the time as an outpatient on weekends and then as a long-term outpatient. In March, doctors found that he'd made a stuffed dummy of himself that he kept beside his bed. "And at one point," Mimi related, "he gave his medicine to the flowers in the room to see if they liked it or not. He would look at how one leaf was greener than the others; he was a scientific person and he amused himself with that. But he knew he was sick and he took his medicine, and after he went home, he took his medicine to even out his moods. [At that time, Mellaril, Elavil, and Librium were the main medical treatments of choice to make patients docile.] He had his psychiatrist to help him, mostly to just change the dosage. Still, he had ups and downs—I don't think they stopped."

In fact, Tom was far more than "docile" when he was released from the hospital; he was a shell as he sat by the hour in front of the television watching sit-coms. Nor were the doctors in agreement about a diagnosis, or a treatment plan: Was his a severe form of manic depression? Schizophrenia? Some combination thereof? Most voted for manic depression, today called bipolar disorder. To Mimi, it was simply "Tom's disease."[7]

Tom's mental collapse had devastated Suzy. Desperately worried, she sought out a counselor through Cal's student mental health clinic.

Her concern was to keep the family from unraveling. Mimi was drinking more, Katie was acting out wildly. Who would take care of her little sister, Maggie, she asked the social worker? Should she, Suzy, quit school and assume the role of family caretaker? Rose Segure was interested in the fact that a 19-year-old should feel so responsible for her family. (Coincidentally, Segure had known Tom and Mimi socially.) Suzy felt desperately torn, but she never forgot the warning Segure gave her. It was searing, but released her: "Your family is a burning building. Get out." And Suzy was to take that advice very much to heart, plotting her own escape, while on the other hand, she continued to play an advisory role with her own mother.

While Suzy—and presumably Katie, who had her own problems—faced the horrible situation for Tom as adults, albeit young adults, Maggie was still a child, nine years younger, and saw the family crisis very differently. "I think it was much harder on my older sisters than on me," she says. "I was still young enough to accept whatever my Dad did—he was just my Dad. I was sheltered, my parents were very careful about how I would feel. I just knew my Dad was 'sick.' And my mother is the kind of person who bucked up when there was a real crisis, so I never had any concerns about what was going to happen to the family, or if we were going to have enough money. I never knew that it was very difficult for Susannah and that she didn't like being at home at that time, until about a year before she died, when she finally told me."

While this agonizing family crisis transpired, Suzy took refuge in her first romance—or rather, a safe, completely platonic affair with a man named Bond Johnson, a teaching assistant for a German class she was taking. The two were drawn together by many interests: books, music, cooking, languages—as well as a snobbish aversion to the pop culture of the time. Johnson was supportive and fun and attractive, a good escort, smart, appreciative of Suzy's brains and admiring her as a woman—or so she thought. Although he and another new friend, Maggie McCarthy, smoked pot, as all the world seemed to be doing then, at least all the world that was in college, Suzy still did not. (A few years later, she did consider taking what she called a "capsule" of LSD, betraying by her quaint terminology how square she was when it came to that common hallucinogen of hippiedom.) She apparently never smoked pot either, concerned about how it might affect her emotionally but also put off by all the Berkeley kids who were "such bores" when they got stoned. "They just sit there staring at their laps," she observed.

But her concern about her emotional balance was key: Apparently she instinctively knew that the family genes favored her own instability. Yet she continued to take Mimi's dexies, the "diet pills" that made Mimi "happy" and that she continued to urge on Suzy whenever she thought she was too plump or too dour, which was frequently. Suzy dutifully took them, wanting desperately to lose weight, but, her mother recalled, she complained that they made her feel "all hopped up, keyed up and unhappy and frustrated." Above all, she was frustrated by the lack of progress with her new crush, Bond. The trouble was that Bond was *too* sensitive and empathetic and adoring. He never pawed her or made cheesy remarks about her figure like the student lugs on campus. But she *wanted* him to hold her, she wanted passion. If free love was sweeping the campus and selected elements of the nation, Suzy remained, like Sleeping Beauty, unawakened.

Eager to get away from the family's problems in the summer of 1965, she enrolled in a summer school Spanish course in Mexico City for a month of intensive language instruction at the Universidad Nacional Autónoma. At 19, she was never to spend more than a few days or weeks at her parents' home again. She was often pulled back to the Shasta Road house by the family drama as much by any ties of affection, but when she returned from summer school, Suzy found another tiny apartment and looked for a job. She waitressed at the Bear's Lair, she babysat, she even got a job for a week as an extra in some forgotten adventure movie shot in Marin County. She was saving as much money as possible that year, because she had an escape plan in mind.

Meanwhile, Tom and Mimi began to pick up the wreckage. Tom wouldn't consider going back to work for a government bureaucracy and he let slip another choice university job, a joint appointment in anthropology and public health at the University of North Carolina: "I turned it down because I knew I couldn't do it," he explained. He was simply not able to handle the pressures of a new job. "But at that time we needed money very badly," Mimi confessed. She found a job as a secretary at the university (shades of the thirties, when she'd typed and filed for a year there) and she took over the family finances—her husband was likely to write checks for things they couldn't afford when he was, she said, "too peppy." As for Tom, he wrote, "After three months I thought I'd see what my brothers on the waterfront could do for me." There was plenty of casual work as a ship's clerk in the San Francisco Bay." So it was to be that this man in his fifties, a doctor of anthropol-

*Susan Savage*

37

ogy, worked from May 1965 to June 1966—an entire year—as a tempo-rary warehouse clerk. Sad irony that both he and Mimi were doing the same jobs as they had nearly three decades before, despite all those years of study and achievement. Yet there was still money—a few years before, Mimi had inherited the Berkeley Hills house in her mother's will, and they had investments as well, but they were not to be touched; Mimi feared for the future, feared that Tom would never again be a steady breadwinner.

Back at school for her junior year in September 1965, Suzy's unhap-piness festered. She was fed up with school, though on the surface she was doing well, taking more writing classes, receiving good grades, including many A's. Again, though, the talented writer with her own by-line on the *Pelican* still received no higher than a B in her writing classes that year. She complained vehemently to her parents about the professors and the students, the mindless class discussions, the overlong assignments. "I just want my BA and out!" she said. But to teachers she remained polite, calm, even obsequious. In one obsessively detailed six-page letter to a Spanish teacher (a class she hated), she covered her crit-icism with a veneer of polite, almost cringing respect. She kept up with her *Pelican* writing, and even made something of a nightclub debut in 1966 at the Hungry i in San Francisco, the club that launched the Kingston Trio, the Limeliters, and Mort Sahl. At the club, Suzy and the rest of the *Pelly* masthead joined singer John Gary (he'd had a recent hit with the song "More" from the movie *Mondo Cane*) on stage for a tongue-in-cheek tribute; there is a photo of Suzy, in her prim librarian's dress, French twist hairdo and heels, feigning a fan's fainting spell while Gary sings.

Deciding to change her major to Italian, since she correctly reasoned that languages came easy to her and she wanted to learn Italian, Suzy began to look at exchange programs abroad that would give her an excuse to go to Europe. More than ever, she dreamed of going away. She would go, she plotted, to Germany and Paris and maybe Italy to work on her languages, as part of the university's education abroad pro-gram. Her sister Katie had been given a year abroad in 1960, hadn't she? Well, now it was Suzy's turn. She couldn't have chosen a worse time in terms of the family's finances—Mimi working as a secretary, Tom a dock clerk—but Suzy was well aware of the nest egg of stocks and bonds that Mimi controlled and persevered in persuading her par-ents to help bankroll her year abroad.

Tom's mental equilibrium was still shaky, but he was already think-ing about getting a "real" job again; he could not go on indefinitely as he was. And shortly after the new year of 1966, he was offered a job at Long Beach State College, near Los Angeles, as an associate professor without tenure. For a man of his training and ambition, Long Beach, at that time a teacher's college, was a comedown, far less prestigious than the research-oriented university jobs he'd so recently been offered and declined. And it would mean another move, to what Berkeleyites viewed as the uncultured south. But Tom well knew that opportunities were fewer for a middle-aged professor with a checkered career who had just had a severe breakdown. With a family and a pile of bills, he took the job.

Was he up to it? It was a gamble. "We didn't know what would hap-pen," said Mimi, "but we moved to Long Beach, leaving Susan in charge of the house in Berkeley, to rent out for us. At first, Tom and I were nervous. For the first semester—the fall of 1966—he wrote down everything that he was going to say every day before he went to class, because he wasn't sure how he'd handle it. It was really touchy, and we didn't know what would happen. He had pills for the depression, but he'd forget them. Then he'd take them again when I asked him to. He was depressed a lot, and when he got a spell it was as if you weren't there for three or four months. He would sit and read books but would never do anything unless he was asked to. I'd go off somewhere else when he was sick like that; I had to get *something* to do—work. I did everything I could think of." Some jobs were unsuited—she tried sell-ing real estate and working in a dress shop, but disliked the atmo-sphere. "I liked working in schools. I was a teacher in a childcare school, and about 1967, I returned to college and got my teaching cre-dentials, and I was a substitute teacher all around the county of Los Angeles. And I worked with the League of Women Voters, too.

"There were not many manic times, but I liked them much better than when Tom wouldn't do *anything*. Because he would get to feeling loose and happy and wild, and he'd buy things and pay me more atten-tion then, and he'd want to *do* things. But then, as it went on, he wouldn't sleep, and I'd get terrorized. He'd go down to the beach, and I didn't know what he was going to do. Whatever it was, he'd do it all night, and he seemed to have a really good time, but it was rough on me. Then later, he would be quiet and just sit and answer yes or no."

All the women in his orbit were affected by his disease differently.

*Susan Savage*

Katie herself was, as it turned out, in the midst of a long struggle with mental illness. "It took a long, long time for doctors to figure out what medication she needed," Maggie says. "She's not schizophrenic, which she was first diagnosed and treated for. She has a very severe bipolar disorder." But stability was, then, far in the future for the oldest McCorkle daughter.

For Suzy, the middle daughter, witnessing her father after the crisis of his manic breakdown was traumatic. "Susannah told me," says Maggie, "that after that time, Dad was just a vegetable. That he was never 'normal' for her again. She was just destroyed by that." Maggie found it easiest to cope. "To me, Dad just got on medication, and then we moved when he got a job as a university professor and spent the last years of his career teaching. He was even the head of his department at one point. He was just my Dad."

During the 15 years that Tom McCorkle was a professor at Long Beach, he did research in a modest way, achieved tenure, and was indeed named department chairman in 1976. He and Mimi and Maggie summered in Uruapán, where at least on several occasions, he brought along students to do field research about modern middle-class Mexican society in the town. Despite his mental problems, Tom was a man's man, liked and appreciated by colleagues and later, by Susannah's husbands. When Professor Robert Harman took his first job at Long Beach State four years after Tom had moved there, he recalls, "Tom McCorkle was the only faculty member to invite my wife and me over. He made daiquiris and margaritas in large quantities. He was a very good host. He was very, very bright. I knew he was a manic depressive. I found him to be a really warm person—that is, when he was in a comfortable environment. But he was ill at ease with people—with students." On the other hand, Tom was to write no more monographs, publish in no more prestigious journals, develop no more adventurous projects. And as his classes developed a reputation for aridity and dryness, students stayed away in droves. Finally, "worn out"—Tom's words—by the job of chair, he took early retirement in 1980.

Mimi was hardly the dutiful little wife helping quietly in the background. Certainly she alienated a good many people in the Long Beach crowd. "She had splashy fallings-out with several people," Maggie says. "I went to a party with her at the end of her life, and Mother told me about a woman there who she said was a rival of hers for Tom in college. Mother was 84 and she *still* held a grudge after all those years! She thought all the women were jealous of her—and maybe they were." Well, she was Lonely Mimi too, isolated to some extent by her husband's disease and also by her own considerable faults and limitations. And yet it fell to Mimi to be the glue that kept the McCorkle family together. She did so, and though Tom at times ridiculed her mind, he also characterized her as his "staunch" wife.

While during that traumatic year of 1966, Mimi and Tom picked themselves up and found a new job and a new start in Long Beach in the summer, Suzy had as little to do with the family as possible. She was making her own plans. She went to summer school and aced Elementary Italian in an intensive course, preparing her, as she hoped, for her European sojourn that fall.

"She came from a seriously messed-up family, which I only knew about in bits and pieces," says Jon Carroll. "This was a time when people were not particularly candid about sharing their family secrets." It was this burden of family, this burden of self, that Suzy McCorkle longed to escape as if she were gasping for air. In Europe, she envisioned freedom, order, beauty. "I was looking," she said simply, "for a saner place to live."

# 1966 TO 1968

# *La Signorina Scontenta*

## *The Discontented Lady*

> Lots of times I walk along the street singing "I Enjoy Being a
> Girl" and "Zippety Doo-Dah." It seems as if I never could have
> been unhappy, and as if I will never be unhappy again. Oh, thank
> you for this year. Love, Suzy
> —Letter to Mimi and Tom, May 1967

Despite the fact that Suzy had saved some money and that Katie had
been given a year abroad, Tom and Mimi were reluctant to agree to
their second daughter's plan to take off for Europe for a year, even
when she promised to take courses at exchange programs in foreign
universities. Ironically, it was Suzy's obvious intelligence that made
them oppose the plan—she, clearly, was the daughter who had a fine
university career ahead of her, and they intended her to get at least a
master's degree if not a doctorate like her father. But she was adamant
about having her break from the course grind, her year abroad like
Katie, threatening to quit school altogether if they did not agree—and
pay for it. She needed their financial support, despite her ongoing
babysitting and waitressing. To her, the university seemed a waste of
time and the source of much unhappiness, from her "affair" with Bond
Johnson that was going nowhere to her sense of being a genuine misfit,
neither a square nor a hipster. And above all, there was her intuition
that she must go away and create to save herself from her unhappy family life and to prove to herself that she was a writer of true talent.

At last, Suzy did wrangle her parents' agreement and, more importantly, their financial commitment to a year in Europe. In late summer,
Suzy formally withdrew from the University of California at Berkeley.

Though she'd agreed to use the year in Europe to perfect the languages she'd studied—French, German, and now Italian—what she really wanted was to hang out, to experience Europe, to drift where she would. Suspecting as much, Mimi and Tom sat her down for a serious talk, urging her not to neglect her studies. At any rate, they added, they couldn't long afford to subsidize what they called her "aimless wandering." The plan eventually agreed upon was that she'd begin by auditing German at the Leopoldsuniversität in Munich for the fall term, then register for the second term either in Paris or in Padua, Italy; Cal had exchange programs in both cities. She'd have enough credits at that point, they calculated, to finish up her bachelor's degree when she returned home for summer school in 1967.

Agreeing to this itinerary, Suzy prepared her bags and in September flew over to Heathrow in England. She had a few days to spend in London. This was the city that was to play such a crucial role in her singing career just five years later, but she had little interest in English-speaking places then. She traveled by train to Vienna, then backtracked, hitchhiking to Munich to sign on at the Leopoldsuniversität to audit classes. Hers was always to be the poor student's lifestyle while in Europe. She was always trying to scrape together enough money to survive, constantly moving from one room with shared bath to another, staying in hot attics and in cold spare bedrooms. Money: There would never be enough of it—never. The need for it shaped her days—the need to get it, but without working for it—and money was a constant topic in her letters home. She was a faithful correspondent. She wrote charming letters, anecdotal letters, pleading letters, explaining letters, wheedling and sometimes angry letters. And in all of them, Suzy asked for money. Money for a better room to live in, a dress, a pair of shoes, a train trip, the oversized bras she had to order from the States, fabric for a dress or a skirt. "How I hate to talk about money, which has already caused much too much distress in our family," she said. But she did talk about it, all the time. However, she also told wonderful, exuberant stories of a young woman of 20, big and blonde and buxom and smart, who was intoxicated by a different way of life, a prisoner let out into the sun. Suzy entertained Tom and Mimi about getting lost in Munich and trying to express herself in German, and the heavy German food. It was not hard to be charming and loving to her parents from far away. "School begins at the beginning of November," she wrote to reassure them as she flitted from place to place all October. "Now I see that I was wittier, brighter, more imaginative, and more humanitarian than my empty-headed high school friends. The very things that set me apart from other kids in high school make my life rich and full and make me attractive to people."

But her moods, as usual, could swing quickly the other way, and her private agony was never far from the surface and would become all too apparent soon enough. For now Suzy was dazzled by the newness of everything around her, her wonderful illusion of escape. "I felt I would crack up if I stayed on in America," she said years later.[1] In the heady foreignness of old Europe, she must have felt that she had freed herself from the dark and lonely feelings that had caused her so much emotional pain. She had always dreamed of having a trusted female confidante, a soul friend, and when she met Katja, a Yugoslav student slightly older than she who was married to a German who was also a student at the university, she was ecstatic. "She is by far the closest friend I've ever had," she confided in Mimi with delight. "I love her very, very much and am already sad just thinking how we are destined to spend most of our lives far away from each other. There's nothing like a close friend of the same sex."

Katja, though, was married, and Suzy was still thrown on her own company a good deal. She found the university lectures just as dull in Europe as she had at Berkeley and cut most of them to read novels in English, voraciously but constantly inspired by them, inspired to write, or to try to write—she threw away most of her attempts. Later that year, she wove Katja and others she'd met into "Cordelia," a story that won the 1969 *Mademoiselle* magazine's College Fiction prize, an important award then for emerging writers. Clearly, the well-read Suzy was familiar with Christopher Isherwood; "Cordelia" has much of the restless, bohemian, poor-artist atmosphere of his *Berlin Stories,* the book that inspired the musical *Cabaret.* In "Cordelia," a group of young artist types share an apartment: "Bill sings, Kirsten plays piano, or we play beautiful records and talk." Into this dilettantish and aimless air, Suzy introduces a disturbing element: the title character, the unstable girlfriend of an acquaintance. As Cordelia acts out, her mental unraveling and just-under-the-surface suffering is conveyed with a curious air of detachment by the narrator, as if she were viewing a play rather than the self-destruction of a human being. "I am very much a part of my surroundings but I am also able to step back and look at them coolly," Suzy told her mother.

By now Suzy had shed that name for what she felt was the more seri-ous-sounding Susanna (the "h" was yet to come). Winter came to Munich, and her high spirits drooped. She was beset with the home-sickness that so often tests young people on their first ventures to see the world. And despite the companionship of Katja, she was lonely. She continued to read enormously. Mornings, she went to the university library to read Tolstoy (*Anna Karenina* and *War and Peace*), George Eliot, Zola, Balzac, Thomas Mann, and Bernard Malamud. Lunch was the important meal of the day—cheap and filling potatoes and gravy at school; she complained they were making her fat. After language classes in the afternoon, it was home at night to her little room in a widow's house, where she devoured more books and tried to write.

There was an opening at Berlitz for an English teacher, but Susanna resisted taking it, explaining to her parents when they urged her to take the job that she realized she'd come to Europe to experience the conti-nent—and to write. "It's not money I want but moral support." Susanna was always a formidable advocate for her vision of things. In the summer, she promised them, she'd work as a receptionist at a hotel on the Costa del Sol, or teach English, or be an extra in the Munich Opera, or a tour guide in Italy. (She did not follow through on any of these jobs.) In the years she was to live in Europe (for she would return in 1969 and stay for another eight years), Susanna became impressively adept at asking Tom and Mimi for money while seeming not to. She asked prettily or nicely or guilt-provokingly, and she asked endlessly. When Mimi, the controller of the purse, dug her heels in, Susanna used her trump card: All right, then, Susanna would say, then she'd sell the stock her grandmother had left her as a nest egg, an unspecified amount of money but something. Loath to let her daughter compro-mise her future security, Mimi invariably gave in and found some cash somewhere, wiring it to the nearest American Express office.

Still, the thousand dollars that Tom and Mimi had sent her off with in September could and did go far indeed in those years. Susanna spent a week in Berlin, where she heard the Berlin Philharmonic, attended a Brecht play, went to art museums and restaurants. There was no singing, no jazz, no whisper of the music in her that was to come—not yet.

Susanna and Mimi had developed a curious kind of intimacy from afar, after much estrangement. Susanna wrote letter after letter—often nearly every day. Some expressed her yearning for a happy fam-ily life:

In our family none of us has done a very good job of making the others feel important, but then conditions were pretty adverse. Oh I want to see you and Tom and Mag, I want to watch sunsets with you in Mexico and sit around a table and make tacos and talk about what's happened that day. We are really a blessed family. There have been bad times, but now we are coming out of the bad times and we are better people for having come through them with love, hope and humor intact. This year I guess we all realized that we do love each other, but we love each other more if Katie and I aren't in the house all the time.

In others, such as this 1967 letter, Susanna appeared to switch roles with Mimi, advising her about her love life with a patronizing tone that she was surely not aware of:

Tom does too love you . . . [only] he is not very demonstrative about his emotions. You just have to learn to look for the proof of love you need in the small, subtle ways. I know from his letters he realizes you are not very happy in some ways (he blames it on menopause and has been blaming it on menopause for at least since I was a junior in high school). I told him you wished he would push the beds back together [you—Mimi—had pushed them apart] after Hurricane Ann swept through our household and tore it up. You are a very very attractive couple.

These advice-filled letters would continue, as in this from Paris in 1969, during Susanna's second European foray:

Remember that Tom was deeply humiliated by his illness, and may be feeling he doesn't deserve to be loved and respected and looked up to by you. He doesn't seem to have too much energy sometimes (I'm sure he wishes he had more energy). I hope you can find nice interesting people (for him to meet) but not people who make him feel challenged (in terms of intelligence, professional prowess, etc.) so that he feels inferior or defensive. Try to remember always that he is a brilliant, sensitive, imaginative, kind man who never fulfilled his potential . . . think of all his dreams, all the things he was going to do and now almost certainly won't. You can be sure that he is haunted by these things.

In January 1967, Susanna turned 21. For her birthday, Mimi wired her $500. Her German term had ended, and Susanna now decided to make her bid for full independence, writing to tell her parents that she was tired of Germany and of Germans. Moreover, she was tired of auditing foreign universities. She had a new plan: She'd spend a few months in Paris, where she'd take French at the Alliance Française, and then head to Italy to study Italian. But no more exchange programs. Nor did she think she'd return to school in the States the following fall. She no longer had, she said, any clear "academic aim." Also, she noted, then-governor Reagan had finally succeeded in shoving through some new legislation in the California Legislature. It required, for the first time, that in-state college students pay tuition. It was too expensive for her now, wrote Susanna.

But her logic eluded her parents: What did she want to do with her life? "Now Dad," she responded to one of Tom's mild admonishments, "you're writing to me like a son again. I'm positive I don't want to go to graduate school. I want to write fiction, not anthropological essays about 'interrelationships of culture, language, and psychology' . . . but short stories." That was her dream, of an unencumbered life as a writer, yet Susanna still longed—as she would always long—for a kind of pre-1960s, pre-feminist happy home life. She fantasized, she told her parents, about being a professor's wife (Bond Johnson's). But her words—"I really feel my sense of importance will derive from the knowledge that I am making my husband, and later, my children, feel important and special"—sounded cardboard, unconvincing.

Her letters at the time reveal a Susanna increasingly plunged in gloom or in an incandescent state of excitement and love for everything and everybody. She was living a crowded life as a desirable young woman with a hectic-sounding shifting series of admirers, adventures, and near-dalliances, some of whom she described to Mimi and Tom, but not all. Though she had been fantasizing about going back to Berkeley and marrying Johnson, with whom she kept up a frequent correspondence, she told Mimi that winter that she was "off Bond for awhile. All the men here think I'm a big gorgeous sexy hunk of woman and I must say that I enjoy thinking of myself as a lusty, healthy woman rather than as a frustrated female intellectual (which I was with Bond)." In her big-sis, advice-dispensing voice, she added to Mimi, "Even if things are much better there in Long Beach for you and Tom than they have been for ten years, it is obvious that you are bored and that your boredom is going to grow into unhappiness unless you can find some interesting things to do. I don't want to sound like a daughter patronizing her mother. [Sounding just that, of course.] You should go out every day if just for a walk, go to museums, lecture series. Many of them are really superb: e.g., bright men discussing Vietnam, race problems, art lectures with slides. Finally though, you need friends. It is especially difficult for an intelligent woman who is also pretty and concerned about how she looks to find female friends." Practically in the next breath, she fell back to an older role, that of needy daughter-suppliant: "Will you please make me some new dresses, send me money for fabric? Also, please don't be mean to me by letter. I accept your way for you and do not persecute you about it and I do not see why you can't be more tolerant. We are just different people who are happy in different ways. Mean things penetrate deep and last long."

Now that Susanna got it that men found her attractive, she needed a lot of attention to confirm her sense of allure, the feeling of power that some women inhale like a perfume, a drug. When she was at Cal, her friend Jon Carroll notes, "she had no idea that she had a powerful effect on men." Well, now she did. Soon she affected a kind of sophistication that was not yet convincing, the ennui of an older and more experienced woman. "Every week I run through men and cast them away— too dull!" There was a constant supply, she told her glamorous mother rather competitively. "It's awful to hurt a person, worst of all when just your very existence on earth hurts him," she added breezily.

One thing she did not discuss willingly with her mother was sex. Susanna had arrived in Europe truly as "an innocent abroad." In high school (a reaction to her older sister's promiscuity?), she'd vowed to remain a virgin until she was married. In college, she amended the rule: She'd make love only if she was in love. But Bond, with whom she was in love, or sort of in love, held her at arm's-length, permitting only a buss on the cheek, a friendly hug. Now at 21, she decided to rid herself of the encumbrance of her virginity, finding a "nice boy" who, she later recalled, kept his socks on throughout the venture, and then stood her up the next night. A fine romance.

There was still the problem of how to justify her time in Europe to her parents and after much heated back-and-forth, she agreed to apply for Cal's education abroad program at the University of Padua in Italy, which would give her the remaining credits she needed in her major. In agreeing to this plan, Susanna was being canny, making sure not to enroll until the following September, which meant she would not have to go home to America for the summer. "And Dad, if that doesn't pan out, I've decided to return to Berkeley to try again," she added.

Meanwhile, she had months and months to enjoy herself. Fleeing Germany for Venice a month after her German term ended in February 1968, Susanna reveled in the beauty of the place and the attention she got. And it was crucial that Mimi, especially, knew about it. "Imagine meeting a man called Donatello! He thinks I'm beautiful." There were many Donatellos appreciative of her ripe form, but she was determined to shed the potatoes-and-gravy weight. She went on Mimi's diet, balancing Dexedrine and Miltowns. "Those diet pills juice me up an awful lot. Everything is so intense and beautiful sometimes, that I think I will go crazy so full of happiness! I am so full of love and wonder that people stare at me as I walk down the street and smile at me without knowing why. I'm so excited now I can hardly sit still. . . . There are no more thundercloud periods of depression, no eating binges. I have something better than beauty: happiness that radiates from me and my down moods are rare here." Speed-induced happiness muted by "minor" tranquilizers, but for Susanna, a rare experience of hope and the sense of so many possibilities in her life. She would chase this golden time, this memory of happy expectation, all her life.

The good times continued to roll. In March, it was on to Paris, where she stayed in a cheap hotel in the Latin Quarter (no shower or bath; she cadged baths from expat friends of her parents who were staying there). She ate jam waffles bought from street vendors while she walked around the streets of Paris, looking at people and doing tourist things. She bought Dior's perfume Eau de Sauvage, "because I am a Savage." She liked French culture—went to hear a lecture at the Sorbonne and to a Molière play at the Comédie Française, but she didn't care much for the French. Frenchmen, she said from her 21-year-old newfound wisdom, "have much less pride and charm than Italians. And you think their women are all pretty until you begin to look at each one individually. They are shrewd, hard folk," she concluded. When Bond Johnson came over with other Berkeley friends, he was friendly, but the romance still went no further and she was—temporarily—crushed. "Men are so important to me that it depresses me terribly to have so many selfish, dull and even evil ones in the same city." But Susanna, again taking Mom's diet–calming pill combos, was restored to her glowing high, and Bond and sneering Frenchmen seemed hardly to matter. "It seems I have everything," she gushed in a letter home, "youth, energy, imagination, a radiant glow from Italy, time and money my parents have given me freely and trusted me to spend wisely."

It was in Paris that winter of 1968 that Susanna had her first faint taste of the future that awaited her around the corner, as a singer of American standards. The French liked old American musicals, and with a friend she went to see the 1945 biography of George Gershwin, *Rhapsody in Blue,* which included bits from his opera *Porgy and Bess.* "I cried and cried—I loved the Negroes who reminded me of my friends in the 'Bear's Lair'—and the music!" she wrote home, a bit quaintly. She had tentative plans to study at the Alliançe Française, but she found Paris unbearable, so she left, as she explained in a letter home, writing from the Costa Brava, where she'd wound up after a cheap and very long train ride, to look into a job that didn't pan out. After early enthusiasm, she greatly disliked Spain—or, rather, Spanish men, whom she found frightening. "They make awful hissing and kissing noises and say really obscene things." Her incredible figure was a constant burden to her; blouses and dresses did not fit, and even the largest brassieres in Europe were too small. "The saleswomen in the stores look at me as if I WERE A FREAK when I try to buy a bra—my size doesn't exist here."

So she hitchhiked back to Venice, the place and the people—generous, humorous, mostly kindly—that she liked best. It was April, warm and sunny, and it was here, she decided, that she would stay, learning enough Italian "to get into the advanced program in Padua in the fall." At the Bar Paolin, in a rather nondescript square off the tourist track, she sat for hours conversing with everyone. There, she heard of a room in an old palazzo (with the important added privileges of permission to use the kitchen and bath), in the flat of yet another widow, this one with three children.

She wrote home amusing descriptions of everything—the fashions of Italy, their shoes and fabrics (these things interested her mother), and the men, of course. People, she said, were fantastically kind to her. She loved the place and the people—and briefly, the children. They were everywhere—in her flat, playing in the squares. "Suddenly I find myself wanting a child very very much," she wrote her mother. "But I realize that it would not be too practical for me to have a child." She spent dreamy days of sunny indolence sitting in "her" café, then the large (60-cent!) noonday dinner she took at the university, afterward reading and writing in her room during the long afternoons before going out to look at art or hear concerts in the evening—Artur Rubenstein playing Chopin at the Teatro La Fenice (half-price seat). "I still love Mozart, I hate Ravel and Liszt and am not too crazy about Bach, in whose music I hear a constant metronome." Evidence of a precise ear, the critical mind, but no exposure to jazz, not yet.

Again, her money was getting low, yet she refused offers to work in a boutique or do legal translations in an office. She'd rather go broke, she declared, than take a job now. It was too glorious a time in her life—and she intended to do some serious writing as well. "For the first time in my life, I can sit quietly with my hands folded peacefully in my lap." Having thinned down (not enough to please her, but enough), she discarded the uppers and downers.

And then, peace didn't last long; it never did for Susanna. Though she had set herself an ambitious reading program of Shakespeare's *Romeo and Juliet, Othello,* and—of course, given where she was living—*The Merchant of Venice,* she hadn't written anything for months. It was too noisy in the widow's flat with the three children. She began to look for a quieter, sunnier room.

Though she seemed oblivious to it, Susanna's dreamy neediness made her a sexual target, but she felt competent to deal with it. "I wonder if you realize how skilled I am at handling dangerous men?" she wrote to her worried father that year, after a teasing mention of a date with an older man. Not long after that, having looked in vain for her quiet, sunny new room, she began a conversation with two Swiss who were sitting at "her" café. When they suggested that their pensione might suit her, she agreed to come have a look. Once there, one of the men lured her into his room, locked the door, tied her up, and proceeded to assault and rape her for what she said was hours. Finally, she managed to escape and ran until she was in a vaporetto, a boat that traveled the canals. On the other side, the conductor began a brief flirtation but, seeing Susanna's anguish, accompanied her to the door of the widow's apartment and waited until she had turned her key and gone safely inside. There, she frantically washed herself and collapsed sobbing on her bed. She told no one, and certainly not the police. She felt helpless, just "some American girl with huge breasts and blonde hair, not even a registered student."

Mercifully, there was one person Susanna could turn to: an older woman, the mother of her landlady in Vienna, with whom she had formed a bond. Susanne Eschmann was a fairly well-off woman who'd had a colorful, committed life. She now lived most of the time in a villa at Lake Maggiore in the scenic northern Piedmont region of Italy. Susanna phoned her to ask if she could come, packed her bags, and hitchhiked there. It was a nightmare journey; she was convulsed with flashbacks as she accepted rides from strange men. Reaching Eschmann's house, she collapsed, sobbing. Eschmann nursed her and, Susanna wrote later, gave her the stark advice of an early feminist: "You are *auffalend,* she said—conspicuous—walk with more decorum, dress conservatively." She foresaw an important career for Susanna as a writer. "And don't marry and have children someday!" she added. "You will never accomplish anything if you do!" The two celebrated with champagne when Susanna discovered she wasn't pregnant.

Returning to Venice, Susanna told no one of the rape—only her second experience of sexual intercourse. Keeping her inner anguish to herself was, after all, part of a pattern she'd established in childhood. In time, she would be able to talk about the rape and its aftermath to her second and third husbands and several close women friends as well as writing about it. "These were the things that she said scarred her," Ingham says. "She could be very naive in a lot of ways: this child-woman split, the underlying part of her persona." Says her third husband, Dan DiNicola, "We visited Italy in '86 and were staying with a friend from her college days in Venice, and she brought it up casually, how two guys had lured her into a room where one had raped her, and then around the same time she mentioned it at dinner at a fund-raiser for Senator Lieberman, brought it up almost offhandedly."

But there was nothing casual or offhand about it in Venice that spring and summer of 1968. Suffering from a kind of post-traumatic stress, Susanna coped by retreating from reality, going every day to the public beach of the Lido to lie there drawing in the sand with a stick, like a child. Again she took a room, in another widow's apartment, and stayed by herself. She felt herself drifting "again and again over a line into madness and oblivion and then floating back to the safety of conscious anguish."[2] But in her letters to Tom and Mimi, she kept up the fiction that all was well. She was writing, meeting people, missing her family, and still reading American novels, she said. She even recommended a book to them, Saul Bellow's *The Adventures of Augie March.* "Like all my favorite novels, it is both very funny and very sad." It was fiercely hot; there was no air-conditioning. "I drink water all morning and write and then to the Lido beach in the afternoon, a pleasant boat-ride away and at night I sleep only in my earrings." She told them nothing of what had happened. But to Bond, she wrote daily letters "crammed with my experiences and documenting my emotional development."

Seeing and speaking only to waiters and shop clerks, she brooded about her future and obsessed about money, writing to Mimi to plead for $350 here, $500 there, masterfully guilt-tripping her parents when they balked. "It sounds as if you are out of money troubles—a new car!" began one of Susanna's campaigns home for an American Express money order. "It is much easier for me, young, single and terribly happy anyway, to economize than for you and Tom and you must never again feel that you are failing any of us kids if you don't support us. You won't have to send me any more money for some time now. So please don't hold grudges. I honestly try hard not to ask for favors from you but it seems whenever I do ask them they are such a big pain in the neck to you that I should just try to do without. I promise I'll think hard before asking you to send me anything again."

Gradually, she re-engaged with her serious writing. "My goal," she wrote them, "is to have at least half a dozen finished, polished stories at the end of the summer. I am kind of lonely, which is very good for working hard. I don't go out much," she added. She was still planning to go to the Padua exchange program and traveled to Munich to see Katja and get her things that she'd left there in storage. At the end of the summer, she went on the cheap to Greece. Though the country was convulsed at the time with violent civil strife, Susanna focused on the domestic details of the place and the people. Then back in Venice, she prepared to go to Padua, saying her bittersweet good-byes to her tall view of church towers and red roofs, the recent, searing violent memories still all too fresh in her mind.

When Susanna arrived near the end of September in Padua, she found the ancient town a charming place, its walls, many of them, still decorated with ancient coats of arms and family seals. Surely this would be a lovely place to study in. But almost immediately, her teachers gave her the nickname of the "signorina scontenta"—the discontented miss. Still in trauma, she buried her fear and shame and concentrated on the school. It was a severe disappointment. She found the program stuffy, slow, unimaginative, and was adamant that she would not live in a dormitory with the other female students—she lasted there two days.

"They are fantastic the way they go to dinner in squadrons of five or six and toast marshmallows (bought at the nearby US Army PX) over candle flames with bent bobby pins as sticks," she wrote her parents. "The class of seven is filled with the same empty-headed childish students who ruined my seminar classes at Cal. If the teacher assigns us a story to read, they protest: 'Oh, geez, it's twenty pages long. Couldn't we do two pages a night or something?' It's like a permanent slumber party. If it comes down to a choice between quitting the program or living in a dormitory, I will quit the program." With the determination that she would later direct at reinventing herself as a jazz singer, Susanna found her own room off-campus over the vociferous objections of the administration; she even found a fellow free spirit, Gloria, who was willing to split the rent.

Though the actual classes were to begin in November, the prep work turned out to be way too elementary for Susanna—she already had learned basic Italian. She decided she'd made a big mistake and determined to quit the program—though she would somehow end up with solid A's for the course. She and Gloria played hooky constantly, going to Venice for concerts and to Milan for opera at La Scala; and finally, at the end of November, leaving altogether for Rome. Rome: the city where she would be awakened to love and to music. But not yet. Still, she and the bohemian Gloria enjoyed themselves. When their cheap pensione room turned out to be a brothel by night, they laughed it off. They hitchhiked everywhere and went out with men, especially married men. It was, in fact, straight out of *La Dolce Vita*—Susanna and her politician, Susanna and her factory owner (linens), Susanna and her car-parts dealer. And most important, Susanna and her architect, Massimo, who was going to Berkeley in January to teach city planning at Cal. And her "Via Veneto playboy. Until he met me," she wrote home proudly. "Two men whose lives I could share happily I think." (A "nightmarish" trip to Naples with Gloria and the former playboy removed him from the wish list, and Massimo disappeared soon after as well.) She sent home another plea for money: "If this makes you short on cash we can sell my stock immediately upon my arrival in the U.S. and I'll give you the money. Here I am," she continued, "twenty one years old and everything going for me, in Rome, losing weight, having a suit made, speaking Italian, with lots of leisure time and enough money in a beautiful and interesting city, meeting attractive men. I'm homesick, though, I want to come home for Christmas, then I'll begin

Cal in January. I want to walk down the street without having men say 'Mamma mia!' at me."

All the Italian men seemed to be willing props for her avid need to be considered attractive and desirable. However, having sex was unthinkable since the rape in Venice. And remarkably, she still day-dreamed about Bond and planned a meeting—he was going to New York, where his family lived, for the holidays, and they arranged for Susanna to stop off there before going on to California. "We are so close," she confided in Mimi, pouring herself into a wifely role modeled on the 1950s sitcom *Father Knows Best.* "We understand each other and love and are made sad by the same things and he really believes in me as a writer. Ever since I met Bond I've been sure he was right for me. I'm about to enter my third year of being in love with him, and he's either beginning to be in love with me back or beginning to show it. It's swell to be gorgeous and charming for all these very appreciative European men, but finally Bond is the one man I really believe in. I want to proofread his brilliant papers, bake cookies for him, hang out his wash and wear shirts, make him laugh and keep his ideas and vulnerability while he fights our way in this tough world." She added, "This is not to be joked about over drinks with friends, okay? Please."

The trouble was, Bond didn't want her to bake and wash and proof-read, much less to make love to. He met her plane at Kennedy Airport. "The moment I saw him standing there," she realized, "I knew what I had not known before, or had . . . been unwilling to admit to myself." Nothing was said, everything was known: He was gay. "I loved him and though I was always sad that he wouldn't ever touch me or kiss me, I was happy to love someone so much." Susanna had her revenge when—still with nothing of consequence said between them—they went to a museum in Manhattan, quarreled, and parted for several hours to cool off. Susanna, she later described, picked up a stranger in one of the galleries and went off with him immediately for a sexual encounter, arriving late to her rendezvous with Bond, flushed and disheveled. Bond was sullen and turned away; it was over between them. Yet Susanna was grateful to Bond. "It was he who taught me that I felt myself to be a misfit, strange, unhappy, insecure, because I was sensitive, and that this sensitivity was a great gift, to be used and developed and left free." Never again did she talk about washing shirts and typing papers and baking cookies for a man as a goal.

When she arrived at the other part of the American world, in Long

Beach, Susanna managed several days with the family before fleeing back up to Berkeley. She loved Christmas—loved its pretty promise of a warm, festive family gathering—but found the status quo of a depressed Dad, critical Mom (especially when she drank, and she drank often), and little sister she never saw because she was always in her room. And Katie. "I sort of feared I'd finish school before her and I think that would have made her feel bad," she confided to Mimi, adding, "I think it's wonderful you and she are getting along so well." This was a short-lived truce. Susanna's sister told her parents she was planning to get married on the beach: When they showed up for the ceremony, there was no one there. She was combative, especially with her mother, in perpetual need of something—money to live on, money for bail for herself or her boyfriends, etc. Mimi fought with her constantly. "And Tom was always hoping that she would snap out of it," recalls Dan DiNicola.

With teeth clenched, Susanna enrolled in Berkeley in January 1968. "There is a great tradition in my family of going to Berkeley—both my parents, grandmother and others," she commented. "It wasn't the right university for me, though." But at the time it seemed a good decision, and at least she could again live free of charge in the Shasta Road house, where she served as rental agent for her parents, finding roomers and managing the property. She was determined to save as much money as she could in order to go back to Europe. Part-time jobs were awful. She worked weekends serving drinks in a tavern "where drunken fraternity boys made jokes about my big breasts, poured beer on me, and tried to follow me home." School was just as bad, long papers to write about scads of mediocre Italian poetry. But she was determined to stick it out and graduate in December. The one bright spot seemed to be her old *Pelican* crowd. She regaled them with her adventures in Europe. Says Dick Corten, "She had total recall and an ability to pull out the languages and play all the characters when she was telling a story from her travels. She was the most dramatically talented in our little group, but very sensitive and easily injured emotionally. Her extremes were more extreme: She was the sunniest personality and very cheerful when she was up; and during her downs, she would retreat into silence." She confided in no one, not even her older-brother pal Jon Carroll. "She was very private; she had other worlds going," Carroll says.

Susanna now found campus life unbearable in every respect except the *Pelican* writing and friends (and Skipitares had gone on to graduate school in what Berkeleyites viewed as low-brow L.A.). It was a painfully hard time for Americans generally that year: There were the assassinations of Martin Luther King Jr. in April and Robert F. Kennedy in June; riots that convulsed many inner cities; and the Vietnam War splitting the country further and further apart. Teenagers in droves were now enthusiastically following Timothy Leary's advice to turn on and drop out; Susanna found their acid-rock music a turnoff, and she found their way of life no less materialist and venal than that of their parents' generation. She despaired, writing that she thought about killing herself by crashing her bicycle into a wall. She consoled herself by withdrawing, singing alone in her room, and writing stories, exactly as she had done as a child. And fantasizing about her life to come, back in Europe, this time for good. "When Susannah would talk about going off to Europe again, we thought she was looking for a different species, almost as if human nature would be different there," Corten observes.

Eating was her great consolation, the binge eating that compensated for the lack of companionship and fun and balance in her life. That year, she said, she gained thirty pounds.[3]

Ironically, given her total lack of interest in her classes and inner turbulence, Susanna got all A's that year (in Italian, Italian literature, two film classes, and, interestingly, Introduction to Music), graduating with distinction in December 1968. Looking ahead, she had booked a seat on another cheap student charter flight from California to Europe. The trouble was that, as was often the case, these flights were few and far between and this one wasn't scheduled to leave for six more months. In the meanwhile, Susanna decided she'd head for Mexico, because two things were crystal clear to her: She wanted nothing more to do with her family up close, and she was determined never to return to America.

Consciously or not, Susanna was modeling herself on the classic American writer-heroes who had gone away and had experiences in romantic places. Well, she already had some and now she wanted more, much more. She wanted adventures and love affairs. But she would be practical, too, more grown-up this time: She would continue to perfect her languages, she would find the kind of work that writers have always done—translating, teaching, typing—but above all she would write. Not just write: She would have what she called a "literary career."[4] Susanna, like all writers, needed the affirmation and the recognition that she was a writer. It was the degree to which Susanna craved acceptance as a writer that was different, just as in a few years she would crave the same kind of acceptance and recognition about her singing—and get it.

Her *Pelican* friends had read some of her short stories and were envious of this next step in her literary career. And a little bit in awe as she made her plans for Europe. "We always knew her as a writer," emphasizes Jon Carroll, who'd edited a stack of Susanna's prose, ranging from biting to witty to—far less often—wistful. "From my younger perspective, I was sure she was going to be a Jean Stafford or Alice Munro or Sylvia Plath. Somebody like that. And she would have, if she had worked on it the way she worked on her music."

# 1969 TO 1972

# Gateway to Jazz

> When I think back about the girl I was at Cal—overweight,
> depressed, working like hell with two part-time jobs and trying to
> keep up good grades—I can't believe I'm the same person. Here I
> am, not a frustrated miserable college girl but a confident young
> woman with settled values which really work for me. This is the
> happiest time of my young life.
>
> —Susanna, letter to Mimi and Tom, 1969

It was in the year 1969 that Susanna was going to fall in love with jazz
and the idea of becoming a jazz singer. But there was no hint at all of
this epiphany in January of that year. Tom and Mimi, who certainly
knew what it was like to struggle without a secure income, had tried, in
vain, to get Susanna to reconsider her plans to become a writer. "We
offered her money to go on for her Ph.D.," Mimi related. But Susanna
would not be swayed from her decision to devote her time to writing
stories—serious fiction. And as usual, she persuaded her parents to go
along. Just for a year, she promised, while she proved to herself and to
them that she was, really, a writer.

As her charter flight to Europe wasn't scheduled to leave Los Angeles for London until May, in those six months Susanna decided to live in
Mexico City and write. After spending a few days with Tom and Mimi
(who were still trying to persuade her to go to grad school), Susanna
boarded a bus for the long ride south to Mexico City. There, she found
yet another rented room in yet another widow's flat, on the busy
Avenida de la Revolución in the heart of the city. But though Mimi was
resigned to Susanna's plan to jettison an academic career, Tom was not.
He shot off a long letter that pointed out—again—the perils as he saw
it of trying to make a living as a freelance writer, entreating her to apply
to graduate school the following September. Just two weeks gone from

59

the States, Susanna dashed off an impassioned response in the middle of January. It was both her declaration of independence and revelatory of her state of mind:

> I was very very depressed, hurt, etc. etc. by your letter. Yes I waited and re-read it and calmed down. But it amazes me that you don't think I know how hard it is to "make it" as a writer. . . . All I can do is work and work and learn and first of all I am going to write about the most pressing things on my mind. I feel so happy and productive now, as if I am using all the things I have to live: my languages, my femininity, my creative powers. I am very gregarious like you Mimi and would rather be with interesting people than shut up in my room writing about things that upset me. Writing is a lonely thing. And I also worry a lot about making a fool of myself. . . . My failures and weaknesses show up in what I write and since I am a person who values privacy and my own self-respect highly, it is a hard thing for me to risk making an ass of myself every time I write a story. . . .
>
> If I'd had my druthers I wouldn't have come back from Europe. I finished college because I knew it was important to you, but 1968 was a year stolen out of my life, just a total waste of time. I now write for several hours every day. Sometimes I get very depressed and think I'm just not good enough, but when I'm at my table writing I forget everything except the feelings and experiences I want to communicate.
>
> I am a writer and always will be. . . . Please try to have faith in me—it is so hard sometimes for me to have faith in my own self. P.S. Don't worry about a wedding for me! I hate weddings. Someday my husband and I will just show up and say hi and have a drink and go away again!

More than a letter, this was a youthful manifesto—passionate, obdurate, full of thinly disguised anger—especially at her parents. It was noteworthy too for the kind of tunnel vision and passion that artists need to succeed, as well as a kind of ruthlessness about her own needs that shaped her approach to her singing career a few years later. Remarkably, too, in only two years, she would be applying the same arguments, the same energy, and of course the same deep need to her declarations about becoming a singer. And with the same degree of conviction that it was her calling.

"Old Father," as Tom called himself, wrote back right away in his characteristically mild-mannered way, which also seems remarkable, given the heat of her letter. "I'm reminded," he wrote, "that you have skills and talent; the letter shows it. Sad that energy that could have gone into a marketable item. . . . Yes we love you." He added prophetically, "I'll put the letter into a folder for a future biographer, calling it 'The Lives and Letters of Brown-Eyed Susan McCorkle.'"[1]

If she had thought to escape to a "saner" country, picking Mexico in early 1969 was hardly the place. Only months before, in October 1968, there had been a disastrous protest by students and some workers at Tlalelolco, a rally inspired by the mammoth student uprising in Paris the previous May. The Mexican event, arguably *the* most significant event in modern Mexican urban history, ended in the massacre of hundreds of students; it was a slaughter of incipient democracy known to everyone but immediately suppressed and denied by the government until decades later. When Susanna arrived in Mexico City, the air was thick with grief, fear, rage, and underground political protests. And she would go on from this hotbed to Paris, which was still reeling from its suppressed May 1968 uprising, and finally to Rome, also enduring a period of tremendous class unrest. But though Susanna sympathized by nature and upbringing with anyone "downtrodden," though she had been encouraged by Mimi to "sit in" for fellow black students in Harrisburg and the like, she had little taste for politics. There is virtually no mention of these huge events in her many letters home over the years of the late sixties and early seventies. Her stories dealt with social satire, intrigue, the inner psychological world of (usually) a female character quite like herself. At 22, Susanna seemed a confused combination of liberated woman and conservative "lady." While championing equal rights for women, she chastised the nascent feminist movement in an unpublished article called "The Decline of American Femininity," arguing for pretty clothes for women and old-fashioned manners between men and women.

And what of the songs and the singing that were to burst from her so soon? "Life in Mexico was empty and dull if I didn't write," she wrote to her parents that winter. Yet singing provided some comfort to her, even then. Not that she sang regularly, and there was no thought of *performing*. Music was a pleasure, was a backdrop. There was no mention of attending concerts, whether of European classical music or folk music. But she would have heard a lot of Mexican music, the ubiquitous guitar and vocal trios serenading diners throughout the country of Mexico, the street entertainers, the powerful and exhilarating mariachi bands: Mexico was permeated with music. But it was incidental to her life. What she did love to do was to *try on a performing persona,* trailing down the greenswards that divided traffic along the busy boulevards of the capital, letting loose with the songs she'd grown up with (and so recently scorned), Peggy Lee's "Fever," "Something Wonderful" from *The King and I,* and other show tunes, and pop hits like "Up Up and Away." "It was," Susanna admitted, "one of my favorite things to do. And no one could hear me in all that traffic." But even if she wasn't heard, the tall blonde statuesque gringa would have been *noticed* singing to herself. Her first rehearsals.

She was still seeking her voice as a writer, working very intensely and in short order, producing two stories that she felt were polished enough to be sent back home to be critiqued by her old Berkeley Hills family friend Cleo Davis. When Davis responded with only lukewarm praise, Susanna's spirits plunged.

But she did not give up. And one of her next stories, not to be published until a decade later as "The Woman Across the Room," is important for what it reveals about her state of mind (and how she felt about her parents' marriage). "The Woman Across the Room" deals with dangerous themes, and dangerously. It has a potent atmosphere peculiar to many of Susanna's stories, a mixture of intensity and aridity and a kind of silent scream that often leads to a violent resolution. Set in a town like Uruapán, where the McCorkles summered every year, the plot is subservient to the characters, as is typical of Susanna's stories. And how she liked to play with identities! In "The Woman," the protagonists are a youngish woman, Pat, and a woman about Mimi's age who is unnamed; both are married and deeply disappointed. When Pat's husband falls ill with "Montezuma's revenge," Pat can no longer wander the picturesque Mexican landscape, fantasizing about her freedom; instead she has to stay and nurse her sick husband. But he does not recover, despite his medication, and Pat discovers that he is deliberately re-infecting himself by secretly eating fresh fruit, the known transmitter of the virus. This shocking twist is typical of a Susannah McCorkle story, as is the voyeurism of the young wife: she discovers this while peering through a crack in the door, watching him wolfing down melon, the juice flowing down his chin and onto the bedclothes. Infecting himself so that he can keep his wife near him! More importantly, "The Woman Across the Room" is one of the first to foreshadow Susanna McCorkle's destiny, ending with a greater shock than Pat's husband's illness. The story concludes with the older woman throwing herself to her death from her hotel balcony. Pat recognizes that the older woman is enacting her own fate if she does not break free of what is making her so very unhappy.

Meanwhile, Mimi "mothered" Susanna from afar in her fashion. "Are you having sex enough? It's important, you know," she advised. Other mothers might worry that their daughters are having sex; Mimi worries that her daughter isn't. Susanna dodged *that* question in her letters home that spring of 1969; though she had short-term affairs, nothing led anywhere.

In the spring, Susanna did find romance, not with a Mexican but, rather, with a French journalist who first tried to pick her up in her favorite café at the National Museum of Anthropology. At first, she was put off by his typical late-sixties gear of leather jacket, Gauloises, and French manner, and when he tried to talk to her, she slipped away from the café to the small theater attached to the museum to watch a film. He followed her in and sat beside her, but afterward, she said she had another appointment and left, walking and singing to herself (by now a daily habit) along the broad grassy median of the Avenida de Chapultepec. This is an indelible and at once a joyous and a troubling image. But the Frenchman was in pursuit. When she stopped at a café near her room for a piece of pie, he reappeared. Susanna agreed to have dinner with him the next day. Not only did they hit it off—she found him hard to resist with his glamorous job as the Latin American correspondent for *Le Monde,* but above all, she was taken by the book he had written about a passionate and doomed love affair, a copy of which he brought her at the widow's apartment. She seemed on fire, he remarked: "J'ai vu toute de suite une lumière dedans." Even his coldly rational Gallic criticisms thrilled her: Her heavy thighs and her lack of beauty, he said, were so fortunately balanced by her beautiful shoulders, eyes, and teeth, and above all, her intelligence.

All of a sudden, she decided that when she arrived in Europe, she would go to Paris to be with him. A fantasy wrote itself easily: Gradually they would form a life together, would come back to Mexico City for his job, then raise a family . . . Yet something in her held back too, some instinct. They would be lovers, but she would not live with him in the beautiful apartment he described. Instead, could he help her find her own place, a room nearby?

It was time to get back to California to fly out of Los Angeles on her charter flight. Susanna left Mexico City again by bus, passing an unhappy visit with her family in Long Beach. They embarrassed and bored her. Maggie spent all her time in her room, Katie called repeatedly asking for money, and her parents, she thought, drank too much. Susanna's acne, which had died down, flared up again. She was nervous about the future. Finally, she and Tom had a large quarrel, ostensibly about women's liberation, and she decided she would never be able to talk to him again about anything meaningful. There was nothing about her family that appealed to her then, which strengthened her resolve not to live in America anymore. Sad but relieved, Susanna flew to London on May 10, then on to Munich, where she visited Katja, and finally, to Paris, where her new lover waited.

As usual, she had barely enough money to get by. True to his word, her Frenchman had rented a room for her, in yet another widow's apartment. It was what she described as a Colette-style boudoir, full of bows and satin and traces of old perfumes, decidedly not Susanna's taste, but he had paid for it. However, she moved most of her things into his place immediately, and they embarked on their affair. It was no good: She felt clumsy and unattractive, could scarcely bear for him to see her without her clothes, and he quickly became disenchanted, so much so that within days, he confessed that he was seeing someone else and asked her to remove her things from his apartment. Back at the "boudoir," Susanna took to her bed, depressed and humiliated.

Then came one of those marvelous moments, an unexpected gift. She received a letter via the American Express office informing her that she'd won *Mademoiselle* College Fiction award for "Cordelia." Along with that came a check for $500, a large amount. Elated, Susanna determined to get back to work on her writing. In no time, she had found another room and bought herself a marvelous Olivetti typewriter with a European keyboard—a prince of a machine, perfect for writing and for the translation work she intended to do to support herself, along with babysitting for American embassy wives. She made no mention in letters home of the affair that had brought her to Paris: "I am meeting some marvelous men. The only trouble is that I think about them too much and yearn for them to call me or else am planning what to wear.

It sure is fun to be a woman." But in reality, Susanna did not seem to be having much "fun" as a woman. Partly, it was her complexion, still broken out from her recent flare-up, and pitted—"revealing my turbulent soul to every stranger in the street." With some of her earnings, she found an inexpensive dermatologist who began a month-long treatment to repair her face by an arduous process called peeling, which removed the upper layers of the skin. While the scaly, then blotchy newborn skin healed, she was compelled to stay indoors for weeks out of the summer sun. "She wrote that she looked a thousand times better," her mother recalled. "She said it was so wonderful not to look in the mirror and wince." In her enforced isolation, Susannah worked on her stories and studied French—and drank rather a lot of wine, observing amusingly: "I notice that if I drink too much or start too early in the day even drinking just a little at a time, by evening I am writing stories full of split infinitives and inconsistent actions, or else typing up an economic report on Tunisia with the carbon paper in backwards." She also developed a new crush, on the dermatologist who was treating her. From the summer season in Uruapán, Tom continued trying to persuade her to *be sensible* and apply to graduate school—or else find a marriageable guy. "A girl must latch onto a reliable man or a reliable career line. Or else look out." Not much help there.

Despite her vow never to return to the States—"I was so into being European and enjoying European culture!"—Susanna was homesick and wrote faithfully to Tom and Mimi, begging them to come for a visit (they did not for several years). Ironically, it was not European culture that called most strongly to her then, despite all her languages and appreciation of European history and art, but a new side of her *own country* she was discovering—at last and for the first time—as an expat. "Not the America I knew, but the one Europeans love," she explained. It was going to the movies and falling in love with old classics like *Double Indemnity* and *Sunset Boulevard,* and more to the coming point, the camp musicals of Busby Berkeley musicals, the Fred Astaire–Ginger Rogers classics. (In fact, these movies were part of America's own art-movie scene, but apparently she'd missed them back at Berkeley.) Suddenly, Susanna was awake to the literary qualities of so many of the songs fashioned by the Gershwins, Irving Berlin, Cole Porter, and the rest. She had not only eyes for the movies but big ears for the songs: "The smartest Europeans took American accomplishments in its popular arts seriously—jazz, movies, dance," she explained. "It was the snob appeal, really, as I spent time with students and artists around my age and they really knew so much about it. I'd hear people in the theaters laughing at the witty rhymes in the movies, and the songs were so amazing and clever. I camped out with sandwiches in art cinemas there, sitting through repeated showings . . . scribbling down lyrics and memorizing tunes."[2]

She had already shown that she could be a ham—the high-school musicals and the mimicry for her *Pelican* friends—and she knew she loved to *sing*. "Walking and singing in Mexico City—where no one could hear, was a release from the solitude of writing short stories, and I guess that's also how I became a performer," she said later. She kept up the practice in Paris, walking through the Tuileries singing the entrancing songs she was hearing in the old musicals at the "art cinemas" she went to.

And then, all at once, Susanna had her artistic epiphany.

It happened, as these momentous events so often do, in a casual setting. She had dropped into the Montparnasse attic apartment of Eileen Stein, an acquaintance from Berkeley. Like Susanna, Stein was living frugally in a tiny maid's room. Trained as a pianist, Stein was hoping to become a singer. She had started listening to old American jazz records in Paris, which was then much easier to do than in the States, where collecting vintage vinyl was time-consuming and not cheap. Not so in Paris: One could get all manner of prized old records for a few francs in chain drugstores. So Eileen Stein put on a record and told Susanna to listen. It was a classic reissue of the 1939 recording sessions featuring Billie Holiday with pianist Teddy Wilson and saxophonist Lester Young. Susanna was entranced instantly with the music. "I Gotta Right to Sing the Blues" contained lines she deeply identified with: "Soon, that deep blue sea will be calling me." That anyone would have a *right* to sing the blues! "Billie Holiday was my gateway to jazz. I immediately became obsessed with her songs, her singing, and her life," Susanna declared. "The odd, unbeautiful sound of her compelling young voice struck me like lightning. She sounded like a woman singing about herself, instead of someone playing a role in a show. I had to hear the same song over and over again, everything about it, her singing, the group. The approach to singing." Eventually the neighbors became infuriated, and Susanna took the song in her head to the park, walking down the long lanes, singing it over and over to herself.

By temperament, Susanna was an introvert. As a writer, she was drawn to the compressed form of the short story, densely atmospheric, moody pieces. In Billie Holiday's singing—and in the material she sang—Susanna sensed a powerful new kind of storytelling, what writer Will Friedwald describes as the "art of the miniscule. . . . Even the tiniest of nuances [in Holiday's singing] assumes epic grandeur; the lightest of inflections takes on tremendous significance . . . her ability to maintain control at super-slow tempi."[3] Susanna continued: "This was different, this black American music. I'd always been brought up to be pretty, sound pretty . . . but I never really wanted to be a singer until then. Billie seemed to be in the room telling us about her life—not singing pretty. . . . Billie Holiday caused me to completely revise my thinking. I felt as if there was nothing separating us." And, this deeply isolated woman added, *I want people to feel that way about me.*

"I waited," she added, "for this crazy desire to fade, but it wouldn't. As crazy as it was, I just could not shake the desire to become a singer. The pleasure of singing and experiencing the emotions of these love songs was so intense I almost cried sometimes. What if I could feel this way most of the time instead of just some of the time? And—make others feel it too? With mounting fear and excitement, I realized that I would have to try to become a singer."

"She knew it would be a good story later to say that she was just translating Italian and French and then one day she heard Billie Holiday and knew she had to become a singer. She knew the reporter would say 'OK, great quote!'" suggests Jon Carroll. But the *why* of this about- face of a decision is complex. Composer and pianist Sir Richard Rodney Bennett, who became a friend in the 1970s before a falling-out later, speculates that Susanna fell in love with the *idea* of being a jazz singer. "The spotlight, the little clubs, the *image* of being an intelligent, heartbreaking singer." But this, he feels, is an entirely different thing from actually *being* a jazz singer. "All the details were right. She had endless curiosity about songs and was extremely hardworking. She had the sound. But," he adds, "it doesn't add up: She didn't have the chops; she didn't have a spontaneous jazz approach." Legions of Susannah's fans, of course, would disagree with this assessment, but even some of her admirers sensed the literary quality of her approach to singing. Says the writer Francis Davis, "When I first knew her in the eighties, I thought that music was some kind of escape from writing for her. But musically, she knew who she was." Adds psychologist Eric Olson, who became a close friend in the late nineties, "She stage-managed everything in her life. She was so skilled and bright and able to do it that it paid off. Musical but also verbal: She wanted to control the story. And she did."

But in the summer of 1969, Susanna was experiencing the kind of high from listening to Billie Holiday (with great poets of the music "singing" behind Lady Day) that most young people then were getting from rock groups. Perhaps for Susanna, singing offered a way out of herself that she badly needed, while writing was a way *in*. There was a new and longed-for catharsis for Susanna that lasted as long as she kept singing, and which would be a help and a source of support to her all her life. Or, that is, until the last months of her life, when she'd stopped singing. "I wanted to get high on singing," she explained about her newfound passion. "You don't even feel the sense of yourself as a human body," she told Roy Schecter, "it's like sailing or hang-gliding."[4] She found she could lose herself while singing as she could in no other way—and was beginning also, even then, to get the attention and acclaim she craved. Her audience was tiny—friends, people in the park. But it was a start. "Getting an immediate response from an audience was very gratifying for someone like me." As a writer, she'd been used to delayed and limited reaction, if at all.

So it seemed that singing from her heart was the missing piece of the puzzle. If the stories Susanna wrote turned up her dark side—the melancholy, angry, frightened, needy Susanna—her singing brought her joy, as it did to her admirers. Like Holiday, she had to *fight* through misery, a sad personal life. And like Holiday, the act of singing *was* joy. The singer Carmen McRae, who knew and idolized Holiday, said of her, "The only way she's happy is through a song. . . . The only time she's at ease and at rest with herself is when she sings." Quite possibly the same could be said of Susanna, whose epiphany was to instinctively recognize that singing lyrics would offer her that same ease of mind, a catharsis. Holiday's music was on the side of hope, was powerfully dramatic with a fabulous sweet-and-sour beauty despite the lack of a great vocal instrument. This, too, Susanna could relate to.

She wrote excitedly to her parents about her newfound passion that fall, asking Mimi to send sheet music; she was going to pursue her singing seriously, she said. Mimi's response was a double-edged sword, encouraging but full of her particular reproof: "It has always amazed me that you seemed to value so little this particular talent!" So here she was, 23 years old, knowing next to nothing about the swing era, jazz

*Haunted Heart*
68

singers, jazz itself, unwittingly following a well-smoothed trail after such singers as Carmen McRae, Rosemary Clooney, and Peggy Lee, to name but a few who had been seduced by the example of Billie Holiday—Lady Day. Yet in Susanna's generation, the trail had grown cold. Few indeed were the vocalists from the sixties who took Holiday as their model—most had probably not even heard her then. None of that mattered a bit to Susanna, for whom Lady Day was like discovering a terrific writer from the past.

It would take more than *feeling* to turn her into a good singer, of course. Still, Susanna already had a lot going for her: a natural ear, a gift for languages, a highly efficient memory, quick, very verbal intelligence. She exhibited all the recent jazz convert's usual symptoms that spring in Paris: running around buying up records, talking about the music, thinking about the music—*high* on the music. She bought vinyl sides by the Ellington band and the small groups of the thirties. Especially, anything she could find with Billie Holiday. She listened to each song over and over, writing down the lyrics, then going on to the next, then walked through the park in the late afternoon, singing the songs softly to herself.

What a difference six months had made! From January to May she had been swinging down Mexico City's boulevards singing old Broadway show tunes to herself. Now she was studying the art of a great African American vocalist in a musical tradition she knew very little about. But Holiday's blend of beauty, world-weariness, and defiance was irresistible to Susanna, and she fell in love with her bittersweet sound and the brilliance of the players. That she had "heard" Holiday right away as a great singer was one thing (many singers had taken Lady Day for their model); that she was moved to become a singer because of Holiday was an altogether different matter. Susanna would go on to find other singers to love—including some surprising ones—Marilyn Monroe and Mae West, Ethel Waters and Bessie Smith. She'd develop a taste also for Mabel Mercer and Joe Williams, for Tony Bennett and Mark Murphy, for Peggy Lee and Lee Wiley and Irene Kral, to mention only some of the best. And then there were the Brazilians: Antonio Carlos Jobim, Elis Regina, and João Gilberto, whom she loved for his relaxed way of singing, what she called "floating" his phrasing across the bar lines of the melody. She set herself to learn Portuguese and became proficient enough to translate lyrics.

But it would always be Holiday who set the standard. Like Lady

Day, Susanna was probably happiest when she sang. "I love being *inside* a song. Some of the happiest moments of my life have been spent there," she told an interviewer. "I definitely became a singer in order to sing sad songs," she added.[5] She was happy singing about sadness.

And she was full of sadness that fall. Her mother gave her a detailed account of her older sister's latest nightmarish acting-out behavior. Her sister was getting sicker, getting in more trouble, the kind of pointless, petty, sordid acts that families who deal with mentally ill members know only too well, events that also serve to distract and wear out the "sane" family members. For years and years now, Mimi had been dealing with a husband ill with manic depression, and an oldest daughter who constantly acted out. She gave away the old car Tom and Mimi had given her to a boyfriend who trashed it, then ended up in jail on assault charges. How could Katie be finagled into psychiatry? Mimi asked Susanna from across the ocean, a continent away. A rhetorical question: (Susanna could do nothing from Paris. "I feel *decapitated*," Mimi wrote, a disturbing word that conveyed exactly how bad she felt. But she immediately added, "Keep happy my love and do good interesting things. I cling so to thinking about you doing just that."

Good and interesting things—yes, but "keeping happy" was as distant a dream as becoming a professional singer. And Susanna still desired, just as intensely as she yearned to sing, to write, and to be published. In a story called "French Lessons" that drew on her experiences while in Paris and then London, Susanna's unhappiness is viewed through the prism of a young woman called Jane. Jane makes her living giving English lessons in Paris and, later, French lessons in London. Jane is English, but in every other way resembles her American creator. Alone during a squalid August in Paris, when "no one in Paris wants English lessons," Jane flees the heat of her room, but finds nowhere to rest. "Miserable old people wandered the streets alone at all hours of the day and night. . . . I walked around as aimlessly as the wandering old vagrants. Where could I go? The museums would be insufferable, swarming with tourists. The most popular parks would be full of those little maggot-men." Finally she is picked up by an old roué who takes her to a café and becomes avuncular when Jane protests that what she is seeking is an interesting life. "Oh but that," responds her unlikely mentor, "doesn't just happen to you by chance, you know. You have to earn it for yourself. It takes a lot of work."

Susanna took this advice to heart just as Jane does in "French Lessons." At the age of 24, she told everyone she was leaving France to live in Italy, her favorite country. Rome was a big city, sophisticated. She was going to try to become a jazz singer there, to "earn that interesting life." The news stunned her friends back home, who had had no hint of this new passion of hers. "But she was a *writer*," exclaims Dick Corten, "She had never sung!" "It came as a total surprise," Jon Carroll agrees. Everyone found her decision shocking, except for Mimi, who of course had been urging her to perform in musical theater ever since her high-school play success in *Bye, Bye, Birdie*. Tom was still adjusting to her declaration that she was going to be a serious writer. Adds Carroll, "It seemed impossibly exotic to do that. I mean, I had *no idea* that's where her career was going to go. When I knew her, it's not like she was sneaking off and singing in clubs or bursting into song. But she was very explicit: I'm going to Italy, and I'm changing my life, becoming a different person. I'm going to be a jazz singer because I say I am. And I'm also changing my name—everything changes except the McCorkle." She was now officially Susannah McCorkle.

In Rome, sunlit and full of beautiful old buildings and vivacious people with dreams, Susannah immediately felt much more at home—for one thing, since she spoke the language better than French, she felt less isolated. "Italians were both friendlier and nosier than the French, and people often asked me what I was doing there," she observed. "In Paris I had been a student, but in Rome I was just another young foreign woman living alone. I was writing, I told them—and oh, yes—I'm a singer, too." But this newfound passion had to be shelved for the moment, as she looked for a place to live and work, though the old pattern of Tom and Mimi's checks, $400 here, $500 there, remained, crucially.

With her two suitcases and not much cash, she found a cheap hotel room and then looked for a place to live and work and pursue a singing career. As usual, she couldn't afford her own apartment, and she took a cramped room—an apartment share—at the Villa Laetitia, located on the left bank of the Tiber River, where streetwalkers plied their trade. Or rather, she found a room in what had been the stables of the seedy mansion, which now housed the Embassy of Pakistan. Behind the embassy, Susannah shared a flat with a tall, beautiful but empty-headed Jamaican model named Peggy. She hated living with a roommate and having to explain to prospective clients that no, *she* wasn't a street-walker, thank you very much. But though she looked high and low for her own place in a more serene location, she could find nothing.

Still, she made friends at the Villa Laetitia with other Americans who encouraged her to follow her dreams. "In Rome you get to be whatever you want. If you want to sing, you're a singer," advised Faye Podell, another American woman renting a nearby apartment. A free spirit, Podell was a divorcée supporting herself by typing manuscripts for Muriel Spark and other English writers living in Rome. An Auntie Mame type, Podell had just given shelter to a talented young painter, which scandalized Susannah's roommate Peggy: He was much younger than Podell—and (more to the point perhaps) an alcoholic. And though the painter ran through his inheritance in record time, ending up homeless and having to be shipped back to the States, Susannah understood exactly why Faye Podell took him in. He was gifted, he was amusing—he was an *artist.*

As for Susannah, she had found a sympathetic ear but was no closer to actually performing than she had in Paris. At first, she picked up work at the Foreign Press Club, translating, editing, and doing research. "They were a seedy but colorful bunch," she recalled. And she found the kind of job that was both implausible and a source of hilarious copy for her diary: She was hired to do public relations for an American rodeo embarking on a tour of Italy. Susannah's descriptions—of the drawling cowboys who hated pasta, the ornery livestock, the unflappable, super-cool Sioux Indians in full war-bonnet regalia who astounded the Romans—show her gift for comedy. In the middle of this *opera buffa,* she placed herself as a kind of a heart-of-gold June Allyson character, gamely trying to hold the rodeo together as it collapses into a heap of dust at a disastrous "dress rehearsal."

She was also older now and less wide-eyed about her ability to attract men. "On my first visit to Italy I was excited to be found desirable by so many men, but I soon realized their ardor had less to do with my appeal than with their need for sexual conquests." She began to develop that necessary skill, so like insect-swatting, that young attractive women who live in a Mediterranean land must acquire if they want any breathing room.

And then, all of a sudden, after asking everyone she met about leads, she got her first singing break, a job on a cruise ship. True, it was off-season, and also true, it was nothing fancy, not a glamorous cruise ship but a tired old Greek liner that took student groups around the Mediterranean. True, too, she was an appendage, an extra tacked on to the weary old Sicilian instrumental quartet in residence. And lastly, Susannah had not been hired as a singer but, rather, as *animatrice*—a cross between a social director and a games-hostess. Yet she was thrilled and prepared herself diligently, buying sheet music for Italian pop hits and writing out lists of the songs she knew, in English, Spanish, French, and Italian. Faye Podell advised her to throw out the plaid, college-girl skirts and blouses that she favored. She borrowed bell-bottom pants and tight sleeveless tops from a woman she knew and took makeup lessons. "Wear bright red lipstick and smile a lot," she was told. The shy sweater-girl at the high school variety show in high heels and a trench coat warbling "A Foggy Day" was now in borrowed hippie clothes belting "Volare."

In her new, sexy image, Susannah went aboard the ship and introduced herself to the quartet of musicians, in English, the Four of the South. The Four had no idea that *a singer* was to join them but shrugged their shoulders and agreed to rehearse with her. While the passengers—all teenagers on a junket—went ashore at Malta the first day, the musicians huddled together, going over charts. There was "Ritmo Affascinante" (Fascinating Rhythm), "Blu Mun" (Blue Moon), "Swanna Ful" (S'Wonderful), "Da Man Ai Love" (The Man I Love), "Sani Saidadastrit" (The Sunny Side of the Street). She sang every night with the Four and with kids who had brought their guitars. And she sang especially for the dancing—hours and *hours* of dancing. She wrote letters of drummed-up enthusiasm home: The crew loved her! The kids loved her! Yet the musicians, she began to see, were far from ecstatic; for them, it was just a job, a routine. "I'll quit the job before I'll let it kill my love of singing!" she declared. Sometimes the sea was so rough that she had to hold onto a pillar to stay on her feet while she sang.

Back in Rome, the management called her in. They were sorry, they said, but . . . she lacked the round-the-clock bubbly personality an *animatrice* needed, the manager said. "You seem to like to sing sad songs too much," he added. Dismayed, Susannah went back to her corner at the villa. "I was a flop," she told Podell. "You had *fun,"* the older woman replied. Soon, determined to keep on singing, Susannah decided to address her musical illiteracy by taking some formal lessons—to learn how to breathe, to sing scales. "I went to Maestro Ricci. He had pictures of Anna Moffa and Joan Sutherland and others kissing him and I knew he was the wrong one, but he insisted he could teach me. He told me to wear a surgical corset and he whacked my jaw: 'Keep your jaw relaxed.' I was so intimidated I couldn't tell him I didn't want to sing opera and after a few lessons, he said I'm so sorry, you will never be a singer, you have a *tiny tiny* thread of a voice. I was so relieved. I said I wanted to sing Gershwin. For this, he said, you have enough of a voice already."[6] In the future, Susannah consulted vocal coaches occasionally, but she was never to acquire formal skills. "If you just let go and make people feel a song, nobody's going to worry about whether you read music or breathe right," she thought, adding, "My favorite singers have a natural rough edge to their sound."

> I wanted to get high on singing again, so I went around to piano bars trying to get work as a singer, making the rounds of the seedy little nightclubs near the Via Veneto. Totally futile. I introduced myself as an American singer available for bookings, but the street-wise club owners and musicians just smiled, shook their heads, and told me I shouldn't be out alone at night. They said, "You're a college girl. Stay out of these bars. You should have a real job with a car and an office." I was a very well brought-up young lady. Only later did I realize that Roman nightclub singers are essentially singing prostitutes, so the club owners must really have thought I was funny. Here I was in these sleazy, squalid nightclubs, with a pageboy and a plaid skirt, saying I was a singer.[7]

There was also the dangerous dark side of being a young woman out on her own at all hours of the night. She was preyed upon. There was the Lebanese businessman who told her he could arrange for her to sing with the orchestra at the Hilton Hotel where he was staying. She sang "Blue Moon" and then had to make a desperate escape. There was the bottom-pinching agent for the always-about-to-open Penny Club, a room continually under construction in the Piazza del Pantheon where she performed weekly "rehearsals" of "Steam Heat" and "Put On a Happy Face" for prospective investors. When he suggested they go together to check out clubs in the remote suburbs of Rome, Susannah was warned off by friends who were sure he had quite a different idea in mind. There were amusing incidents, too, such as her audition for an Italian company of the musical *Hair*. While everyone else at tryouts was dressed like a hippie in keeping with the show's theme, Susannah modeled herself more on Jane Fonda in *Klute,* wearing a miniskirt and (borrowed) white boots and choosing to sing the wildly inappropriate "Strangers in the Night." (Needless to say, she didn't get the part.) Rejections, failures, the sordid and the funny: To her it was all worth it, part of the game. She was, Susannah wrote, on a high, one of her soaring phases, intoxicated by a happiness greater than any she'd ever known. Convinced that she was meant to be singing, she determined to find a way.

At the same time her singing was suffering setbacks, Susannah had a stroke of luck. Hanging out with other expats at the Foreign Press Club, watering hole and unofficial job and apartment exchange, she met a British journalist named Andrew Hale at the bar. Hale had rented a sprawling suite of offices and wanted to rent out three rooms down the hall from the rooms he needed for his work. The location was fabulous: the bell tower of a beautiful seventeenth-century monastery, which, aside from a few stray clerics, had been converted into apartments. A few blocks from the Piazza Navona, 5 Via Arco della Pace was a romantic aerie approached down ancient arched and cobblestoned streets, next to the pretty old Chiesa della Pace (Church of Peace). The rent was inexpensive. Was Susannah interested?

Oh, was she. She signed on and immediately moved from her cramped share with the vacuous model. Susannah loved everything about the place: the dramatic entrance through its huge, dark green wooden door guarded by a portiere, the hundreds of worn old stone steps past beautifully designed cloisters. She bought cheap used furniture, put up posters and plants and rag rugs. She even had a phone, something of a luxury then in Rome; Hale had it installed, asking her to take his calls for him. Above all, she loved being at the top, with the sun and the views of Rome: "The city is ochre and golden, drenched in sunlight, dotted with beautiful old churches and fountains," she wrote. Her bell tower was a magical place to her, a haven where, at last, her dreams of writing and singing seemed to come alive as never before. "Anyone who got to live in a place like this, I thought, had a right to expect an interesting life for herself."

The bell tower and the Piazza Navona nearby became her living spaces. No computers then, no cell phones, very little on television. As for music, no CDs; tape recorders and record players were big and cumbersome. What a place in which to come of age! The piazza was a beautiful ancient oasis, closed to the traffic that clogged so much of the city, a magnet with its Bernini fountains—not one but three beautiful fountains—and the delightful church, the Sant'Agnese in Agone, with an equally delightful legend: The martyred Agnese, it was said, covered her exposed nakedness with a miraculous, luxuriant growth of hair. There was a constant, shifting population of buskers, mimes, and portrait artists, their patrons, the tourists—including, in 1970, throngs of hippies, druggies, artists, and hangers-on. The piazza's cafés, in particular a small café overlooked by tourists, became Susannah's headquarters. She loved the life of the place—the long, unhurried meals with food and much wine and conversation and love affairs being the main forms of entertainment. "Rome," she decided, "was a perfect city to begin my career in."

She was, especially at first, often alone. In the mornings, she worked on her stories. During the afternoons as it got hot, she would sit for hours with her books and papers, reading and writing until dusk with her frugal *spremuta di limone*—a pitcher of water and fresh-squeezed lemon juice. She was reading hugely, as she always had, especially fascinated with the women writers of the recent past, so many of them, as did not escape her, rebels themselves: Isak Dinesen, Djuna Barnes, Katherine Anne Porter, Jean Rhys. It was the generations that followed these women, above all, *her* generation, Susannah knew, who could really live as independently as men without being considered social outcasts. Sipping her lemonade at the café, Susannah wrote of that time, "The reasons women once had to have men—for social acceptance, for children, for financial support—were gone now. Singing was more physically exciting and more emotionally rewarding to me than men anyway in those days." A bit vainglorious, the kind of comment Susannah was apt to make when she was not quite sure of her ground. Yet she more than half-believed it.

Susannah had gone, in just a few years, from musing about a future as a professor's wife and homemaker, to staking out a career as a writer and singer. But at the same time she was as desperate—it is her word—as ever for romance. She fantasized that a lover—or Lover—would be the antidote to "the misery that was my constant companion. Sometimes it actually lifted for days or even weeks at a time." In the meantime, she had fallen in love with Rome, with her tiny, ancient piece of it. It would remain one of her favorite places for the rest of her life, if only as a memory.

Something else she craved was a confidante, a soul friend, as she had hoped Katja would be. In June, she found that friend when Faye

Podell's niece, Thea Lurie, an aspiring journalist from New York who was Susannah's age, came for what she thought would be a brief visit, after which she planned to rejoin her French boyfriend and move with him to New York. But Lurie, like Susannah, fell in love with Rome and with an Italian. And she met Susannah. Podell had arranged for the two women to meet at Susannah's café in the piazza; Lurie went reluctantly, busy with other plans, other people. But the two women hit it off right away. The friendship between them was a constant, though while Lurie made and kept other long-term friendships in Rome, for Susannah, she says,"others came and went." Susannah paid tribute to this intimate friendship in a story called "The Bearer," where Lurie, named Rachel in the story, becomes an idealized female Other. "I can't imagine life without Rachel's friendship," she wrote.

Thea Lurie now decided to stay in Rome and work and love, breaking off with the Frenchman and letting go of tentative work plans in New York. Trained as a journalist, she picked up freelance work for a variety of news agencies and at first shared an apartment with another young journalist, Sylvia Poggioli, who was to become a European correspondent for National Public Radio. Soon she found her own place and then lived for a time with her Italian boyfriend during the 11 years of her stay in Rome. Steadily, she built a career, doing secretarial work for an English writer, translating film scripts, working on documentaries for Italian television, teaching English, writing for the *Daily American* and for the Italian newsweekly *Panorama,* and then a foreign correspondent in Italy and the Middle East, before returning to New York in the early eighties. Freelance work wasn't hard to find in Rome, certainly easier than in Paris. Susannah, too, picked up translation work—an art book, a series of lectures on Kierkegaard (she who distrusted philosophy so, declaring: "I believe in people, in human relationships, in feelings"), even knitting instructions for an English women's magazine. And, like practically every broke American *vagabundo,* she gave English lessons.

Throughout the three years she lived in Rome, Susannah kept an account of her life in a diary contained in a stack of Italian school copybooks, which she worked up at the end of her life into an uncompleted manuscript for a book she called *Secrets in Piazza Navona.*[8] Because she wrote so much about her life then, a clear picture emerges of her mental state. She chronicled her long-standing mood swings, the exhilaration when her self-confidence soared, followed by the crashes during which she doubted herself and, at times, became suicidal. This perhaps unwitting journal of a manic depressive is indeed full of secrets; only her most intimate companions ever knew of the emotional struggles she lived with. But there were also delightful passages about all kinds of characters she met up with, brilliant and acerbically drawn sketches.

"Work and friends, rather than food and eating, became the focal point of my existence," she added.[9] She dropped thirty-five pounds, again. At first, she resorted to diet pills, but she couldn't tolerate the way they made her feel, and she was amazed to find she was no longer resorting to binge eating. Surrounded by the drug culture, she stuck with wine. Though she once thought of taking an LSD "capsule" that a visiting professor from Berkeley offered, fortunately she did not; the wine was enough to tip her precarious emotional balance at times and bring on the blues. At such times, Susannah would take to her bed for days at a time, where, in her words, she was "riddled with fears and complexes."

How to reconcile this woman with the luminous, bright, caring, vivacious Susannah who attracted so many people in her life? The statuesque blonde who could be seen daily at the Piazza Navona? "She spent a lot of time in her favorite café, writing, giving English lessons and attracting quirky characters," Lurie remembers. There were few hints of the melancholy that often consumed her, or of the dark impulses that pulled her from the light to the shadows of her psyche where she had been traumatized. "She had a kind of a darker side about certain sexual things," says Englishman Keith Ingham, her musical partner and lover when she later moved to London. Susannah told him about how she gradually realized that her landlord, the journalist Hale, was having sex with women in his office next to her apartment, especially after he traded Susannah a love seat for a foldout cot that she was using for seating. At first, she told Ingham, she was uncomfortable and slipped away to the piazza. But then her curiosity got the better of her. "Susannah told me she would watch them make love, somehow, through a crack or whatever in the wall," recalls Ingham. "Crouching down and peering at them." Ingham's sense that Susannah had a tendency to gravitate to the darker side was shared by the Italian musician Francesco Forti, who became her friend and then lover later on in Rome. "I've felt intuitively that you want or are expecting violence to be done to you," Forti said after she related a dream where she was badly hurt and in pain.

The period after the cruise ship work ended was another difficult time for Susannah. There was little opportunity to pursue the singing she was determined to do. "Discouraged," she wrote, "I eked out a living as a translator and teacher"—again, translating whatever came to hand—romantic stories for an Italian magazine, a play, business documents, but also writing, the first draft of what would be her most accomplished story, "Ramona by the Sea." And, with her hunger for affection as well as gift for hyperbole, Susannah wrote, "I feel very very happy that my friends are surrounding me and care so much about me."

At 24, Susannah had had a string of admirers, short-lived affairs, but never anything lasting. Through her Piazza Navona crowd that first summer, she later told Keith Ingham, she met an architectural engineer called Marcello (Vittorio in her diaries). Marcello was successful, tall, dark, much older—in his forties—the first man, Susannah said, to make her feel beautiful physically. But she held back for a while: He was too arrogant, too passionately possessive. He scoffed at her artistic ambitions. "I don't see how you can go on living the way you do. Get a real job!" "I need to do the things that I love," she replied. "I give it in my writing, and I give it when I sing. It's so heavy, it's too much love to carry and not to give."

Marcello's somewhat sinister qualities attracted her and calmed her insecurity. "The world is violent. With a man I feel protected, sheltered," Susannah wrote.[10] Marcello provided perfect melodrama for her—days and nights of lovemaking and a beginning of acceptance of her own voluptuousness. Often they would go to his summer house in Saturnia, "a mysterious area redolent with sulfur springs," as Susannah described it. Ideal for a man who, as she described, had "an interest in monsters and rites of black magic." Alone at his country place for hours, sometimes days, she worked steadily on "Ramona," then titled "Ramona in Southland." Capturing the interplay among the adults and children as mental illness crashes against the barricades of their middle-class life, "Ramona" was searingly honest and well-crafted, announcing a new writing talent. It was also an unblinking and unflattering portrait of her family. "They didn't like that story," Ingham says, with British understatement, adding, "Susannah's dwelling on unhappy times scarred her." And quite possibly Susannah's airing of family unhappiness in her writing scarred *them*.

It isn't an easy task to maintain a reader's interest with a main character who is a pudgy, sullen, introverted teenager, but Susannah manages to convey the sense of an inchoate world of urgent emotions under the surface of ordinary things. Like nearly all of her stories, "Ramona" is strong on atmosphere, feelings and insight, with carefully selected detail and a limpid, honest prose potent with her own freshly gathered, important discoveries.

Brooding, angry, depressed, overweight Ramona feels doomed, in a family she despises—as does the sibling in the story, who like Maggie, for all her protestations of feeling that her parents were fine and dandy, "survived by going in my room and closing the door." Ramona has an emotionally remote father. Indeed, she feels invisible to him, especially now that she has crossed the threshold from girl to full-breasted woman. (It is worth noting that later on, after Susan became Susannah the singer, while she would do everything she could to make herself be admired, from carefully watching her weight to rigorous exercise to skin peels, contact lenses, breast-reduction surgery, hair stylists, makeup stylists, dressmakers, etc., she would continue to think of herself as unattractive.)

And above all, Ramona has a mother—and what a mother! Instead of recognizing Ramona's anguish, she criticizes the weight she's gained and the clothes she wears (unflattering and messy). A pretty and patronizing woman, the mother takes Dexedrine to be "happy" and ignores her daughter's sullen sarcasm.

The story is almost painfully claustrophobic, as if there is not enough oxygen among Ramona's kin to keep anybody in the family healthy. Ramona has come home from college for a visit to her family's house, which is near the ocean. There, she does nothing—or, rather, she broods, lies around the beach, hangs around the house, and privately criticizes her mother: Ramona is passive about everything in her life. And yet, Susannah's gift as a storyteller is to draw the reader into that life.

Tension builds as Ramona's visit continues. She declares that she hates college, hates the empty posturing, as she sees it, of her fellow students in their Free Speech Movement protests, hates their playacting in rallies against the Vietnam War. The "sexual revolution" that has swept into the sixties has only worsened her anxiety. Ramona has recently begun a disastrous affair with a good-looking man who is impotent with her, but he flaunts his conquests with other women even as he keeps Ramona on a string. (This unsavory character seems the only truly fictional one in the story—there is no evidence of Suzy ever dating such a man.)

The climax of the story comes when Ramona's father, until then a dimly seen, seemingly inconsequential figure, erupts with a frightening display of crazy energy; unraveling into psychosis, he at one point attempts to break down the locked door behind which Ramona cowers, terrified of him but also fearful for him, as he is at last taken off to the hospital. "For Christ's sake, don't let what happened to him happen to you!" her mother shrieks at her. But Ramona comforts herself with fantasizing about death. She "could imagine dying, but she could not imagine killing herself." Not yet.

Meanwhile, Susannah was struggling with her affair with the sulphurous Marcello, telling herself she felt totally secure with him, though she well knew that it would probably not last. Marcello played a kind of Henry Higgins to Susannah's Eliza Doolittle, a part she struggled with. No, she told him, she did not want to be spoon-fed Italian history and philosophy, and no, she didn't want him to pay for plastic surgery for her nose and her breasts. Above all, she wouldn't give up her dream of becoming a singer. "You're too intelligent and ignorant. A dangerous combination," he told her. The summer affair, an explosive physical passion, collapsed.

Susannah could never stand rejection (once again a man she'd been vulnerable with had criticized her looks), and following her lifelong pattern, the plucky spirits and resolve of the recent past were instantly wiped out. Back at the bell tower she stayed in bed for days and days, unable to stop the wracking sobs, the black despair. Then she received the news that her *roman à clef* in miniature was a College Fiction finalist, along with a check for several hundred dollars. (After publication in 1973 in *Mademoiselle*, "Ramona by the Sea" was reprinted in *Prize Stories 1975: The O. Henry Awards*.) Her spirits lifted, just as they had after her Frenchman broke with her and she learned that "Cordelia" had won a prize. But this time, the elation did not last as long. She was still reeling over the breakup with Marcello, and had just been fired from a new job at a magazine, for "lacking commitment." Even more discouraging, she could find no singing work. Even her beloved Piazza Navona had lost its appeal. All she wanted to do now was to sing Billie Holiday thirties swing songs with a swing band. That, she said, was the entire scope of her ambition.

It is not too much to suppose that with no outlet for her singing, the truth that she had fashioned for herself: that she must sing as she must breathe and eat and sleep, imprisoned her in a dilemma without an exit. But there were no gigs; at least, none to lift her spirits and none that she could hope to go looking for in her current psychological disrepair. "I began to spiral down into depression," she wrote that fall of 1970. "It seemed to me that I failed at everything I did. Jobs. Men. I was alienated from my family and my country. My money was running out. There was really no point in my continuing to exist. I was disgusted with myself."[11] She considered methods to kill herself: cutting, poison, or a dramatic dawn leap from the bell tower?

But first, Susannah decided she would write about herself, leaving behind a work to be remembered by. Though still heartsick and thinking of her coming end, she began to pour her frustration into words, as she could not do—not yet—into music. The words came furiously fast as she wrote, eating little and losing weight. Soon she'd outlined the plot of a novel she called *The Quitter,* "a mystery about my short and unsuccessful life." The book was planned to be about a new tenant of the bell tower who begins to seek clues about the mysteriously vanished previous tenant, gradually coming to realize that the previous tenant and she were *one and the same person.* From deep depression, the pendulum of her emotions had swung the other way as she concentrated only on *The Quitter.* In a letter to Mimi in a thick file of Susannah's writings her mother kept, Susannah wrote, "I separated myself from the world a little more," though, she added, she was careful to maintain her customary routine, going every day to the café, sitting there as she always did, meeting friends—"in order," she explained, "to avoid any conspicuous change of habits that might cause my friends concern, evoke their suspicion, lead them to guess what I was trying to do and try to talk me out of it." This was always to be her modus operandi, and she became extremely adept at it, an actress of normalcy, of calm, to all but the most intimate of her friends (and, sometimes, convincing even them, as she did, in fact, at the very end of her life). Aside from professionals whom she sought out—therapists of one stripe or another, and a handful of others—no one knew of her suicidal fantasy life, nor of the manic-depressive illness that forced her into acting the part of normal living, a subterfuge that is of course well known to the mentally ill and, in their way, to many alcoholics and drug addicts too. It became a kind of game and could even be fun at times. "I fooled them all," she said, by keeping her "normal" routine, even going out on the town one evening with a group and singing old Mexican boleros "with gusto" at a Spanish restaurant, strumming a guitar to tapes of the new music craze, bossa nova, and trying to teach herself Portuguese phonetically. Yet what brought Susannah out of the darkness, she acknowledged, were the connections with people, her new and important friendship with Thea Lurie and her other friends, her deep and abiding curiosity about the people she was meeting at the piazza. That and her desire to keep singing, her absorption in writing about the adventures and personalities she was witnessing. It worked, that time.

Then suddenly, this latest serious inner storm was over again, as a season of hurricanes subsides to blue skies and calm waters until the next round of tempestuous weather. And Susannah simply forgot about killing herself, and about writing *The Quitter*. Well, not completely. Soon after her brush with suicide, an acquaintance did try to kill himself. Susannah heard of it and rushed to help, visiting him at the hospital, comforting his distraught wife. "Although I have never tried to kill myself, I have wanted my life to end, several times," she wrote to him sympathetically, after he'd been flown from the hospital back to his native England. She wanted him to regain his zest for life; she exhorted him to work at cherishing what was dear to him. Paradoxically, Susannah was comfortable in the role of rescuer and nurturer, good at salving her friends' wounds, at cheering them up, while diverting attention from her own pain. Her empathy for others was a lifelong trait, one that endeared her to many.

She still yearned to sing, but as the winter of 1971 gave way to the softness of spring, there were still no singing jobs. She had to earn money, so she placed ads in the newspapers offering to teach English, calling herself a "persone serie," to distinguish herself from the call girls who advertised. She was her old analytical self, wondering why "we" American women were so "emotionally starved" that they were willing to accept "almost any man" who showed them attention. She had begun to see Marcello again, if sporadically, but Susannah was also seeing other men—a noncommittal Greek intellectual, a Swiss documentary filmmaker who was "perfect, intelligent, kind, sociable, talented, etc." She wrote about a strange fantasy telephone affair she had, replete with the identity twists that fascinated her, in part 2 of her story "French Lessons." A woman had called in response to Susannah's ad offering English lessons and asked Susannah to give her private lessons in her apartment—and, as she was a painter, to pose for her. Sensing something off, Susannah refused, but the caller persisted, and they began an intimate telephone relationship in which they soon were discussing details of their sexual experience, their likes and dislikes—an early kind of phone sex. Rather than terminating the conversations, Susannah became intrigued and willingly answered the increasingly intimate questions put to her, albeit in a passive and offhand way. At last, the caller declared that she was a lesbian and was anxious to meet Susannah for a tryst. When Susannah refused, she called back, confessing that *she* was actually a man, named Bruno. To sound like a woman, Bruno went on, was simply a trick of the voice, and he demonstrated his "voices" until Susannah was convinced it was really he playing both parts. "It would ruin everything for us to meet. It's so good this way: just two voices, no obstacles in between," she explained, but at last, agreed to make a date. Inevitably, Bruno turned out to be disappointing, short, and mean-spirited.

Her life, though, was about to improve, and the music was about to begin. Through a psychologist taking English lessons with her at the café on the piazza and who thereby learned of her aspiration to sing like Billie Holiday, she was introduced to a friend of his, an amateur saxophonist and clarinetist who loved jazz. Francesco Forti, from an old wealthy Jewish family, was a teacher in his early forties who was devoted to the music of Sidney Bechet and the swing-era stylists. (Throughout his life, says his sister, Angelica Forti-Lewis, Forti continued to search for new musical forms; at the end, he was exploring Jewish sacred music. One of his sons, Sebastiano, followed in his footsteps, becoming a jazz saxophonist.) Forti invited Susannah to Basin Street, a little nightclub where swing musicians hung out. Entranced, she stayed until three in the morning. She began to hang out with Forti, who invited her to his apartment, where he would hold jam sessions. She sang "Baby Won't You Please Come Home," "Come Rain or Come Shine," "Careless Love," and "St. Louis Blues." Susannah felt better than she had in a long time. "For me, singing the blues is requited love. I was soaring—I was really up high and free."

For Susannah, Forti was the missing piece—a musical guide, a partner to soar with. On a practical level, his complicated private life pulled the clarinetist in a dozen directions. He had four children by his first wife, a son with his then-common-law wife Donatella—a devoted though emotionally volatile woman (divorce wasn't legally viable in Italy until 1974, after which Forti married Donatella)—not to mention

Forti's adoption of Donatella's daughters. But he was to become irresistible to Susannah, this big, dark, sensitive man with a receding hairline. Together, they built a great and fantastic plot of a romance, a romance worthy of an opera, full of clandestine meetings, agonized partings, long declarations of undying love, guilt and conflicted feelings, scenes of weeping and shouting. "My feelings for you will never change," Forti declared. But for some time the affair remained a platonic one.

Enthralled as she was with Forti, Susannah continued her liaisons with others—with Peter, the Swiss filmmaker, with Marcello the architect once more. There was a final disastrous scene between them—more Italian opera—after she agreed to meet Marcello at his summer house in Saturnia and arrived to find a woman she trusted, a Mexican journalist called Dolores, in bed with him. Trapped in the remote countryside with the pair, Susannah became, she wrote, "traumatized, hallucinatory and suicidal." Hitchhiking back to Rome as soon as it was daylight the next day, she crawled into bed in her bell tower, crushed by Dolores's perfidy and Marcello's cruelty. There she stayed for days, until at last she felt well enough to venture out again.

She saw the gentle, vacillating Francesco Forti again and made music with him. Though they had been careful not to make love, one evening he announced that he would leave his family for Susannah, though theirs was still a friendship only. "It is the music that has drawn us together in an almost mystical way. . . . For me, music is Francesco," she wrote. She could not, she went on, commit to one man, as she hardly knew herself yet. "But I need him so much. Maybe we could make it work, maybe he will love me for who I am, not who I could be." She told him secrets. "I said I would have to have at least two or three long love affairs to know what I wanted and what I could give to a man. I said I was pretty sure I was meant to live alone. I said I was capable of leaving Rome the next day and never coming back, or of killing myself." All of which would come true someday.

Forti was her first living link to the music, and in turn, her singing enchanted him. Thus bonded, they now went around Rome together constantly, haunting the few clubs that played jazz—Basin Street, the Folk Study Club, jam sessions in hotels, an audition for a jazz club that had not yet opened. With Forti, she most enjoyed the innocent meetings at his large apartment when his family wasn't there. He played his horn and she sang for hours. Forti introduced her to the various camps in jazz: the "trads," or traditionalists, who stuck to jazz of the twenties and thirties and loathed the modernists, or "beboppers," of the forties and fifties, and the "free jazz" movement spearheaded by saxophonist Mario Schiano. The Italians also had a unique style of their own, which they called "jazz of the night," a lyrical and melancholic jazz that grew up after World War II. Forti, who'd been schooled on Sidney Bechet and Bessie Smith, was nevertheless hungry to hear all schools of jazz, eagerly attending the rare concerts of visiting Americans like Thelonious Monk, Chet Baker, Dizzy Gillespie, and Bill Evans.

Thus his tastes inevitably shaped Susannah's. Forti took the view that she should learn jazz from the ground up, starting with his beloved idols, getting a thorough foundation in blues and jazz and as a singer, especially concentrating on the great Bessie Smith. This Susannah did. She familiarized herself with the old repertoire, sang "Careless Love," the twenties blues standard, Forti accompanying her on clarinet. It was not easy to make the transition from Lady Day to the Empress of the Blues; at first, Bessie Smith sounded heavy, impossibly old-fashioned. But as Susannah educated her ear to a different sensibility, she began to get Bessie—with her, too, the lyrics were vital. Soon, Susannah developed a credible if somewhat startling imitation of Bessie. And something else was happening: Others were beginning to hear her, to listen to this new singer. "I was very introverted and I didn't have much confidence in myself. But I felt sure of myself in Rome." Forti's support gave her a start.

Like teenagers, the two would play and sing wherever the music was happening, then sit holding hands and eating ice cream at one in the morning. Susannah would go home to her bell tower and cry, at once happy and frustrated. It was inevitable that Donatella learned of their friendship. One afternoon, behind dark glasses, she arrived at the outdoor café where Susannah hung out, to confront her. Susannah then invited her to her apartment, where there was another operatic scene. Promise me, said this woman dressed in a long black skirt who kept her sunglasses on, whose hands were trembling, that you will not be lovers. Donatella seemed to think his family was the only obstacle preventing him from being with Susannah, recalled Susannah.

By that fall, Susannah had broken her promise, writing, "In moments of weakness I succumbed gradually to his beautiful love for me, which bathed me in warmth like the winter sunshine in the Piazza Navona. I let him love me. That I am so alone that I need his love desperately is another matter. But how can I regret feeling such an intense love for a man? 'You're my last love,' he says. Not young, not handsome, not so sexy, not dynamic, but the man I love." Susannah was, Forti wrote in a stream of daily letters to the bell tower, "a blonde Viking but very dark inside, the *brava ragazza* [accomplished young woman] of Piazza Navona." She was grateful to him in turn, for he had awakened her. "How come I always thought I was so ugly before! I'm beautiful. I'm beautiful!" It was an affair of furtive meetings; it had to be, with Donatella, desperate to hold him, suspiciously hovering, Susannah aware that she had broken her promise, Donatella suspicious. In her diary, Susannah wrote, "He believes we are fated to be together. I fear we are doomed to be apart." (She was very often accurate in her predictions.) Once again, Forti said he would leave his wife and family to be with her. But this time, his wife found out and, says Lurie, freaked out, going to Susannah to beg her to give up her husband for the family's sake. Forti responded: "It is absolutely impossible to renounce our friendship and making music together."

But Susannah had to put all of this passion and drama on the back burner for two long months, when a family crisis called her back to California, the last place she wanted to be. There was drama of a different sort in Long Beach, where Christmas and New Year's were far from festive, as Susannah wrote. "Tom and his manic pontification, Katie's childish cruelty. And Mimi drunk, trying her college cutie lines on her party guests on New Year's Eve." Her parents had begged her to return to help deal with a difficult situation. The previous summer, even as Susannah took up with Forti, Katie had given birth to a baby; the father was Mexican, either a rancher's son or a ranch hand (the McCorkles weren't sure), whom she'd met in Uruapán on an unsupervised trip there. Mimi had written to alert Susannah to the fact and to put her best face on the situation: "It is a marvelous thing to make a baby," Mimi wrote. But Katie was still very unstable; she was apt, as Susannah later recalled, to go walking around au natural outside on the beach with the baby. Tom and Mimi wanted Susannah to go down to Mexico and find out the extent of the damage that Katie was rumored to have caused to the family reputation—as Susannah wrote, "to scout around and see if Tom and his family are still acceptable in Uruapán." So Susannah flew down there and stayed with the Trevinos, her old family friends. "I sat in their rose garden with my favorite foods, the sun, the peace. I wish I could have spent all my time in the garden, but

instead I had to go out into the town and find out what my sister did
. . . . Well, I heard the stories, how she went out alone with the crowd of
drinking, whorehousing lazy sons of rich ranchers and screwed them
all the same night in the Hotel Mexico. Did she do that? I don't know,
I don't know. I wish I could say I don't care too, but I do. It kills me.
What's going to become of her? But on to other things, no use hashing
over *that* again."[12]

Before that ghastly mission, Susannah had gone up to Berkeley to see
friends and especially to meet Forti's sister, Angelica Forti-Lewis, who,
as it turned out, had been living in Berkeley since the sixties. Susannah
made a lasting and positive impression on Forti-Lewis. "Susannah was
one of the nicest people I ever knew," she says. "Her goodness was
incredible. She didn't want to hurt Francesco's family. She said that she
and Francesco were so much in love that they didn't even acknowledge
it." Susannah wrote Forti letters, she told Forti-Lewis, that he would
pick up at her apartment every day, to avoid interception by his wife. "I
have never received such letters before and probably never will. These
are things that can only happen once in a lifetime," he wrote back.

Back in Rome in February, Susannah continued her clandestine
meetings with Forti, even as Donatella continued to suspect and entreat
and break down. All three of them were at fever pitch. Forti complained that everybody wanted a piece of him, that between his job, his
music, and his family, "it seems like I'm a cow always being milked."
His first wife, Sylvia, had had to be hospitalized for pneumonia, and
was suddenly involuntarily detoxed from the pills she'd "gotten used to
taking, becoming agitated." Meanwhile, Donatella continued to
unravel, presenting what he told Susannah were "hysterical symptoms." In March, Forti left abruptly for a trip to Africa with Donatella,
who had had a breakdown, hoping to calm her down, but was constantly tortured by thoughts of Susannah. "I feel obligated to my wife,
yet I have this attraction and connection to you through our music."

Something had to give. As her love affair with Forti became more
and more untenable, Susannah looked for other opportunities to sing.
Her experiences on her own, without Forti, were disappointing. To visiting American musicians, she was just an available young woman who
fancied herself a singer. She was devastated. Meanwhile, she had to
work. The cobbled-together English classes, the occasional translation
or sale of a short story, the remote possibilities of paying jobs as a
singer—none of these, she admitted, were long-term solutions. Her

European friends encouraged her to apply to become a simultaneous translator for the Common Market (today the European Union). "The plan," Susannah explained, "was to make a lot of money working very intensely for several days a week doing simultaneous translation." It would be a well-paying job with full benefits for the first time in her life, which would also leave her time to write and pursue her singing. Yet she balked, unable to make the commitment, to study for the rigorous exams in Brussels. "They kept calling me from Brussels to reschedule my exams and I just didn't go. After singing, I couldn't see myself talking about cheesemaking in four languages!"

Instead, she followed a tenuous slip of a lead toward a singing career. In June 1972, while at Sperlonga, an Italian fishing village popular with tourists, she had an affair with a British sound technician who was working on a movie in Rome. "Though he thought I was crazy to want to be a singer of old songs, he generously offered me his flat in London to live while I tried to sing, advising me not to give up my place in Rome since I was sure to fail." At Sperlonga, she'd also met Maurice Rosenbaum, a *London Daily Telegraph* journalist who reviewed folk singers. After singing for him, he said he'd introduce her to people in London who might be able to help her. She was thrilled to hear that Rosenbaum knew the poet Philip Larkin, who contributed jazz criticism to the *Daily Telegraph*. She'd brought with her to Europe a copy of *The Whitsun Weddings,* a book of his poetry, and had already written the poet a fan letter, after which she'd discovered his collection of record reviews, *All What Jazz: A Record Diary, 1961–1968,* while browsing for books in Rome's U.S. Information Library. With the new Rosenbaum connection, she immediately wrote to Larkin again. "I am," she wrote (after reminding him of her previous letter), "a singer of traditional jazz and blues (pre-1945 music, which I understand is what you like best too.) . . . I know no one there. Do you know even anybody I could listen to jazz records with, because I need someone to share jazz with?"

It was an audacious but brilliant move, and if it did not quite swing open doors for her in London, it did keep them from slamming in her face. Larkin, famously prickly, a country-mouse librarian, might seem to have been an odd choice to reach out to for jazz contacts in London, but, as she said, she knew no one. Larkin wrote back right away. "Jazz," he told her, "is at least as important to me as literature. It sounds most courageous of you to come to London to sing with traditional bands." He added quickly, "I'm afraid the possibility of our meeting is remote."

But he gave her a name: John Chilton, "a first-rate traditional trumpeter part-author of a magnificent book on Louis Armstrong" (and, later, of a number of other books about jazz). The same day, Larkin wrote to Chilton, cautioning him: "She may be an almighty fool and bore for all I know, but she *sounds* sensible enough, if a little brash. I suppose I am slightly touched by the idea of an American girl setting out to conquer London as a jazz singer. Perhaps she has money."

With that slim contact and a place to stay, Susannah headed for London to find somewhere she could *sing*. Writes Chilton, "We met when I was minding my wife's book shop, The Bloomsbury Book Shop. After a general chat, during which she mentioned her work as a translator and her short-story writing, she said she would like to sit in with some jazz musicians while she was in London. At that time, together with saxophonist Bruce Turner and a rhythm section, I played once a week in a jazz pub, The Crown and Anchor, in Islington, London. I invited Susannah along, but it was some while before she took up the offer; in the interim she went back to Italy." Same thing when she went to the hangout for jazz lovers, Dobell's Record Shop, on Charing Cross Road. Brian Peerless, a drummer, worked part-time at the shop then and remembers that Susannah came in and, after mentioning her correspondence with Philip Larkin, asked about jazz spots. Besides the Crown and Anchor, Peerless suggested New Merlin's Cave. In the same conversation, she admitted, says Peerless, that she was a great Billie Holiday fan and that she sang a little.

Now that she knew there was some kind of jazz scene in London—and was convinced there was virtually nowhere for her to sing in Rome except with Forti—Susannah returned to Rome at the end of August, determined to move on. But still conflicted and full of doubt. That fall, she took as much freelance work as she could to scrape together money for the move. Her love affair seemed dead in the water. She was down on herself. "I wondered if I were a writer who liked to sing and that was all." When her landlord gave her notice that he wanted her bell-tower apartment for himself, she realized she had no reason at all to stay in Rome any longer.

"I decided that I wanted to go to an English language country so that people would understand what I sang. To try while I was still young so if it didn't work out I wouldn't be frustrated and bitter when I was forty. I had no encouragement," she added. "I just had to do it. I felt driven, like a crazy woman. I used to lie in bed shivering. Why am I doing this? I don't even know if I'm any good. Why am I going to another city and starting from zero there? I'll try now, then I'll probably fail, but I'll know I really tried. I said goodbye to my friends, the man I love, and Piazza Navona, and headed for London with a broken heart and a fierce will to succeed as a singer."[13]

Writing was an important outlet, but singing was her calling. "Singing had become my only hope, all I had and all I believed in." And in London, her life as a singer was about to begin.

# Foggy Day

Music was the best thing that ever happened to me—the missing
link. It was like finding my tribe, a family I never knew I had.
—Stan Britt interview

No sooner had Susannah arrived in London and stowed her things in
the vacant bedroom of the Kensington Gardens Square flat being lent
her by the sound engineer she'd met in Sperlonga than she received a
telephone call from Donatella Forti. Shouting and weeping over the
phone about the love letters between Susannah and her husband that
she'd found in his briefcase, Donatella begged Susannah to stay away
from him. Forti, Susannah wrote in her diary, stood by the phone listening to Donatella and wringing his hands, and followed up with a letter of farewell. Donatella, he wrote, was now "miraculously" better. In
the next line, he wrote, "I wish always to be near you in the world of
music, where our feelings are real." It was the most potent kind of love
affair, the one that can never be. And both of them treasured the memory for the rest of their lives.

Meanwhile, the physical passion between them may have been over,
but the relationship simmered. Despite her distress over the end of her
love affair with Forti, Susannah was back to the usual grind of finding
paying work. She quickly got bread-and-butter jobs, typing and translation jobs she could complete at home on her trusty Olivetti typewriter.
And within weeks, also, she'd found a literary agent to represent her in
England. Patricia White of the Deborah Rogers literary agency would
represent her for more than a decade. And within that year, Susannah
started getting stories sold to the fairly lucrative market of women's
magazines in England and their far-flung lot of subsidiaries, from
South Africa to Finland. Most important, she found a place to sing, at

the 606 Club in the King's Row, a small, all-night, hip coffee bar where artists and jazz-lovers and night people hung out. Though it wasn't a paying gig—she got tips only—she was getting exposure. "A lot of musicians and nice, bright, funny people go there and I now go there almost every night after work. I sing to the most appreciative and responsive audiences I've ever had," she enthused in a letter to Thea Lurie in Rome. "It goes on until 5, 6 or 7 every morning." She also began an affair with the owner of the club.

The affair was over soon, in March. "About two months longer than usual," Susannah later remarked wryly to an English friend. But she was far more interested in her singing career and spent all her free time checking out the small but active London jazz scene. In March, she began dropping into the Crown and Anchor and New Merlin's Cave when John Chilton and his group played there. "On a Saturday night booking there that spring," recalls Chilton, "Susannah was featured with a pickup band consisting of myself on trumpet, Dave Jones on sax and clarinet, Laurie Chescoe on drums, Pete Corrigan on double bass, and Keith Ingham on piano. She sang a few numbers with us." (These songs, Susannah wrote in her diary, were "I Love My Man," "Sunny Side of the Street," and "Exactly Like You"—all straight from Billie Holiday.) Chilton, like most musicians who heard her, found Susannah's singing to be "promising, even though it was almost a caricature of Billie Holiday's style; her presentation at that time certainly needed polishing. On the evidence, I would never have guessed that she would become an accomplished performer. However, she practiced incessantly, sat in whenever and wherever she could, and effectively learned some difficult songs."

The best of the small group of London jazz players heard in her a kindred spirit. "People were saying, 'Ah, she's nothing but a Billie Holiday copyist,'" says Ingham, who would accompany her for a decade, "but what I heard underneath that was a singer who had a wonderful understanding of the lyric, nice time, and a nice sound. I thought, if she only could get off this Billie Holiday kick, she'd be really great. And she did. Susannah basically developed her own great natural talent for interpreting any song she thought had a certain substance or appeal in it." Bruce Turner, a superb saxophonist and clarinetist and eccentric who led a group called the Jump Band at New Merlin's Cave, told her, Susannah reminisced, "'You're really good. Do you want to sing with my band every Wednesday?' So I immediately had a singing job. It was unbelievable."

Still, she was barely able to support herself on the odd translation and two or three pounds a night plus tips with the Jump Band, and was back to sharing somebody else's digs and dressing in cheap, secondhand clothes—then favoring long, flowing dresses with flounces and cap sleeves. "I often got fired because they said I was too sad. They wanted more beery, cheery songs. But I always found another place to go." She made the rounds, all of them—strip joints, West Indian clubs, after-hours clubs that sold illegal booze and drugs. Places with names like the Mandrake, the Star, and Garter. Anywhere that had at least a piano she could sing with. The music she'd fallen in love with and had to sing, she told someone, was better than love, because there was no pain in it.

One of the places where she sang—and was fired from—she chronicled in "At the Keyhole Club," a short story she wrote about those early days, calling herself Alice, a youngish, struggling singer in London pubs at the low rung of show business. Alice is in fact a kind of Sally Bowles–like character, and the Keyhole Club could be a later stand-in for the Kit Kat Club made famous in *Cabaret.* As told through the eyes of Alice, the atmosphere of the place, its characters and their demimonde doings, are at once innocent and decadent—as is Alice/Susannah herself. As the story opens, Alice has just been fired from a gig and looking for another. Her only requirement of a job is that she can earn enough to keep body and soul together by her singing. She finds such a job at the Keyhole Club, a dingy "hostess club" in upscale Mayfair, where she's surrounded by strippers, a slick Eastern European emcee, and a pianist sidekick called Earl. While Earl is described as a washed-up alcoholic, Alice is fond of him because, she says, "We both love old songs." But their performances go unappreciated, not to mention unnoticed. Still, she soldiers on—it's a gig—until things fall apart, as they inevitably must. First Alice (who, like Susannah, has a huge bosom) overhears a conversation among the strippers, in which the strippers trash her physical endowments with bitchy accuracy in dialogue that reads as if she'd lifted it from a bad real-life moment. Next, she is fired. But the worst moment comes when she discovers that she has misread ol' romantic Earl: He robs her of her pay packet as she is getting ready to go.

And there the story ends, a picture of the unlovely world in which Alice must toil to do what she feels compelled to do—sing. But that describes only one side of Susannah's life then. The other side was equally sad, and lonelier. In the second half of her story "French

Lessons," Susannah writes about those first daytime months in London: alone and lonely, doing her freelance typing and giving private language lessons. "I knew no one and had no desire to meet anyone," she wrote. "I slept too much and ate too little. With nothing in my present I relived the past." (There is a fairy-tale ending to the story, however, when the narrator realizes that her little patch of London is not gray and pointless, and then immediately embarks on a relationship with a good and kindly man whom she had previously rebuffed.)

Despite her initiative and success in her writing and at least the promise of singing work, moving to London from Rome proved to be a very difficult adjustment for Susannah. Despite the end of the affair, she and Forti continued to write constantly. There was also the dawning realization that, despite the 1972 hit movie *Lady Sings the Blues* introducing Holiday to a new generation, her generation, she was going to have to go beyond Lady Day homage to become a "real" singer. "British musicians said, 'You're a kid and it's great to love Billie Holiday; but, you're American and you owe it to American jazz not to recreate records but to do something of your own.' I took that very seriously." So said Susannah, but she was nowhere near ready, she thought, "to dare to sing in my own way."[1]

The London jazz world was tight-knit and very knowledgeable, matter-of-factly reverencing the American jazz players and vocalists whom most Americans neither knew, nor cared to know, anything about. That and the generosity and acceptance Susannah found worked in her favor, convincing her that she had done the right thing in coming to London to sing. From very early on in her stay, there were John Chilton, Brian Peerless, Bruce Turner, Keith Ingham, and Richard Sudhalter. American-born Sudhalter, a cornetist and bandleader, was also a journalist and author of several books about music, including one about his first inspiration, cornetist Bix Beiderbecke, and Hoagy Carmichael. Eight years older than Susannah, he had settled in London with much the same plan, to carve out a career in Europe as a writer and a swing-era style jazz musician. The ambitious Sudhalter put together groups such as the New Paul Whiteman Orchestra, the Anglo-American Alliance and Jazz Without Walls to play in various settings the kind of music he loved. It wasn't long before he had Susannah sitting in as the "thirties chanteuse." Sudhalter had it in mind to become a great accompanist, playing obbligatos behind a vocalist in the manner of another idol, cornetist-trumpeter Bobby Hackett, who played beautifully behind the singer Lee Wiley. Susannah seemed perfect for the role. When Sudhalter got bookings for his group in Copenhagen for July and August 1973, he urged the agent to let him bring Susannah as well. In Copenhagen, Susannah and Sudhalter appeared on stage with the great saxophonists Dexter Gordon and Ben Webster, and spent one memorable afternoon in Webster's apartment. "We spent hours there, listening," Sudhalter remembers. "He sat at the piano and talked about the economy of phrasing, of making a little of a lot."

But of all the musicians she was meeting, Keith Ingham was the most influential in every way. A self-schooled pianist with a tremendous knowledge of great popular songs, especially those from the first half of the twentieth century, Ingham was born in 1942 in London and came from a working-class family. A brilliant scholar, he went up to Oxford on a scholarship, where he studied French and Russian before switching to classical Chinese. Funnily enough, it was his tutor in ancient Chinese, David Watkins, whom Ingham credited with whetting his appetite for jazz. "After we'd done these Chinese texts, he'd put on these Bessie Smith 78s on his wind-up gramophone, sit and drink wine and talk about Bessie and Tommy Ladnier, Joe Smith, Louis Armstrong. It was lovely." He'd taken piano lessons as a boy—classical, of course—and then joined a jazz-based band as a teenager, though his family disapproved. (Much as pianist Marian McPartland's very proper English family had been shocked at her love of jazz in the forties.) "I loved all kinds of music," says Ingham. "Fats Waller, Tatum, the two-handed piano players, then Nat Cole, Ellis Larkins, Tommy Flanagan, Hank Jones. Most of my favorites, I found, were also great accompanists." After graduation, Ingham utilized his skill with Chinese, working undercover for the British government in Hong Kong, but on his return to England he decided he would pursue his true passion and become a jazz pianist. "I began to play in nightclubs in London. My father thought it was a lot of noise, but things were taking off for me."

Though bebop and then, in the late sixties, Coltrane, were all the fashion, Ingham wasn't excited by it. "I was a little bit of a fish out of water, though there were a few others like me. This Coltrane stuff was coming in, and every saxophone player played like him—for three-quarters of an hour, just playing on a cycle of three chord changes. Absolutely boring to me. Louis Armstrong and Sidney Bechet, with their embellishments on melody, they really sang on their instruments—like the great opera singers. Jazz is a vocal music. Well, I was more interested in this way of playing, and I also had a particular interest in songs. With Susannah, I played the songs I never otherwise got a chance to, by Vincent Youmans and Cole Porter and the like, on a level of sophistication far beyond the ability of the average jazz group to play. Most jazz musicians have a repertoire that's pretty minimal—endless repetitions of the same tunes."

With Forti, Susannah had been urged to broaden her listening. Ingham pushed her further. "I lent Susannah records and tapes by Ethel Waters—I think Susannah learned quite a lot about how to use her dramatic flair from her—and Mildred Bailey, Lee Wiley, Connee Boswell and the black blues singers, and Julia Lee, early Ella, early Sarah Vaughan and Carmen McRae; also a lot of males: Jack Teagarden, Johnny Mercer, Nat Cole, Mose Allison. Most people's style comes out of an amalgam of other things, a synthesis. Susannah just absorbed all this material. She was the quickest study of anybody I've ever heard."

As much as the singers she listened to and learned from, Susannah's emerging style came straight out of the songs themselves. "As long as there was a good song involved, she'd do it," Ingham says, "even if they were sung by apparently unlikely people like Marlene Dietrich and Alice Faye, an underrated singer of great warmth, with a fine understanding of a lyric. Susannah never liked to do the 'cutesy' things except to send them up, like her Marilyn on 'Diamonds Are a Girl's Best Friend.' And if she didn't like a song, there was no way you could get her to do it. She had a very instinctive sense of what would work for her. She never read music, but she'd find different ways of doing a song, maybe a little darker sound in the harmony, a little sadder and bluesier. But her real forte was that she really understood a lyric and could put it across wonderfully, particularly if it were a great writer like Johnny Burke, Johnny Mercer, or Yip Harburg. Most jazz singers haven't a clue what they're singing about most of the time."

Before they knew it, she and Keith were steady musical partners. Ingham (like Forti) was married and had a family, a small child then. But his wife, Marina, who'd been an au pair from France when she met Keith playing piano at a party, was no Donatella. "Marina would come along to see Susannah—she knew the musical thing between us, and then she was French and they have a different attitude anyway." And Ingham was no Francesco Forti either; he made no secret of his liaisons with other women, whether married or not.

It was an exhilarating time. All at once, it seemed, Susannah's fantasy of being a singer was falling into place, as a number of people appeared to help her. Peter Boizot, a businessman who loved jazz, was one. He wanted live music in his new chain of Pizza Express restaurants. "Piano and voice was ideal, a small group," Ingham says. "So we began to work in various Pizza Expresses, one on Dean Street, another on the King's Road, a third on Fulham Road—spots that attracted a post-Beatle audience which was becoming a little more sophisticated, and which had money to spend. Among them were dress designers like Mary Quant, BBC scriptwriters and broadcasters like Benny Green and Peter Clayton, and restaurateurs. They loved lyrics, and Susannah was the only singer in London singing Rodgers and Hart and others of their caliber. She was like a little treasure, and within months, she created this little niche and networked it." In this group of literate music lovers was one who helped Susannah's career enormously. Chris Ellis, a singer (or "crooner with a bit of swing," as he describes himself), was also a record producer for EMI. In fact, "this wonderful man," as Ingham calls him, may well have been the one and only record producer who could (or would) have helped the unknown Susannah McCorkle at that time. "Chris's World Record Club series, originally mail-order, had done much to revive interest in popular music as it was before—as Chris put it, 'the rock set in,'" explains cornetist (and sometimes trumpeter) Digby Fairweather. "And keep in mind," he adds, "that the early seventies was a time when even stars like Ella, Tony Bennett, Carmen McRae, Sarah Vaughan, Sinatra, struggled to hold on to an audience and record good material." Jazz and the American songbook and their venerable interpreters were like little boats washed out to sea on a tidal wave of the Beatles, the Doors, the Rolling Stones, Led Zeppelin, and so on. But Susannah, unlike the stars, didn't have to struggle to retain her crown. She just had to find a few places that liked, or didn't mind, the music she wanted to sing.

Recalls Ellis, "She was seated at a table by the piano, in the late winter of 1973 at the Pizza Express on the King's Road. She sat there silently as Keith and I chatted and he duly played any request I made. Then, Keith invited her to sing and I think I must have gasped in astonishment for what emerged from this tall, blonde girl was pure Billie Holiday circa 1936."[2]

But like Ingham, Ellis sensed that Susannah had the potential to be much more than a Holiday imitator. He, too, began to spend time with her, listening to and talking about music and singing. "I'd play all the great versions of a tune, and then I'd say, 'Now I want Susannah.' Soon, not only could Susannah identify singers from the swing era after a few notes, she was beginning to sing classic songs in her own way, suggesting different tempi, burnishing the lyrics with care. I told her something I'd heard: 'A singer should be at the service of the song. That's an artist versus a performer.' I had never dared to hope that such a striking and exciting stylist would emerge," he adds frankly. "She so desperately needed and wanted to learn about the sort of music she wanted to sing. I could suggest a song, and she'd try it exactly—this was in an attempt to find her repertoire. She thought her voice was so young and girly, but I told her she'd grow into certain songs." There were then, and would always be, songs that Susannah found that raised some eyebrows. Yet usually most listeners conceded she was right to sing them. "When she sent me a new record a few years later," Ellis recalls, "I noticed 'By the Time I Get to Phoenix' was on it, and I was more than dubious. But when I heard it, I realized she knew what she was doing! She had an instinctive taste for lyrics."

Where Susannah needed the most help was with the performance side of singing, in manner and dress. She had a stiff, at times almost frozen physical attitude on the bandstand. "I stand there and sing, eyes glazed over. I want to do more but be genuine. But I've been afraid I'll just make a fool of myself," she confessed to Ellis, who adds, "She had very little confidence in herself as a woman and no idea at all of how to make herself attractive. She acted like a plain girl. I told her, 'You slump and move badly, though you've a damn good figure. Stand up straight.'" She found a performance coach, went to movement classes, to Elizabeth Arden for professional makeup. And she got the idea of studying film clips of singers, to see how they moved. But, disliking what she called the "worked out gestures" of many vocalists (she mentioned Peggy Lee), she turned to actors, studying the way women like Simone Signoret and Patricia Neal moved. "They were doing almost nothing but were really present, and from them, I learned to just trust my face. I'm on fire, but only in the song. I want to connect and have the audience feel," Susannah confided.

"Oh, she was painfully shy of her own body," Ingham affirms. "She was very, very self-conscious. She had a voluptuous type figure at that time, and she was conscious of men looking at her, not just listening to the music but wondering, 'Can I go to bed with her?' A woman singer is vulnerable out there, whereas I can hide behind a piano—more protected. It takes a lot of courage to be a singer."

"Keith," says Ellis, "worked with her long and hard and was just as much a perfectionist." Indeed, it was impossible to imagine Susannah's career developing in a meaningful way without such a musician behind her. Inevitably, perhaps, she again fell in love. By the summertime, Susannah even moved into the Inghams' apartment while Keith's wife and son were away for the month of August, visiting her family in France. Susannah rationalized this awkward arrangement, knowing that Marina accepted that Ingham "saw" other women and that by now, she either suspected or knew that Susannah and Ingham were having an affair. In an understated British way, Ingham describes the love affair as "fun and spontaneous early on; a nice physical relationship." Though Susannah continued to miss Forti and what she called their "mystical communication," as time wore on, she wrote, "I can see now what a weak man he is, how he is doomed to frustration and melancholy by his own nature."[3] She was, of course, enjoying the exhilaration of her new affair with Ingham. "He understands, appreciates, and loves me in every possible way," she rhapsodized in August, "and I am amazed at the effect it has on me."[4] However, long-term prospects for the love affair were poor. "I wasn't cut out for marriage," Ingham concedes. "More to please my parents, I had got married before Susannah. I told Susannah I had other girlfriends and I wasn't going to stop having them." Other musicians who knew him at the time concur. "He was a bit of a ladies' man," agrees cornetist Digby Fairweather, "young and handsome and phenomenally talented."

Still, Ingham was willing enough to live with Susannah. In the fall, he left his wife for a sunny, affordable sublet he'd found with Susannah, who summed up that period they first lived together in one word: "idyllic." She and Ingham were working five nights a week, so she did not have to take in typing. She would get up at noon, do the day's shopping, read, listen to music, practice scales—and, of course, write. Tom and Mimi stopped by London to see Susannah and meet Ingham in the course of a long-anticipated trip to Europe. But Susannah was all nerves, recalls Ingham. "She thought they weren't being nice to me and became furious." But Ingham remembers the visit quite differently. He liked Tom McCorkle a great deal. "He was tall, gaunt, dour-looking and he reminded me of another Tom—your expatriate poet, T. S. Eliot. He was very quiet, a taciturn person, but we both liked P. G. Wodehouse, and we would talk about Bertie Wooster and other characters and scenes from those books we'd enjoyed. They were very kind, very nice. Of course, I only saw them for a few days. Susannah put her mother down, but Mimi didn't pretend to know anything about this sophisticated world of songwriters."

After her parents departed, Susannah not surprisingly fell into a funk, writing about the doubts she now had about her relationship with Ingham. "He seems," she sniffed, "tiny compared to me and his tastes (in everything but music) are bourgeois." As was her habit, she fictionalized the relationship and its problems, looking back to the previous summer when she'd stayed with Ingham while Marina was in France. In "The Lover Who Got Locked Out of the Garden," a Susannah-like single woman (not young, still attractive) picks up a married man at an avant-garde play and sleeps with him that night in his flat—his wife being away on a trip. They embark on an affair. She is a part-time typist living in a modest bedsitter with seemingly no relationships apart from him. Though not much seems to matter to her, it is very important that she not be humiliated or even embarrassed, as happens as a result of their curious affair (for example, she is turned on by his "colorlessness" and his "ugly tie"). When one day a neighbor refuses her access to the common garden at the back of her lover's building, the narrator responds by walking away from the whole affair. "She was actually refused entry into the locked garden out back," Ingham acknowledges. "And yes, she was bitter about my not leaving my wife right away for her." But "The Lover," like all her fiction, achieves its power not through plot but from the charged, storm-brewing atmosphere. As in most of Susannah's stories, there is the common thread of the unhappiness of the main character, an underlining of depression: "She wondered how many unloved women were working away in their kitchens, tired of studying their disappointed faces in bathroom mirrors."

Not surprisingly, asking Ingham for his opinion of a draft of "The Lover" provoked an argument; he was unsparingly frank. "Her stories sort of rambled on," he recalls. "There was no real conclusion, and they were suffused with unhappiness. The first part of that one seemed, I thought, to be lifted from a John O'Hara story I knew; I made her rip it up. Then," he admits, "I regretted what I'd said, though she had asked me. My comments produced a violent reaction of Sarah Bernhardt proportions of sobbing on the floor. But I couldn't offer her constructive criticism. That was the beginning of the rift between us. She was furious at me a number of times for things I said about her stories." He had no way of knowing how serious Susannah was about her writing, no notion of how raw her nerves were when she felt criticized. But he quickly learned. "Whenever she got a bad notice or a rejection of a story from the agent or something, Susannah would be absolutely crushed. Devastated by adverse criticism." He adds: "Soon, the relationship began to sour." Susannah began to complain that Ingham was sabotaging her performance, that he would mutter negative comments to her between numbers, tell her how awful she looked. Told that she objected to others after their breakup that he went so far as to deliberately play things in the wrong keys or at the wrong tempo, Ingham, who has teamed well with a range of singers from Barbara Lea to Joyce Breach to Rebecca Kilgore, is indignant. "Nonsense!" he says, years later. "Never! That would be the worst kind of unprofessionalism."

But for all the sense of slights and hostility she felt, Susannah was as determined to make a real success of her writing as well as of her singing. She coveted the idea of producing a published book, a novel— that, she thought, was the true test and the ultimate source of legitimacy as a writer. And she had one in mind: *The Quitter,* the book about dual identities that she'd begun in Rome. "It was in the works, but slowly and in a very formative stage," says Pat White, her English agent. "Over the years, the novel was always going to be finished, and sometimes it was worked on. But her singing took center stage. Though we sold a few short stories to magazines—I remember the South Africa, Sweden, and U.K. women's magazine market—the novel never happened."

"Susannah told me that she was complex," Ingham says, "but I didn't realize how complicated she was, and how much extra baggage she brought with her. And for all her lack of self-confidence, she was haughty and defensive with the average blokes that liked music, the 'regular guys' in the record stores and pubs—and with certain friends of mine. She made them uncomfortable; they felt there was this screen up and no warmth behind it." This was a criticism her third husband was to make as well.

Yet their physical bond remained tight. For the first time in her life—in her late twenties—Susannah had a steady, live-in sexual partner—and she thrived on it. "She'd seemed like a 'goody two shoes' at first, but she changed and became very sexually free," Ingham goes on.

"She did things she'd never ever have envisaged. I remember one cold snowy morning—she was going out to the paper seller very close by. I said, 'Why don't you put your beautiful fur coat on with nothing underneath?' She did—and she wouldn't have done that before, ever. And another time, we went to Venice where she had been sexually assaulted. She wanted to face that, to exorcise it, I believe. We were on the Lido, sunbathing among the rocks, and she wanted to make love right away. I was terrified of the police: In Italy and Spain, they'd throw you in jail for that sort of thing, and it is hard to get out. But we did— we found some rocks and hid behind them and made love." Then, at a house party to celebrate a friend's marriage in a cottage in Bordeaux, "Susannah was being a bit manic about sex," Ingham says. "She'd discovered it, and she made a point of discussing her intimate life with one of the couples, who were having difficulties. It made them and me uncomfortable. But she was a bit of an exhibitionist and flaunted her experiences. Well, she and this other woman didn't get along. One day, it was Susannah's turn to take the mile walk to the bakery for croissants and so on. And the other woman came into our bedroom and she seduced me. She was trying to get back at Susannah, I'm certain. Susannah found out, but I lied about it."

Notwithstanding the sexual freedom she found with Ingham, Susannah confided to being "impossible to live with and full of dark, secret thoughts."[5] Having shared with Ingham about the childhood voyeurism that had extended into adulthood in Rome, Susannah began to urge him, he said, to act in certain sexual games. In particular, Ingham says, "She would always be after me to bring a woman in the room and have sex with her while she watched from the closet. She said she needed it for her writing, that she'd been in a closet with her doll at a party when she was young and a couple, grown-ups, had come into the room and made love and she'd watched from the closet." Though details blurred over time, she added that it had happened during a trip with her family, while staying in a hotel in Claremont, California. "She needed it reenacted, she said," adds Ingham, "and she'd get angry when I wouldn't do it for a story that she was going to write. So finally I did it, but I didn't feel comfortable."

In their several years in London together, Susannah and Keith accumulated a store of amusing-only-after-the-fact incidents typical of itinerant jazz musicians in an era generally inimical or at best indifferent to jazz. For instance, their first steady gig in the fall of 1973 at a soul food restaurant dissolved quickly; as Susannah wrote, "the English white clients want more of a Stevie Wonder hand-clapping act, so out we go." That was followed by a strip club—food for "At the Keyhole Club" story: "I only sing there," Susannah said wryly. In the spring of 1974, they thought they'd found a steady gig, at a club called April and Desmond's. "It was a big gay club next to Harrod's, called that after April Ashley, the first Brit to have a sex change sometime in the fifties," Ingham remembers. "She'd been a merchant seaman, and this fat Desmond was her partner. April took a shine to Susannah and wanted to make her into a dramatic singer—you know, torch songs, dramatic things like 'Cry Me a River.' April would throw her arms up in the air and tell her, 'You have to reach for the stars.'" Susannah was soon fired. "I'm an introverted singer who stands still and concentrates," she declared, "not a Monroe or a Dietrich or a Judy Garland who is all show and vaudeville emotion."[6]

But always, a gig was a gig, and her next was a Marilyn Monroe show. She and Ingham were hired to promote a new boutique called Biba's on the Kensington High Street where, as Ingham put it, "all the dolly birds bought their little skimpy outfits." Susannah swallowed hard and agreed. "She had to dress and sing like Marilyn Monroe, as a promotion for Norman Mailer's recent book about the actress," Ingham recalls. "Biba got a white baby grand in the window and had Susannah poured into a glittery, skintight dress, and Mary Quant did the makeup. Susannah sang 'I Want to Be Loved by You' and the rest of it, two half-hour shows a day for a couple of weeks. It went over very well, and we were paid well." But dealing with the "role" of Monroe brought Susannah to a fresh understanding about show business, and about identity. Stripping off her makeup, wig, corset, and gown after the gig one day, she wrote, "I realized that without all this stuff Marilyn Monroe was unrecognizable when she walked the streets. It was eerie." The implication was that for her as well, performance, with its opportunities for exhibitionism, was fraught. Her bread-and-butter gigs were pub dates. "Places where these loutish guys hung out, you know, the kind who talk without consonants," Ingham recalls. "I remember she said to me, 'Did you see those men looking at my breasts? You should do something to them!' I said, 'Well, they're going to look, you know. I mean, what can I do, really?' She was bothered by her breasts—they were National Geographic–type breasts—but her figure was fabulous when it was all dressed up." And when she was in a good mood, she could be quite funny about it. Once, Ingham recalls, he came home to find Susannah dressed up in a Playboy bunny costume, complete with ears. "I'm your bunny for the night!" she told him.

Their sublet flat was taken back by its owner, and while waiting for another living space to open up, Susannah was offered a room in Chris Ellis's house. She quickly grew miserable, feeling terribly isolated, without much work. Then, as Christmas neared, their new apartment became available and she and Ingham moved back in together. Not surprisingly, these two—she who had never maintained a relationship with a man, he who did not want monogamy—quarreled often. "We'd have big fights over my supposed insensitivity," Ingham says. "I loathed that pseudo-liberal Berkeley stuff she'd learned. She'd say, 'You're a typical pompous European ass.' She liked what she called 'sensitive' men." They had a huge fight right before Christmas and Ingham left the flat in a fury, not coming back or calling her over the holiday. Susannah was bereft and finally ran him to ground in a club where he often played. She sang "Billie's Blues," and they made up.

Yet she didn't love him; she was clear about that in letters to Thea Lurie in Rome. He was "too bossy and lower middle class. But I've never had the feeling of someone coming home to me or of me going home to someone and I like it." Just then, too, she was arranging to get married. For Susannah, who'd later make a reputation as a "bruised romantic," this marriage was strictly business. If she were to marry a Brit, she could then get a work permit and wouldn't have to leave England every six months. She'd found a taker in William George Stone, "a layabout wastrel," she called him (Ingham in his blunt fashion describes him as "a gay junkie"). She'd met Stone hanging out in the 606 Club and proposed to pay him about 200 pounds, a tidy sum that Stone accepted readily. For the "wedding," Susannah, in a thrift-shop dress, met Stone at the Register's Office in Chelsea. It was January 14, 1974. And that was the last of Stone as far as she was concerned. "After two years, if there was no cohabitation, you got an automatic divorce, which she did before she left London for New York," Ingham recalls. "A lot of people did it. Later the Home Office cracked down."

Work permit in hand, Susannah could get singing jobs more easily. She wrote from time to time to Philip Larkin, who responded from the country encouragingly, as in a note in April of that year about a recent gig: "I was very happy to hear that your venture had paid off. I was half-afraid you might end up singing to cinema queues—not of course through lacking talent but through lacking breaks. What you say about lyrics seems profoundly sensible, and ought to be more widely accepted. I hope as you get better and better known it will be! Kindest regards, Philip Larkin."

Around that time, the Fortis, incredibly enough given the recent love-triangle-generated hysterics, came to London on a trip and made a point of going to hear Susannah sing at an informal Pizza Express gig, with Ingham on piano. Not surprisingly, he was not well disposed toward Francesco Forti, but the odd couples made nice over wine and pasta. "I think she wanted him to hear how much she'd progressed and that his encouragement and faith in her—or whatever it was—had had some fulfillment," Ingham recalls. "He seemed a sensitive, shrinking-violet kind of guy, and the wife was just there, one of these long-suffering people. And then, I did hear a tape of him playing. He reminded me a bit of Mezz Mezzrow, a clarinet player of the twenties and thirties. The music was sappy and lacked technique." For Susannah, having Forti hear her was a triumph, though she had given up the idea of ever being lovers again.

Both she and Ingham were beginning to make names for themselves. Chris Ellis was able to get them recorded on a project devoted to Cole Porter tunes. They were in fine company, joining Elaine Stritch, who was then based in London, actress Patricia Routledge, actor Ian Carmichael, and the Mike Sans Singers. Susannah was given three songs, with Ingham providing the arrangements and accompaniment: "I'm in Love Again," "Don't Look at Me That Way" (with a beautiful bossa nova backing), and "You'd Be So Nice to Come Home To," plus one verse on "Let's Do It." They rehearsed in an Abbey Road studio with session musicians, then recorded in July and again at the end of August.

It had taken just a year and a half to make her record debut, and when the album came out, Ellis's faith in her was confirmed. "The results were very, very good," he says. "The reviews were highly favorable to her in the prestigious magazine *Gramophone* and other publications. So people began to take notice"—people such as the lawyer for Cole Porter's estate, who was so taken with Susannah's interpretation of "You'd Be So Nice to Come Home To" that he pushed for her to get a part in an upcoming Broadway show with Porter's music. Though the audition fell through, the buzz about this fresh-sounding, literate-sounding new singer continued. Interestingly, there is little trace of the Billie Holiday mannerisms in the Cole tunes, though many faulted her for too closely imitating Lady Day for a number of years to come.

Soon after, Susannah set off as part of a rare tour of England and Scotland put together by Dick Sudhalter, with Bobby Hackett. "Susannah had sent Hackett a tape of us and, once in England, he made a point of telling us both how much he liked it," Ingham remembers. Indeed, both Hackett and Sudhalter insisted on using Susannah, an unknown, on the tour, though the tour promoter was pushing to use an English singer with a recognized name. "Dick said, 'No, Susannah's the only one who sings in the right idiom and if she doesn't do it, we're not having the tour.' Which was an amazing stand to take," Susannah recalled later to Roy Schecter. Of the slim amount of taped performances surviving from her first years of singing, the single cut of a fresh, young-sounding Susannah and Keith live with Hackett in Swindon on October 6, 1974, is of great historical interest.[7] The tune is "A Woman's Intuition," a lovely, wistful ballad that Hackett had recorded with Wiley, for whom it was a favorite (Wiley also recorded "Intuition" on her last recording, *Back Home Again,* in 1971). On the tour, Hackett praised Susannah from the bandstand as the best thing since Billie Holiday. Several years later, he told the veteran DJ Dick Golden the same thing. The quote wisely went to the top of her résumé.

But Susannah was all nerves on the tour, which had begun badly at the Roundhouse in London. "There were no monitor speakers, so she couldn't hear herself and was off pitch, and the people were restless and didn't like her," Ingham recalls. "At intermission, she was in her dressing room, downcast, but bright red in the face—she would always color up when she wanted sex. And we did, right there, and then she went out on the second half and was terrific." Susannah confided in a letter to Lurie that she "dreaded being with Keith—except for making music and making love."

She was gaining a lot of singing experience now. In February 1975, she and Ingham were in Edinburgh, at the Traverse Theater, where she sang, among others, "Mad About the Boy," "Basin Street Blues," and "What a Little Moonlight Can Do." And they performed live on a BBC program later in the year.[8] They played often at the Pizza Express in Wardour Street in SoHo, a swing-jazz hangout, with cornetist Digby Fairweather. "I remember thinking that her performance was impressive, a kind of stylistic cross between Billie Holiday and—noticeably—

Marilyn Monroe," Fairweather recalls. "She was visually striking and in many ways a very beautiful woman, slightly gawky but handsomely bosomed and with a soft face and a complexion less smooth than might have been expected. I began to work after that with Ingham and McCorkle fairly often, at times with Ron Russell's Jazz Band, a South London-based Dixieland group. At pubs and clubs like the Glazier's Club, the Crystal Palace Football Club, Keith would bring Susannah to sing with us, though she didn't seem to really like a free-wheeling Dixieland setting." But Susannah would rise gamely to the occasion, as when a group led by clarinetist Wally Fawkes, with Keith and drummer Brian Peerless, badly needed a singer for the new mayor of Camden's civic reception. She hopped on the Underground and was there for the second half of the evening. "And she did a wonderful job," Peerless says.

Meanwhile, Chris Ellis was working tirelessly at interesting EMI—which was flush with funds from hits by the Beatles and other pop groups, some of them produced by Ellis—in recording Susannah. But despite her promising debut on the Cole Porter record, the EMI people weren't interested, so Ellis paid out of pocket to have some all-important demos made, to persuade them to change their minds. In the summer of 1975, Susannah and Keith went into the studio and recorded 22 numbers—an hour and ten minutes' worth of demos. "She could be moody," Ellis says, "but she wasn't difficult professionally in the studio. She knew how she wanted things done there and she was firm, but she didn't fly off the handle. And, she did know that producers have to have the final say."

What Ellis didn't see was the Sturm und Drang at home before the recording. "At a performance, if she thought she hadn't sung well," Ingham recalls, "she would lie on the floor and sob. I'd think, 'My God, how am I going to get her out of this?' Gradually she'd come around—I'd give her a glass of wine or something." Susannah knew she was difficult. "I manage," she wrote, "still to have some incredibly desperate and black moods. I drive Keith crazy by worrying so much about things." Yet, she went on, "Until recently, Keith's attitude toward my depression and self-doubt was anger, ridicule and everything else that made me feel worse." They argued a lot, and she would storm out of the house to an all-night restaurant, where "I'd be calmed down by friends who hang out there. But lately, he's been much more helpful."[9] Indeed, Keith found that if Susannah recorded a song on tape, then studied every element carefully, she was far less anxious. And this process worked wonderfully on the reel-to-reel tapes that were made in the Abbey Road studio, such songs as "Sweet and Lowdown," "Don't Smoke in Bed," "The Second Time Around," "This Funny World"— and, many thought, "I Love a Film Cliché," a number by lyricist Dick Vosburgh (it would be part of the hit show *A Day in Hollywood, A Night in the Ukraine*) that required Susannah to draw on her natural mimicry, acting out the lyrics, actually bits of well-known film dialogue ranging from tragic to slapstick.

But the demos went nowhere at EMI, languishing for decades on a shelf until, by chance, Ellis came across them after Susannah had died. Pulling out the long-outdated reel-to-reel tapes to listen, he was astonished at the brilliant recording debut she'd almost made. "I was taken aback: Everything was there, in place, already." In a tribute to the new girl singer who had popped up on the London scene a quarter of a century before and meant much to him personally, Ellis released the songs on a CD called *The Beginning: 1975.*

Susannah was in a hurry, feeling "old to begin" a singing career, she told Ingham, needing to fast-track her career anyway she could—and not indulge in the nerves that often threatened to overtake her. She craved a recording under her own name, real gigs that paid well. But the year was full of disappointments—the demos leading nowhere, a good club job falling through, her up-and-down feelings about Ingham. By now—two years after arriving in London—she was setting her sights on New York. Even in the mid-seventies, a low period for jazz, marginalized by rock, with fewer venues for singers than ever, the city was still the epicenter of the music and its business. She very much did not want to go there on her own, unsupported, but Ingham was wary of leaving England and, in particular, his son. On the other hand, his estranged wife Marina worked for Air France and could get cheap tickets, which would mean he could get back to England for visits. But as he thought about whether or not to make the break, Susannah decided to go by herself. Though she was terrified of singing without Ingham's support, she was quite clearly unhappy living with him. Says Fairweather, "I always thought the relationship was a case of mistaking the musical rapport for something else. He was not a chauvinist, but very sharp."

Susannah in New York that fall of 1975 spun from high to low daily. She found and lost a singing job, auditioned but didn't get a part in a

Broadway-bound musical, took a lover—the owner of an uptown jazz club—and lost him when she lost her gig. After an uncomfortable few days at her friend Gloria's Village pad, she moved into the bohemian Chelsea Hotel, which she loathed, then found a cheap studio apartment nearby on 15th Street, where she went from crying inconsolably to a high again after she got some copyediting work, the possibility of a job teaching languages at the New School, and, best of all, the promise of a good singing job in December with Dick Sudhalter. Mimi plied her with care packages—practical household gadgets, mostly, but also "things like little shortie white gloves—the kind I used to wear to high school dances," giggled Susannah. And out of the blue, Ingham, in the process of getting his divorce from Marina, called and proposed to her. Her automatic divorce from Stone would come through in a few months, so both she and Ingham would be free to wed, but Susannah was hesitant, remembering the conflicts between them, and she stalled. Ingham visited. "I'd come over on weekends and I'd stay for about four days. I remember we had one big fight when she wanted me to go see her friend Gloria belly-dance. I wanted to go see Ellis Larkins, one of my absolute favorite pianists, who was playing along with Al Haig at a club called Gregory's. 'No way,' I said." In the end, they were not to marry for several more years. But it was a boost to her self-worth to know that Ingham had proposed.

Susannah was marking time, waiting for her gig with Sudhalter, who was also trying to crack New York and who had lined up the December job at the Riverboat, a club at the bottom of the Empire State Building. Gary "U.S." Bonds, the rock singer, was the headliner, with Sudhalter and his group, called In the Spirit of Bix, and Susannah on vocals, as the second line.[10]

Though Sudhalter was willing to work with Susannah, they did not get along well, according to Ellis—"both were perfectionists"—while Ingham attributed most of the friction to arrogance on Sudhalter's part. "He loved and knew a lot of songs, but in London jazz circles he had an air about him: 'I'm-an-American-jazz-musician-where-do-you guys-come-from?' Mild-mannered people in London wanted to deck him." As did, apparently, Susannah on one occasion, when she felt that Sudhalter had crashed her gig at a Pizza Express and shoved him hard in the chest to get him off the bandstand. "And she never offered a word of explanation or apology," observes Sudhalter, who may well have been miffed when Susannah began asking Fairweather, rather than him, to play horn with her and Ingham. "Susannah would have been a means to an end for him—he hoped to get gigs on her coattails," Ingham thinks. Still, Susannah felt grateful then for the Riverboat job. "Dick was very helpful," she told Roy Schecter a few years later, in 1981. "He really seemed to love my singing and believe in me," she added. All that was to change not long after.

Sudhalter, having combined music journalism with his career as a player for years, was well connected with the press. Not that reviewers could have failed to have noticed Susannah, or at any rate the spectacular photo of her that appeared in the ad for the "Bix" group. She out-Marilyned Monroe, all long blonde mane and a tight, spangly dress in spectacular chesty profile. The buzz was on. She met New York musicians and critics: Benny Goodman came by, so did Marian McPartland. John S. Wilson of the *New York Times,* who was to follow her career with unflinching honesty, was polite, *Village Voice* jazz critic Gary Giddins was kind: Susannah was "a refreshingly unpretentious vocalist who understands the strength of understatement." It was Whitney Balliett, longtime jazz critic of the *New Yorker,* who gave her the gold star. While acknowledging some shortcomings, in particular intonation problems that would always be a challenge, he praised her "fondness for rare and unblemished songs"—like "Pinch Me," a Wee Bonnie Baker favorite, "You're Not My First Love," and "The Trouble With Me Is You," an old Nat Cole number—and concluded that she was "a performer of inestimable promise." This was a phrase that Susannah treasured like a love letter. "Inestimable promise!" Susannah not only collected songs the way some women, as she once wittily remarked, collected furs or jewelry, she also collected good notices.

Dick Sudhalter continued to do Susannah good turns. "He said, 'Come to the Carlyle hotel tonight. Marian McPartland's playing there and I told Marian all about you and she really wants to hear you sing again,'" Susannah recalled to Schecter. With McPartland were two friends, the kindly disposed Balliett and the imposing composer Alec Wilder. "I was excited and nervous," Susannah recalled. "I went there in my little raggedy clothes, in the snow. I almost fainted—all these important people in music. [Wilder had recently published his highly regarded book *American Popular Song,* in which he had eloquently argued for their serious consideration.] They asked me to sing and I did and they really liked my singing. I was very nervous." She sang "Easy Come, Easy Go" and then Wilder's tune, "I'll Be Around," as the composer held his head in his hands, looking pained—simply his habit when he was into concentrating. "Alec Wilder was a wonderful character. He talked to me for a while and heard me on another occasion and also said very nice things."[11]

After the Riverboat gig, she had no major bookings, just a little work at Upper West Side restaurant-pubs like the Fugue, the Atrium, and Broady's in the winter of 1976. The *Times'* Wilson caught her at Broady's in February—worse luck: It was hardly the right ambiance for wistful thirties ballads, nor was Susannah, especially without Ingham to anchor her, able to rise above the noise and general barroom atmosphere. Though Gary Giddins called her the "choice of the week" in his column in the *Village Voice,* Wilson decried her "flatly stated delivery." Crushed by his review in the *Times,* she later told her friend Roy Schecter that she broke down sobbing, which Keith Ingham confirmed. But then, she added, "Alec Wilder called and said, 'Wilson has cloth ears. Don't listen to that man. We can hear also what you're going to be—wonderful.'" Ol' cloth ears, however, was to write some glowing reviews about Susannah later, when he felt she'd grown as a singer.

Though Sudhalter had hired Susannah at the Riverboat and introduced her to many musicians in New York as he had in London, they never worked together again. Watching Susannah network and vie for coveted engagements and befriend influential critics and journalists, Sudhalter felt cast aside. "She was all career," he says. "She would jettison people all the time." Certainly at times even Susannah's close friends admitted she lacked tact, as when she brushed aside the offer of a Scottish journalist friend of Ingham's whose knowledge of jazz was admittedly slight but who had been trying to help publicize Susannah as a favor. "No thanks—I don't need you anymore," Ingham recalls Susannah telling the journalist after she became a bit more established. In the jazz world, both fiercely competitive and yet relying on a cooperative spirit among musicians, many singers and players recall examples of what they call Susannah's self-promotion and ruthlessness—accusations never made, by the way, by her non-musician friends (including the many critics and DJs whom she cultivated). "I liked her," says Marian McPartland, who praised Susannah's "unique style that you can always recognize." "But," adds the veteran performer, "she always talked about herself when we had conversations—what do they call that? Narcissism? So I didn't talk to her that often." While Susannah was only doing what every artist who comes to the big city does—promoting herself—the fierce intensity and single-mindedness of her drive, along with a certain maladroitness, put off some people, and created a pool of ill will.

Though Susannah had created a stir and was admired by critics like Balliett and Rex Reed and Alec Wilder and musicians who caught her singing, singing jobs were still scarce in the late seventies, and she was lonely in New York. "I missed Keith," she said. In London, Ingham had signed a contract for several albums with EMI and urged her to come back in May and record a couple of tunes on his first solo project, *The Music of Richard Rodgers*. With nothing happening in New York, she agreed. "I came back to London with the idea that he'd come back to New York with me," she told Schecter. She sublet her apartment in Chelsea and packed her bags. Back in London, she re-recorded two little-known gems she'd done on her EMI demo the year before. "A Lady Must Live," with lyric by Lorenz Hart, from the 1931 show *America's Sweetheart,* is a delicious blend of little-girl and world-weariness—a mixture that was a constant element of Susannah's appeal as a performer—on bits like Hart's risqué scansion on "with my John or my Max, I can reach a climax." The second tune, "This Funny World," was sung by the star Belle Baker in a rare 1926 Rodgers flop called *Betsy* and features a soft melancholy Susannah would burnish to a high gloss as her career went on. For his Richard Rodgers album, Ingham won critical praise for the authority and accomplished harmonic sense of his playing, and Susannah for her "delicious voice, good phrasing, and beautiful pitch." On the strength of that performance and Chris Ellis's tireless work behind the scenes, she was offered her own album for EMI. (Before they'd commit to a multi-record deal with her, the EMI brass said they wanted to see how an album of a popular composer's work would sell.) Ingham suggested she record an album by the composer Harry Warren, still alive but nearly forgotten after a long and impressive career writing for movies. "He never had a Broadway hit, and there's a snobbery in the belief that the greatest American composers all have to come out of Broadway," Ingham, as passionate an amateur historian of the sweep of popular music of the earlier half of the 20th century as he is a pianist, points out.

Susannah and Ingham recorded *The Music of Harry Warren* in two sessions at the end of August 1976. It was a remarkable feat. There was no official budget. Ellis once again fronted money for the studio rental and for the musicians, all friends who'd worked with her before: saxophonist Bruce Turner, drummer Johnny Richardson, and bassist Len Skeat. Ingham, as usual, provided the arrangements. The budget didn't allow for official rehearsal time and sound checks. They simply got together informally, talked about the music, and ran through the tunes. The joyful easy, jazz-swing feel Susannah achieved on the Warren recording is all the more impressive a production given what had preceded it. After receiving the Harry Warren album, the composer sent a glowing letter to Chris Ellis:

> I am often asked whether or not I enjoy hearing new versions of songs I wrote long ago. It depends. I don't like arrangements which distort the melodic line and destroy the original harmonies. I certainly do like to hear new arrangement made by talented and tasteful musicians, such as those on this album . . . I congratulate you for what you've achieved with this album especially with the beautiful singing of Susannah McCorkle. I am both pleased and grateful. Harry Warren

While the record was a critical success, EMI still felt that Susannah's work was too "uncommercial," and the label backed out of further recording arrangements. It has not released Harry Warren on compact disk.

With three records out between them, Susannah and Ingham felt they were ready for better bookings, more record dates. But it was still slim pickings. Things took a turn for the better in the fall after an ill-omened cruise ship booking that gave nearly everyone aboard dysentery. Then Ellis brought along his neighbor, the veteran jazz agent Ken Pitt, to hear the duo at the Taverna Syrtaki on South Moulton Street. Pitt had handled many performers visiting England from the States, from Mary Lou Williams and Teddy Wilson to Sophie Tucker to Mel Tormé. At that time, Pitt was representing Cleo Laine. "Keith began to play," remembers Pitt of that October night in 1976, "then a girl singer began to sing, and my attention was drawn toward the unusual voice I was hearing—certainly not one that one would expect to hear in a Greek restaurant! At the end of their set, Susannah and Keith joined our table. I learned from Susannah that they were having difficulty in getting worthwhile bookings and that even the gig in the Greek restaurant was due to the generosity of the owner, who was an ardent fan of theirs." Pitt agreed to take them on as clients.

With this boost to their careers—they hoped—Susannah's spirits soared. Things were definitely looking up. They'd found a new flat they loved in Chelsea, a peaceful little place with a patio out back facing Brompton Cemetery, a park-like expanse of some 40 acres. Next door were a couple and their two sons with whom they became friendly, and Susannah soon had a confidante in Frances Bendixson, a jewelry designer about 10 years older. Years later, Susannah wrote fondly to her, "I see you as you were when you came into my life, with your pageboy, muted green clothes, great legs and great shoes. How happy I was to meet you and spend time in your garden with you that first day! You are the most special person to me in England." In point of fact, Susannah had longed to have a close woman friend in London, but without much success. "My friends' wives liked her," Ingham notes, "but she made them uncomfortable." With Frances Bendixson, a somewhat motherly figure, Susannah soon established an easy rapport. Both loved to go on long walks in the "park," and loved girl talk. "About clothes and hair and skin and makeup, as neither of us had very good skin and she took a lot of trouble when she was onstage," Bendixson recalls. "She was very self-conscious about those big breasts of hers, and on stage she felt that she really needed clothes that were specially designed for her. I think she liked her figure but felt very vulnerable. When she walked down the street, all eyes were turned on her all the time. She had a fabulous figure and a very beautiful walk—regal, languid, elegant."

They especially formed a bond when they discovered each had had a difficult relationship with her mother, and in a long short story called "Caroline's Mother" that Susannah wrote for her friend after Bendixson's mother died, Susannah wove together negative attributes of both their mothers into a portrait of a monstrously controlling maternal figure from whom the young woman, Caroline, eventually runs away—as both Susannah and Frances had done, though years later Caroline's mother exacts her revenge by showing up on Caroline's London doorstep and taking up right where she left off, domineering Caroline up until the moment she dies. Thus again, as in so many of Susannah's stories, freedom or release comes only with death, though even then there is an ambiguous note, as Caroline sits staring gloomily at the Brompton Cemetery park across the street.

But now Susannah and Keith's career together was on the rise. In January, they were reviewed at the Syrtaki by Robert Cushman, the musical-theater reviewer for the influential weekly *The Spectator.*

Cushman loved them, describing Ingham's piano as "powerful, discreet, pungent, plangent" and Susannah as a "girl rather than a woman singer, knowing but vulnerable [who] values every song for itself. She chooses them well. . . . Her wit, like that of many of the best singers, is deadpan." Cushman, like others in England and on the Continent, viewed Susannah through the lens of a chanteuse, a singer of songs first and foremost, though one for whom jazz was the driving spirit. Yet categorizing Susannah would remain a difficulty and often be an impediment to her career: Was she really a jazz singer? That was the important question to answer for some, while to others, it was beside the point. The Cushmans, Robert and Arlene, became friendly with Ingham and Susannah—she was usually clever about handling well-placed journalists—but Cushman kept his critical eye on the ball. "When she did understand a song, she was very good," he says. "But a lot of songs she didn't get the comic sense of. For example, after she met Dick Vosburgh, the comedy writer, and sang his lyrics to 'Film Cliché,' he said, 'She hasn't got a sense of humor!'" The dry, puckish, fast wit Susannah could exhibit may have evaporated that day; when Susannah was tense and driven or feeling down, her wit took on an acrid flavor. Mastering Vosburgh's tricky, demanding lyric to "Film Cliché" might have added to her performance anxiety. Adds Cushman, "She was so intense, and she achieved a lot partly through sheer willpower."

Susannah and Ingham were still earning their bread (or pita and pizza) at the Syrtaki and Pizza Expresses—places, said another reviewer in January, that were "all uproariously crowded, full of revellers intent on playing musical chairs. A girl like Susannah needs a supper club." Friends from that time remember many a time when Susannah was overwhelmed by the clatter and the chatter in the pubs, as she would be, later on, even in fine supper clubs. "I remember," recalls Digby Fairweather, "a time she stopped a song midstream and said, 'Keith! Will you tell these people to stop talking while I'm singing?'" Agrees Frances Bendixson, "She was really insulted if people talked through her performance, and she'd get agitated and twitchy if the audience was noisy." Of course, no one has more memories of Susannah stressed-out at the gig than Ingham. "She'd admonish the audience. I'd say, 'Just ignore them, just sing, that's life,' but she wouldn't. In Munich at Oktoberfest, we did a gig. That's the worst time of year for performers. She was up there trying to do Bessie Smith and so on, while those beer-swilling louts were banging on the table, and she lost her voice for the rest of the week. She was very down."

For some time, Susannah had craved a booking at Ronnie Scott's, London's top jazz club, where the best musicians and singers performed. Her attempts to crack the club were met by indifference. Not only was she little known, her repertoire was from an unfashionable era. But now she had Ken Pitt in her corner and Pitt had known Ronnie Scott forever, all the way back to 1949, when Pitt ran a swing club in Southall where Scott had played saxophone. At first, Scott's manager, Pete King, was not encouraging, Pitt remembers, but he pressed on, reminding Scott himself of how far Susannah had come from her tip-singing days in 1973 at the 606 Club, where Scott had often hung out. Finally they made a deal that winter, bringing in Susannah and Ingham in a trio setting as a second booking. The money wasn't great, and reviews were mixed, but it was a foot in the door. Other bookings followed: at Peter Langdon's Brasserie, off Picadilly, where the fashionable and the famous went—Susannah's fan Mary Quant the designer, Mick Jagger, Michael Caine.

And there were more recordings. In March, Ingham recorded his second album for EMI, *The Music of Jerome Kern.* Once again Susannah sang lovely, neglected songs: "Nobody Else but Me," from a 1946 revival of *Show Boat,* and "Why Was I Born?," a bittersweet ballad introduced in 1929 by torch singer Helen Morgan. It might have been Susannah's theme song.

She began to concertize, a far more congenial métier, and she was booked by Pitt at the Country Cousin in April, two weeks at Quaglino's in May, weekends at the Portman Hotel. She was now commanding about £80 a night in take-home pay, a far cry from the £2 or £3 at her first jobs at the 606 Club. BBC broadcaster Peter Clayton produced a concert of Johnny Mercer songs by the pair at Pizza Express in April, both a sell-out and a succès d'estime; they followed up later in the year with a concert of Ira Gershwin's lyrics. The Johnny Mercer concert bore other fruit, catching the attention of Black Lion Records producer Alan Bates. (EMI seemed permanently uninterested.) Bates asked them to do an album of Mercer's music. Delighted, Susannah and Ingham combed through their large collection of Mercer songs, "offbeat songs as well as ballads and brighter numbers," she said. (Many years later, Mercer's widow sent Susannah a never-published song she'd found, and she recorded the bluesy "A Phone Call From the Past" on one of her last albums.)

For the Mercer album, Ingham sketched thirties-style arrangements for the six musicians, including Fairweather on trumpet and cornet. It was a happy, almost a carefree recording experience, Fairweather says. "There were very few second takes. She loved the material and sang it with relish, from Dixieland standards like 'At the Jazz Band Ball' to reflective ballads like 'Skylark' and the witty hoop-jumping, 'My New Celebrity Is You.'" Still, it was not a perfect date. Pitch problems plagued Susannah. "On 'One for My Baby,'" Fairweather adds, "Susannah's tuning strays noticeably at one point. But perhaps she and Keith felt that the overall feel of the performance made up for that momentary lapse." Possibly because she and Ingham were trying to re-create the intimate Billie Holiday–Teddy Wilson small-group sound, Susannah sounds far more like Billie Holiday on *The Quality of Mercer* than she had on the Harry Warren and demo sides. It clearly suited Susannah, who delivered the clever songs with relish and a clear delight.

Listeners responded enthusiastically to the Mercer record. "To the joy and amazement of Susannah, Keith and myself," Fairweather says, "they started getting airplay and excellent reviews, including in the States." The album went on to win her two Grammy nominations and achieved something of a cult status when released in the States (under the dull title *The Songs of Johnny Mercer*).

As her career looked up, Susannah found herself with less time and energy, and less interest in the odd typing job and private language lessons. Both she and Ingham were struggling to earn a living, pooling their pay and living frugally (and of course, he had a child to help support as well). When Tom and Mimi sent her one of their periodic checks to help out, this one for a couple of thousand dollars, derived from the sale of some land, she wrote not only to thank but to reassure them, albeit defensively. "Ever since I've been here I've made a living from music. Not a rich one. Let's say like a secretary, and that's okay. Plus I'm doing what I love. Remember that. The money you sent is waiting in a savings account in New York." For, having tested the waters in New York, she was planning on going back permanently, and soon.

With that in mind, she squared her shoulders and wrote a second letter to her parents, asking for another, more substantial "loan":

The past six months I have really begun to hit my stride with audiences and enjoy performing in a way I hadn't since I was about ten and doing skits for my schoolmates. I have also become very good at selecting my material and adapting it to my particular abilities. I've never felt more ready to tackle New York. All the omens are good, best of all, a real resurgence of interest in good songs and in jazz. I've made fresh starts so many times in so many cities, but never in my life have I had such hope and high spirits about it. . . . I'm very good at managing money . . . but we are going to have massive expenses getting settled. . . . If you are prepared to loan us money I think I could safely say we could have it paid back in five years. We haven't had a lot of work in the past couple of months, but what we have had has been prestigious and we have been very very successful with audiences.

Susannah didn't exaggerate about the praise she'd received. In the small, influential circles of listeners and critics, she'd attracted the approval of Philip Larkin, Chris Ellis, Robert Cushman, and jazz-loving Pizza Express owner Peter Boizot, and practically the whole, if small, circle of swing-era jazz players in England, including the touring American legend Bobby Hackett. And her brief trip to New York had won praise from no less a critic than Whitney Balliett and the attention of columnist Rex Reed. Eminent composers Alec Wilder and Harry Warren had showered her with praise. But neither did Susannah exaggerate her and Keith's plight, the dead-end-seeming spot they were in, living in London. In deciding to make the move, she'd been especially encouraged by Chris Ellis. "I nudged her to leave London and go to New York," he says. "London audiences weren't for her—there weren't enough people for her kind of music. I felt that the only place where her work would be fully understood and appreciated was in the USA, and that with the good publicity going for her, she had the opportunity of getting work there. It was the right thing to do. I gave her her chance—I recorded her. But she had the talent. She did it."

Susannah was eager to go back to New York, not only because of her career but because she was homesick: "Not for the America I knew, but the one Europeans loved," she stressed. Still, there was the still-unresolved issue of her relationship with Ingham. There was little love lost between them now. "Once the passion between us wore out, there was very little in common outside of music," he says. As Susannah had confessed to Thea Lurie the previous year, "Sometimes I wonder if I want to love anyone anymore." Yet she couldn't imagine herself making music without Ingham supporting her at the piano.

So, despite her misgivings, she bent all her persuasive powers to convince him to come with her. He temporized, but finally agreed to join her in a month, once he'd settled his affairs. In the meantime, they continued to argue. Trying to salvage the relationship that autumn of 1977, he wrote her a mea culpa: "As our music became richer, deeper and more satisfying so our relationship deteriorated to a degree which horrifies and frightens me now. When you needed me, I wasn't there, I was in my safe world of the piano, keeping you out yet again."

But as she boarded a plane that October to return to New York—with a number of well-received recordings and reviews and a good singing job lined up in a top New York club—Susannah couldn't help but feel hopeful about the future. Once they were in New York, they'd recharge their energy, and their careers would blossom. She was almost 32 years old, he was a few years older; she felt they had to do it now.

And after decades of neglect, the music Susannah and Ingham loved was moving from the margins, with singers of standards finding steadier work after the long drought of the sixties. "The nostalgia craze was soaring," wrote James Gavin in a book about cabaret, "creating an audience eager to give the old stars the attention that they craved."[12] Mabel Mercer, the doyenne of intimate standards, had opened the St. Regis Room in 1972 and had starred in a popular television special with Bobby Short and others, signaling a new mood in New York. Clubs opened: Soerabaja hosted Hugh Shannon and Bricktop, Brothers and Sisters featured Barbara Cook, Bobby Short made the Café Carlyle his home, and fans filled Reno Sweeney's and The Ballroom. Susannah's generation had rejected standards and their singers as dated and square, but the sixties' kids were growing up now. With Ingham in New York, she would be in the vanguard of the new generation of singers and musicians bringing fresh interpretations to the great old songs. She was seasoned, and she had a booking at a big club lined up. She had albums on her résumé, advance praise, and had made sure that important critics and reviewers in New York were aware of what she had been doing across the pond. What could go wrong?

She was about to get a rude awakening.

Little Susan McCorkle
at the family home in
Berkeley with her doll
"Country," who accompa-
nied her everywhere.
(Family photograph)

Tom McCorkle and
Mimi Manchester in love
on the campus of the
University of California-
Berkeley in the mid–1930s.
(Family photograph)

Susannah in Venice, summer of 1968. Though she looks radiant, it was one of the worst summers of her life. (Family photograph)

*(above left)* Susan McCorkle as a choir member of the John Harris High School Girl's Ensemble as a senior in 1963. Second row from the back, third from the left. She was also listed in the senior class "hall of fame." (from *The Pioneer,* yearbook, John Harris High School, Harrisburg, PA, 1963.)

*(lower left)* One of Susannah's first gigs as a jazz singer in May of 1971 in Rome, at the Folkstudio club. At her right is clarinetist Francesco Forti, her first important love. (Photo per Thea Lurie)

Pianist Keith Ingham at a solo performance in 1982. He was Susannah's first long-time musical partner and second husband. (Photo per Keith Ingham)

Susannah with pianist Ben Aronov at the jazz club Struggles, in Edgewater, New Jersey, circa 1984. (Photo by Roy Schecter)

After Susannah's wedding to Dan DiNicola in August of 1991, they posed with his children. Left to right: Jeff DiNicola, Roy DiNicola, Dan, Susannah, Anne DiNicola. (Photo per Thea Lurie)

Susannah singing with her regular trio at HMV, a music store in Manhattan, in the summer of 1999. Pianist Allen Farnham was her last long-time musical partner. Not shown: bassist Bill Moring, drummer Tim Horner. (Photo per Allen Farnham)

Mimi and Tom McCorkle with Susannah in 1988, celebrating their fortieth wedding anniversary. She sang "The Folks Who Live on the Hill." She cried, they didn't. (Family photograph)

Susannah with Thea Lurie, her closest friend, in 1999. They met in Rome in 1970 while both were beginning their careers, Susannah as a singer, Thea as a journalist. (Photo per Thea Lurie)

"The Songbirds of Jazz" was the billing for singers Maxine Sullivan, Carol Sloane, and Susannah in the winter of 1983. Critics liked the group but the three did not get along. (Photo per Thea Lurie)

Susannah's literary side. At the prestigious MacDowell Colony with other writer Fellows in August of 1983. (Photo per Thea Lurie)

With the critic Rex Reed, an important champion, circa 1977, fresh from London and desperate to succeed. (Photo per Thea Lurie)

Being hugged by the drummer Roy Haynes after an Algonquin performance in 1999. A number of esteemed jazz musicians dug Susannah—Joe Williams, Tony Bennett, Phil Woods, to name several. (Photo per Thea Lurie)

Susannah straddled jazz and cabaret. At the Firebird cabaret in New York in 1998, with friends Hubert and Jackie Osteen, and performers Andrea Marcovicci and Mark Nadler. Both Jackie Osteen and Mark Nadler became very close to Susannah. (Photo per Jackie Osteen)

## 1977 TO 1984

# The Hungry Years

I wish everybody would let me alone to sing my little songs.
—Susannah to DJ Bob Jones

October 1977: A hopeful time for Susannah, with a lot of singing prospects back in New York. The Harry Warren album was due for release on an American label; she had a booking lined up at the Ballroom, a key club in downtown Manhattan; and she was networking like mad, meeting musicians, club owners, managers, record producers, writers to talk to. Yet she also observed how many on the New York jazz scene were unimpressed with a singer concentrating on the old standards and repeated her complaint that while what she thought of as "jazz" was "the music of the intelligentsia," in America it was dated. But by "jazz," she was not seen as referring to the modernists and post-bop players, nor the experimental vocalists: *that* scene was narrow but definitely alive and in no wise dated. Indeed the problem in New York was precisely that to many, jazz *meant* cutting-edge, meant avant-garde. In focusing on the music of the past, Susannah herself, in their view, was dated. This was an argument, a tension, that would continue. And meanwhile, one by one, the plans she'd counted on fell through. She faced a great disappointment when the powers-that-be at EMI and Black Lion in London wouldn't allow a release of certain tunes she'd recorded to be included as part of Alec Wilder's monumental, forty-part radio program called *American Popular Song.* "Wilder told us there was one singer that he was unable to obtain," said producer Joel L. Siegel. "We guessed Sinatra, Peggy Lee, etc., but he said no: Susannah McCorkle." Next, the big nightclub date was canceled, with no other good booking in sight. "It seemed as if I had been jinxed,"

Susannah told Roy Schecter. "Everything fell through. I was miserable. I really was under a cloud for about two years."

She chronicled her state of mind in "The Woman in 2B," a story published a year later.[1] In the story, an unnamed, married protagonist in her thirties, like Susannah, arrives in New York from England to look for an apartment for herself and her husband, who is soon to join her, as Ingham was soon to join Susannah. In the process, the woman meets a landlord who has a place for rent; then, although he is described as a crass man, she agrees to have dinner with him. They immediately embark on an affair, which the woman describes as enjoyable even though she is repelled by his crude table manners and the sex "toys" she comes across in his bedroom. When her husband arrives from London, she breaks off the affair without explanation, though she is aware that the landlord follows her around and spies on her. Everything is coated with a veneer of affectlessness, of drifting.

It was another piece of autobiography. Susannah, while hoping to continue to sing with Ingham, was not, she told Lurie and other friends, at all sure she wanted to stay with him in New York. But then Ingham did indeed come to New York in time for Thanksgiving, full of misgivings and not much cash. "I came over with £50, about 80 bucks. I left an apartment that I had with my first wife and my son Alexandre, who was then about three. Susannah had said to me, 'You've got to come here too,' and I knew that I did. Susannah was right, and I'll always be grateful. But I was naive when I got here. I thought that Susannah had been doing well. I thought, 'She's going to be working, and it's going to ease the way for me.' But she hadn't been working at all!"

He nearly turned around and went back to London, but after a teary emotional scene, they reconciled and moved into the apartment she'd found, a three-room place for $350 a month on the Upper West Side. Today West 85th Street off Columbus Avenue is a tidy block with neat brownstones and a school at the end of the block. But then, it was a slum. "A bad drug street, as we soon found out," says Ingham. "There was a pimp on the bottom floor of the building, a super who repeatedly would get drunk and come pound on our apartment door, shouting, 'I'm gonna kill whitey!' Across the hall was this black hooker in her fifties, drunk and yelling, and this girl who lived in the apartment below was into sadomasochism—Susannah knew about it, I didn't. For somebody who hated violence so, Susannah was very curious about what was going on there, somebody being whipped and handcuffed and so on. It was an awful place. But we were stuck, and we had to find the rent. Her parents sent her money, but that wasn't enough. And Susannah did work a little—she was singing in this little place downtown, the Village West."

In time-honored fashion, Ingham dodged the powerful New York City Local 802 of the American Federation of Musicians union, which had a long-standing rule against immigrant musicians: "You couldn't work in the city until you'd sat out for six months or something. But I did play. At Jimmy Ryan's and Eddie Condon's, and then I auditioned for this restaurant, Ambrosia, on East 60th Street which Susannah had learned of from a coat-check friend of hers. These two women, a couple, were looking for a pianist and I got the job because I played a lot of tunes; it was a lovely steady six nights a week on a little baby grand. Benny Goodman came in, and I started working with him also. And Richard Rodgers came in. I remember thinking, 'He doesn't want to hear his stuff, he's heard it endlessly.' But up comes the note from him to the piano: 'Could you please play some of my songs?' I began to play the lesser-known ones like 'Little Girl Blue,' and he wrote a note, very appreciative. He came back a lot and brought in theater people. So I was the breadwinner, and that job lasted about two years, until Ambrosia closed. At the same time, Susannah began to get a few more little singing jobs here and there. And she would work as a secretary or typist. [For a year, Susannah worked as a secretary to an eccentric rare-coin dealer, an experience she soon worked into a new novel.] She had somehow met a therapist called Helen Aronson, a Polish Jewish refugee, and did some office work for her, I think in 1978. I don't know if Susannah was in therapy at all with her, but Helen, now deceased, did tell me in a conversation that Susannah had very crazy tendencies. 'She's just plain nuts,' she said. 'Be careful, there's a lot of anger suppressed there.' Well, I never noticed *that*. To me, Susannah was a person who shrank away from *any* kind of violence. She even hated debate—what we would call different opinions."

While Ingham quickly found a niche and a paycheck with his steady restaurant gig, Susannah was having a rough time, and it affected her emotional state terribly. Scraping together a reduced fee from her freelance clerical work, Susannah took Aronson's advice and found an amiable psychotherapist named Roberta Todras, who remained friendly with her after Susannah left off therapy with her. "Initially, I helped her with her image of herself, then with pre-performance anxiety," Todras says. "She felt she was not attractive enough, and how she looked was very important to her. She was continually putting herself down while trying to make it. She moved in and out of depression. She had demons. She struggled to be cared for. I worked with her on accepting herself." Too often, Susannah wrote, she blew up her setbacks into "some terrible pattern leading to a descending gloom, everything falling through."

*Crazy tendencies. Demons.* In "I Was a Compulsive Overeater," written in 1977 (one of a number of articles she wrote on spec for *New York* magazine of which she eventually sold just one, a funny portrait of her plumber, in 1979), Susannah was bluntly truthful, writing about her cycles of binge-eating and fasting—hating herself the whole time. Drugs were never an issue for her—she no longer even took "diet pills"—but she was sensitive to even a moderate intake of alcohol. Not a "problem drinker" in the way of her mother, during periods of stress, when she sought to relax with a few drinks, Susannah was apt to break down crying, or, on occasion, act out. Psychiatrists note that for persons who have bipolar disorder (Susannah's later diagnosis), even one drink can tip their delicate balance and, among other effects, influence them to do things they might not otherwise. And if Keith Ingham is to be believed, this did happen to Susannah—she did indeed act out. The tangle of Susannah's and Keith's mutual needs was made knottier by wine, says Ingham, citing an instance during the hot summer of 1978. Susannah had gotten a part-time job as rental agent of her building, which featured cheap apartments, and decided to show a prospective renter their apartment on the top floor. "I was in the bathroom shaving. Naked. The girl kicks the door open, and she has a view of the bathroom and me. When I come out, she's in the main room and the sun was streaming in, shining through this girl's dress and she's not wearing anything underneath. Well, we opened a bottle of wine, and things took off from there with the three of us. It just happened spontaneously. As it happened, she turned out to be a hooker, and they threw her out. And there were some other threesomes with the S-and-M girl who lived below us, who'd be mildly tied up. Again, we'd had some wine."

How far all this was from the good girl with the white gloves, from the shining, achingly romantic persona who fell in love with Billie Holiday's gorgeous grit. How far from the exquisite sensitivity and the finely wrought combination of innocence and world-weariness that would win over so many fans! But Susannah was bound to Ingham by a complex of needs, and above all her drive to sing. "She told me she married Keith because she needed a piano player," says Dan Moran, her last lover of consequence. She was as yet far too insecure to work with anyone else regularly. Her then-friend, pianist and composer Richard Rodney Bennett, took her to an informal hangout where singers went for fun, but the veteran accompanist found playing for Susannah "deeply uncomfortable. She did 'My Old Flame,' and all the time she was anxiously listening to the piano, worried that she was going to lose it." Those first years after her move to New York constituted a nadir, a time in her life when meaninglessness and hopelessness panicked her, when self-loathing got the upper hand, when she did things that surely appalled and frightened her, so counter did they run to her cherished romantic ideals. Susannah was pulled violently by the undertow of the manic depression that she as yet neither recognized nor accepted. Like an alcoholic who is still in denial (and much of the curve of her disease parallels the downward curve of alcoholism), she could only run from the truth at this time in her life, thus pulling herself further down. Soiled, her shining, bright, romantic longings. Messy, the emotional life of this woman who had a passion for organization and control.

All the more remarkable then that when Susannah finally had a chance to sing in public, she was, as one reviewer said succinctly in the spring of 1978, a "sensation." At a Monday-night showcase at the important club Reno Sweeney's, she was a standout among a dozen hopeful performers. "She looked and sounded gorgeous and was in complete possession of her material," wrote a critic, adding that Ingham was "simply brilliant." At the Copacabana Club soon after, Dick Sudhalter, soon to become the regular jazz critic for the *New York Post*, praised her but had misgivings (as had Ingham) about her choice of Neil Sedaka's "New York City Blues" (from his 1974 album *The Hungry Years,* another of her favorites then). "It simply contains more pain, anger and sheer grit than Miss McCorkle's voice could handle," he wrote.

There was never unanimity about Susannah among the cognoscenti, about her talent, her selection of material, or even the way she looked. Dan Morgenstern, a dean of jazz criticism, recalls coolly, "I first heard her at Eddie Condon's when she was new to New York. George Simon [the writer and big-band critic] was very enthusiastic. I was not. And I was surprised to see dirty fingernails!" "She didn't know how to dress then, and you would see her early on with oily hair, unkempt and awkward," adds a singer who met her then (a criticism that no one would make of the groomed and coiffed Susannah in her 1990s diva days). John S. Wilson of the *Times*, who'd been polite about Susannah in reviewing her Riverboat performance in 1975, now wrote that he was "puzzled about her choice of show songs and occasional contemporary songs that seem to leave her at a loss," adding that Susannah seemed "overpowered by her jazz accompaniment." Wilson gave her another mixed review two years later after hearing her at a club called Barbara's in the Village. "He did positively single out her version of the Arthur Schwartz–Dorothy Fields song 'Alone Too Long,'" Ingham recalls. "But he ticked off her clumsy movements, her stiff arms, and said one of her gestures was pure ZaSu Pitts"—referring to the twenties and thirties film comedienne whose trademark gestures included fluttery hands, plaintive eyes, and "Oh dear me!" Wilson's remark particularly hurt because Susannah had worked hard on her stagecraft, taking movement classes and studying actors and singers on stage.

"After the ZaSu Pitts remark," Ingham continues, "Susannah had one of her convulsive fits, sobbing on the floor. 'I hate this man.' She told me she wanted revenge, that I should take a gun and go down and shoot Wilson. I tried to comfort her. I said, 'Susannah, please, maybe he's trying to help you, he's pointing out something you need to know, because I don't think Wilson is a vicious critic. Everybody gets knocks—look what the great artists have been through, Louis Armstrong, Duke Ellington, everybody.'"

John Wilson was not being cruel. Susannah had after all been singing for only half a decade when she decided to face New York, where Wilson, Morgenstern, and their colleagues had been brought up on the great jazz singers of the forties, fifties, and sixties. She had no way to come to terms calmly with her limitations. In a few years, Wilson was to give her a glowing review. "Everything has fallen into place," he wrote. In the meantime, she'd have to pay her dues along with everybody else, something she was ill-equipped to do.

At least there were London bookings to depend on. In the winter of 1979, Ken Pitt had put together a month's worth of engagements for Susannah and Keith, posh one-nighters and three weeks at Ronnie Scott's opposite saxophonist Johnny Griffin, at double their last fee, and a BBC interview with jazz journalist Stan Britt.[2] Speaking in a breathy, tightly enunciated expat accent (many Americans commented on

Susannah's unplaceable if slightly foreign-sounding speech), Susannah declared in the interview on March 7 that she would not play "old basements anymore," a dig, presumably, at the humble Pizza Express pubs that had given the duo their start. "There's always something—a mike breaks down, waiters whizzing by. I just can't sing there anymore—it's too amateurish." Observes her old friend Jon Carroll, "But the reality of life as a singer of jazz songs is you play lounges with waitresses moving around and serving drinks. People yell requests from the audience, and that's how you earn your money, get your public. I know it was hard for her to deal with that aspect of show business. Out there in the world of people who own nightclubs, they don't care how many obscure Cole Porter songs you've discovered and revivified. They care whether you're putting butts in the chairs. It's a cold world."

Keith Ingham agrees. Mentally wincing over Susannah's swipe at the Pizza Express—why alienate the owner Peter Boizot, a jazz lover who hired them and paid them good money and who also owned the more upscale Pizza on the Park?—Ingham countered Susannah's objections in a firm tone: "From a musician's point of view, it's fine." Next Susannah was saying aloud that she and Keith were still struggling to make a living at their music, though they had hopes of having a new record out soon, which would undoubtedly lead to bigger and better things. (They saved money in London by staying in the basement flat of Richard Rodney Bennett's Victorian Gothic house in "then unfashionable Islington: Sir Simon Rattle [the conductor] now lives in it," says the long-transplanted-to-New York Bennett.)

Back in New York, Susannah faced the same struggles as usual in finding gigs, though work picked up a bit in the spring, when she was booked at a hip club in Bucks County, Pennsylvania, and more importantly, at a new jazz club in the Village called Abingdon Square, where pianist-composer Dave Frishberg, whose music she would champion, also played. But Abingdon Square soon closed and the Pennsylvania club didn't call her back. Now Susannah set her sights on California. She and Ingham flew out to Los Angeles, where she planned to network for bookings in area clubs. Meanwhile, she and Keith stayed with her family in nearby Long Beach, where Ingham gained more insight into the McCorkle family dynamics. "There was friction among all the family members," he recalls, and Susannah and Tom sparred over their accomplishments. Tom hadn't published anything big since *Fajardo's People* at the time of his breakdown, though he was hard at work on a long-cherished dream, a "Mexican" detective series. He'd almost finished the first, called *Death of a Macho,* and was planning the second, *The Long Siesta,* though he complained he was able to write for only two hours tops on a good day now. And he had no publisher. "He resented the fact that she was published," Ingham emphasizes. "She had published close to a dozen short stories by then in the English women's magazine market, besides her O. Henry award-winner 'Ramona by the Sea,' and had a new piece coming out that fall in *New York,*" he recalls. Having been through hell and back with his own psychiatric problems, Tom must have harbored some resentment at the unsparing portraits Susannah had drawn of him and Mimi in "Ramona," though he was not one to admit it. He usually withdrew into a bleak silence around his wife and daughters.

Tom at 66 was almost at the end of his career, and it was not a triumphant exit. It was painfully clear to both Susannah and Ingham, when they visited one of his classes, why he was being, in his words, "pressured to retire by his department." His classes were sparsely and indifferently attended. Ingham, with his Oxford education, was distressed for Tom. "He was depressed. I was appalled—these louts lounging in their chairs, chewing gum," he says. Tom's mental condition, diagnosed variously as "schizo-affective," "bipolar," "schizophrenic," or "manic depressive," had made it a challenge for him to teach since he took the job at the college in 1966.[3] The classes that Ingham and Susannah visited were among the last he was to teach.

When it came to Susannah and her mother, Ingham was perplexed. In years to come, Susannah was to describe her mother in witchlike terms. Theirs was—largely—a silent mother-daughter psychic fight, as was her relationship with her father, but with Mimi, there were also eruptions, shouted arguments, tears, and accusations. "Mimi *was* a bit of an airhead," he recalls, "and she probably did have a drinking problem. But she was also a wonderful seamstress, and at various times she made beautiful gowns for Susannah and was very proud that Susannah would wear them to sing in and look great. She was trying to help her in her way. But Susannah hated her mother, despised her for her competitiveness. Both her parents, I think, would feel awkward around her because she'd put them down at every opportunity: 'You don't know what I'm doing,' she'd say, 'or what I'm singing.'"

Ingham also met Susannah's older sister Katie during the visit. "She was the one who was really crazy, I could see that," he says. "Still, Katie was able to hold down a job as a nurse's aide, I believe, in a hospital [she had finally gotten some kind of nursing degree or certificate], and the grandparents cared for her cute little illegitimate kid, Carlos, while she was out at work." Tom and Mimi continued to raise Carlos until he was about 13. "But he was wild even then," Mimi said. "He felt the world was against him." Eventually, Mimi kicked out her oldest daughter and grandson.

Returning to New York, wrangling with her British album producers, and borrowing money from Ken Pitt and others, Susannah was at last able to lease the Americans rights to both her Johnny Mercer and Harry Warren albums, to be distributed in the States by Inner City Records. For the Mercer album, sometime producer-critic Joel L. Siegel and photographer Bradley Olman provided liner notes and cover photograph, gratis. The result was a big splash in the then-small pond of American aficionados for "that kind" of music, a critical success and a crucially important move forward in Susannah's career.

Finally, Ingham and Susannah, envisioning their careers taking off, decided to get married. "I did have my green card by then, so the marriage was not for that reason," he explains. "But getting married did stabilize my status, as I was traveling in and out of the country a good deal." For the occasion, on December 5, 1979, at City Hall in downtown Manhattan, Mimi flew in. (Tom did not, for he was in no condition to travel, Mimi said.) Afterward, they had a small reception at the apartment—and when everyone had gone, Susannah said, the newlyweds had another of their frequent arguments, in part perhaps stemming from her dependence on Ingham, who was her arranger, her pianist, her musical director, her ticket to becoming known. But even as she hated her need of him, she planned her next record with him, something she hoped would broaden her appeal. However, the project they settled on was one for the cognoscenti. It featured the lyrics of a man who'd been known in previous decades as "the social conscience of Broadway." E. Y. "Yip" Harburg had written the lyrics to many Broadway shows, most famously *Finian's Rainbow*—and the film *The Wizard of Oz*. As it happened, Harburg lived only blocks from them in a commodious apartment facing Central Park, the location Susannah perennially craved and never achieved. Harburg agreed to meet with them there and was so impressed with the couple's thorough knowledge of his songs that he invited them to copy music from his personal collection. "He was left-wing, liberal, also witty and profound," Ingham recalls. "And he was very amenable. When we said we were going to do an album of his songs, he actually changed some lyrics for her on 'Thrill Me.'" Harburg, like Harry Warren and Alec Wilder, were bowled over by Susannah's exquisite handling of the material.

The album that resulted, *Over the Rainbow: The Songs of E. Y. "Yip" Harburg,* recorded in January and February 1980, was a wonderful, close collaboration between Keith's excellent arrangements and accompaniment and Susannah's superb readings of the lyrics, an ironic success since these two partners were increasingly estranged in their private lives. Released by Inner City, *Rainbow* furthered their reputations (*Stereo Review,* for example, chose it as the magazine's "Best Record of the Month" in January 1982) and brought Susannah much new notice. Her biggest fan may have been her father, who found the project irresistible. "A spectacular achievement," he wrote her after he heard the record, "To me," he added, "your intelligence is the unique thing that you have more of than all the others."

But as often happened following a major creative effort, Susannah's mood dipped once she'd made the record. She was restless and increasingly impatient with Ingham's stalwart and exclusive love of the old songs. She took the scattered criticism about *Rainbow* very much to heart. One critic cited its "decidedly retro feel"; another called it "the music of your grandmother's generation." Being associated with "your grandmother's music" was emphatically not what she wanted. More and more, Susannah felt hemmed in by Ingham's taste. He was perfectly content with the great songs of the past, while she wanted to at least explore the songs of the present. More than that, Susannah craved musical independence. About upcoming bookings in England in the spring of 1980, she wrote to Ken Pitt, "It is important for me to build a solo name, both Keith and I agree. I don't have the kind of ego that I want to be a star," she added. Then, "The marquee should read *Susannah McCorkle and the Keith Ingham Trio—*not *with.*" While such wording may seem a distinction without a difference, nevertheless it signaled that she wanted to be elevated a notch above the accompanists, like better-known vocalists.

Back in the States, her professional life began to look up. She sang at Reno Sweeney's again, had other bookings lined up, and was planning a new album—but *her* way, not Ingham's. Happily, the two had found a much better place to live, at a well-maintained complex on West 86th Street off Central Park called the Parc Cameron, though Ingham was always working and rarely at home evenings. Ironically, less than a year after their wedding, she and Ingham were no longer a couple except for music. He'd met another Susan (Brown) while visiting in England, and they had fallen in love. For her part, Susannah was "seeing" a series of men now, too. "Musicians like Warren Vaché, Ron McClure, probably others," Ingham recalls. "I like talented, interesting men," she wrote candidly to her mother, "and would rather have short involvements with them in hopes of finding one who isn't crazy and can build something more lasting with me than settle for someone who is nice, attractive, but basically bores me."

She also now plunged into her writing full-speed, trying to make a living from stories and nonfiction articles. She already owed money to her parents and friends like Chris Ellis and Ken Pitt. Now, on the strength of the sale of her profile of the plumber to *New York,* she tried developing a series of other thumbnail sketches of odd characters she met. "If one pays off, I'll send you the money right away," she told Pitt. She was able to sell one or two, but the amount of work involved was huge, and most of them, like her compulsive-eating article and another called "Assault in Central Park," while providing invaluable looks at her life and state of mind at the time, didn't get placed.

In "Assault," Susannah wrote a first-person account about a frightening encounter while she was race-walking in Central Park in the late summer of 1980. As she strode around the path in late afternoon, she thought about her plans: "I'd be home in time to watch the sunset from my window, take a shower, make a nice salad for dinner, listen to music. Maybe I'd go out with friends later on, or maybe I'd just stay home and read. I was feeling great—peaceful, fit, happy with the way my life was going both personally and professionally." Then a man lunged at her from behind a tree. "I did the only thing I could. I screamed for life." Now, Susannah had been doing vocal exercises faithfully for years at that point. When she screamed, the park listened. "It was a piercing, gut-level cry for help. It couldn't possibly be misconstrued," a man who came to her aid told her. Susannah's conclusion, that New Yorkers were a "family" and that she was part of a great city, was unconvincing. She *had* been lucky, she had been rescued, but what about the man who attacked her? Was he not also part of the "great city"? Susannah, curiously, did not write about the feelings that come after such a traumatic event, the fear and panic that can overwhelm the victim. Perhaps she could not face the old feelings from her past assaults and rape that must surely have been revived that afternoon in Central Park.

Her nonfiction efforts not paying off, Susannah concentrated again on short stories and the novel in progress. She complained of the din from the street and the neighbors, of Ingham's hours at the piano. But she would never find it easy to work at home no matter where it was. She was always looking for what she called a "neutral place" to engage the muse. During those first years in New York, she prevailed on a series of friends. "She often asked if she could come to my place to write when I was away working a lot in England, particularly in the summers," says Richard Rodney Bennett. "I was always being told how awful it was at home with Keith, how badly he treated her, and how she couldn't write." By the early eighties, she was lugging her typewriter over to Diane Mich's, a new friend who had an apartment on the East Side and was away at work during the days. "I'd come home from work, and we'd talk," says Diane, soon to marry and become Diane Mich Feldman—and Susannah would then often use the Feldman place when they were away in the summers. The habit of wanting to write away from home was one she kept for the rest of her life.

Her English agent Pat White placed many of her stories abroad, in England in the popular *Woman's Journal* and *Woman,* and in a host of subsidiaries—*New Idea* in Australia, *Female* in Singapore, *Svensk Damtidning* in Sweden, *Sarie* in South Africa, where she had to use an Afrikaner pseudonym (Susan Kruger), and a dozen others, and also continued to encourage Susannah to complete her novel in progress.[4] Then Susannah found an impressive American champion in Doubleday acquisitions editor Jacqueline Kennedy Onassis, who was much taken with Susannah's music and wit after hearing her on a program with DJ Bob Jones on WNEW radio. Recalls Dan DiNicola, Susannah's last husband, "Susannah liked to tell the story of coming home one day and hearing a breathy voice on her answering machine, claiming to be Jackie Onassis, telling her she'd been impressed by 'Ramona by the Sea'" (Susannah had mentioned it on the broadcast, and Onassis had checked it out in the 1975 O. Henry Awards collection). Though Susannah thought somebody was putting her on, she called the number back—and it really *was* Jackie O. At the editor's request, Susannah eagerly assembled a group of her short stories and her novel in progress, a psychological mystery called *Closer to Home,* that Susannah described in summary: "A heroine called Lynne has just left her husband. A woman in her mid-thirties, at that terribly tenuous stage in which she knows that it's best over, but she still has strong feelings for the man and keeps slipping back." Thirtysomething Lynne takes a job working for a "millionaire kid coin dealer, a doomed figure . . . of undeniable brilliance in a given field, but [living] an existence that is childlike, destructive, even tragic, while Lynn yearns for a constructive, happy life by the end of the book." Although Kennedy Onassis wrote several letters, telling Susannah she was "enchanted by the glow in all your stories . . . you have a wry understanding of human relationships," she wasn't too excited about the plot of *Closer to Home*. "I wouldn't tangle with a mystery if I were you," she advised. "One doesn't wish to read on and see all those grisly things happen. . . . If you should decide to change the focus of your novel, I should be happy to see it. . . . Is it too boring to wish for a happy ending for that young woman with whom the reader sympathizes?" But although the character Lynn might wish for happiness, Susannah could neither write such endings, nor—more to the point— even plot a novel in such a self-conscious way. Very few of her stories ever ended smoothly or happily.

But Susannah felt encouraged to keep up with her fiction, and in the fall of 1982, she won a highly coveted residency at Yaddo, the artists' retreat in Saratoga Springs, was accepted back in May, and went the following year to the equally prestigious MacDowell Colony, in New Hampshire. A brilliant array of writers, musicians, and visual artists had preceded her at these havens: Sylvia Plath, Katherine Anne Porter, James Baldwin, Alice Walker. That autumn, she enjoyed the company of others, many of whom would make names for themselves—Allan Gurganus, Bob Shacochis, Clark Blaise (married to writer Bharati Mukherjee), and Richard Price, with whom she had an affair. Ingham came to Saratoga Springs to perform with her and visited Yaddo, but he came away unimpressed. To him, "it had an artists' prison atmosphere." But to Susannah being accepted in such selective company was a tremendous vote of confidence in her writing.

Along with her writing career, Susannah was making real progress with her singing career in the 1980s, beginning with a job subbing for singer-pianist Dardanelle, who was a regular on weekends at the Cookery. The club had been put on the map in the seventies by the great jazz pianist Mary Lou Williams, who was followed by blues singer Alberta Hunter. In 1980, Dardanelle needed a couple of weekends off because of some minor surgery. It was Susannah's friend, jazz fan and fledgling promoter Joel L. Siegel—he who had only recently written the album notes for the U.S. release of Susannah's Mercer album—who convinced owner Barney Josephson that Susannah would be a great sub. For the two-week opportunity, Siegel went to work, helping Susannah get free publicity shots and a donated new gown. And most importantly, "leaning on everyone I knew in New York to come to Susannah's gig," so that nearly *tout le jazz New York* was there the night Susannah opened, with Ingham, of course, anchoring the piano, and Harvey Swartz on bass. The place was packed both nights, and she was such a success that Josephson decided to keep her on regularly, bumping Dardanelle from the spot. Susannah was ecstatic: "It's my best booking so far and I have a new friend [Siegel] to help me," she wrote home. She updated her repertoire, including standards like "I've Grown Accustomed to Her Face" (she sang "to *His* Face") and a quaintly amusing number from the twenties called "When I'm Housekeeping for You," as well Harburg's "If I Only Had a Heart," but some jazz tunes, too, such as the Peggy Lee–introduced "Some Cats Know," and Dave Frishberg and Bob Brookmeyer's "Useless Waltz."

Heavyweights came and heard and were impressed: composer Arthur Schwartz, critic Francis Davis of the *Atlantic,* and the already-smitten George T. Simon, who raved of her New Year's Eve 1980 performance in the *Post,* "Oh Susannah really shines . . . she is new and unusual, she is delicate and twinkling." (Even Wilson of the *Times* liked her this time, praising the way she treated the lyrics.) Writer Chris Albertson was equally enthralled. He wrote glowingly of her in *Stereo Review* several times, including a cover feature on her in March 1984. But none could top critic Rex Reed's dream review on November 12 that year, after which everyone must have felt duty-bound to go hear her, but which almost certainly created a backlash of envy among Susannah's fellow singers. Reed wrote, "She's a great new singer on the jazz circuit, and her struggle to carve a career has not been an easy one. She has the soul of a Billie Holiday, the sultry wisdom of a Sylvia Syms, the spirited sweetness of a Peggy Lee, all rolled into one disarming musical package," with "impeccable taste, an uncanny ear . . . a luscious voice . . . a poignancy that is rare among singers with her age and experience, and a sensual, intimate style. . . . She's pretty as a peach in a spring orchard."

Ingham, the stalwart, elegant, and knowledgeable musical safety net for Susannah as a singer, was hardly mentioned. Just like Teddy Wilson for Billie Holiday, or Tommy Flanagan for Ella Fitzgerald, he rarely got a nod from the "music writers" and, also like Wilson and Flanagan, was seldom granted solo elbow room. It was all about Susannah now. That was show business. She was arriving.

And she was starting to acquire some fans from her own generation. "WNEW regarded her as the youngest and freshest of their standard-bearers," says Roy Schecter, an ardent student of American singers of standards. The radio station was one of the few places on the dial playing jazz and standards in New York. Among its DJs: Jonathan Schwartz (long at WNEW, first as a "rock" DJ, later featuring American popular standards) and especially Bob Jones, on whose popular nighttime program *The Milkman's Matinee* Susannah, always sparkling and articulate, became a favorite guest in the seventies and early eighties (and later on WQEW). In the late seventies, singer Ronnie Whyte brought along Susannah's then-unknown *The Music of Harry Warren* London import to an appearance on *Milkman*. "He gave his hour to her!" Jones says. Susannah's exuberant, Holiday-small group-inspired version of the rhythm-and-rolling "A Quarter to Nine" became a favorite of Jones's audience. But Susannah was a favorite of more narrowly focused broadcasts as well, such as *Everything Old Is New* Again, hosted by David Kenney on WBAI and Jim Lowe and Company, on WVNJ. When DJ Lowe hosted a celebration of the songwriters Jule Styne, Burton Lane, Mitchell Parrish, and Cy Coleman in 1982, Susannah—and Ingham—wowed the crowd. "Sophisticated Lady" lyricist Mitchell Parrish wryly noted that he'd planned to sing the song that day, but thought better of it after hearing Susannah's gorgeous version.[5]

Roy Schecter, who stayed a fan throughout her career, first heard her at the Cookery. Weaned on Sinatra and a lyrics lover, he recalls Susannah's impact clearly at the club: "People came in the restaurant to find a big-boned, slim, voluptuous woman with big shoulders, full of vibrant energy and enthusiasm. And along with her, this short, erudite, reticent Brit—Ingham. They were all about the song, the music. Later, her presentation became more sophisticated, but at that time, she just stood still and sang. And they *loved* it. That was it."

Susannah's success that fall of 1980 and winter of 1981 at the Cookery was exhilarating, but in soaring high, those on the ground felt she rather forgot about them. Joel Siegel had worked hard to put her initial gig together, spending money on travel, printing, postage, and phone calls to launch her. "He is terribly nice, enthusiastic and assertive,"

Susannah told Ken Pitt. "He wants to be my manager and is doing up press kits for me." After the success of her initial Cookery gig, though, Siegel says, "Susannah dumped me for Linda Goldstein, who had come in from the West Coast. She was representing Dave Frishberg and expressed interest in representing Susannah as well. Linda was broke, so Susannah wanted to give my management fee to her. [Goldstein later hit it big managing Bobby McFerrin]. Like a dummy, I agreed, because Susannah was my friend." Goldstein, though, quickly bowed out of managing Susannah, and she and Siegel resumed their relationship.

Siegel invited Susannah and Ingham to come to Washington, D.C., where he was teaching, to perform for a film class in November. "They came up with an excellent program of songs from forties musicals," he remembers ("The Hollywood Blondes—Great Songs Made Famous by Legendary Ladies of the Silver Screen").[6] It was followed in February 1981 by a concert of Irving Berlin songs at the Corcoran Gallery, where Siegel was producing an American Songwriters series. But the relationship between manager and singer, already damaged, quickly disintegrated. The concert was on a Sunday afternoon at 4:00 and Siegel suggested she end the show by 5:30. "Because Washington is a very early town. But she wasn't done until 6:15; when people began ducking out around 5:45, she felt that they were walking out on her, even though I had explained the situation in advance." Susannah's overlong concert had now made them late for a dinner party across town, but as they were passing the One Step Down, Washington's longtime "insider" jazz club en route, Susannah insisted on stopping to ask about work. "Can't we spend just one hour without worrying about your career?" Siegel recalls asking. "She became furious with me." Soon, they parted ways. Not long after, Siegel began managing singer Shirley Horn, who was coming out of retirement in her native Washington. "It's a shame I haven't found the right agent yet," Susannah said mournfully in May to Ken Pitt, adding prophetically, "It's going to be a lifetime battle." "This kind of parting of the ways happened quite often," Ingham comments.

Her wit and talent and the compelling charm with which she told her stories in song drew many to her, but the "up one moment and down the next" of Susannah's personality was already confusing some, just as the way she found acceptance with key folk of invaluable service to her career, such as Bob Jones, Chris Albertson, and Rex Reed, did not endear her to her peers. When Rex Reed commented in a review that

Susannah "already has forgotten more than most of the shlocky cabaret belters in town have learned," other singers were bound to wonder just whom he was referring to! The singers who did know her already had reservations—for one thing, there was the ambition she wore on her sleeve. Singer Carol Fredette remembers Susannah in the early eighties. "Hanging out in the clubs, usually alone, with a glass of white wine, doing her homework—listening to seasoned saloon singers like Buddy Barnes and Charles DeForest who had great repertoires." Wrote Reed, she "collect[ed] useful tunes the way housewives collect discount coupons." "I think she wanted to be a major star," says Richard Rodney Bennett. "She was terribly needy. But if you go into singing this kind of music for lots of money and success, that kind of ambition can only go so far. And then, she was always telling me tales of woe, about how people misused her, abused her."

Singer and pianist Daryl Sherman heard of Susannah after meeting Richard Sudhalter in 1979, when Sherman was performing at the Sheraton Center. "Susannah was able to convince you that she was eager to learn, grow, talk about music—everybody responded to that. Hey, all of us are ambitious. But it's how you do it. At social events, there was Susannah, darting around the room, zeroing in on the more important people, ignoring the less important, controlled—nibbling and sipping, that's all—and exuding what at the time I perceived as great confidence. I felt a cordiality from her, but not much interest in getting to know me, and I always found little footing for a direct conversation with her. And not snotty, but condescending: 'Oh, Daryl, I love that little song of yours'—whatever it might be. And once she said to me, 'Oh, *I* don't work in clubs anymore. I just do concerts.'"

"I found her aggressive," states singer Barbara Lea, whose career in the early eighties was proceeding slowly, but who had *New Yorker* critic Whitney Balliett in her corner (Balliett didn't write much about Susannah after early praise). Claims Lea, "She took a couple of jobs from me: a Johnny Mercer concert [in 1981 at Lincoln Center's Library for the Performing Arts] and a club date at Stephen's in Chapel Hill. Tommy Gwaltney, the clarinetist, told me Susannah said, 'Oh well, Barbara can do that later.'"

Sometimes she would alienate writers still unknown, just beginning their careers. Writer James Gavin was initially put off by Susannah at their first meeting, after a performance at a cabaret program at St. Peter's Church in New York. "She said rather curtly after a few moments talking to her, 'There are a lot of other people here waiting to speak to me. I can't spend any more time with you.'" Writer Will Friedwald, who became a noted author about jazz singers, was a college student hanging around the clubs and soaking in the scene in the early eighties. In the next decade, he came to most of her Algonquin shows. When Friedwald reminded Susannah they'd met early on in her career, he says, "She only asked, 'Were you an important critic then?' I said no, I was just a college kid. She said, 'Oh, no wonder I didn't remember you.'" Once successful, she became friendly with both men. Gavin became a confidante.

But it was her fellow professionals who had the most pointed reservations about Susannah as a singer. Sherman remembers Susannah sitting in at a club called the Conservatory in 1979. "I'd been hearing great things about her, but I thought: 'Her pitch isn't good, she can't sustain a note, and she's awkward.'" The very gifted jazz singer Carol Sloane sent Susannah a good-luck telegram when she learned of her weekend Cookery gig in 1980, but quickly became disenchanted with her singing. "I found her sets at the Cookery boring and uninspired," says Sloane. At the time, she was living with the brilliant but alcoholic jazz pianist Jimmy Rowles, who could be mean-tempered. In his time, he'd accompanied the greats—Billie Holiday, Sarah Vaughan, Carmen McRae, Ella Fitzgerald. When Sloane put on Susannah's Johnny Mercer record for him to hear, she says his response was immediate and violent. "He heard just a few opening notes, abruptly stood and shouted 'No, No!,' stomping out of the room." (Singer Jane Harvey is said to have had a similar reaction about a year later when she heard Susannah at Michael's Pub. She ran out of the room, crying "The emperor's new clothes!") Jazz singer Anita O'Day gave Susannah "zero, zero stars" on a jazz "blindfold test" after hearing Susannah's version of "My Foolish Heart." "Why doesn't she fill the spaces?" O'Day grumbled, "What about all the time that's in between the lines with nothing happening?"[7] Other singers said she strayed off-key and missed notes, and that she could sound braying, coy, too languid. Even Susannah's great champion, Rex Reed, who compared her voice to "red fingernails tearing through white taffeta"—a ravishing image—found limitations. "She didn't swing; rather, there was an inability to swing," he says, adding, "because she couldn't or wouldn't let herself go."

And when Susannah was faulted by some critics or other singers, it did not seem to occur to her that she might have been at fault in any way. She either fell apart, sobbing, according to Ingham, or fashioned herself into the role of wronged party heroically continuing to fight the just cause (her career), the unfairly treated victim of mean-spirited and jealous folk, the one always taken advantage of and misunderstood. (So convincing was Susannah in this role that her friends and loved ones agreed wholeheartedly.) But at the same time, Susannah's psychological—indeed, her biochemical—state was fragile and constantly shifting (what Roy Schecter described as her "up and down"). As remarkable as the progress that Susannah had made was, she was acutely aware that she was still a relative neophyte in her demanding field—she'd been singing seriously for only seven years, without formal training. This fed her massive insecurity. "I got her gigs at the 92nd Street Y and so on, with other singers," Rex Reed recalls, "but she thought all the other singers were getting a lot more attention."

But there were other musicians who were attracted to Susannah's singing, especially to her gift with a lyric—pianist Marian McPartland, for one. She wanted Susannah to play with her and invited Susannah to have a starring role with her at a concert in 1981 and later, on the radio show, *Piano Jazz,* hosted by McPartland.[8] The concert was a celebration of Alec Wilder's music a year after his death by the Eastman School of Music's Arrangers' Orchestra in Rochester, New York, with which Wilder had had a long association. Susannah was thrilled by the opportunity. She loved concertizing, with its implications of serious listening, and she loved being thoroughly rehearsed: There was far less room for surprises that way, and she could relax. Rayburn Wright, a seasoned jazz-orchestra arranger, gave Susannah a free hand in choosing material, which she then sent in "basic arrangements"—worked out by Ingham—to be orchestrated. She especially loved singing "If Someday Comes Ever Again," with its Johnny Mercer lyric, a ballad that, she wrote, inspired in her "the feel of a faded childhood. I thought of a merry-go-round figure, sang it to Keith and he wrote out something, it was like dreaming an arrangement."

The televised production for PBS, one of a very few of Susannah's concerts to be filmed, reveals her strengths—and the obstacles still before her. To a partially filled concert hall, Susannah at first sang and moved stiffly, her gestures hammy and tense, her gaze flickering with nerves; and, too, her fussy blue dress was too prim and her fluffy, ingenue pageboy distracting. The camera also wasn't very kind in revealing her uneven complexion under the heavy makeup. But, after she had warmed up, Susannah sang convincing and exquisite versions of Wilder's ruminative ballads, "Trouble Is a Man" and "It's So Peaceful in the Country," his paean to nature. She felt "transported" by the occasion, Susannah said afterward. All the pizza parlors and strip clubs she'd sung in had led to this moment, and it was worth it. For the moment.

The televised Wilder concert with McPartland nudged open more doors for her. Lowell and Helen Manfull, then professors of theater arts at Penn State, saw the PBS show and tracked down Susannah to open the Central Pennsylvania Arts Festival in State College, in the summer of 1982. "She was a big hit," says Manfull, "and came back to sing twice more in subsequent years."

But a Michael's Pub appearance in October 1981 (with Ingham, Al Gafa on guitar, Steve La Spina on bass, and Joe Cocuzzo on drums), got very mixed reviews. This was a high-profile date at a big club, which Susannah badly wanted and needed, although the place was known for its often shabby treatment of artists and audience. As had other performers, Susannah tussled with the club's owner, Gil Weist, about the sound system and other aspects of the room. Moreover, the club insisted she exclude the contemporary numbers she so wanted to sing to reach out to an audience beyond what she called the "camp" of nostalgia. Eventually, she was allowed to do the show her way. The *Times'* Wilson moved from tepid to warmer, while Rex Reed in the *Daily News* levitated: "Some girls have a pretty voice and no sophistication or intelligence. Others have virtuosity . . . but no heart. Rarely does a singer have all of these virtues in the same package, and that's what makes Susannah special. It is impossible to believe she hasn't been singing for 50 years." But there was also a nightmare of a review, by the *New York Post*'s cabaret reviewer Curt Davis, who slammed her on all counts: "This is background singing and as such is acceptable, but as cabaret it is eccentric and indulgent."

For Susannah, this was cause for meltdown. She was sure Richard Sudhalter, who'd become the *Post*'s jazz reviewer, was behind Davis's attack, either influencing Davis or using him as his literary "beard"—a claim she knew impossible to prove. Although Sudhalter had given "Suz," as he'd called her, good notices, he'd recently reviewed her performance at a Jack Kleinsinger–produced concert more negatively.

"Her intonation is wayward even at the best of times," he'd written. By then, there was very little goodwill left between the two.

Recalls Richard Rodney Bennett, "At the time, she was telling me how badly Dick Sudhalter treated her; he was living with Daryl Sherman, who was the salt of the earth, and Susannah thought all the good things were going to Daryl." "Sudhalter *was* arrogant," Ingham allows, "but underneath that niceness she had, Susannah was ruthless." There is evidence to support this. In a letter she wrote to Ken Pitt right after the bad *Post* review, Susannah made it clear she was talking about Sudhalter without naming him. "A dreadful man . . . now a jazz critic, unfortunately, once a friend and leader of a band I sang with in London who is simply gunning for me professionally (he admits it's due to jealousy but keeps doing it anyway), wrote me a poisonous, paranoid letter which I found waiting for me when I got back. . . . Friends [advise] me that this man is so despised that he can't do me much harm. He is a worm and a creep."[9] This was the man who, when she was completely unknown, had gotten her the job on the Bobby Hackett tour, had introduced her to Ben Webster, and in New York, to Marian McPartland.

By now, Susannah was getting far better reviews as a jazz singer (as opposed to a singer of nostalgic, jazz-based songs) in England. As she planned that spring of 1981 to play Ronnie Scott's again in 1982, she tried to position herself even more independently from Keith than the previous visit. And she wanted significant money for the date, too. To Ken Pitt, she wrote:

Please just use "Susannah McCorkle" [on the announcement in front of Ronnie Scott's club]. That's what we always do when it's my gig, particularly now that I'm getting busier and don't always work with Keith. I am sorry to say (in strict confidence, of course) that Keith has been so difficult since things started going for me that I have come very close to splitting from him professionally. . . . Out of loyalty I am trying to keep working with him, but in view of his constant threats (e.g. if I record with anyone else he'll never play for me again, etc.) it is hard and I am always billed only in my own name now, both because it makes sense (we are in no way a team onstage, it is me backed by a group) and because with his bad temper and my need, now that things look so promising, for stable and reliable people around me, I cannot guarantee that I will always work with him. I was still hoping for the best with Keith, but, because of the kind of person he is, am preparing for the worst.

"Susannah was doing what we call 'a wobble,'" explains Pitt, who had been working on putting together a tour for the duo to India, of all places, as well as London clubs. Shortly after her letter, he wrote back that the tour had fallen through and that Ronnie Scott's was balking at her new salary demands. "It feels schizophrenic to have people in the know telling me I'm going to be a star and then not being able to pay the rent!" Susannah wrote back, adding that Pitt should set up a European tour. "She tried to be 'helpful' by sending details of her CV," adds Pitt, "all of which were known to me."

But the tension was easing between her and Ingham, very likely because, after being on a waiting list for nearly two years for a studio apartment in the building where she still lived with him, one had at last become available. She was thrilled at last to get her own little aerie on the sixteenth floor, she told Pitt. "Now, just the idea of being able to work in peaceful silence whenever I want to is intoxicating," she went on. "I am glued to my desk, have written tons of letters about article proposals, singing work, etc. We are getting a divorce right away, it should be final in a few weeks, so that Keith and Sue can marry. Miraculously, his attitude toward me has changed completely since we went to the divorce paralegal who handled it. Sue has noticed this too— Keith is considerate, polite, even friendly to me now!"

But just how entwined Susannah continued to be with Ingham she documented in a story called "Harry's Wives," written as they were parting and soon afterward. While there is the predictable laundry list of complaints about an ex-spouse by Kay, the Susannah-like main character, "Wives" also explores the kind of curious—and spurious—solidarity that can spring up between former and present wives. Kay and Lucy, the fictional Sue, seem much more a pair of teenaged girls than grown women, though Kay is a professional musician (a pianist) and Lucy a mother-to-be. As they become friends, they fix each other's hair, put on each other's makeup, have long, secretive chats. Their chats, unsurprisingly, revolve around Harry (Ingham), a trumpet player who kicks up a thick coat of resentments and unhappiness by his very existence. Kay muses about her marriage to Harry to the new wife, how she "simply kept to herself, playing the piano and listening to records if

Harry was out, reading when he was home" (much to her disdain, he liked to spend his spare time watching "sport" on television). As the story winds down, the pregnant Lucy leaves Harry and comes to Kay for comfort, and the two women cry in each other's arms over their failed romances. "He'll never really care about anything except his music, will he?" exclaims Kay, crying "for the lonely girl she herself had once been, and for the man whose greatest happiness was playing 'Getting Sentimental Over You' with his eyes closed." The fact that Harry finds his greatest happiness through his music seems a weak indictment to make against a musician! Susannah had become a singer herself to be "transported." But writing "Harry's Wives" was, as writing always was for her, a way to explore and then purge, as she hoped, some negative feelings. She told Pitt, "Now I'm out of my marriage and feel really good about the future!"

After she got her own apartment and the divorce, Susannah's social life took off. She lost weight and took up race-walking. "She was a bit on the heavy side at first," says Diane Mich Feldman, "but became slim and very groomed." She made another new girlfriend, Ellen Mullins Bollinger, who met Susannah when she sang along with Tony Bennett at a new hangout called Broadway Joe's. "We clicked, and we often went out with another friend, DJ Jim Lowe, to hear music everywhere," Bollinger recalls. "She said she was highly sexed. There were various men, oh yes, lots." Adds Richard Rodney Bennett, then a confidant, "Not just musicians—inappropriate men: a Romanian doorman, that kind of thing, I remember her telling me." "The funny thing was," Ingham muses, "she didn't like her body. She felt she was a slave to it. She said she hated the urge to mate." In a story she wrote during that post-divorce time called "Waiting," Susannah muses through her unnamed protagonist, "I wanted a companion, not just a lover."

All during the ups and downs of her hectic personal life in 1981, Susannah had been working on a new departure for her, an album she hoped would take her career to a younger audience. Recorded in November 1981 and released the next year, *The People That You Never Get to Love* stressed contemporary material. (The album was titled after a 1979 Rupert Holmes song.) Susannah set herself against a trend of that time. While pop singers were "crossing over"—Carly Simon's *Torch* (she called it "pre-rock songs") that year, Linda Ronstadt just ahead with *What's New* in 1983, *Lush Life* in 1984, and *For Sentimental*

*Reasons* in 1986, and then in 1991, the best-selling *Unforgettable* by Natalie Cole—Susannah was going in the opposite direction, from standards to pop.

Ingham had very little interest in the contemporary material she chose for *The People That You Never Get to Love.* Susannah defended her choice of Neil Sedaka's "The Hungry Years," declaring that in the song, the struggling years had real value, that there was something worth fighting for, and out of that fight came happiness. Susannah's faithful fan, Roy Schecter, agreed; he found her so compelling on "The Hungry Years" that he thought it was one of her signature songs. Not so to Ingham, forever faithful to swing-era standards. "The song was all about how we were happy early on, then things fell apart—very self-pitying and depressing. And like Wagner's *Ring,* 'The Hungry Years' went on and on, for like ten minutes instead of four, and hardly any tempo at all." Nor was he happy with the Paul Simon material she chose, "Still Crazy After All These Years." "That stuff is identified with him, and that's a problem," Ingham protested.

But Susannah felt she had to face the chronic dilemma of the jazz-based singer head-on, a dilemma that has grown as the years go by—stick with what the vast number of listeners think of as dinosaurs and risk being seen as precious and irrelevant, or incorporate new material into the performance and risk seeming ridiculous (the great Ella singing "A Hard Day's Night," etc.). (A risk, some would argue, that cuts both ways, when pop and rock stars record their "jazz standards" albums, to mixed reviews.) For her *People* album, Susannah selected the wheat from the chaff, including a recent Oscar Brown Jr. song, "The Call of the City," Dave Frishberg's "Foodophobia," and Blossom Dearie's "Bye Bye Country Boy," as well as a few standards and one Brazilian number. But if the title song gained her the new fans she craved, it confused (probably inevitably) most of her established audience that was accustomed to a diet of standards. In particular, Holmes's musical musing, about the missed opportunities for real romance that people imagine as they go about their everyday lives, was long on lyrics and short on melody, a literary treat for Susannah but a musical plod for Ingham. In the short run, though, Susannah's "modernizing" paid off and reviewers mostly loved the album. Wilson wrote in June 1983 in the *Times* that Susannah "has found out what she is and who she is and how to project that discovery," and Douglas Watt in the *New Yorker* singled out "the apt choice of material."[10] The record won a Stereo

Review Record of the Year in 1983, too, alongside Wynton Marsalis's *Think of One* and Michael Jackson's *Thriller.* Best of all, the songwriter himself, Rupert Holmes, dubbed her "spectacularly splendid." For the moment, she was on air.

Susannah thought Holmes, composer and singer of the huge pop hit "Escape (The Piña Colada Song)"—and a polymath who has gone on to a successful career as a playwright, screenwriter, and, recently, a novelist—was "spectacularly splendid," too; in fact, she had fallen in love with him while disentangling more and more from Ingham, who had his own new love affair to tend to. Susannah had hopes of a project she could do with Holmes to be called "The Philharmonic Goes to the Movies With Susannah McCorkle." "It was a heavy thing," recalls her friend Ellen Bollinger. "Holmes loved her, and I know he affected her deeply, but as I recall he was duplicitous about his marital status, and he became remote." The philharmonic project—which she'd hoped would feature newly commissioned arrangements by Holmes and others—remained a dream. There was seldom the money to fund her dreams.

Despite her feelings for Holmes and ideas for musical projects, Susannah was still involved with Ingham for musical support. They'd gone to London and played Ronnie Scott's again in March 1982, after which she wrote to Ken Pitt, "I have been enjoying a period of great serenity and productive work." But by July, she was sinking again, anxious about money and her career. She hadn't gotten the money she wanted from her last two-week engagement at Ronnie Scott's, but she wasn't giving up. "Some of my friends, like Dave Frishberg and Blossom Dearie, have played London (specifically, the Pizza Express in SoHo) for very good money and conditions. . . . Since I am known in the jazz and song world there, I'm hoping for similar treatment. I think people at Ronnie's and the Pizza Express may still think of me as a local girl who stays with friends, doesn't get much money, etc., but things really have changed." The soul of patience, Pitt responded with yet another of his soothing letters. But, he says now, "Susannah was never wanted, never invited by any venue owner. I had to do a selling job on each one. Because she always did a splendid job, she could get a return booking, but only at a modest increase. Her drawing power had yet to evolve—she did not put English bottoms on English seats." Marketing Susannah would continue to be a hard sell, despite her growing acclaim and accomplishments. The nerves and the drive to succeed that so often translated to imperiousness, occasionally to scenes, put off London clubs to a degree. But more to the point, Susannah's audience, captivated by the romance and nostalgia that had drawn them to her initially, wasn't hard-core jazz, which followed hard-bop, avant-garde, scat-singing.

What Susannah didn't confide to Pitt was her worsening private life. She did so in part to her London friend Frances Bendixson that summer of 1982. "She told me she sank deeper and deeper into depression. Just too many bad things happening at once." Her brief affair with Rupert Holmes was over (he was, Susannah said, "a talented and dear but a hopelessly screwed up man"), her American label, Inner City Records, had just declared bankruptcy, and there had been cancellations of concerts as well as magazine articles turned down. Worst, though, from Susannah's point of view, was what she termed the "sabotage attempt of an obnoxious man now a critic"—very likely, Dick Sudhalter.

As carefully hidden from the world and her friends as it was, here was clear evidence of the struggle that Susannah went through repeatedly from adolescence on: the nagging, insistent perfectionism, the fear and loathing of herself, the drive to accomplish as a way of vanquishing the shrill putdowns of the inner voices, the distracting and distorting of reality created by her chronic, still-undiagnosed biochemical imbalance. But Susannah was a fighter and vowed not to give in to the dark side. She was then reading Sylvia Plath's diaries with a jolting sense of identification and copied out Plath's entry from October 1, 1957, into her own journal: "I cannot ignore this murderous self: It is there. Its biggest weapon is . . . the image of myself as a perfect success. . . . I have a good self. . . . My demon would murder this self by demanding that it be a paragon." Afterward, Susannah reflected, "It was actually Sylvia's diaries that started me on the road to recovery." With a chilling ability to circumvent her own manic-depressive core, Susannah added with the curious, not to say spurious, logic that would drive her all her life: "Because I saw how she wrecked everything by wallowing in her depressions and practically making misery an art form."

She was aided in her belief that she could overcome her own deep lows by the swing toward elation and by winning prizes. In the fall of 1982 her mood definitely improved by being ranked third in the world among female jazz vocalists, at least in England, in *Jazz Journal International*'s reader's poll (first and second places went to Sarah Vaughan and Ella Fitzgerald), and having *The Songs of Johnny Mercer* chosen by the same publication as its "jazz record of the year." She was just as vulnerable as ever to negative criticism, however. When the veteran British jazz journalist Max Jones made cool remarks about her talent, she told Roy Schecter, "He's not a very good critic. Sort of a joke, not someone to be taken seriously." Schecter remarks, "It was difficult to be critical of Susannah. She could be tough in that way: You're either for me or against me. She'd tell stories about allies who she then turned into enemies. I felt there was a paranoid streak there, part of her illness."

By 1983, she and Ken Pitt came to an amicable parting of the ways. By then, Pitt was semi-retired to care for his ailing mother. "I fully appreciate your insecurity and belief that perhaps you are 'missing out' somewhere, somehow," he wrote to her, after she told him she was sure she could get a good deal more work in England and the Continent. "I have explained to you the economic facts of life but if you still feel that you would like to seek the help of others then please enlist it." It was to be as Pitt said, however: Job offers were few and far between for Susannah after that.

By the early 1980s, Susannah was working frequently in a number of small, good jazz clubs. She had learned a great deal in the London pubs, but it was in these New York (and New Jersey) clubs where she worked hard at becoming a jazz singer. Says Amos Korn, who owned Gulliver's, "More than any other singer I've ever heard, she had a narrative ability. She picked the better songs, and she simply sat on a stool and told their stories." Korn puts his finger on one of Susannah's abundant gifts, which is an ability to shape narrative in a nuanced, well-paced fashion. She knew this about herself: "I am a storyteller," she said, time and again. "The difference from other singers was clear—she couldn't hide her intelligence," agree Gary and Phyllis Gates, who later became friends of Susannah's.

"However," adds Gary Gates, "she had a wooden presence on stage then." The trouble was that Susannah might be wooden one night, and cook the next, but at that point in her career, she was not yet accomplished enough to be able to cloak the fear that may have been the greatest block to a consistently looser performance. The real limitation for many then was pinpointed by reviewer John S. Wilson: "She is most comfortable when she gets away from songs that lend themselves to jazz treatment." This seemed the case at Gulliver's, then in West Paterson, New Jersey, in the fall of 1982, where she was backed by Ingham, Harvey Swartz on bass, and Ronnie Zito on drums. She seemed energetic rather than swinging when tackling up-tempo numbers like "Come On, Get Happy" and "The Lady's in Love With You," while she was far more beguiling on witty standards and ballads— "My New Celebrity Is You," "So Many Stars," "No More Blues," "Where or When."[11] At Struggles, another New Jersey club, this one in Edgewater, she worked with pianist Mike Abene, who subbed for Ingham, and got a rave review from the local paper, developing a following among those who loved her repertoire—she became known for never repeating a song during her three weekend sets a night and for almost never forgetting a lyric. Again, Susannah's readings of slow numbers were radiant and soulful, but she strained on up-tempo tunes. The strain was also evident in her difficulty working in saloons. Roy Schecter recalls that she chided him for ordering a meal during her set. "She said to me, 'Roy, I was completely unnerved—you were *eating* while I was singing.' I told her, 'OK, but you really should try the linguine, Susannah—it's great here.'"

When she was offered a two-week gig in January 1983 on a bill with the two veteran jazz singers Maxine Sullivan and Carol Sloane, Susannah accepted with alacrity. The trio, billed as "The Songbirds of Jazz," was first to play a week at Charlie's, in Washington's Georgetown neighborhood, the friendly restaurant-bar owned by guitarist Charlie Byrd, a club where she'd sung for a month of Mondays in the spring of 1981. Arriving in Washington the day before they were to open, the singers went to the club to rehearse with pianist Stef Scaggiari. "The pianist was only available until five o'clock to rehearse," remembers Sloane. "Susannah said, 'Can I go first?' So she did—and at 4:45 she said to us, 'OK, you can have him now.' Gave us fifteen minutes!"

Susannah's gaffe was followed by others, perhaps because Susannah was so anxious about making a success of this unprecedented chance to sing with two more seasoned jazz singers. She put her foot into it with Maxine Sullivan, apparently. Sullivan was a wonderful, if underappreciated African American singer with an effortless, swinging delivery. But it had been a long time since she'd enjoyed a hit record. "Loch Lomond" was recorded in 1937 and made her a name, but afterward, though she had a career in radio and movies, she'd left the business to raise her children, returning to performing in the late sixties. A bit later, after the Sullivan-McCorkle-Sloane engagement, Maxine Sullivan paired with Keith Ingham, who partnered with her on several critically acclaimed albums in the later 1980s. "She was put off by Susannah. She told me that Susannah treated her like a servant, asking her to fetch and carry stuff," says Ingham. Worse sparks flew between Susannah and the gifted jazz singer Carol Sloane, who was known for her chops and had paid a lot of dues.

Recalls Joel Siegel, who caught the "Songbirds" one evening at Charlie's, "There's Maxine Sullivan wandering around with a clipboard, urging patrons to sign a petition for a Duke Ellington postage stamp; Carol Sloane having cocktails at the bar with friends, a borrowed Redskins cap on her head; and Susannah collecting addresses for her mailing list. Promoting herself." Says Sloane, "At each venue"— Rick's in Chicago after Charlie's—"Susannah would open the show, I'd follow, and Maxine would sing the final set. And we three were expected to sing a tune together." (The songs they traded choruses on were "Somebody Loves Me," "The Lady Is a Tramp," and "Baby, Won't You Please Come Home.") "This," Sloane says, "became a source of embarrassment for Maxine and me and the audience when Susannah attempted to scat sing." And Susannah was made aware of her lack of this skill. "I'll never be a musician. I just don't have it," she moaned in a letter to her parents. "She was deeply insecure that she wasn't as good as the musicians," Ingham confirms. "She needed comfort and self-assurance."

But in point of fact, reviewers in Washington gave all three singers a thumbs-up, though in Chicago, a writer declined to enthuse over Susannah, referring to her as "the vo-do-de-o girl"—a comment she never forgot. Nor did she forget Sullivan's words to her after their last set together, in the dressing room, "Honey, you shouldn't be trying to sing jazz. You need to go into those supper club kinda places." This was prescient, though it would be six more years before Susannah opened at the Algonquin's Oak Room, the epitome of "those kinda places."

After "Songbirds" Susannah returned to Washington in February with Ingham for a performance far more suited to her strengths: a program at the Corcoran Gallery with the Susannah-esque title "Dreams and Fears in American Popular Song," heavily weighted with then-recent tunes including Frishberg's "Wheelers and Dealers," Billy Joel's "My Life" and "New York City Blues," Dory Previn's "You're Gonna Hear From Me," and Rupert Holmes's "Special Thanks." She and Ingham were barely talking anymore, but the show had to go on and they moved it next to a club called Stephen's After All in Chapel Hill, North Carolina. There Susannah, who had not yet given up the idea of attempting to scat-sing, met up again with Carol Sloane, a formidable scatter. Remembers Ingham, "Carol, who was to follow Susannah at the club, was there, and she sat in one night with Susannah. When she scatted, Susannah tried to do the same, but her attempts fell flat—literally. Susannah was jerky and jumpy." After the show, the two singers had a fierce argument, cutting to the heart of the matter of jazz singing. "I maintained she was not a jazz singer because she was incapable of swing and she did not improvise," Sloane says. "She had obvious discomfort in the jazz setting." Susannah was wild: She saw herself as singing from the heart and soul, in the tradition of her mentor, Billie Holiday, who did not—as countless people have noted—scat sing. But, as Richard Rodney Bennett points out, "with Billie Holiday, there was an instinctive recreating of a tune, not something you learn from a recipe." Unlike Sloane, Bennett is among those who feel that Susannah had an ability to swing, but he concedes she lacked "a spontaneous jazz approach." Was Susannah or was she not a jazz singer? The question comes up repeatedly, and the answer, it seems, lies in the ear of each listener.

"We became truly estranged after that conversation about Billie Holiday," Sloane says. "In those days Susannah appeared to me to possess steely determination and even some ruthlessness. I had no idea of the fragility of her mental health." When, a few years later, Concord Records, the largest and most important of the independent labels representing jazz musicians, signed Susannah as their "new" female jazz singer after Rosemary Clooney, Sloane was surely displeased.

Back in New York, Susannah tried to put the encounter with Sloane behind her. The singer's criticism had cut deep, but it did not deter her. Writing to her parents that spring, she declared, "I am now very happy to be making my living both writing and singing—I love the balance." However, to say that she was "making my living" was stretching it: She still depended on the checks that Tom and Mimi sent intermittently. Now back in the Bay Area, where they'd bought a smaller house in the Oakland Hills, Tom still tried to pursue a writing career, but the lack of response to his mystery novels from editors and publishers put him in a slump, and he often "forgot" to take his medication until prodded by Mimi and his doctors. By 1983, he wrote gloomily, his income from writing was "zero." Still, there was more money around than there had been for a long time. He and Mimi had sold the Shasta Road house—although, he wrote to Susannah, in a letter accompanied by a generous check, they were in the middle of a lawsuit with their brokers and thus financially constrained. Tom felt guilty about Susannah, whom he'd last seen at his youngest daughter Maggie's wedding in 1982 (Susannah had sung "Summertime" a cappella, spurning the band her sister had hired for the reception). "This is an attempt to even up for things we have done for Katy and Maggy [sic], something we have lost sight of with you away at the other side and that I, at least, hadn't noticed until I saw you at Maggy's wedding."

The check helped Susannah concentrate on finishing her novel *Closer to Home,* a reworked draft of the manuscript she'd sent Jacqueline Kennedy Onassis several years before. She'd made her way through half of the new version the previous summer in 1982 in Saratoga, "at my friends' funky Victorian hotel," followed by six weeks at Yaddo, where through a friend she hooked up with Gail Hochman, a New York literary agent, after several others had declined to represent her (though Patricia White remained her English agent). In the summer of 1983, she was halfway through *Closer to Home* and eventually completed a 450-page draft that she sent to both Hochman and White. "My memory of the manuscript Susannah sent was that it was very rough and unformed and that she was unhappy with it," says White, who concurred with Kennedy Onassis that the novel "wasn't remotely ready to be submitted." Thus informed, Susannah was determined, she wrote back to White, to "polish" her manuscript. "I am hoping to devote time to it this summer and have it ready for the fall [of 1985]." But though force of character and atmosphere could carry along her short stories very well indeed, shape (i.e., plot) and especially a satisfactory conclusion eluded her in the several novels she was to work on. She never completed *Closer to Home.*

Musically, in 1983, Susannah was again at work on a new album. "I suggested that Susannah do a tribute to Leo Robin," Ingham says. "She loved him." Robin teamed up with Ralph Rainger at Paramount Pictures to write a number of terrific songs, such as "I Wished on the Moon," and, with Jule Styne, he wrote the lyrics for the Broadway show *Gentlemen Prefer Blondes.* "But he was a forgotten lyricist," Ingham adds.

Inner City Records was willing to distribute and market the record, but Susannah would have to pay production costs. She found backers through a friend she'd made hanging at P. J. Clarke's after hours with DJ Bob Jones. Financier Andy Lipman who sent around a prospectus and rapidly put together a group of investors. Ingham provided the arrangements gratis for the December 1983–January 1984 sessions. "I got Al Klink for the date," Ingham says, "a wonderful saxophonist who'd been with Glenn Miller. While he often didn't get mentioned on the notes to albums, he was the kind of guy who just went into the studio, blew marvelously, was paid well and then went home." Invited to sit in at the recording studio, Roy Schecter remembers how "in the rehearsals Susannah was very particular. She had a highly critical mind, was incredibly bright, and she did want to be in control. At the session, she didn't tell Klink what to play, but where she wanted him to solo. It worked out well."

Though the recording had gone smoothly, Susannah hit a wall with Irv Kratka of Inner City Records, who surprised her by saying he wouldn't issue the record unless she committed to a three-record deal. But Susannah had grown disenchanted with the company's accounting policies and was reluctant to sign on. (Subsequently, Inner City declared bankruptcy.) Without a record company, *Thanks for the Memory* was in limbo, its title eerily prescient—it was Susannah and Ingham's last album together.

After the recording was done, they traveled to the West Coast for a series of concert dates in California and Canada. Tony Bennett was on the airplane Susannah took to Los Angeles, and she sought his advice about an enticing career possibility. "Susannah is a creative and wonderful pioneer, a very daring singer," said Bennett of her later, adding that Susannah always chose to sing the best material. "She doesn't compromise." Now, she told him, producers of the successful musical *Nine* were putting together a road company and wanted her to audition for the female lead, the part of the wife Luisa, which Maureen McGovern had played on Broadway. *Nine* was a show that strongly appealed to her, this story about an Italian artist in his forties suffering a midlife identity crisis and torn among the women in his life. Should she try out for the part? "She told me Bennett said no," relayed Mimi. "'I think guys like us should just sing. It would be the same thing, over and over, night after night,' he told her." She let go the idea of *Nine*.

She wanted the first of her California concerts to signal her arrival as a singer of substance in the land of her birth. Opening at Cal Tech in Pasadena, she presented a paean to Hollywood called "Movie Blondes of the Silver Screen." Reviews for the ambitious program of 19 plums plucked from the thirties—ranging from Dietrich's "Falling in Love Again" (in English *and* German) and Mae West's "A Guy Who Takes His Time" to Doris Day's "Ten Cents a Dance" and Marilyn Monroe's "Diamonds Are a Girl's Best Friend"—were mixed. Susannah had a "tremulous vibrato," a local reviewer complained. But the influential West Coast critic Leonard Feather was smitten—with Susannah, that is. As for the program, he dismissed the material as "trifles," and particularly sharpened his quill against his fellow Brit, Keith Ingham: "A pianist, shall we say, of the old school. His solo number ('Hurray for Hollywood') marked the nadir of the evening."

In San Francisco a few days later, "Blondes" played to a packed audience, recalls Susannah's college friend Dick Corten. And there, on hometown turf, it was Ingham who got the better review. "Philip Elwood of the *San Francisco Examiner,* a respected critic, was very complimentary about me and the trio but not quite so glowing about her," Ingham recalls. Indeed: Elwood hit the same refrain—and nerve—that Carol Sloane had a year earlier and that a number of reviewers and even fans had mentioned—that Susannah had a rather wooden, or tense, approach. He hailed Susannah for having a "superior voice," but could she be thought of as a jazz singer? Not if jazz singing comprised "the sound of surprise," Elwood concluded. Susannah, he wrote, "is very, very studied. . . . Were she thrust into a jazz jam she might be lost." Adds Ingham, "The review also featured a photo of me rather than of Susannah—and that really ticked her off, and so it did other times, too, when the musicians got a good write-up and hers wasn't as good. And if things weren't going quite right, she'd blame the musicians—most singers can be like that—and sometimes musicians do make mistakes. Well, I was between her and the musicians, trying to defuse the situation by humor. As one example, we'd been asked back at that club Stephen's, in Chapel Hill, and she was attracting a good crowd and got a very good review, but when [veteran jazz singing duo] Jackie and Roy came in, Susannah got nervous and began blaming the musicians. In front of them, she said to me, 'We can do better on the second set!' I replied, 'How do you want the next song, then—too slow or too fast?' And Jackie and Roy laughed." To Susannah, these were examples not of Ingham's humor but, rather, of his meanness to her.

In March, with the publication of a cover story on Susannah in *Stereo Review,* Ingham reached the breaking point. "It was all about her start and London and so on," he says. "And she never even *mentioned* me! I called to tell her what I thought, how disappointed I was after all the work we'd done together. I said I wasn't going to work with her anymore. She said not a word. She acted stunned. But once we had this break, I had nothing to do with her." He did fulfill a commitment to accompany her in the summer of 1984 at the Pennsylvania arts festival they'd played before to great success, but that was it. "She would occasionally call to borrow some music, but I was quite brutal about it. I wouldn't talk to her or see her.

"With Susannah," he continues, "I had the happiest year or two when she was discovering music and was putting her life on the line with these songs, trying to continue a tradition that she loved. But by about 1982 or so, every song had to relate to something totally in her own life somehow, everything had to be from a point of view that she agreed with or was about her, and she wouldn't sing many, many songs because she objected to them. The spontaneity and the fun had gone out of it, and it became rather mechanical, always performing the same way. In a cabaret act, too, there's no space for the musicians to solo." Susannah addressed this very point in an interview with Stan Britt on the BBC in London. "Giving Keith solo space, the audience might think I forgot the words. And I'm interested in communicating, not in being one of the guys anymore."[12]

So there they were, living at the same address for what would turn out to be the rest of her life, awkwardly meeting in the elevator, the lobby, on the street, but never really speaking to each other again. "She was haunted by knowing that he lived in *her* building," says violinist Linda Fennimore, who also lived in the Parc Cameron and who became Susannah's race-walking partner. "She *hated* Keith and said repeatedly that he'd said cruel things about her singing, like, 'If it wasn't for me, you'd never be anywhere.'" "She thought Keith was her enemy those last years," concurs her next husband, Dan DiNicola. "She burned all her letters from him in front of me." Susannah continued to get her revenge in the press, downplaying Ingham's importance in her life and early career, and sometimes omitting him completely from her résumé. When interviewed for *Jazztimes* by Leonard Feather, for instance, she referred to the "nice group of middle-aged British musicians who really nurtured me." If "middle-aged" was meant to be a sly dig against the unnamed Ingham, Susannah was on shaky ground: Her ex-husband was just six years older than she.

Though Ingham's third marriage ended unhappily, musically he went happily on his way. For 10 years he played solo piano at the Regency Hotel, and he has made more than 80 albums. He especially liked working with Maxine Sullivan. "That was great. We did an album, *Great Songs From the Cotton Club by Harold Arlen and Ted Koehler,* which was nominated for a Grammy." (More salt in the wounds: The album, and his happy association with Sullivan, came out within a year after his breakup with Susannah.) Ingham went on to record with many singers, including Peggy Lee on an album of rare Harold Arlen songs, called *Love Held Lightly.* He continues to record with various combinations and with singers Barbara Lea, Joyce Breach, and Rebecca Kilgore. As for Susannah, "I only count the happy hours—the memories of when we were in London."

Many fans who fell in love with Susannah's singing in the early years confess that they still miss the pairing of McCorkle and Ingham. "We always felt she was at her best with Keith—inspired. He taught her so much," says Helen Manfull, adding significantly, "From a *musical* point of view, Susannah was on stronger ground with Keith as her musical director than in later years." Reviewers often singled out Ingham's work with Susannah: Douglas Watt, for instance, in reviewing *The People That You Never Get to Love,* said, "Miss McCorkle has the further advantage of being supported . . . by an unusually fine pianist named Keith Ingham who is able to supply, with unfailing skill and sensitivity, precisely the right, enhancing accompaniment to each song." Despite expressing hatred for Ingham, Susannah was not unaware of how valuable his musicianship was to her. As she told Roy Schecter, prophetically, "It's probably the most important professional partnership either of us will have in our lives."

But in the spring of 1984, Susannah's career and private life were poised to take off in exciting new directions.

# I'll Take Romance

She was looking, I thought, for somebody to come along to rescue
her from herself.

　　　　　　—Keith Ingham

She was tempted to gravitate towards darkness, desperately looking for love. Yet she was an old-fashioned girl with a girl-next-
door quality.

　　　　　　—Dan DiNicola

For Susannah, falling in love was a wondrous, fearsome experience.
But when she was down, the newness of love seemed to be no more
than the preface to another crashing disappointment. "She *desperately*
wanted to be loved," says psychotherapist Roberta Todras, who treated
Susannah during the eighties. "A mind-altering experience, a deep
yearning for some kind of acceptance that would make her whole." A
way to love herself.

In late winter 1983, not long before Ingham made the final break
with her in April, Susannah had one of the most important meetings in
her life, a lunch with a man she'd met a couple of years before while
performing at the Van Dyck, a jazz club in Schenectady. Dan DiNicola
was a tall, dark, intense man in his forties, a television features reporter-
writer in the Albany-Schenectady-Troy area. Though he'd never heard
of Susannah and was far more interested in hard-bop instrumentalists—he was an amateur trumpet player—DiNicola had dropped by
the Van Dyck to listen to Susannah for an area arts roundup he was
preparing. "I never listened to the lyrics until Susannah," he says. "And
I couldn't believe what I heard. We sat down and did an interview; then
I didn't see her again for a couple of years: I never happened to be in
town when she was." In early winter of 1984, Susannah was up at

Yaddo, the artists' retreat in Saratoga Springs, working on her novel. It was not far from DiNicola's beat, and they ran into each other again in town. This time, something clicked and they made a date to have lunch in New York when he'd be there on business. "February 25, 1984—I still remember it well," DiNicola says. They talked for hours, discovering they both were romantics, passionate about music and literature. A former high-school English teacher, he'd had a poster of hero Leo Tolstoy hanging in his home office. Was Susannah his Anna Karenina? "Something about you is fragile, despite your sturdy character, those accomplishments you earned. . . . You are strong," he wrote that spring, adding the magic words, "yet something inside me wants to protect you, nourish you." Perhaps it was this above all that made this energetic, smart, outgoing man irresistible. He would be the lover (and eventually, husband) that she craved, as she'd told her mother in explaining her divorce from Ingham. "Nothing is more important than loving one person and being close. That's why I got myself free: Because I want to love and be close to one man and grow old with him too." More than that, DiNicola would also be the protector she craved, the schmoozer and negotiator and fighter—the manager she had never had.

By the time Susannah and DiNicola fell in love, she was coming into her prime as a singer. "She shows constant evidence of improvement—in delivery, interpretation, balance of her performances, range of her repertory. It doesn't stop," enthused Wilson in the *Times* over a Fat Tuesday's appearance with pianist Ben Aronov, whom Ingham had recommended and who was to play with Susannah for five years. At Fat Tuesday's, Susannah's repertoire included "You Must Believe in Spring" in tribute to Mabel Mercer, who had just died and whose velvet-and-pearls approach and literary acuity with a lyric made her the object of Susannah's devotion: "It's just a matter of reading a book out loud and with sense, with full stops and commas and the sense of what you're singing about," Mercer had confided to Whitney Balliett about her singing style. Susannah had met her a few years before while singing at the Van Dyck and was invited to pay a visit to Mercer's farm nearby. Susannah liked to remember how they sat on the porch overlooking the farm, singing together.

Just how well Susannah was singing was documented on a precious few extant video- and audiotapes of performances. How glorious she could be, for example, singing on a WNEW live broadcast, brilliant on a standard like "Autumn in New York," sexy and signature-wistful on "Where or When," definitely intelligent on "For All We Know." Her rendition of the nearly endless, and endlessly clever, choruses of "My New Celebrity Is You" was a tour de force; she gave a beautiful, heart-broken rendition of "What's New?" and an outstanding a cappella reading of the verse to "As Time Goes By." And there was her contemporary material as well. She breathed near-melodic life into "The People That You Never Get to Love," relished a flush of Frishberg tunes, and ended with impressive takes of some of the obscurer old gems: "It's Anybody's Spring," "It's a Pity to Say Goodnight," "What's Been Done Before." Not that there weren't problems. Her performances were still marred at times by wavering intonation, a tendency to turn strident on up-tempo numbers and consistently overreach for high notes at the end of a song—as if she found it hard to let go of the experience she had just created. But Susannah was often otherwise singing so exquisitely that it didn't matter.

Yet she still wasn't getting that many good jobs, and DiNicola was understandably perplexed and chagrined. "I had thought she was a big artist when we met, but I soon realized that very little was coming in from singing. She had a little money and an inexpensive studio apartment—that's about it." DiNicola made it his business to get Susannah work, and he found himself at home among the rough-and-tumble of managers, agents, clubs. He was already writing a column on movies for the *Schenectady Daily Gazette* in upstate New York, and doing features reporting for the local CBS-TV affiliate. "So the inside stuff of the music business, positive and negative, didn't take too long to figure out. It was my life," he says. "I found there are two types of people who run clubs and venues: the sleazeballs, and the bumblers, nice people who mean well but get bamboozled by agents who just want their commission. Few really care about the artists. The manager at Fat Tuesday's told us Susannah made more for them than Dizzy Gillespie, because Dizzy cost so much. But she didn't appear there enough. Money, that's all they care about." And promoting Susannah was all DiNicola cared about. If some found him too rough-edged and opinionated, others appreciated his efforts. "He was very good for Susannah," Roy Schecter says. "At the gig, he'd be nervous, pacing around, want everything to go just right. It was touching." Another big part of his job as manager, DiNicola found, was shielding Susannah from the unpleasant aspects of the music business—particularly rejection. "If a gig fell through, it destroyed her, and she would disappear into her room for days," he recalls.

Susannah now had *Thanks for the Memory: Songs of Leo Robin* on tape, but there was no record company to release it. DiNicola got to work looking for a label. He called Bill Stillfield in California, whose label, Pausa, had been reissuing inexpensive Capitol recordings; DiNicola helped put together a three-record deal for Susannah with him, beginning with *Thanks for the Memory* in 1984. He also helped Susannah set up her music-publishing company, an important way of securing copyrights and capturing royalties. Susannah called it Skylark.

With DiNicola helping her, Susannah sensed a turning point in her career as well as in her private life and joked that now that jazz—her kind of jazz—was "in," she was all of a sudden hip, not camp. She made another record for Pausa in June 1985, called *How Do You Keep the Music Playing?* with financial backing again lined up by Andy Lipman. Rather than the "songbook" approach, spotlighting a single songwriter of the past, she recorded a mix of old and new songs, as she had for her *People* album. Along with ballads, a Brazilian number, a novelty tune, and a Frishberg tune, "Blizzard of Lies," she included the pop hit "By the Time I Get to Phoenix." *Keep the Music Playing* would win her acclaim, including good reviews (Leonard Feather voted her "singer of the year") and another *Stereo Review* Record of the Year award. There were still those who didn't like the mixed-bag approach, though. And if many of her listeners loved her ability to peer into the heart of a standard like "There's No Business Like Show Business" and give it an entirely new interpretation, others felt that her recasting of the Irving Berlin song as a pull-out-the-stops heartbreaker was *de trop*. "Show Business" had been a rousing anthem immortalized by Ethel Merman, but Susannah, who discovered long-forgotten additional lyrics, found its dark edge: it was the same dark edge of depression that she found and identified with in its creator, Irving Berlin, she later said in a long article she wrote about him. Said one musician involved with the recording, " 'Show Business' was joyless, as if she were not having any fun." (Ten years later, she recorded it again, still a song essentially about loss, but this time a subtler version, with a lightened background of reeds and rhythm.)

Susannah's way with her musicians was still problematical. Richard Rodney Bennett, a prolific composer who had written, among other things, dozens of film scores and many arrangements for singers, produced two arrangements for the album *People That You Never Get to Love*—"Blizzard of Lies" and "By the Time I Get to Phoenix." It was not a happy experience. "She knew exactly what she was doing and what she wanted," he says. "But I've never had an arrangement where every single detail was worked out. She told you everything: 'I want a pause here, then a tremolo there, two beats rest here, then this.' She was very professional about it, she paid me for the arrangements I did, and when she wanted alterations on one, she paid for that too. But it was like making a frock for her. I've never done anything like that." Asserts bassist David Finck, who worked with her often in the eighties: "She was disrespectful of musicians—many musicians have this opinion. There's the story of her hiring [legendary saxophonist] Al Cohn to play sax on the *Keep the Music Playing* date, then asking him to play his solo over and over. 'Al, that was great, but could you do it again, a little slower?' *Al Cohn!*" Adds James Gavin, "Many musicians didn't like her. She presented herself as an authority but seemed to have come out of nowhere—and it was resented. She was aggressively intellectual, like a college-girl upstart. She hadn't got her act together yet. Her pitch was often off, and her time could be unsure. She wasn't a musician! But what do musicians know or care about singers? She was interested in the *emotional content* of a song, its lyric, and her performance."

"The era of the passive, polite girl singer—that's over," comments longtime DJ Dick Golden. Despite the negative rap that some players gave Susannah, others appreciated what she was getting at. Pianist Dave McKenna was one. He met Susannah when she dropped by to visit a Cape Cod supper club where he played nightly during the summer, and he invited her to come by a piano bar in New York called Hanratty's in the fall. "Dave would drop what he was doing and go into a sumptuously harmonized rubato version of 'Oh, Susannah.' She would always graciously accept this tribute with an ear-to-ear smile," Golden says. "Then he would coax her up to the stand, and they'd do a few tunes together with Susannah sitting on the edge of the piano bench." Other veterans who esteemed her include saxophonist Phil Woods, who dug her while on the same bill in Denver, and bassist Ray Brown, who recommended her for a job in Los Angeles, where the seasoned trombonist Al Grey was backstage while Susannah was singing. (Backstage also was Dan DiNicola, who recalls a young singer approaching Grey for advice about her craft while Susannah was onstage. "Grey said, 'Listen to her. That's jazz. That's the way to sing,'" says DiNicola.) Another fan was drummer Roy Haynes, says DiNicola. Yes, adds pianist Allen Farnham, who accompanied Susannah for most of the 1990s. He remembers that Roy Haynes, along with other well-known musicians, always made a point of dropping by to see her shows when they were in New York.

In the mid-eighties, Jonathan Schwartz hosted *New York Tonight,* a short-lived television program on what was then the new medium of cable.[1] A lifelong devotee of the music (his father was composer Arthur Schwartz), Jonathan Schwartz had become a popular DJ in the seventies on WNEW and for a time was trying for a career as a singer too. Probably this is why during an interview, after the usual banter, he asked Susannah why on earth, given how lonely the life is, she became a singer. In reply, Susannah smiled a bit wryly. "I am never closer to people than when singing," she said.[2] And she meant it—she who had missed closeness with other people all her life, despite her relationship with Ingham and other intense, if short-lived, love affairs. But now—when she was nearly 40—it seemed that at last she would not have to depend on singing to bring her closeness. She had found not only romance but a true partner.

Yet she was uneasy with the domestic arrangements that each couple has to work out. "She saw herself as a singer rather than a housewife focused on marriage responsibilities," says therapist Roberta Todras, whom Susannah was then seeing. "And," Todras adds, "she wanted to live in New York City, while she realized Dan had a life in Schenectady, upstate."

In her way, Susannah tried to become part of DiNicola's upstate life. When she met him, his personal life was unsettled, with a second marriage on the rocks and soon to end. His first marriage had also ended in divorce, after producing a daughter, Anne (23 when Susannah entered the picture), and a son, Jeff, 22. DiNicola had adopted his second wife's son, Roy, then 16. Soon after the one-year anniversary of their first lunch date in New York, Susannah moved into a small apartment upstate with DiNicola, on the top floor of an 18th-century row house in the Stockade, Schenectady's colonial-era district. Soon, Roy DiNicola remembers, he returned from a year abroad in Germany, moving into the small room at the back of the cozy apartment. But inevitably, it was not a cozy arrangement for any of the three. Roy was a teenager; his parents were in the process of a divorce. "And," he says, "I hadn't met Susannah before that." DiNicola and Susannah decided to buy a house together. Where else but Schenectady? DiNicola had roots there, family, friends, work; New York City was out of the question unless he found a job there, which was unlikely. And DiNicola, who liked Schenectady, assumed that Susannah would too, once she settled in. Practically speaking, in his view, what difference did it make if she flew to her engagements out of the Capital Region rather than New York?

They moved into their house in December 1985. As ecstatic as a child with a new toy, Susannah wrote her parents a letter from "my desk in my own study in my own house!!! It is an unbelievable feeling to own a house after all these years of living like a student. I can sing scales without anyone hearing me, everything is decorated and arranged just the way I want it. . . . It's really a once in a lifetime house, full of wonderful period detail—tile kitchen, sunroom with oak-framed arched windows, oak woodwork in perfect condition, original floors, solid doors, iron doorknobs, etc. . . . I feel so domestic. Last night I put up a Christmas tree covered with old fashioned ornaments I've been collecting and Monday I'm going to bake and frost ginger cookies in my own home! From all the side windows we can see the park with lots of trees (frosted in snow right now—beautiful) and a rose garden. And thank you so much for helping to make this house possible."

"We each put $10,000 down," DiNicola explains. "Tom and Mimi helped her with her $10,000. I would pay the mortgage and the taxes, but we co-owned it."

The house (where DiNicola still lives) is a cozy late-Victorian on a postage-stamp lawn across from a big, pretty park. He remarks, "Still, she had to flower up reality! She went to some pains to acquire a different address for the house: Niskayuna, which she felt had more cachet than Schenectady."

Meanwhile, Susannah had kept her studio apartment in Manhattan, one room with a fold-out bed and a tiny kitchen and a bath. She commuted—though, as time went on, she stayed longer and longer in New York. Her apartment finally came to represent the wedge that was her ambition, the consuming demands of her singing career, in the marriage.

But not at first. Things were idyllic at first. It was Christmas, her favorite season. She seemed born to sing Christmas songs. Her version of "The Christmas Song" on CBS's *This Morning* was pure honey. Everyone who knew her then remembers Susannah trying hard to be domestic. Like an old-fashioned newlywed, she collected recipes, baked homemade bread and pizzas, and, always, made cookies at Christmas. "This cookie project grew into a big production; it took days and days," DiNicola recalls. "Freeform gingerbread cookies. Very social, people in. . . . It was too much. But she wanted it that way. It was a meaningful tradition for her."

Once the Christmas and New Year's holidays—and her 40th birthday—had been celebrated, Susannah's mood fell again. In a letter to her English agent, Pat White, she seemed to be barely holding back a major case of the blues:

"I have not been able to establish a rhythm of writing in spite of all the things I've done to help me get back writing again. Being close to a man after so many years on my own is—after all the happiness and romance of it—a huge adjustment, especially because we live three hours apart. But I am getting used to the benefits of a small-city life (at least for weekends and summers!) and think my writing will improve with my new stability and my quiet life up here. My time is so chopped up with all my travels [and] the usual ups and downs of an adult (usually) relationship and trying to work out how I should be with Dan's 17-year-old son, who lives here this year, that I am feeling pretty muddled. Instead, I'll work on a short story till I can get my balance again and concentrate for long periods as one needs to do on a novel. When anyone asks me how the book is going, I feel attacked and exposed for the non-finisher that I so far am. . . . I wish I could just sleep all day like my cat."

Her idea of stability would always include a room of her own, where she could think and write, and in her Schenectady house, she loved her cozy little study upstairs with a window overlooking the little green square of the backyard and a pretty, old-fashioned roll-top desk to sit to. In the winter of 1988, she made a last-ditch effort to wrestle *Closer to Home* to a finish but finally gave up. "I know you must be very disappointed in me for not having justified your early and lasting support of my work and I am disappointed in myself too," she wrote White, adding ironically, "I could handle writing, singing and unsatisfactory love affairs, but not writing, singing and a stable relationship. Finally I decided to make my peace with not writing and hope that by being calmer about it, I could resume it more easily one day."

She was right about the greater demands placed on her by "a stable relationship." Not only those of a mate, of course, but also the demands, though intermittent, of being a stepmother to two twentysomethings and a teenager. For DiNicola, the only child of Italian immigrants and a devoted father, family was everything. And when they decided to live together, she, in his phrase, "came into my family."

This blended family had had its full share of upheavals and crises. Speaking of his older half-brother Jeff and half-sister Anne, Roy DiNicola says, "They had an awful time of it growing up. Dad and their mother got married because they had to, very young. And it was volatile between the families. Their mother tried to kill herself when they were in the house and was in an institution for awhile. They've been through a lot, but they are well-adjusted kids." Roy had his own family problems, particularly with his German-born mother, who became an alcoholic. "I was a sophomore in high school when my parents were getting separated, and I decided to spend my junior year in Germany, so I left home in July of 1984, and my mother left for Long Island." His mother was in poor emotional shape, so when Roy returned to Schenectady the next summer, he had nowhere to go but the little apartment that Susannah and his father shared: "And I was forced to find a way of getting along with Susannah. She wasn't warm with kids, but we found a way to work it out."

Jeff had graduated from college that summer of 1985 and come back home too, living alone in what was the family house before it was sold (his sister, Anne, was in Japan). Less easygoing than Roy, he found it harder to accept the presence of yet another woman in his father's life. "I felt a lot of resentment toward Susannah—I feel close to both my biological and my stepmother and an allegiance to my stepmother. Anne thought that Susannah was great for Dad, but she was far away, in Japan," he notes. "I saw myself as the victim of circumstances. Susannah was resistant and uncomfortable about family things."

"I wasn't paying attention to Jeff," admits Dan DiNicola. "I was so involved with Susannah and he didn't feel as if he had a family. And Susannah was not particularly attuned to that—it was not part of her nature." Adds Roy, "Dad was torn between the woman he loved and the family. He would defend her, and he would market her for us. For example, he sent me an article about her as a singer. I told him he didn't have to do that!"

As in so many families, holiday gatherings intended to serve as a time of renewed closeness and good cheer were also a stage on which to act out family conflicts. And there was a lot of pent-up tension in the DiNicola mélange. "Dad always wanted family around," Roy says.

"Lots of food and wine and talking for hours around the table. That's his favorite thing to do. But it was not Susannah's." Because the traditional rich foods—the hams and creamed vegetables and pies and cakes—tempted her into binge eating, Susannah responded by reconfiguring the menu. "She'd stock up on food from the whole-foods store," Roy continues. "No stuffing in the turkey—a bulgur wheat dish instead. Dad's favorite food in the world was pumpkin pie, but no pumpkin pie. I saw, too, how she had a hard time eating moderate amounts; with chocolate, she'd polish it all off." "She'd eat, be depressed about it, then leave us gathered at the table and go upstairs," Jeff recalls. "She would henpeck my father about how to eat—how to dress, too."

Jeff was point man in family confrontations with Susannah: "She left a note for Roy when he was staying with them during a summer vacation while he was in college, about how he should not treat the house like a hotel and lecturing him about cleaning up after himself. I called Dad: 'What the hell is this?' But Dad was supportive of her. I'd also get annoyed because Susannah would always talk about people in terms of what they did—like 'So-and-so, she's an author.' I told Roy, 'She's a phony; she thinks she's better than everybody else.'" "She could come off as rude," Roy agrees. "She was smarter than the average person, and she felt you had to have an interest, a passion. Jeff and his wife Kim and later my wife Holly and I would joke that she was stuck with us," Roy says. When the family all went to a baseball game at Fenway Park in Boston together—Dan was and is a huge sports fan—Susannah pulled out a book and started reading. Kim recalls explaining to an incredulous Jeff, "Well, she's *eccentric*."

Susannah's relationship with Anne wasn't much easier. After studying Japanese in college, Anne had gone to Japan in 1984 intending to stay for a year, but ended up getting married and opening her own small language school. Consequently, she saw Susannah less often than her brothers, though she made regular visits to the States. "Susannah loved the idea of a family," she says, "but it was difficult for her to be around people for long periods. I would come to visit and she would be fine one-to-one. But with the family at the dinner table, her head would go down, as if she were bored. Then she would leave, just go to her room. Same thing in Japan. She came twice to Japan, once with Dad in 1989, and once alone in 1991, during a jazz tour. That first trip, I had a big party—Dad gets a lot of energy from people. Susannah didn't like it—she excused herself and went up to her room; she spent a lot of time there. On the other hand, she needed a lot of attention. She liked smaller groups. On January 1, her birthday, six of us went out to dinner, and she was the focus of the party."

"For my marriage to Kim in November of 1988," recalls Jeff, "Anne came in from Japan and we got a call from her in tears. It was the day of the rehearsal dinner that Dan and Susannah were hosting, and they were having a big fight. Then, after the wedding, Susannah left early during the reception. Everything, I thought, had to revolve around Susannah and Dan."

DiNicola had his own issues. "Very few of her friends came or stayed at the house," he says. "Schenectady is a blue-collar kind of town, essentially, and she'd say, 'Who'd want to stay here?'" Nor did DiNicola's friends interest her—except for artists and writers. "She didn't try to hurt people, but she did, with her aloofness," he explains. "A social misfit, fussy about conversations. However, when they got to know her, she'd be fine. I think I helped her with that."

Those first years were strained, but remarkably, this group of people from difficult backgrounds and different temperaments managed to build a web of affection and care and love for each other. "As time went on, my father would speak more openly about her shortcomings," Roy says. "And over the years, Susannah grew to appreciate a family where all loved each other—she said so. As we realized that Susannah might not be temporary in our lives, we got to know her more." "She'd come off as a very strong, self-confident woman," Jeff observes, "yet I got to know that she always doubted herself in everything. And she was frustrated seeing other singers who she said were clearly less talented making a bigger living."

At first, the DiNicolas rolled their eyes at Susannah's complaints about her parents, especially Mimi. After all, they'd had their own difficult mothers. Dan DiNicola, like Ingham before him, was at first amazed to see Susannah's reaction to her parents. Not long after they'd fallen in love, they visited Tom and Mimi, who'd moved into a new house that year, in pretty, garden-filled Oakland Hills, minutes away from Berkeley. Mimi sought solace in cocktails, while Tom just sat. He had been in retirement about four years, and his condition had noticeably deteriorated. He did odd jobs around the house; he read a bit; at night he was visited by bad dreams. His doctor, in a report for his medical insurance company, cited his "visible psychopathology, his rather conspicuous obsessive personality type which constricts his lifestyle and thought."[3] According to DiNicola, while visiting her parents, "Susannah would sit in a chair like a fetus, totally alienated from her surroundings"—or, Susannah might have argued, totally *insulated* from her surroundings. As she wrote with rare deep candor later in a book proposal, "Because of the effect on my father of his prolonged, unacknowledged depression and breakdown, I took my own tendency to depression very seriously and vowed not to let it push me too over the edge."[4]

Susannah's relationship with Mimi would continue to be rocky. Three years later, in 1987, Susannah and DiNicola planned a vacation with her parents to the Napa Valley after she'd completed a successful week's performance at San Francisco's Plush Room. The trip was marred by a heated argument between Susannah and her mother, as a letter dated that November 28 reveals:

> I felt terrible that I said what I said in anger in the heat of the moment. But I am deeply relieved that the importance (rather than the anger) of my words penetrated, because I have been extremely concerned about you for quite awhile now. I have wanted to bring up the subject of your drinking, but I have been discouraged from doing it by other people and by my own lack of confidence in our ability to communicate with each other. We just never have had an affinity for each other, but on my side, at least, our lack of closeness doesn't mean I don't care deeply about what happens to you . . . Love, Susannah

To celebrate her parents' 40th wedding anniversary the following year, Susannah tried to smooth over the relationship with them by putting on a little concert in their garden. "She hired a pianist, and she sang 'The Folks Who Live on the Hill' and cried, but her parents didn't respond at all," as DiNicola remembers. Mimi was still angry at Susannah, and she had to deal with Tom's chronic and debilitating depression, which fluctuated between bad and worse: "I am doing no writing or other constructive work," Tom complained to his doctor, "and I don't know how good I might be in a crisis. I seem very slow in all my processes and my wife complains that I seem depressed and don't want to do things. It looks like I am of little use to anybody the way things are." His medication had cut out the manic part of his illness but had left him little to live for. Sitting for hours on end in his living room, nursing a cocktail and smoking, Tom worried about his children discovering the truth of his condition. Though he had compiled a thick file relating to his hospitalization and years of treatment for manic depression, and needed the documentation in order for his medical insurance to accept his claim of disability, he was unable to find it. "I think I may have destroyed my documentation in preparing to move from Long Beach to the Bay area," he wrote his psychiatrist. "Because I wished to spare my daughters the pain of reading about my experiences." Susannah, of course, fully aware of the history of his mental illness, was distressed beyond words at seeing her father's condition on her visits to California.

She seldom saw her sisters, even on her infrequent trips to see Tom and Mimi. Katie drifted and crashed in and out of the family, and Maggie was now Maggie Pinson, married, with a baby, Alice, living in Texas, and alienated from Susannah. "I had gotten a job at the university, nothing very exciting or lucrative, but solid," she says. "Susannah had great scorn for a straightforward, career-ladder person." A few years later, when Maggie and Alice visited Schenectady, the two sisters quarreled. Maggie said she didn't like DiNicola, and Susannah countered that Maggie's husband was a "six-pack guy, beer and a football game on TV," Maggie recalls. "We'd try to correspond with each other by mail, and then we'd get mad at each other and stop. I used to dread getting her letters. They upset me. And, she probably felt the same way. That's the kind of relationship we had."

But Susannah worried privately about each member of her family. She worried about what she saw as Maggie's listlessness, a passivity that she thought might mask the depression that seemed to run through the McCorkle genes. In New York, she sought out a support group for families of schizophrenics to assist her in dealing with Katie's ongoing crises and her parents' continued involvement in them, especially their efforts to help raise Katie's young son, Carlos. She worried about her mother's drinking and her harshness. And of course she worried about her father. "Tom loved his daughter," DiNicola asserts. "He sent her $100 or $150 a month from his disability check, and always renewed her *New Yorker* subscription. But he withdrew." In fact, Tom had long ago ceased to be able to offer steady emotional support, the only thing that Susannah really wanted from him.

DiNicola's job of managing Susannah's career worked out well at first. In the late eighties, she was appearing at Pizza on the Park, the high end of the London "pizza joints" in which she'd started her singing career. Chris Ellis came to hear her. "She was happy to have someone to take over the business side for her—it was a *great* relief. She hadn't had a manager before, and she hated having to negotiate for herself on business deals." Generally, however, Susannah didn't want to say that her husband was her manager. It was supposed to be temporary but, in fact, Susannah never did have a manager apart from DiNicola. Putting her best face forward, she told Leonard Feather a few years later that she was "too much of a maverick and a free spirit [and] unless you're making huge money you are not going to get an agent and a manager. I don't even know whether I'd want those now."

But it was DiNicola who made the phone calls, hundreds of them, DiNicola who argued about dressing rooms and salaries and airfare and publicity; DiNicola who took care of the dozens of details that can build or break a performance. Susannah was a perfectionist and continued to have a hard time with saloons and the typical club ambiance: the hurly-burly of the clinking of glasses, the laughing and chatting by inattentive patrons, the ringing of the phone and the cash register, the waiters taking orders. And for a singer, out in front, vulnerable, there was the quality of the mikes to be considered, the placement of the sound system, the temperature in the room. Eventually she drew up a closely written list of demands of several pages. A typical jazz musician like Ingham had shrugged and told her to ignore it all, to rise above the fray. But DiNicola, in his own words, "was the enabler, trying to make everything nice for her." With mixed results, say some. "Dan's intense personality accentuated her nervousness. It added to the neurosis," says a recording-industry insider. And some of Susannah's friends thought he was too possessive. "I found Dan DiNicola extremely domineering," says Lisa Dawn Popa, who sold CDs for artists in the Algonquin lobby. "She was nervous around Dan. She loved talking to the people who came to her shows, which helped sell her CDs as well. But with Dan, she didn't hang out. They just packed up and left." "I think he actually harmed her career," asserts Diane Mich Feldman.

Susannah was not easy to work with. For a manager, whether husband or not, she could be wearing. "Tough and perplexing," as her old friend Andy Lipman puts it, "not ruthless, and she had a heart of gold, but prickly, certainly." DiNicola agrees: He was often frustrated. "She would always insist on starting a show with an esoteric song, instead of a crowd-pleaser, despite my pleading with her," he says. "And I'd tell her to let loose with her singing more than to have every word perfect. She was very strict about that. Once we had an argument before a show, and she went on and forgot the words to a verse and scatted. *Scatted*! Afterward, she said to me, 'You see? Because of the fight, I messed up.' I told her it's okay! She'd take big risks with the songs she chose and in her life—but *not* with the performance."

Indeed, Susannah's vocal performance was still a puzzle for many. Don Heckman of the *Los Angeles Times,* who was to become a big admirer, gave a mixed review of her performance in August 1986 at the Vine Street Bar & Grill in Los Angeles. Leonard Feather, who admired what he called her deep understanding of lyrics and natural acting ability, was not yet the huge fan he'd soon become. That year, he decried her "somewhat dated sense of jazz phrasing . . . and a limited feel for harmonic variation . . . not the stuff of which great jazz singing is made." Others agree. Linda Fennimore, a neighbor who was Susannah's race-walking partner, is a jazz violinist who first heard her at the Park Ten in 1988, a restaurant at which she'd sung since 1985. Her response was guarded. "I loved her approach, her dedication, but she was not a singer you'd sit back and listen to."

But Susannah had a plan, a vision of what she wanted to do vocally, regardless of how some folks took it, even if she had to alienate people in the process. In the fall of 1986, for example, she made another record called *As Time Goes By,* part of a vocalist series for CBS/Sony in Japan. With her were jazz heavyweights: Billy Taylor on piano; Victor Gaskin, bass; Tony Reddus, drums; Ted Dunbar, guitar; and Jimmy Heath on tenor saxophone. Trouble began when she rejected all but two of the long list of tunes, many of them associated with Billie Holiday, that the producers had sent her to choose from. Her insistence on her own choices brought a clash with Billy Taylor. Later, she dismissed the entire project as "the contraband Japanese album." Referring to the notion of simply showing up in a studio to sing with a combo, she said, "I hate the whole concept." She never did *that* kind of album again.

If Susannah was unhappy with *As Time Goes By,* her next album for Pausa, *Dream,* cut in early December that year, was a far happier experience; everything here was arranged and thought out, all the songs she chose had a pensive, misty-eyed atmosphere.[5] *Dream* was another album graced with a great tenor saxophonist, in this case Frank Wess, whose sound, however, seems too virile for Susannah's pastel delicacy. Again, she mixed new and old: Paul Simon's "Train in the Distance" and Lieber-Stoller's "Longings for a Simpler Time," with standards like "All of Me," vocalese à la King Pleasure (based on a tenor solo by Illinois Jacquet: Susannah enjoyed singing set pieces to jazz solos) and the Lil Hardin Armstrong twenties classic, "Just for a Thrill," and the obligatory Brazilian bossa nova, here Jobim's "Triste." "This isn't singing, it's vocal artistry," cooed one critic.

But *Dream* quickly turned into a nightmare when Pausa Records went bankrupt not long after releasing the album. "One of the people working there turned out not to have been paying composer royalties," DiNicola says. But DiNicola had been courting the owner of a then-new label for some time: Concord Records' Carl Jefferson. A wealthy car dealer, Jefferson (nicknamed Jeff) was a jazz lover who started his own label in 1972 to record his favorite swing and bebop players, along with running the popular Concord Jazz Festival (and then a sister festival in Japan, Concord-Fujitsu). There were other independent labels who recorded vocalists, but Concord was the largest, going on to release more than 700 records in Jefferson's lifetime. And it had the most jazz cachet. Though both Ken Pitt (who had long represented Mel Tormé, a Concord artist) and another Concord artist, Marian McPartland, had put in a good word to Jefferson about Susannah, it was a meeting between DiNicola and Jefferson in San Francisco in 1987 that finally clinched the deal; the timing was right. Allen Farnham, who became Susannah's regular pianist a few years later, was a distant cousin of Jefferson's and worked on the promotion side of the company then. "This was the golden age of CDs, when they were new in the late eighties and early nineties," he says. "Everybody was getting a CD player, and all the record companies were reselling their catalogs as CDs, including Concord." Jeff, according to Susannah, told her he'd looked around and found that she was the only young singer with a track record. (Subsequently, Jefferson signed a number of other younger singers.) Farnham, who describes Jeff as "gruff," "crusty," and "cantankerous," describes the softening effect Susannah had on the older man. "When he met with Susannah and Dan, he just stared at Susannah—it was like Dan was not there. There were guys like him who fell all over her and thought she was so sexy; then there was another crowd she left cold."

For her first Concord album—the first time she had a budget behind her and could get beyond bare-bones accompaniment—Susannah consulted with Chris Ellis. She was eager to do what she called a "foreign album"—ballads from Italy, Mexico, France, Germany—but Ellis suggested she table the idea for the moment and concentrate on recording several tunes short enough for radio airplay. "You have a very special talent for warm, slightly rueful songs—e.g., 'Darn That Dream,'" he pointed out. (Like Keith, Ellis didn't care for current pop, but he'd seen how Susannah had made silk purses out of contemporary numbers like "By the Time I Get to Phoenix" and knew she'd go for an eclectic range of material.) *No More Blues,* as the album was titled, was her biggest success to date, a solid seller and *Stereo Review*'s 1989 record of the year. Besides the title song, the English version of the Brazilian tune "Chega de Saudade," there was the usual mix of standards and new material. It was a very strong offering, with Gerry Mulligan's "The Ballad of Pearly Sue," Louis Armstrong phrasing on "Swing That Music" and "Everything's Been Done Before," Lester Young–inspired vocalese on "Sometimes I'm Happy," and Dave Frishberg's amusing "Can't Take You Nowhere."

As was his custom, Carl Jefferson teamed her with musicians from the Concord "family": Bucky Pizzarelli and Emily Remler on guitars, Dave Frishberg on piano, and, as her musical director for the date, the clarinetist and tenor saxophonist Ken Peplowski. Though he later worked with her again, Peplowski told other musicians afterward, "Anyone who once records with Susannah is not eager to do so again." Responds DiNicola, "The rapport wasn't there." However, Jeff had assigned the two to work together, and that was that. But the clotted atmosphere of tension and Susannah's nervous fussiness in the studio, as if she had her life on the line, added up to a bad experience for other sensitive souls. Frishberg, recalls Richard Rodney Bennett, telephoned him after a day in the studio cutting the record. He was staying at a hotel not far from Bennett's apartment on the Upper West Side and, though they didn't know each other well, he wanted to drop by. "It was about five in the afternoon," Bennett says. "He came in and I thought he was going to start crying, he was so unhappy. 'I had the most terrible, terrible day,' he said. 'I was playing for Susannah McCorkle, and it was so awful!' He was *really* upset, and to top it off, he said that Dan DiNicola came over at one point in the session and told him, 'This is really going to help your career, you know.'" Frishberg, though he did not record again with Susannah, performed at least once with her after the difficult *No More Blues* (they traded choruses on "Guys and Dolls" and "Let's Call the Whole Thing Off"). And they were certainly cordial. Susannah continued to record Frishberg's compositions often for the rest of her career.

DiNicola handled as much of the business end of Susannah's career as he could, but he was juggling his own demanding job and was often on the road himself, doing interviews and putting together profiles for his television show in Albany. Often Susannah had to take care of the finances herself, setting fees and figuring profit margins at clubs, trying to keep track of expenses. She was careful with money, and her negotiations with her sidemen provided a frequent irritant to already problematic relationships. "In 1989, she asked me to play Fat Tuesday's," David Finck recalls, "and she offered me, like, half my usual fee for that club, and I said so. She got upset." Lee Musiker, who succeeded Ben Aronov as Susannah's pianist, from 1987 to 1989, reported a contretemps with her to Finck. It was an argument about money. "He gave her a receipt for his taxi ride to the airport and said he wanted payment—in cash," Finck says. "She said she wasn't going to pay, then started crying."

However, there were good reasons for Susannah to be careful about money: As the leader of her group, she faced wildly uneven pay rates among different gigs. Some jobs were generous and covered all her expenses, but many of them didn't, requiring her to cover sidemen's expenses such as hotel rooms and meals. And in the late eighties, Susannah felt greater pressure than ever to be prudent about money. At that point, after all, both Inner City Records and Pausa had gone bankrupt, and she was suing for the rights to her six records released by those labels. In 1989, she was successful, and later they were released on CD through Concord. But in the meantime, she was losing years of potential royalties. (So did Keith Ingham, who had both done the bulk of the arrangements on those albums and anchored on piano. He got paid nothing. "Zilch," he shrugs. "But it's far in the past now.")

For all the hard work that DiNicola and Susannah put into her career, and despite the accolades (in one flyer, for example, she included Francis Davis's praise of her as "The Best Jazz Singer of Her Generation"), she still wasn't getting the booking she wanted. "The clubs liked cutting-edge scatters like Betty Carter," DiNicola explains, "and Susannah was a jazz singer in the old Billie Holiday tradition." It seemed harder than ever to establish the kind of audience she sought countrywide. Susannah and DiNicola chafed at her sometimes chilly reception.

"She was often being reviewed by someone who didn't get it," he complains. Susannah, who was careful not to be negative about other singers publicly, was known to rail in private to family and friends. "It's to the point now that if you're black and scat, then you're a jazz singer," she bemoaned one night. Although she and DiNicola had no hard evidence that she'd lost out on jobs because she didn't fit that profile, they felt they had plenty of circumstantial incidents to back them up. To be called a "dewy-voiced archivist," as she was by *Esquire* in a "round-up of girl singers" in 1988, was a backhanded compliment.

Part of Susannah's problem was that it was still hard to place her as a singer. She might sing a hip Frishberg tune like "Blizzard of Lies" or "My Attorney Bernie," then turn to an obscure Irving Berlin or Leo Robin song, before moving to a pop tune. Audiences, as well as club owners, were often confused—or indifferent. To jazz club owner Amos Korn of Gulliver's, the difficulty for Susannah had nothing to do with her. It all came down to the bottom line. "By the late eighties," he says, "most jazz clubs looked at it from a business point of view, and they didn't think that Susannah could cut it with almost any audience."

More and more, as the eighties progressed, Susannah was drawn to concertizing, rather than gigging. "She was always trying to find a niche," DiNicola says. "The concert with Marian McPartland in Rochester was the impetus for a series Susannah did with symphony orchestras in '85." Backed by her trio, Ben Aronov, Steve LeSpina on bass, and Joe Cocuzzo on drums, in a variant of the program she'd developed with Keith, and with another unwieldy title—"Susannah McCorkle Takes the Symphony to the Movies"—Susannah toured with the Rhode Island, San Antonio, Rochester, and, finally, Springfield symphony orchestras. She'd pared her long program down, however, so that it included just nine songs, including Berlin's "Let Yourself Go," Gershwin's "They Can't Take That Away From Me," Warren's "42nd Street," and Arlen's "Blues in the Night." Susannah and her rhythm section took a jazz approach to the tunes. But, as DiNicola points out, "These concerts attracted the kind of older, unhip crowd that goes to the symphony pops concerts for some light entertainment, not jazz. So she was caught in the middle, and she wasn't a hit."

Presciently, *Daily News* reviewer Douglas Wyatt noted: "Her real forte is with the cabaret genre because of her elegance," adding that her "sly, caustic wit and rollicking theater delivery" well suited the genre. Susannah had begun by learning songs from the great musicals of her childhood, had stood out in the first (and only) musicals she performed in as a teenager. She had a feel for such songs, was one of those singers who uncover the emotional heart of a Gershwin tune, a Berlin song. And that was both the problem and the solution. In an elegant atmosphere with a rapt, schooled audience, Susannah was usually a hit. At the Plush Room in August 1987, the top venue for cabaret/jazz-based singers in San Francisco, she wrung an admiring critical review from the *Chronicle*'s Gerald Nachman: "In her candy-box valentine-red dress, big sorrowful eyes set in a raw-boned but welcoming face, she looks at first like a farmer's daughter at the prom—not quite comfortable in her sexy gown or, for that matter, on stage," he began. "Then," he added, "things start to happen."[6] But she needed more such venues, many more. A golden-seeming opportunity, a March 1988 concert called "Jazz Meets Pop," filmed by a local PBS affiliate at the Proctor Theater in Schenectady, turned to dust; Susannah's performance was unevenly brilliant and inexpertly produced. She would play the theater again, but had no more offers of headline television shows.

By now, Susannah's career was pushing the limits of the mid-list jazz singer: She was not a star, but she was becoming better known, with a distinct presence as a singer and a growing following. Though Susannah complained in a letter to Ken Pitt that she wasn't getting "enough promotion from Concord [Records]," she added that she noticed doors were opening for her now after the release of her first album for the label.

Susannah was also garnering more positive attention from serious critics and writers. The critic Francis Davis visited her in Schenectady in 1988 for a feature article he was preparing about her for *High Fidelity* magazine. Davis had been a fan since hearing, by chance, Susannah's rendition of "Fools Rush In" on her Johnny Mercer album a few years before. "I realized it was more than good—here was someone who really cared about these songs," he says. When he learned that she was a published writer, he naturally was curious to see some of her work. "She didn't want me to see her stories." Finally, she allowed him to, "after much coaxing." After reading "Ramona by the Sea," Davis met with Susannah again for more conversation and was stunned when Susannah admitted that, like the unkempt Ramona of her story, she'd been a compulsive overeater. "'It's like being a drug addict or an alcoholic,' she told me, 'except you can't say you're going to cut out food entirely.' After that, Susannah sent me a long letter, taking back some of the things she said. I did think she was insecure and I saw the downside." Davis was among the small group whom Susannah took at all into her confidence, a group that had a hard time reconciling the "trim, confident figure," as one put it, of the performer with the dark, often agonized characters she wrote about and claimed to identify with.

Though she'd tamed her compulsion to overeat by sheer force of will, she still struggled with her body image. Not long after Davis had his conversations with her in 1988, Susannah made a momentous decision. With the encouragement of therapist Roberta Todras, she decided to undergo breast-reduction surgery, something she'd longed to do for years. No matter how sternly she dieted, she still had outsized breasts: "Sylvia Plath in an English barmaid's body," to quote her college friend Jon Carroll. "She was extremely self-conscious at the size of her bosom and the wrong sort of attention it brought her," says Richard Rodney Bennett, "and she was pleased by gay men's attentions and happy with their companionship, as presumably they wouldn't react to her in that way."

The surgery went well, though afterward she was still large-breasted.[7] From then on, Susannah built an ever-slimmer body, rigorously dieting all her life and at times becoming too thin, though she was far more at home in a thin self.

But after the surgery—by a cruel irony or a lucky happenstance—a routine checkup revealed a lump in her breast that turned out to be malignant. "They probably could detect the lump *because* she'd had breast-reduction surgery," Todras points out. Everyone reacts differently to cancer: Susannah responded with rage fueled by uncontrollable fear, and agonized over whether her cosmetic surgery had exacerbated the disease or even caused it. Her doctor in Schenectady wanted to operate right away; if there was any lymph-node involvement, it was urgent to excise it. But Susannah said no: She had three weeks of tours coming up, including an important, two-week engagement, a first for her, at the Fairmont Hotel in Chicago. She and the doctor argued, she and DiNicola argued, but Susannah was adamant. First she would fulfill her engagement. And every night that she sang—she was transcendent, never better, it seemed—and every day she race-walked and ate her organic health foods. She felt strong and powerful. The cap was a "Tribute to Johnny Mercer" in Denver, where, admired one reviewer, she sang the old songs "as though she had just found them in an attic." "I came back to Schenectady convinced that my music and spirit had turned the thing around," she wrote.

But the lump had not melted away. Nor had her rage. "She was angrier and angrier," says DiNicola, who had traveled with her during part of her Midwest trip and watched her come off the stage after a performance seething. Now, back home in Schenectady, she could postpone reality no longer: She must start treatments. "I felt horrified, terrified and totally alienated, plunged into the world of cancer," Susannah wrote. "I was devastated, disbelieving, furious and enraged that my life, always a struggle both professionally and personally, now seemed utterly impossible. . . . It was a surreal trip of public highs and private madness. On the road I was dealing not only with my horrific news but with a piano player with a cocaine problem. The strong inner core I had developed as a child in a dysfunctional family simply wasn't there any more. I lost the will to live and barely survived this episode. I hardly knew the crazed person I became."

"Susannah blamed her cancer on depression, and she blamed her depression on Schenectady," says Jeff DiNicola. "She perceived cancer as, 'It's an imperfection, and I can't have any imperfections.'" And she blamed Dan. "He was angry and afraid rather than sympathetic," she wrote in a journal. "Didn't hold me when I needed to be held then, early on, just after I'd got the news. He represented the whole, healthy world that didn't have to have cancer."

Susannah underwent a lumpectomy, with the welcome report that there was no lymph-node involvement—the best possible news in the circumstances. Yet her rage and depression did not lift. "The surgeon got frustrated with her," DiNicola recalls. "He had just had three patients die of the disease, and Susannah was getting the best outcome there was." She kept fighting the oncologist, too. No, she told him, she would not undergo chemotherapy. "I didn't want to poison my whole body when something was only in my breasts," she explained. Adds DiNicola, "She didn't want to lose her hair."

Crucially, she then began taking Prozac to treat her anxiety and depression. "She was suicidal, and I referred her to a psychiatrist who prescribed antidepressants," Todras says. What is not known is whether she had yet been diagnosed with bipolar disorder. At any rate, along with psychotherapy and antidepressants, her friend Andy Lipman recalls that she began at that time to experiment with alternative medicine—in particular, homeopathy. Remarkably, given the extreme turmoil in her life, Susannah was, says pianist Allen Farnham, "relaxed and composed" during a gig in Hawaii she played with him in November (their second together) for some Japanese businessmen whom Carl Jefferson brought together for a Concord-Fujitsu jazz party. No doubt her medications were responsible for helping her composure, but only in part: With musicians—indeed, with the whole "outside world"— Susannah always maintained a samurai-rigid code of behavior that sealed off her professional from her private life.

"No longer do I break down and sob, as I have so many times these past months," she said, before consenting to take seven weeks of radiation treatments starting in December at Memorial Sloan Kettering Cancer Center in Manhattan. Then there were the bills to pay. She and DiNicola were living together but not yet married, and Susannah was responsible for her own medical charges, and many items were not covered by her insurance. As usual when she was in straits, she turned to Tom and Mimi. Explaining that she had "been absolutely suicidal" that autumn, she asked them for money to cover "mental health care." As they had always done, be it ever so reluctantly, her parents sent her the money.

It would be years before Susannah could bring herself to disclose her illness to anyone outside her immediate circle of family and several intimates. Although she would later become an advocate for breast-cancer survivors, well into the nineties Susannah was convinced that public disclosure of the disease would damage her career. Meanwhile, as she was to write, "I face the future in the notoriously treacherous field of music, feeling thrilled and terrified, blessed and cursed, to live a singer's life."[8]

# Sunshine Susannah

Susannah is one of those people who will never be widely popular.
The reason is the general public doesn't appreciate real quality,
and Susannah is real quality.
　　　—Singer Joe Williams to Roy Schecter, circa 1990

"The music world," Dan DiNicola says often, "is a mean, ugly world."
And one from which, in contrast to the euphoric sense of finding her
"tribe" when she started singing in London, Susannah felt estranged.
Where did she fit in? she asked. Neither the jazz world nor the cabaret
people seemed to accept her as one of them, she felt, though she did
have friends in both. After several years of working diligently to get
Susannah into good jazz clubs, DiNicola had met with limited success.
Concerts weren't easy to secure, and after the mixed reception of her
"Silver Screen" program, the most congenial setting with the most
appreciative fans was, she found, the elegant rooms of upscale hotels,
such as the Fairmont in Chicago and the Plush Room in San Francisco.
She still tried to get bookings in jazz clubs, too, but she wanted the
name clubs, like Yoshi's in Oakland, Fat Tuesday's in New York. No
longer was Susannah just a "girl who just wants to sing my little
songs," as she had described herself in the past. "I think later on she felt
she had to be more show business," says Amos Korn, where she'd cut
her Jersey jazz club teeth. "Now she'd come with three different
gowns for the sets, and she'd have problems with the sound system—
feedback—because she'd insist on being in front of the speakers to
move around and be more choreographed." Concurs Chris Ellis,
"Early on, she wasn't so self-conscious about everything in a song having to relate to her, but later, everything had to have a meaning; everything was very, very serious." Yet she was perfect in a performance in

1990, well served by the smooth, tradition-minded Jim Cullum Jazz Band, relaxed and vibrant in a medley of Hoagy Carmichael numbers, "Hooray for Hoagy," and another called "Hollywood Jazz: Music from the Movies," featuring Academy Award losers that became great standards.

And she set her sights on one hotel room in particular. By the late 1980s, the prize venue in Manhattan for jazz singers who sang standards was a particular cramped and dowdy room: the Oak Room at the Algonquin. The Algonquin Hotel, smack in the middle of New York, is a place rich with literary and theatrical ghosts: Round Table regulars like Robert Benchley and Dorothy Parker, guests like Eudora Welty and Noel Coward (who always stayed in "their" rooms), characters like *New Yorker* editor William Shawn ordering Cheerios for dinner and the great comedic filmmaker Preston Sturges passing to his reward while in residence. The hotel had been rescued from ruin in 1946 by oil magnate Ben Bodne, who kept the library on "their" floor of the hotel filled with first editions of New York writers. But with the advent of World War II, the Oak Room—then a flourishing cabaret shoehorned next to the busy, noisy Blue Bar—was closed down. It had remained dark until 1981.

Another character—and cabaret is all about characters—had successfully hounded—his word—the hotel to reinstate evening entertainment. "In the thirties, the Oak Room always had entertainment," recalls Donald Smith, a publicist and great friend of Mabel Mercer. "That lasted until 1942, and then it had a flourishing pre-theater dinner, but by 8:30 P.M., it was closed up, chairs on the tables. The Blue Bar off the lobby in the Algonquin had the longest cocktail party in New York City, and they thought the Oak Room would affect business there." To the tiny stage with its postage stamp platform and badly in need of a facelift, Smith brought in Steve Ross, pure cabaret gold. He was a great success, as were Michael Feinstein and Andrea Marcovicci later, and made the Oak Room a great asset for the hotel, through subsequent changes in ownership, management, and behind-the-scenes drama. Smith became known as "the man who saved cabaret." But more jazz-oriented singers also had important starts there: Diana Krall, Harry Connick Jr., John Pizzarelli.

Susannah and DiNicola thought she would be a perfect fit at the club, with one foot planted in jazz stylings and backing, and the other in the American songbook—cabaret's bible. But DiNicola was repeatedly rebuffed by management. Finally, in 1989, after then-manager Anthony Nuttle and his staff listened to one of her CDs, they agreed to hire Susannah—says Arthur Pomposello, then maître d' of the Algonquin's Rose Room dining room, but soon to be promoted to manager and booking agent of the Oak Room. It was he who convinced Nuttle to hire Susannah. It was a spectacularly good booking, encompassing the entire holiday season, from November 27, 1989, to January 5, 1990. While Susannah meticulously planned her show, calling it "Men, Women, and That Old Devil Called Love," with pianist Lee Musiker and bassist Dick Sarpola (Musiker left in late December and Ben Aronov came in to replace him), DiNicola worked tirelessly with the expensive publicist he'd persuaded a reluctant Susannah to hire. Says DiNicola, "I went to every concierge at every important hotel and said we'd comp them if they let their guests know about her."

At the dress rehearsal of the show before opening night, DiNicola and Arthur Pomposello sat in the back taking notes. "She didn't like suggestions from others," DiNicola says, "but after some changes—shorter intros to the songs, omitting some songs, having the piano play behind her while she talked, which she wasn't used to—the show was great." Agrees Roy Schecter, who saw Susannah perform dozens of times from the early eighties on, "It was one of her best shows—the concept of the show was very strong and well integrated."

But was it jazz, or was it cabaret? To write up the show, the *Times* did not send jazz critic John S. Wilson, who'd been writing about Susannah since the seventies, but its cabaret reviewer, Stephen Holden. In one fell swoop, "the paper of record" shifted Susannah from her roots—the African American vocal aesthetic of Billie Holiday, Ethel Waters, and Bessie Smith, her first singing role models—to being compared with theatrically trained vocalists such as Karen Akers (with her "cultivated chic and heartfelt expression," wrote Holden) and Andrea Marcovicci ("breathless fervor" and "immense charm"). DiNicola would always maintain that Holden gave Susannah's debut at the Oak Room a mixed review because "he didn't get Susannah, like many other people who run the cabaret world." Another who didn't "get" Susannah as a singer was Donald Smith, who hadn't favored her Algonquin booking in the first place. "It was always pleasant with Susannah, but I felt she wasn't comfortable in the cabaret setting. She didn't make eye contact; she was distant. She sang beautifully, her repertoire was interesting, but in cabaret, the emotional connection has to be intimate.

Cabaret is revelatory—a very revealing process." And this was a chronic complaint about Susannah, even when she was at the top of her form in the nineties. Explains Andy Lipman, "Susannah didn't seduce an audience. She made them come to her on her terms. She had her standards and wouldn't change them." James Gavin sums up the broader issue: "Susannah's way of singing—and she's not the only one—is unfortunately perceived as a no-man's land by a lot of people. The jazz clubs will think you're cabaret; the cabaret people will think you're too 'jazz' for them to handle." "Susannah," DiNicola concludes, "fell through the cracks."

She would always struggle with her place in the world of cabaret, the world the Oak Room had rapidly come to rule during the last part of the 20th century. Disdaining cabaret singing as "precious" while continuing to laud what she called the "lack of pretension" that she loved about jazz, Susannah tried to define—and defend—what she felt made her a jazz singer, telling Leonard Feather in an interview, "I like a performance based on an inner intensity instead of an overblown, obviously theatrical kind of presentation."[1] Paradoxically, in her quest for a heartfelt performance, she relied ever more on a script—every note worked out, the talk between numbers memorized. If it made for a smooth performance, it was also an approach that, many musicians felt, sacrificed the jazz aesthetic of flexibility and surprise. Says Tim Horner, Susannah's favorite drummer from the mid-nineties on, "I've worked with many jazz singers—Helen Merrill, Carol Sloane, Ernestine Anderson, Mark Murphy, Joe Williams. They allowed for variation, for musicians to do something on a tune. Susannah I saw as a cabaret artist. You had to do the show the same way every time: *Nothing* was improvised, and if one thing was out of place on her arrangements, she knew it. She was very nice and respectful. But I never had a conversation with her about musical things." Unless she was thwarted, felt threatened or undermined or upstaged (as with Ingham and Musiker, Hank Jones, and Carol Sloane, to name several), Susannah was pleasant if businesslike with her peers. She did not sit around talking about music, except when working with a collaborator, her pianist usually, but also with musician-arrangers like Rich DeRosa. However, Susannah did not read music and did not behave as one of a group of musicians.

But as she grew as a cabaret-based performer, some of the musicians who accompanied Susannah during those later years seemed to understand her drive for perfection and were sympathetic to it. Says bassist Steve Gilmore, "She was very, very good at what she did. She picked such good material, and her soul was connected to it. I really enjoy being extremely professional, so I didn't feel constricted. She wanted things exactly right, and I did that." Adds DeRosa, "With her, you're going for the art—you know, like Miles Davis versus Doc Severinsen."

Despite the divisions and reservations of critics or players, Susannah went over very well with Oak Room audiences, which was the most important thing, of course. If she was less adventurous as a singer within the cabaret context, the benefit for Susannah was that when all the externals were right—a good audience, functioning sound system, backup players—she was, in her words, "transported. I nearly always have an out of body experience." Especially, she admitted, "on the sad songs."[2] Holden's observation that Susannah was "far from the most charismatic or relaxed singer" around was countered by his praise for her excellent taste, her wit, and her intelligence. Attendance, which had been slow at the start, picked up. "Susannah was a phenomenal success; it was her happiest time," DiNicola recalls. "She was on commission, and she made some really good money. And then there was a separate fee for a New Year's Eve show." The Algonquin booked her for the following post-Thanksgiving through New Year's of 1990–91; *Life* magazine featured her as one of the best younger singers of classic American popular song (others included Maureen McGovern, Andrea Marcovicci, Karen Akers, Cassandra Wilson, and Michael Feinstein). Everything was looking up.

Susannah's new show for 1990–91 carried one of her unwieldy titles: "The Politically Correct Chanteuse: Time Capsule Songs for Women by Men." This was an idea, says Lisa Dawn Popa, who for years sold CDs for artists at the Algonquin during intermissions and who was a sympathetic ear for Susannah, that was suggested during a conversation she had with Andrea Marcovicci. Susannah had serious fun parsing some old song lyrics for sexist content. She'd refused to sing certain songs in the eighties, on the "my man beats me, treats me awful mean" theme that Billie Holiday had famously, and plaintively, sung, and she'd cut out songs mentioning smoking from her repertoire (like "Two Sleepy People," with its line, "Here we are, out of cigarettes"). But she'd become restless, declaring in the nineties, "As the whole politically correct thing mushroomed, there was more and more [song material] that had to be left out." She even decided to sing "Billie's Blues" again—

"because it's a beautiful song," she explained. "I got some boos. But that is the song and women do still allow themselves to be beaten today and so I decided I'll try to understand this point of view, this having a great undying love."[3] For her 1990–91 holiday show at the Oak Room, she chose not only classic women-as-victims-of-love songs, but amusingly outdated songs, like the obscure Betty Crockerish romp "When I'm Housekeeping for You." Reviewers of "Politically Correct" were positive if not enthusiastic. In the *Times,* Holden, warmer now, assessed Susannah astutely: "She has the jazz phrasing of Billie Holiday, refined carefully into a pop style." She had problems with pitch, he added— and there was her presentation, gawky and uncomfortable. (A National Public Radio critic was a bit more cruel: Susannah, she said, looked the part of "a schoolteacher, updated, with spaniel-like brown hair.")[4] There was fretting among the musicians, too. Bassist Sean Smith recalls how he and her new pianist, Ben Aronov, chafed at the nightly post-show meetings Susannah insisted on holding, with notes of everything that had gone wrong. "That was draining," Smith says.

There were unqualified successes. Susannah did a ravishing voice-over for a television program called *Letters From the Heart,* produced by DiNicola, featuring letters from wives and lovers to servicemen in World War II and sang a shimmering "I'll Be Seeing You." "That was another happy time," says DiNicola.[5]

But happy times did not, as usual, last long for Susannah. "Susannah was such a success," DiNicola says, "that Andrea Marcovicci, a singer connected to the monied Park Avenue world—her father was a prominent physician—decided she wanted that time period from then on. Susannah lost out." Not so, says Marcovicci. "I would never take another singer's time slot." Rather, she says, it was Arthur Pomposello who proposed the schedule change. Not without a fight. DiNicola and Pomposello thrashed it out. "He was pompous," DiNicola declares, "and if he knew you had a weakness, he'd exploit it. Susannah didn't have the leverage, and he knew it." Pomposello sees it differently: "Andrea Marcovicci was our strongest draw. Always, regardless of anything, no matter if there was a blizzard, or what time of year."

Pomposello gave Susannah a post–Labor Day gig, from mid-September to October, in 1991 and again in 1992, when she was paired with the legendary Julie Wilson and Maureen McGovern on the cover of *New York* magazine. But soon after, "deeply humiliated and reduced to tears" after a loud stag party at the Blue Bar next door drowned her out while Tony Bennett and his guests were in the audience, she stormed out of the Oak Room, vowing not to return. (Four years later, in 1996, emphasizes Pomposello, "she was thrilled to be back." She would continue to play the Oak Room for the rest of her career, for a total of twelve stints.)

Respect and money. So much had to do with one or the other. An Oak Room is not, at base, that different from a Pizza Express in one respect: It is a place that sells food and liquor. Early fall and later, early summer, "was not the best time to play the Oak Room," DiNicola points out. "Pomposello would increase the minimum [that is, the number of chairs that needed to be filled] giving Susannah a percentage of the house." Unsurprisingly, Pomposello disputes this. But one thing is clear: The Oak Room was the top of the heap—both performer and place added luster to each other. And for a singer, playing there could be parlayed into other things—publicity, better draws, more money record sales, concerts—and there were few of the big elegant venues left, neither the downtown clubs that had thrived through the eighties nor the venerable rooms like the Empire Room at the Waldorf-Astoria. So the Oak Room was the queen of cabaret in New York, as Susannah was to discover when she left it.

Susannah cut her second album for Concord in February 1990, with the rather obscure title *Sabia* (though *sabia* is a noun meaning "songbird" in Portuguese, it is far more commonly known as a past-tense form of the verb *to know* in both Portuguese and Spanish). The album is full of beautiful songs. For years, she had longed to do a "foreign" album of her beloved Brazilian numbers—especially the loose, relaxed, and slightly flattened approach of João Gilberto, a singer with whom she'd fallen in love in the early seventies, along with Billie Holiday and thirties swing. Also hovering around *Sabia* is the ghost of another singer, the Brazilian Elis Regina, who had died of an accidental cocaine and alcohol overdose in 1982, at 36. Regina's singing and aura had been another magnet for Susannah.

Brazilian songs have been *de rigeur* for most American jazz-based singers, but none of Susannah's contemporaries studied the sounds and spaces around the music with more sympathy than she (her slight American and noticeable Italian tinge did not detract). "I'm not totally fluent," she said, adding amusingly, "I feel I could easily have a love affair in Portuguese but I couldn't buy a postage stamp." She even performed a slyly exuberant version of Sondheim's this edge-of-camp bossa nova parody, "The Boy From . . ."

But *Sabia* was far more than a group of songs sung in foreign languages. It was a long project that engaged her skills as a translator and writer as much as a singer (she fashioned English lyrics to more than half of the eleven songs on *Sabia* (eight were on the cassette, three more were added to the CD). It was a long-held dream of Susannah's to write her own words to the Brazilian songs she'd fallen in love with as a fledgling vocalist in Rome. And she greatly disliked most of the English translations extant, especially of Antonio Carlos Jobim's melodies, complaining that the English versions were banal, Tin Pan Alley lyrics. To her that kind of approach was "criminal," great songs set to hack work by American lyricists looking to make a fast buck. She didn't name names, though jazz writer Gene Lees, who penned some fine lyrics in English to Jobim songs, did. In album notes to a Jobim CD reissue, the lyricist Norman Gimbel had reduced the opening line in "The Girl From Ipanema" from five to three notes. In Lees' opinion, this "completely destroyed the swing."[6]

Though she tried to stick to the original ideas expressed in Portuguese as much as possible, this was often hard to do. "P'ra Machucar Meu Coraçao" (by Ary Barroso) literally means "to bruise or crush my heart." In Susannah's English translation, titled "The Day We Said Goodbye," she decided to find a way instead to convey a corresponding sense of the loss. For Jobim's "A Felicidade," or "Happiness," she wanted people to understand that it was really, ironically, about sadness. Her new lyric to his "Vivo Sonhando" was also wistful: She called it "Living on Dreams." One of her most successful poetic turns came with Luis Bonfa's well-known "Manha de Carnaval," the principal song from the film *Black Orpheus*. Originally translated by a small battalion of lyricists into "A Day in the Life of a Fool," Susannah treated "Manha de Carnaval" as an impressionist picture of sadness she titled "Sunrise": "Lavender, rose and gold, the colors of dawn unfold / sweet moment you long to hold / as it passes by."

The paperwork alone of finding and writing for permissions from publishers and composers, including from Jobim himself, was a large task. Though Susannah assured Carl Jefferson that the agreements needed from the Brazilian songwriters were as good as done, Concord was still waiting for the documents after the recording had been made—and could not be released until they were in hand. When Jefferson blew up, furious at the thought of having to record much of the album again in Portuguese (though Susannah had recorded several alternate "takes" of songs in the original Portuguese), she called everybody she knew in the business, pleading and begging for the rights. And she got them, to all but two of her new English versions—luckily, she'd also recorded an all-Portuguese version of each, then included in the album. She chose an Italian song as well, the beautiful ballad "Estate," which she'd heard sung by João Gilberto while living in Rome; Susannah reworked it as "Summer," with new verses in both English and Italian.

For the album, Susannah had outstanding musical support. Lee Musiker's crisply adventurous obbligatos, Emily Remler's fluid guitar, and an excellent rhythm section, including a Brazilian drummer and percussionist, added spice to otherwise largely wistful, dreamy song stylings. She'd envisioned a soft, sexy Stan Getz–ish sax sound behind her. "She wanted Scott Hamilton, but Jeff [Carl Jefferson] wanted Scott to be Rosie Clooney's player," recalls Allen Farnham. "Jeff wanted Ken Peplowski with Susannah. But there was still the problem of chemistry; it wasn't right. Susannah asked me how to talk to Carl about getting Scott; she was so skillful with language but would agonize over how to approach him. And he was a hard-headed businessman, and he'd complain about Susannah's demands, the expense. I gave her a script of what to say, and Carl finally let Scott play on the album. It was a one-shot deal, but afterward, Jefferson loved the record. His mother was Portuguese, he said, and used to sing to him in the language."

If it was an album she could be pleased with, there was loss connected with it later that year. Tragically, Emily Remler, a heroin addict, died at just 32. And it was shortly after that Musiker, Susannah's musical director as well as her piano player, quit over money. "A complicated issue," comments Farnham, her later accompanist, who managed to work it out with her. If Susannah was making thousands a week at various gigs, she had thousands in expenses as well. "Musicians ask for more money when they play with a singer than with a group," he explains. "In turn, the singer might overpay the musicians by overestimating her take and end up with little for herself." This was often the case with Susannah, for although DiNicola performed many duties of a manager, she was very often in charge of working out the details, including paying accompanists. "It took her awhile to come up with a formula that was fair and would work," notes Farnham. "And Susannah hated being ripped off."

After Musiker departed, Ben Aronov worked with her for a couple of years. But on her next recording for Concord in September 1991, the luminous *I'll Take Romance,* Jefferson paired her with legendary pianist Hank Jones, who had accompanied many vocalists, including a stint with Ella Fitzgerald in the early fifties. Jefferson had assigned guitarist Howard Alden as musical director of the date, and Frank Wess was on hand with his strong, soulful saxophone. For this date, Jefferson, DiNicola, and Farnham were all in the studio. Farnham had moved back to New York from California, to pursue a career as a pianist, but was still working part-time for Concord. Susannah, says Farnham, "laid down *I'll Take Romance* with Jones. But Susannah didn't like the way he was playing behind her." Recalls DiNicola, "She said something like, 'Can I not have so much [piano playing] there, and I want this here.' She wasn't going to be intimidated. She respected him, but she had her charts and she knew what she wanted."

So did Jones. When they broke for lunch, he took Jefferson aside. "He said, 'I'm leaving now; I'm not coming back.' Carl was furious at Susannah and chided her. And now there was no pianist. Susannah turned to the obvious choice in the control booth: Farnham. "And wasn't she lucky?" points out Richard Rodney Bennett. Farnham was able to distance himself from Susannah's demands and was eager to work with her. He provided her with strong, steady pianistic support from then on, including the kind of arrangements she felt most comfortable with. But he was aware of the prickliness. "You don't talk that way to Hank Jones," he recalls. "She *dissed* him. And she drove some other pianists crazy. They'd want to do their own thing. She'd remind them not to overplay, so she would be front and center, showcasing the lyrics."

The arrangements were minimal, some done by Ingham years before, several by Musiker, one by Ben Aronov, and the rest done on the spot. "So I just jumped in," recalls Farnham. All went well—until the end of the session. "We're doing a piano-and-vocal duet," he says, "a tune called 'Where Do You Start.' She's in the booth and I'm in the studio, so I can't see her. On the master, you can hear Susannah start to cry, then she's sobbing—losing control. In the engineer booth, Carl is saying, 'What's going on?' Dan rushes in, and Susannah, sobbing, explains, 'I thought of my best friend going through a divorce, and I was her on the tune.' That never happened again," Farnham adds, "though on the tearjerker ballad at the Algonquin [usually 'The Waters of March'], she would summon up the emotion and always take out her handkerchief after and wipe her eyes. If it was acting, it was Method acting. But at the record date, she was really crying."

On the resulting album, which includes the title cut with piano by Hank Jones, after Jefferson swore everybody to secrecy on the date ("Jones wouldn't have known or cared," Farnham says), there is no hint of the turmoil behind the scenes. And Susannah had found her favorite accompanist. From then on, she recorded only with Farnham, although she performed with other pianists. Bill Mays, many felt, was a wonderful complement to her, and, says Rex Reed, she would have loved to work with Alan Broadbent, who'd recorded so marvelously with the late singer Irene Kral, one of Susannah's favorites.

As a musical partner, Farnham was a boon, providing what Susannah both wanted and needed. He had jazz in his soul and flashes of brilliance and wit, but no shocks; he was steady and dependable and discreet, concentrating on the music at hand. "In concert, she used to go for the flashy opener and at first, they were too fast. We used to call them 'tempo ridiculoso,'" remembers Farnham. "But it evolved into more variety of tempi, the opener, then an easier second tune, an easy ballad, and a real tearjerker ballad later and a trio feature. This kind of program is very standard with singers. But in the ten years Susannah and I were together, things got better. She really knew later how to grab her audience."

It is a mark of Susannah's highly disciplined, divided self that although she partnered with this perceptive and sensitive man as much as with any other person, Farnham knew little about her constant inner turbulence. Susannah had made her music, and all of its attendant business, her world apart, her refuge; he was her musical arranger, director, and pianist—it was as simple, and as complex, as that. She worked well with him, and often happily, on the shows for the Algonquin. Farnham first worked with her on *Autumn in New York* in September–October 1991; thereafter, he and Susannah met to look at the music together, after she had selected the material she wanted on the basis of lyrics that fit her theme. "She got an electric piano in her apartment to transpose on, and that was great. I'd take the basic tune and change harmonies, and she'd tell me if she didn't like it. I'd do the arrangements while she'd cook or clean or whatever, then we'd go over them. She paid me by the hour for the arrangements. If she thought a musician was fair with her, she'd be fair. I didn't haggle; that's why we worked well." "But," he adds, "she never upped the money."

Susannah's bad fairy really bore down on her during a trip to Japan in the fall of 1991. At first, it seemed to be a terrific break for her when

Carl Jefferson booked her on the Concord-Fujitsu Jazz Festival. This was a yearly event that he'd successfully coordinated with the computer company in Japan. But from the beginning, everything seemed to go wrong. Booked for October 27–November 11, Susannah was loath to lose a booking she'd made in Myrtle Beach on October 26. "But they're a day *behind* us in Japan," Farnham drily observes. Having arrived in Tokyo right behind the wire, Susannah found that the Japanese promoters were accustomed to scat singers like Carol Sloane and Ernestine Anderson who were willing and able to sit in with whatever band of all-stars was on the bill. They did not understand that she was different. She had Farnham as anchor on piano, but was expected to sit in with the Scott Hamilton Group. "But then, she fights for her own slot with her own musicians," Farnham recalls, "and so now, it's thirty minutes before the set and she's scrambling for musicians! Barney Kessell doesn't want his drummer, Chuck Redd, who she's used to, playing with anyone else. That's completely reasonable and customary. Then she asks Akira Tana, but it's extra work and he wants to get paid for it. And she can't find a bass player. So now Susannah is in the dressing room, and she's turned out all the lights. At last, Carl Jefferson says he'll pay Akira Tana, and she gets a bass player and she goes on. All this for only two songs a night!" Then there is the reaction of the Japanese jazz fans. Farnham, who has lived in Japan, speaks Japanese, and has a Japanese wife, explains, "It was a fiasco. It's a racial thing: Black is the real thing with them. The Japanese didn't recognize her. I get that too when I go there." On this point, Susannah's stepdaughter Anne agrees. This was a further nudge to Susannah's deep insecurity as a jazz performer, which some might cast in terms of race, others in terms of chops, still others in terms of sensibility or aesthetics. For sure, Susannah did not forget that Japanese jazz audiences tended to prefer soulful singers trading choruses with the band to her sculpted delivery.

Surprisingly, given the pile of negatives, Susannah in performance was anything but a fiasco, as a videotape makes clear. Her up-tempo "Lady Is a Tramp" and the Mercer ballad "P.S., I Love You" are beautiful, serene-seeming, accomplished renditions. After the concert, she visited with Anne at a hot spring where a Japanese woman played the traditional stringed instrument called the *shamisen.* There, relaxed and happy, Susannah talked about how attentive she found the Japanese audiences. Neither Anne nor Farnham was about to tell her that Japanese audiences are always attentive, regardless of their feelings about a performer. "But," adds Anne, echoing Farnham, "the promoters in Japan resisted having her back. To them, I think jazz was only men and black women."

Though they lived together as man and wife, Susannah and DiNicola had not formalized the relationship and continued to waffle about getting married. As part of the couples counseling they went to before their wedding in August 1991, Susannah shared with DiNicola a revealing "wish list" for their future. She wanted "to be valued as an artist by my peers and the widest possible audience I can reach" and "to earn enough from my work to live comfortably and not be afraid of being poor in the future." Fair enough and nothing extraordinary there. But she was concerned about DiNicola's obsessive nature, she continued, and above all, she was afraid about herself: "I'd like not to be afraid of getting cancer again, of becoming a compulsive eater and getting fat again, of losing my mind and wanting to die again."

She also expressed reservations about her relationship with Dan. And it was understandable that both looked at a third marriage with trepidation. Still, says DiNicola, "We loved each other too much to split up." "I'll probably dress up and Dan will probably wear blue jeans" (he wore a jacket and tie), Susannah joked about their wedding on August 11, 1991. They hosted a reception the next day at the Adelphi Hotel in Saratoga Springs, for a small number of friends and family, followed later in the month by another reception in a New York hotel, at which Susannah asked singers Carol Fredette and Bob Dorough to sing. Mimi and Tom flew in from California for the wedding. At the reception in Saratoga Springs, Thea Lurie was excited to finally get to meet Susannah's father. But Tom was a mere husk of himself by then. "He said nothing, there was nothing—no reactions, not even a brief toast to Susannah and Dan. He seemed emotionally shut off," Lurie recalls. It must have taken a great effort of will for him to get on the plane and fly cross-country and have to deal with loud New York and all these strangers. "I'm sorry things are so hard for you now," Susannah wrote to him later that year, after receiving a bleak letter.

And though they were married, Susannah now lived in her Manhattan apartment, visiting Schenectady occasionally, having told DiNicola after her treatments for the cancer were completed in 1990 that she associated Schenectady with getting cancer and couldn't live there half-time anymore. Both traveled a lot for their work. "I have a commuter marriage," Susannah used to say. "I have a fragmented life." "She would come to Schenectady for long weekends during the summer, when it was too hot in New York. But she wouldn't arrive until late Friday night," DiNicola says. "She would do a bit of writing, she worked on her music, or just lie around with her cat. Or she'd go off and visit friends she'd met through me—Bryan Nielson, Marion Roach Smith the writer, the Barretts—he was a sculptor. And often I had to leave on Monday on a trip, which didn't leave much time together. So there was great strain sometimes for me as a husband as well as a manager. I loved her, and I believed in her art and her integrity as a musician. I tried to be objective, to separate my feelings from her art."

Some New York friends saw things differently. "He didn't like to share her with the world," says one. "In New York, he'd call her every fifteen minutes. Susannah was sympathetic with his insecurity; she didn't complain about him. But it seemed Dan was jealous of her career. And I don't think he liked her to be recognized more than he was—he wanted the canary in the cage." Not so, says another mutual friend, Christine MacDonald. "The sticking point was that they were not living together continuously," she says. "Why couldn't they have found a place midway between Schenectady and New York? But Susannah had her support system in New York, and in Schenectady, Dan was a star—more people know him around there than her."

The Susannah who could be prickly and *All About Eve*–ish often showed her tender, caring side with the man who was arguably her biggest love. "She did do thoughtful things for me," says DiNicola, who was able to show his vulnerability with Susannah. "She bought me a Raggedy Andy doll; I'd lost mine when I was a boy. And she encouraged me in my writing and my work. But often she wasn't there, as for my 50th birthday. And then, when I had walking pneumonia, she called, but she didn't come, though I was sick. On the other hand, when Rex Reed got sick, she was all solicitous and took him soup. It wasn't that I was angry or resentful of her New York life—it was more I was sad." When Susannah's New York friends visited the Schenectady house on rare occasions, the tension between the partners was thick. Susannah's friend Ellen Bollinger, also newly married, paid a visit in the mid-nineties. "I thought the house was cold, the couple unaffectionate," she remembers. Agrees Christine MacDonald, "It was very clear that she and Dan were having trouble. Neither," she adds, "wanted to compromise about moving."

Then, a bombshell not long after they married: Susannah discovered she was pregnant. She called to tell DiNicola, but she was not, she felt, delivering good news: She was 46 years old and deeply worried about the cancer recurring as a result of having a baby. As a former Catholic, DiNicola didn't like the idea of abortion but said he'd support that option if her health were endangered. Susannah, who knew she could always depend on her closest friend, called Thea Lurie for help. Lurie dutifully accompanied Susannah on doctor visits. Some thought the hormonal changes of pregnancy could trigger a recurrence of the cancer; others did not. "Within a week, she'd made up her mind," DiNicola says. "She wanted to do it alone, by herself, and she did. This hurt me hugely—I wanted a say in it." Adds Lurie, "Susannah was great with kids but she never wanted a child of her own. She told me from the time I knew her in her twenties that she didn't want to have a baby."

She doted on step-grandchildren and friends' kids, lighting up when she performed for children (and drawing them easily into the show). Her first step-grandchild, David, was born the following year, in March 1993. (She would have been acutely aware that his birth was close to the time when her own baby would have been born.) Jeff and Kim DiNicola's winsome, smart little boy charmed Susannah. When he won a part in his grammar school's production of *Over the Rainbow,* she was thrilled. But she loved children in small, controllable doses, as did Mae West, about whom Susannah wrote admiringly later. "I never wanted motherhood," Susannah quoted West, "because you have to think about the child and I only had time for me. I was born to be a solo performer, on and off stage."[7]

The abortion and, more to the point, the way Susannah handled the abortion left a deep wound in the marriage. But despite all the stresses and difficulties, Susannah and DiNicola still loved each other. "I'm married to a very special man and feel busy and appreciated in all that I do which is a great feeling," she wrote in the early nineties. It was still enough then.

In February 1993, it was back to the studio to record *From Bessie to Brazil.* This time Susannah pushed Carl Jefferson to let her include some contemporary tunes along with the standards. This eclecticism continued to bewilder many and divide her audience. "As always seems to happen with this tremendously gifted singer," a reviewer observed, there was "the odd, strange lapse of judgment as to the kind of song she can get away with."[8] Susannah was all over the place, the review continued, with what it called an "embarrassing 'My Sweetie Went Away,' a misplaced tribute to Bessie Smith, and a wincingly cavalier 'Still Crazy After All These Years.'" Then there was her selection of Ethel Waters's "Thief in the Night," complete with flapper-era hip black patter—"the first rap music," the liner notes coyly stated, along with a beautiful Brazilian number, the obligatory Frishberg tune, and a new and improved "People That You Never Get to Love."

For the first time, too, a number of songs feature Susannah's voice cushioned by expanded arrangements, an octet of four horns with piano, bass, guitar, and drums. Rich DeRosa prepared two of the arrangements and would work on most of her subsequent albums. "She knew what she wanted," he says, echoing Ingham and Richard Rodney Bennett. "I never saw crying or temperament, though the studio is a stressful situation. A perverse problem of jazz is that it's too much about the players, too self-indulgent. She would say to them, 'I need you to think about the storyline,' which usually meant to be more subtle. And yeah, she'd get frustrated, but at herself, not at the musicians." Adds saxophonist Dick Oatts, who recorded on several of her albums, "She didn't want anything to detract from the general message of the tune or the arrangement, and so she would forget she had these incredible musicians. The last date we did, there was a tune with lots of chord changes and a furious tempo. I had a solo and felt that it was a feat to get through it. Afterward, she said, 'Dick, do you have to play so many notes?'"

Explains DeRosa, "There would be a budget for larger orchestrations on about half the album, and often we'd build on and expand a trio arrangement that she'd use in performing. I enjoyed the assignments. Allen [Farnham] and I would split the arranging chores. He and Susannah would develop the keys and the concepts; then one of them would contact me and ask me to put a song into such-and-such a key in such-and-such a style. For vocals, you're scoring to text—which style best conveys the imagery? I do a lot of underscoring for theater music. Susannah once said she liked my thinking about the notes being subservient to the lyric and the drama. I especially like the way the arrangements I did for her on 'A Friend Like Me' [on *From Broadway to Bebop*], 'Something to Live For' [on *From Broken Hearts to Blue Skies*], 'You Do Something to Me' [on *Easy to Love*], and 'I'd Rather Lead a Band' [on *Let's Face the Music*] worked out."

It seems odd that, in the liner notes of *From Bessie to Brazil,* no mention was made of Jobim's "Aguas de Março/The Waters of March," though that would become Susannah's signature song. No other song so completely allowed Susannah room to express her feelings. "She would mesmerize audiences with it," DiNicola recalls, "and when she finished she would hear a deafening silence and then incredible applause—it was the only song she had to encore." With its flowing bossa beat, "Aguas" has the rhythm of the road built into it, the plodding of the long journey of life. With its haiku-like verses, the song is layered and enigmatic, like an impressionist painting. Characteristically Jobim, it is a powerful meditation fashioned from a few notes, a study in contrasts, whimsical, earthy, mysterious, and also hinting at times of harshness, of violence. Susannah would surely have heard this song, written in 1972, the year that she decided to pursue a professional singing career, and recorded by the composer on *Jobim* and, especially, on the near-perfect *Elis and Tom,* on which Jobim and Elis Regina approach the lyric playfully to a humming and cheerful rhythmic background, almost as if languidly throwing a ball back and forth in a kind of existential singing game.

There is a whole literary subtext to "Aguas de Março" too, one that Susannah loved, a kind of transformation of the everyday, ordinary happenings that Jobim described around him while on his ranch in the *campina,* the dry backlands, during a stay at the end of the rainy season. With the end of the March rains comes the mud, and new green life. But there are oblique references in the song to death and violence as well. Brazilians, DiNicola says, told Susannah that the song also referred to the murder of an acquaintance of Jobim's; perhaps it was also linked to the score he was writing for *Chronicle of the Murdered House* (in English), a movie adapted from a Brazilian novel by Lucio Cardoso about the corruption and violent decline of the old feudal Brazil.

There are really two "Aguas de Marços," the first in Portuguese and the second, dictionary in hand, by Jobim in English, 18 verses where he set himself the challenge of avoiding the "Latinate" vocabulary upon which his native language is built. Susannah had long relished the idea of providing a newly edited English translation, and Dan remembers her polishing both Jobim's and her own new verses on a train in Japan in 1989 as they traveled to visit Anne, along with the other lyrics that appeared before "Aguas" on *Sabia.* Though Susannah, recalls Anne, was quite pleased about her revamped English lyric and received permission to record it after she contacted Jobim's lawyer, after the composer died in 1994, his estate, stung by other banal translations, barred any new English versions of his songs. Though Susannah's excellent translation of his "Caminos Cruzados," which she titled "faint Music," was heard in concert, she was never allowed to record what she called "the best love song ever written for people over forty."

All the more happily, then, that her version of "The Waters of March" was recorded. If it was part of Jobim's genius to fashion Portuguese poetry out of the everyday—"A stick, a stone / It's the end of the road / It's the rest of a stump / It's a little alone"—Susannah's gift was not only a subtle substitution for a number of awkward word choices. Her version—"A stick, a stone / It's the end of the road / It's feeling alone / It's the weight of your load"—even more importantly heightened the contrasts of emotional shifts projected by physical descriptions. The song tells a primordial story, and for Susannah (as quite probably for Jobim), the emergence of the earth from winter to spring signaled the lifting of depression. For her, the beauty of "all the tiny things" that Jobim had made note of in his song (a list that she tweaked) was a homecoming of the self, a rebirth of the human spirit. As for Susannah, she was coming out of a very difficult, dark period, her own winter into spring during the time she focused on "The Waters of March." Indeed, she was recovering from not only her breast cancer, but her visceral reaction to the fact that she had cancer. The intensity of her fear was coupled or intertwined with the disease she lived with, the bipolar condition of her biochemistry that fed the great downs and the soaring ups. She was, in this song more than any other, singing pure autobiography. "We don't talk about death, about killing ourselves, in a pop song, but the Brazilians do," she noted.[9] And how much "The Waters of March" was a soul-searching lament about the bondage of self as well as a celebration of freedom from psychic bonds, became clear only after her suicide. "What an irony that the song meant an affirmation of life to her," says Dan.

Susannah introduced "The Waters of March" in performance in the spring of 1993, shortly after making her new recording. Her new show had a typically unwieldy title: "From Bessie to Brazil: 60 Years of Great Songs, Songs of Survival and Hope." Rather than at the Algonquin's Oak Room, it was presented at Tavern on the Green, a large and popular restaurant at the edge of Central Park; she'd accepted an offer there after the loud stag-party fiasco at the Oak Room, but she was again bedeviled by tough externals at the Tavern—as were others who sang there. "It was a really terrible room to sing in," says Roy Schecter, who was, as always, in attendance, "large and noisy and surrounded by topiary." Farnham emphasizes, "The room was really a restaurant with entertainment just added. That's a crucial distinction. There was a nine-foot Steinway grand piano in the middle of the stage—where Susannah would normally be standing. But they wouldn't move it. And there was a bad sound system, which they didn't fix. And they wouldn't tell the people to be quiet, so Susannah did. The booker said that because Susannah complained so much, they didn't want her back." Farnham adds that Susannah did return a couple of years later to Tavern for a smoother run. But clearly, it was not a superior alternative to the Oak Room.

Rainbow and Stars was another of the precious few top cabaret venues in Manhattan, where she appeared in March 1994, after a successful pairing with Jonathan Schwartz two years before. But if Susannah hoped that it would turn into a lucrative steady engagement, she miscalculated on several counts. First, her program's very breadth could be confusing, even if she was, as Rex Reed proclaimed, a "great singer whose artistry has no parameters." After a jazzy "Don't Fence Me In" and "Is It an Earthquake?" she offered "One of the Good Guys" ("Girls" in her case), an unhummable new song by David Shire and Richard Maltby Jr., Randy Newman's "You Ain't Never Had a Friend Like Me" from the movie *Aladdin,* the forgettable "He Loves Me," and a thirties medley, including a verse from the first song that Susannah had heard Billie Holiday sing, "I Gotta Right to Sing the Blues," followed by Bessie Smith's "I Got What It Takes" and, finally, a flat Louis Armstrong imitation of his "Everything's Been Done Before." Where were all the beautiful ballads?

She also reinforced the reputation she'd developed as demanding and difficult, known for hushing patrons and for complaining publicly about bad lighting, sound systems, and so on. "Management was left reeling," James Gavin says the room's publicist, David Lotz, told him. "She left the stage because something was wrong with the lighting on stage, saying, 'When they fix it, I'll come back.' People *cringed.*" But Susannah felt she was simply asking for her due. Says Oak Room manager Arthur Pomposello (Susannah returned there the following year), "Susannah was the most difficult artist I ever dealt with—such a perfectionist and a touch of the neurotic. Everything was so finely tuned." Others she worked with concurred. Photographer David Lubarsky, who frequently produced covers for Concord and shot portraits of CEOs, met a tense and untrusting Susannah when he worked on her Gershwin album. Echoing Pomposello's complaints, Lubarsky says, "Of the thousands of persons I've photographed, she was the most difficult. I can usually disarm a subject." Still, the resulting cover, Susannah in profile at a gauzy lace-curtained window, was lovely. When she did establish rapport with a photographer, the prickliness and demands dissolved. Photographer Carlos Spaventa found her easy to deal with. "She approached me, after I met her at one of her shows." Spaventa, a jazz fan and a photographer, was stunned when she requested that he shoot her next cover. "I specialize in Paris and the French countryside, not portraits of people. But we both enjoyed the photo sessions we did." Spaventa was to shoot five album covers in all.

If managers were "left reeling" by Susannah's behavior at Rainbow and Stars, she didn't know about it—or simply ignored it. She told an interviewer not long afterward how the club "loved her and wanted her back."[10] But her nerves remained paper-thin. Many of her friends recall incidents in which she interrupted shows with a complaint. In June 1997, remembers Christine MacDonald, who'd traveled downstate for her show at the Oak Room, "She stopped the music. Either the temperature wasn't right or it was the lights, and she said it wasn't fair to the audience." Agrees her friend, entertainer Mark Nadler: "As long as the room was quiet during her show, she wouldn't care if anybody in the place bought a drink." The bartenders and waiters might remind her that they were only doing their job, but for Susannah, the right atmosphere was essential. "When the audience is quiet and realizes they are part of the show," she reasoned, "they become part of it." Says bassist Steve Gilmore, "We called her 'the whiner' after a bit on *Saturday Night Live*. She complained about little things. And the sound and lighting checks! You'd arrive somewhere all tired, and the band would be kept at the place forever, going over every single thing." Hating road food, she brought her own or else stocked up at a nearby health-food store. Sometimes she'd refuse to stay in the lodgings provided. Her stepson Roy recalls that when she was booked to play near his hometown of Boston, she called him begging him to find her another place.

Her drive for perfection brought results, of course. Susannah never permitted herself to be good enough; she always drove for the best possible performance, sound, look. Photo shoots were hugely fraught—she prepared for them, she confided in one photographer, "as much as I prepare for a recording." Candid shots of herself, even old family photos she came across, "she'd tear up instantly if she didn't like them," DiNicola says. By 1994, the flattering, gamine-glamorous look that many came to associate with Susannah had evolved. The close-cropped haircut and careful makeup, the long-practiced-to-perfection sunshine public persona, the model-chic thinness achieved by a permanent diet of steamed vegetables, whole grains, and vigorous exercise, the glittering gowns. For her 1994 appearance at Rainbow and Stars, Susannah wore sleeveless black velvet with a plunging neckline and black gloves halfway up her arms, heavy black jewelry and thick, perfectly applied makeup. At 48, she was finally a femme fatale, ready for the prom.

Then there was the contract she worked up in later years. Many stars are famous—infamous—for their demands and stipulations. A Peggy Lee or a Mel Tormé left no doubt: The dressing room was their *room*. Tormé's, for example, had to be painted a certain shade of green, and a limo had to be waiting outside at all times with the engine running, to whisk him to wherever he wanted to go. It was treatment for somebody with clout, a star. Susannah's contract, at one time posted on her website, with its pages of meticulous attention to detail, even to the choice and exact placement of the sparkling water she drank onstage, was a document not just worthy of a star but also eloquent of the kind of parallel universe in which Susannah lived, in her head.

But how often could Susannah get a contract like that? Not from the Oak Room, to which she returned in 1996, after touring heavily in 1995 but without a new show. The Algonquin's Barbara McGurn describes the Oak Room contract as "boilerplate, two pages. Informally, artists might ask for something: water, food, room temperature—most like it cool. If we can accommodate, we will. But it's not like rock stars, whose management often seems to think it makes them look much more important to ask for all these things." In short, Susannah's website contract was mostly a wish list.

After appearing at Rainbow and Stars, Susannah went into the studio in April to cut a new record, an eclectic group of songs she called *From Broadway to Bebop*. Along with standards, there were an old-time Brazilian piece by Carmen Miranda, a show tune by Shire and Maltby Jr., and, reflecting DiNicola's jazz enthusiasms, pieces by James Moody, Chet Baker, and Bill Evans. From the time she'd signed with Concord, she and DiNicola had pressed Jefferson for expanded, orchestral backup on her records, and on the *Broadway* album, Jefferson agreed to the compromise of several octet arrangements. But Susannah dreamed bigger dreams, world-class arrangements by such as Don Sebesky and Gunther Schuller. She recorded Sebesky's "I Remember Bill" on the *Broadway* album, and they discussed his working with her on her next album. In 1995, she also corresponded with Schuller about another album project for which he would be the arranger, in which she would be backed by a standard jazz orchestra for several tunes, and one including strings and French horns for others. But though both men were willing to lower their usual fees, after Jefferson balked at the still-higher expenses involved, neither project came to anything. Sebesky, hearing what a reviewer described as the "bland, Concordesque" octet arrangements behind Susannah on her subsequent album of Cole Porter songs, told DiNicola that he'd flung the CD across the room in frustration.

By the 1990s, for all her achievements—the bookings at the Oak Room, a recording contract, a stack of admiring reviews, and a growing audience—Susannah still saw the glass as half-empty, as much a victim of self-doubt as she had been as an unknown starting out in Europe. She also missed the easy companionship and camaraderie that she fantasized her peers in the music business enjoyed with each other. But it was not to be for her. "She would try so hard to get people to like her that they thought she was a phony," DiNicola says. "That Doris Day persona—she wore her heart on her sleeve. Then there was the fact that she was so smart, brighter than most people. Intelligence can be viewed as arrogance." Susannah's manner, concurs Thea Lurie, could seem to be off-putting.

And she could be tough on singers also, particularly when she was with trusted friends who were critics. "Anything she said had to be off the record," notes James Gavin, who remembers several conversations in which Susannah did discuss other singers in a less-than-flattering manner. "I remember Peggy Lee's show had just closed, and Susannah said, 'You can't quote this, but I think she needed a good editor.' Another time, she did a wicked imitation of Alberta Hunter—who she didn't like as a singer. Susannah was a talented mimic." When a critic friend from London mentioned liking Andrea Marcovicci very much, he recalls that Susannah snapped, "Everybody I know thinks she's terrible." Rex Reed goes a step further. "Susannah almost never had a compliment for a girl singer—only if it was a man." Were there exceptions?

"A few. She did love Irene Kral, and Sylvia Sims, and she was crazy about Jackie Cain of Jackie and Roy. But that was about it, I think."

It will hardly come as a surprise, then, that most of Susannah's fellow singers found her off-putting. Says singer and pianist Daryl Sherman, "I couldn't relate to the diva mentality." "She could be very flattering," adds another, "but it often seemed shallow and insincere." A typical complaint was that of singer Chris Connor, who telephoned Richard Rodney Bennett to vent: "I don't know why, but Susannah never gets in touch with us unless she wants something from us!" Bennett himself was another who felt he was given the brush-off. "Susannah called and said, 'I never see you anymore, I miss you,' and in the next breath, 'Oh by the way, I'm going to London—do you know a good pianist there?' and that was that." Her neighbor and race-walking partner, jazz violinist Linda Fennimore, likes to quote the late veteran bass player Milt Hinton, with whom she apprenticed. "Milt would say to me, 'Help people to learn what you want.' Well, Susannah wouldn't share with other musicians. She tried to control as much as possible of her environment."

To be sure, Susannah had her devotees. Younger singers—Karen Oberlin, Rebecca Kilgore, Jane Monheit, and others—paid her the compliment of close imitation; Kilgore actually mailed a fan letter. But many of her peers, like Mary Cleere Haran, were distant, DiNicola says. "She was like the little girl not invited to play in the sandbox." But the question remains: Was it a matter only of the "mean, cruel, tough music world," as DiNicola views it—a world rife with high-pitched competition, envy, intrigue—the squabbling over the crumbs and slivers of the little showbiz pie? Or did Susannah bear some of the responsibility for her isolation, her place "outside the sandbox"?

Neither her admirers nor critics were aware that underneath the "Susannah Sunshine" exterior—the nickname that California friends gave her—lay something quite the opposite, although *sunshine* unwittingly but perfectly describes one symptom of the disease she was suffering from, bipolar disorder—later specifically diagnosed as Bipolar II. According to Kay Redfield Jamison, an expert on the disorder and a sufferer of bipolar disorder herself, what distinguishes Bipolar II from Bipolar I is that the manic episodes are less severe. (Susannah's father had suffered from full-blown mania as well as periods of major depression.) When Jamison describes the lesser manic state, she seems to be describing Susannah: "Hypomania is usually ebullient, self-confident and often transcendent, but it almost always exists with an irritable underpinning.... The certainty of conviction about the correctness and importance of their ideas, the intense and impulsive romantic or sexual liaisons ... the expansiveness, energy, risk-taking."[11] What her friends observed as an over-the-top exhilaration, dangerous in its intensity. And then, of course, came the crash, where the lows were every bit as low as in Bipolar I.

Only a very few, very close friends were privy to parts of the picture of Susannah's biochemically based disorder, or disease; only Lurie and Keith Ingham and Dan DiNicola and one or two others knew of the extent and intensity of her mood swings and their corrosive effect on her sense of self, and self-worth. "There is a very very somber side to me," she told a California friend, Brad Kay. Even fewer people—her therapists and her husband and best friend—knew anything about her suicidal thoughts, especially since the cancer. "She was a tortured soul. She talked about killing herself," DiNicola says. Meanwhile, remarks the singer Karen Oberlin, who greatly admired Susannah's work, "It must be hard to carry on while considering suicide."

Or seeing a loved one prepare for it, and, since 1993, Susannah's father had been doing just that. As members of the Hemlock Society, the assisted-suicide organization, Tom and Mimi had been readying for such an eventuality for some time, as Tom had been in increasingly poor health, after several strokes and the recent discovery that he had lung cancer. "The children came to visit, and then they all knew about it, what he was planning," added Mimi, emphasizing, "When he decided to kill himself, he wasn't crazy." The whole event became something of a tragicomedy in several acts, as relayed by Susannah several years after the fact to her dressmaker, Lorraine Ruggieri, a mothering presence who became, especially late in Susannah's life, a sometime confidante. First, Tom explained to Susannah that he was going to delay his death until after her performance at Rainbow and Stars in the spring of 1994, because, he said, he didn't want to upset her. Next, he was all set to carry out precise instructions for suicide on a particular day, but then the washing machine broke and Mimi asked him to wait until he'd repaired it. Finally, in 1994, following a method suggested in Derek Humphry's book *Final Exit,* Tom ingested a quantity of pills he'd stored up and tied a plastic bag over his head.

"Later, there was a kind of memorial service for Tom," Dan DiNicola recalls. "We went to Oakland, and Katie, Maggie, Carlos, and other friends sat around the dining-room table and told stories about

Tom." Susannah talked about how her father had been happiest when he'd been working with his "brothers" on the docks as a shipping clerk or on faraway anthropology projects when he was young. "She knew that death was a release for her father, but she was upset," DiNicola adds. Then, in 1995, Susannah's aunt, Dorothy Manchester Beals, followed suit with a planned suicide. Mimi was as supportive of her sister's action as she had been of Tom's, explaining, "Dorothy was 94—she couldn't read or move anymore."

Susannah continued to work at building her career. But club, radio, TV, and concert dates continued to be erratic, and would remain so until the end. Allen Farnham, for example, was booked for just 12 dates with her in 1995, many of them only for a weekend or a single concert. From 1992 to 1995, her stepson Jeff, an attorney, handled all the negotiations of her contracts. "The Algonquin was the really profitable performance," he recalls. "But other than that, mostly I saw how hard she had to sell herself to get back just a little."

According to Dan DiNicola, out pounding the club pavement, in the period he represented her, at least, Susannah lost gigs because of her race. "I didn't tell her when one festival turned her down because, they said, she wasn't a black singer who scatted." Jeff confirms this. And somehow, the information leaked out, of course. In a rare burst of openly expressed bitterness during one of her worst "down" periods later in 2000, Susannah told her friends Sigi Schmidt-Joos and Kathrin Brigl in an interview for his *Showtime* radio program in Berlin that she was often told by jazz clubs that they weren't interested in hiring white jazz singers. But it was probably more complicated than that, as she knew. There was more competition now, and most of it was younger. Susannah had always straddled categories, and the chronic difficulty of *placing* her limited the venues. "Susannah was too cool and hip for cabaret and not cool or hip enough for the jazz world," asserts DiNicola. Reviewers who didn't like her were usually polite, though occasionally some were revealing of the prejudice against Susannah, one saying that in performance she was like nothing so much as a "jazzed-up Martha Stewart."[12]

Limited in traditional venues, Susannah was encouraged by friends in the advertising business to turn her energy to breaking into the lucrative world of voice-overs for commercials, and she enjoyed some success initially, speaking and, at times, singing for such products as Xerox copiers and Nestlé Tollhouse Cookie Dough.[13] But trying to get work in voice-overs was as competitive, if not more so, than singing gigs, and eventually she abandoned the idea.

Far more to her liking was getting back to her writing. After years away from freelance efforts, in 1994 she worked up a book proposal about her life as a singer. She added, "But what I would really love to do is a book about the singers and songs of the '20s, '30s and '40s, so perhaps I can bring that in, too."[14] An editor friend, Fred Allen, was now at *American Heritage* magazine and encouraged her to work on long pieces dealing with music. The result, over the next several years, was profiles of Ethel Waters, Bessie Smith, Irving Berlin, and Mae West. But another promising project—a series of radio biographies of jazz singers for which Susannah would write the script, host the show, and sing the songs—fell through.

Continuing to worry about her income, she considered developing a workshop for colleges on singers and singing, contacting her old *Pelican* college editor Dick Corten in Berkeley to see if he'd introduce her to the film connoisseur Albert Johnson, a local Berkeley legend, about working with Johnson at the university on a program about Broadway shows and their songs—she'd built a card file of the lyrics to more than three thousand songs by then (and once learned by her, almost never forgotten). Her workshops for young children and high-school students were more promising, but presented different challenges. "She liked kids, but they could be a tough audience," recalls Farnham of gigs at libraries in Harlem and the Bronx. Then Concord Records linked with the Borders Books and Music chain, to bring Susannah to various stores for free lecture-concerts. "The thinking was that hundreds of people would come and many would buy her CDs, but there were usually only a few. And she was good at those lectures, really good," Farnham says.

In 1995, Susannah lost her second "father," the crusty and contentious but trustworthy and admiring Carl Jefferson of Concord Records. After she flew out West for his memorial concert on July 10, a marathon event that included virtually everybody who had recorded under Jefferson (she sang "They Can't Take That Away From Me"), Susannah sat for a radio interview with DJ Paul Conley, discussing the two men who had died recently, both so important in her life. While about her father Tom, she said only, "He was a closed man, not emotional—he didn't express his emotions," she had depended on Jeff. He had ruled Concord as a fiefdom, she commented. His dictates sometimes clashed with her own strong-willed vision of what she should record, but he was the kind of man to whom she felt she could go in a crisis.

After a trip to Italy in August with DiNicola (she bypassed Rome), Susannah was back in New York in early September to record the Cole Porter album, *Easy to Love,* before her Oak Room stint. But the album didn't quite gel, perhaps because it was the first time Carl Jefferson was not there. Nick Phillips, a trumpet player and producer who'd been working for Concord since 1987, was now managing album production for her, a three-day process once she'd selected her material and set the arrangements: two days in the studio and another day to re-record and mix as needed. "I tried to be a calm presence in the studio so she could focus and relax and perform at her best," Phillips says. "She could be very emotional, quite neurotic in the recording studio." Susannah remained totally instinctive—she never knew the notes of the scale or her range except by singing until she found a place where she was comfortable. And her pitch was not great. "She was a little flat sometimes, in the Brazilian mode," Phillips observes. "She worked really hard at it, but intonation was not her main focus. Susannah was interested in the lyrics, the language, and her ear was great *that* way."

On the arrangements, she would defer to Farnham and Phillips, who handled the details. "Some musicians could handle her demands, like wanting a different style on a particular record; others not," Phillips admits. "Allen and I acted as her interpreters in communicating to musicians." But DiNicola was also always there for support and feedback, and some saw him, pacing and intense in the recording booth, as sending Susannah's already high nerves higher. "She'd say, 'I feel all your energy, Dan!' I'd have to kind of serve as a middleman," Phillips recalls. "Nick," says Diana Lang Phillips, a friend of Susannah's who'd married the producer, "was more than a producer. He was an ally, a friend. There were some really difficult times in the studio, and he helped her to focus without losing it."

She does not sound at her best on the *Easy to Love* album, seeming to strain noticeably and move from wistfulness to the perilous shores of self-pity. What a reviewer called her "Achilles heel" of choosing the wrong tempo is evident on "Anything Goes" and "From This Moment On." She is out of tune on "Night and Day," and after a great beginning on "You Do Something to Me," her rendition of the tune simply loses conviction. The problem lies at least in part with the arrangements, the band sounding remote, suspended in space, as on "Who Wants to Be a Millionaire." Yet there are gorgeous takes here, too, of "Goodbye Little Dream," "Why Don't We Try Staying Home?", "Weren't We Fools?", "Just One of Those Things," and "Easy to Love."

By the time Mimi came out to Schenectady that Thanksgiving of 1995, Susannah was sinking into a depression, and her mother's behavior pushed her further down. The family had already observed Mimi's sharp tongue with her daughter, as when she flew out East for Susannah's second Algonquin appearance in the fall of 1990 and, afterward, remarked only that she didn't like Susannah's dress. Mark Nadler, Dan DiNicola, and even Keith Ingham long before saw Susannah's competitiveness with her mother—the college catch, the "campus cutie." "That white-gloves persona—trying to please a woman she despised," DiNicola comments. Mimi's criticism was, still, devastating. After a long holiday dinner that November, Mimi drank too much and let Susannah have it again. "We were in the kitchen talking," recalls Anne, who'd flown in from Japan. "And Mimi said to me, 'You speak Japanese and Russian—so difficult!' 'Well, Susannah speaks Spanish, Italian, French—and some Portuguese,' I reminded her. 'But that's just Romance languages,' Mimi said. I think that Mimi was jealous because Susannah got the limelight. Mimi was mean."

Mimi's problems with alcohol were an old story to Susannah. She'd written her a letter in 1988 pleading with her to stop. "Susannah and I talked about how a lot of people in the 1950s got soused; it was a different era then," DiNicola suggests. "And yes, both her parents drank, but Tom did it differently. I thought Mimi was an alcoholic." Mimi had another, loving side, the side that sent Susannah letters of praise and admiration, the side that sent her checks and kept all the reviews of Susannah's performances and recordings in apple-pie order in file folders at her desk. But Susannah, of course, never knew which side was going to emerge.

By the Christmas holidays, Susannah wrote to her London confidante Frances Bendixson to note that she was having "one of her bad winters." Her plunge into depression was abetted by the recent death of 43-year-old singer Nancy Lamott from uterine cancer. "I live in fear of getting [cancer] again and am very threatened, frightened and saddened by every female's cancer death," Susannah confided.[15] Like Susannah, Lamott had had years of obscurity when she came to New York. And like Susannah, she began to get real acclaim, especially after the release of a Johnny Mercer CD in 1992, about a decade after the American release of Susannah's Mercer album—both singers' albums plugged by an enthusiastic Jonathan Schwartz on his radio program. And then sadly, yet again like Susannah, Lamott put off cancer treatments, despite the pleading of loved ones and doctors, until she'd completed an important singing engagement—the Fairmont in Chicago for Susannah, the Oak Room for Lamott. Except in the latter's case, it was too late. She died not long after.

After a three-week engagement at London's Pizza on the Park in January 1996, Susannah was invited back to perform in Europe by her friends the jazz journalists Siegfried "Sigi" Schmidt-Joos and Kathrin Brigl, who interviewed Susannah a number of times for their radio program in Berlin. They invited her over to sing at a 60th-birthday celebration for Schmidt-Joos at Quasimodo's, Berlin's big jazz club, and then arranged for her to appear at an outdoor summer concert with the well-known RIAS jazz big band. For this rare overseas performance, Susannah put together a fine program, using excellent German musicians. Yet the concert was a mess. She'd hired Rich DeRosa to expand existing trio arrangements, but when the big-band charts were discovered to lack rhythm-section parts, she was forced to omit a number of her songs. The mishap, Allen Farnham says, was through no fault of DeRosa's: Farnham and the bass player and drummer had simply worked out the rhythm on the spot, without writing it down. Rather, the fault lay with Susannah. "She didn't have a musical director—me—to work it out in Germany, because she had decided there wasn't enough money in the budget to bring me over to Europe. And the band leader over there told her they couldn't spend the time working out the missing parts. She was mad at Rich DeRosa, but she hadn't been thinking clearly and she brought it on herself."

Though she was cast down by the disappointing concert in Berlin and came back to America with what her stepson Roy calls "these horrible downs which Dad couldn't get her out of," her work, as it had always done, served as both a distraction from her troubles and an antidote. Her Porter album became the basis for "The Passionate Cole Porter," which she brought to the Oak Room that June, after a triumphant opening at the now-dark Yvette Wintergarden in Chicago. Audiences loved her "Censorship Medley," in which she restored risqué and double-entendre lyrics that had been x-ed out: "Six sinful hits in their unexpurgated original version that were denied radio air play."

She also had a delicious new writing project on Irving Berlin to burrow into. Being Susannah, she was fascinated not only with his incredible body of work—the amazing marriage of his music and words—but with "the history behind them and how they got written." As she had explicated Porter's life through his music, his obsessions through his love songs, now she looked into Berlin's bouts of deep depression, which he fought with hard, creative work until late in his life. Her *American Heritage* piece about Berlin, "Always: A Singer's Journey Through the Life of Irving Berlin," published in 1998, was Susannah's only writing about a songwriter. Among the favorable reviews, none was more touching than a letter she got from her mother. While composing the letter to Susannah, Mimi wrote, she'd had to stop and gather herself together, because she'd been so moved by the struggles that Susannah depicted that she began to cry. "I'm so proud I'm your mother," Mimi concluded. But it was not enough to make a dent in Susannah's feelings of being unloved by her mother. Says her sister Maggie, "She hung on to hurts from many years ago; she never forgot *anything*." Above all, Susannah still grieved over the lack of consistent affection and acceptance she'd so yearned for as a child.

*Let's Face the Music: The Songs of Irving Berlin,* Susannah's sixth record for Concord, was recorded in late October 1996. As she had with her Cole Porter album, she'd searched out alternate and forgotten lyrics to some of the songs. Her voice is more interesting on the Berlin album—huskier, looser, more mature—and the arrangements are a better fit. A refashioned "There's No Business Like Show Business" is leavened with a softer, slightly Latin background, the words beautifully limned. The impeccably phrased album won praise, including 3.5 stars (out of a possible 4) in a *Down Beat* review.

At the end of November, Susannah appeared on *A Prairie Home Companion,* the popular NPR radio show. She was at the top of her game now, many felt, and a tape of her during a set at Jazz Alley in Seattle that year confirms it: Singing "The Waters of March," she is polished, confident, sincere, believable—a creation of her own fantasy, slim, glittering, and youthful-looking at 50.

Yet videos of performances from the period telegraph something else as well—that there is something not quite right. Is it the clenched jaw, the ramrod-straight posture, the gaze that looks away and over the audience, never *at* it? Signs that she is perhaps holding herself together with a rigid iron will—the same will that had forged her into a singer in the first place? The careful, choreographed gestures? "She was self-conscious about her appearance—oh my, yes," DiNicola says. "For example, she had a wandering eye that was not quite focused, which was operated on more than once." Most photographers learned to tip-toe when they had to shoot Susannah, for record covers or other promotion material. They and her closest intimates really knew about the effort and strain it always took Susannah to put herself together. Most people were kept at a distance, including musician colleagues. "She was genuinely considerate and so careful about asking everyone how they and their family were," recalls bassist Steve Gilmore. "But she didn't like to talk about herself."

There *were* times Susannah reached out and revealed bits about herself to new people. Baby steps. Photographer Barbara Singer managed, after much persuasion, to have Susannah sit for a long photo session in December 1996. "When she came to my studio, she told me, 'I've had a hard life.' Though Singer took great pains with the pictures, Susannah didn't want them released when she saw the results. "Because the lighting and the lens I used showed the coarseness of her complexion," Singer explains. "But I think I got her soul in her eyes." There was a lot of pain in that soul, and Singer had caught it.

A couple of months later, after the photo shoot, Susannah confided to Jackie Osteen that she was feeling "thoroughly demoralized" because of what she called a bout of flu: She had recently decided to go off Prozac. It had been, she told her, "a wonder drug," helping her to "avoid committing suicide." But she could no longer bear what she called the "cumulative disturbing side effects." In Schenectady for the Christmas holidays, Susannah and her friend Christine MacDonald from Saratoga Springs planned a trip to Mexico right after Christmas to celebrate Susannah's 50th birthday on January 1st. They put the whole thing together quickly, a family reunion of sorts. DiNicola, who was loath to take vacations, reluctantly agreed, and MacDonald, Mimi, Susannah's nephew Carlos, and Roy and Holly DiNicola all decided to fly down to the colonial city of Oaxaca in southern Mexico. (With a brand-new baby, Jeff and Kim took a pass.) Arriving before the others, Christine MacDonald and Mimi McCorkle spent time sightseeing together. Though Mimi was famous among Susannah's friend as a Mommy Dearest, Christine saw another side of Susannah's mother as an attractive and affectionate woman.

Mimi once talked about how she got along well with her daughter when she was a "happy singer." But Susannah was not often a "happy singer" on that Mexican vacation. Her mood swings and the push-and-pull between her and DiNicola was obvious to those around them. "Susannah was a great deal of fun, but then she'd get very uncomfortable and pushy," MacDonald remembers. She and DiNicola seemed relieved not to be together. Then came Susannah's birthday dinner. "She hated that her birthday was New Year's Day," says Roy. "Growing up, she'd felt that she had got no recognition that it was her birthday: Her parents were just hung over from New Year's Eve." She planned carefully for the right kind of birthday party in Oaxaca, an authentic Mexican New Year's Eve. What she got instead was a restaurant with what Roy calls blaring rock music. "She wouldn't have been able to get through that without going into a depression," he remarks. "But she found a better place, quiet, with good food and champagne, and made everybody leave the noisy place. And we did have a much better time."

The trip to Mexico was a farewell, and perhaps Susannah knew it would be: the last big family get-together of DiNicolas and McCorkles. Sprinkled through the albums made in her last years with DiNicola are direct references to what Susannah was feeling. There was the little-known heartbreaker by Cole Porter, "Weren't We Fools?" in which Susannah seems to predict lasting regrets over the end of her marriage, and a year later, sung as a stately and immeasurably sad ballad, the Irving Berlin song, "Let's Face the Music." Susannah, said Rex Reed, was always "searching for [a] daddy, then resenting him when he loved her."

# Faint Music

I am in such a strange state that I feel a terrible lack of confidence in everything I do, that I have "lost it" as a singer, a writer and a human being, and just want to go into hiding until my spirit comes back. . . . I feel like a shell of myself.
  —Conversation with Jackie Osteen, 1998

After returning from Mexico in January 1997, the long-simmering tension between Susannah and Dan DiNicola began to boil over. When Dan's daughter Anne, home on a visit from Japan, joined them on a trip to Montreal later in the year, Susannah, she says, "was being a pain. I didn't yell at her, but I let her know it. But Susannah hated confrontation of any kind and withdrew stonily." Back in Japan, Anne wrote Susannah a letter that shows an important dynamic in Susannah's illness: "Your refusal to apologize for anything and the fact that you acted so wounded put me in an even bigger fit. I just wanted to get away. . . . You portrayed yourself as a victim without making any apologies." If in denying responsibility for having a part in a conflict, the victim can feel confirmed in being the wounded one, the price is alienating others. "I stayed angry at her. I wish I hadn't but I did not include her in my life during her last years," says Anne.

Susannah and DiNicola had been consulting Philip Romero, a New York City psychiatrist. Romero warned Susannah that her habit of going into a room and shutting the door for hours, sometimes days at a time, had done damage to her marriage. "At first we'd see him regularly, later occasionally, separately and then together," DiNicola says. Romero had a reputation for brilliance, albeit one soon to be tarnished. He and some of his patients allowed writer Paul Solotaroff to tape-record and take notes of their sessions for about a year, and the pseudonymous results appeared in a book.[1] Solotaroff's book was immediately controversial and became more so when a *Village Voice* article identified Romero as the therapist character, making the charge that the doctor had taken compensation for his participation and bent several ethical guidelines.

DiNicola saw signs of Romero's questionable judgment well before that scandal broke: "He started missing appointments in '96. Susannah said she recognized the signs of substance-abuse problems, having dealt with musicians for decades. Sometimes he wouldn't show up at all. Other times, he'd be very lucid in his suggestions." Adds Thea Lurie, "Susannah thought Romero was talking them through what he called a 'guided separation,' to help them work out the problems of their marriage." Such a trial separation, Susannah hoped, would allow them to clarify how they could better balance each other's needs. "Your father and I aren't perfect," Susannah told Roy, "but I know he's the best I'll ever have. I'll never find anyone like your father and so I think about that when we think of splitting up."

But, DiNicola explains, "When she explained her plan to Romero— that, for example, she would go to ball games with me if I'd go to the ballet with her, he cut her off and told her the marriage was really over. Susannah was *still* willing to go for a trial separation, but I was not. I said no. I always felt I had to protect her from bad news—if a job fell through, for instance. Life was always uphill for Susannah and when she was down or upset, I'd try to fix things. Her happiness was dependent on her hope for work. In time, I got more and more tired of it." Still, he did agree to go with Susannah to meet with Romero one last time, in the late spring of '97. "He never showed up. Susannah took what she saw as a betrayal by her doctor very hard. She was really upset and angry with him," DiNicola recalls. "And then, Romero just disappeared." In fact, the therapist, under pressure, had voluntarily surrendered his medical license and checked into a Pennsylvania rehabilitation clinic. In time, he was to have his license "provisionally restored."[2] After Romero resurfaced, DiNicola continued to see him for private therapy sessions from time to time.

The final split between Susannah and DiNicola came soon after Romero disappeared. Susannah had long struggled with what she called his "Type A" personality. "She loved Dan, but they could never reconcile their different rhythms," says Lurie. "She wanted calm play time together that included walks in the park, visits to museums and the ballet, and these were not interests he shared." Above all, Susannah longed for romance. "She liked that illusion—the little girl part, believing in 'love,'" observes Roy Schecter. "In the singing, it's an innocent quality mixed with the sexiness. Listen to her sing 'I Can't Give You Anything but Love.' It's as if she really meant it." "She was such an incurable romantic," concurs Francis Bendixson, her London confidante. "And I think Susannah got bored with men," she adds. "My impression is that she was highly sexed and could get antsy."

So could DiNicola. "I felt stifled, I was not having a life, and I was bored and bothered by it. I worked a lot, getting gigs for her. And very often, for what? One example: I got her a gig in D.C. Then I rushed down from work so I could be there in time for a sound check—Susannah could be buried by the instruments. There were two sets. Afterward, I would have liked to go out and have dinner, talk, be with my wife. But she'd still be talking to customers at 1:00 or 2:00 A.M., and I'm hungry and now there's no place open to eat, so it's back to a motel room. I said to her, 'I'm getting nothing out of this. I do all this for you, but you only come up to the house in the summer.'"

The final break came in her studio apartment in Manhattan in May 1997. "I felt I was propping up her career, and it was exhausting. I told her it just wasn't working. Her unwillingness to come to Schenectady. The depressions. The eagerness to get back to New York. Of course, we had fun in New York—staying in the apartment. And while we were splitting, I brought up the abortion. It was such a source of sadness for me. She hadn't seemed bothered by the abortion at the time, but now she bawled and bawled, just terrifically. I left her apartment. Later, as I was driving back home, I called her on the road and apologized."

So Susannah cut her ties to DiNicola and, especially, to Schenectady, a town she detested. (After a conversation about the place, the veteran lyricist Fran Landesman, of "Spring Can Really Hang You Up the Most" fame and other hip-yet-sensitive lyrics, wrote a song for Susannah she called "Suicide in Schenectady." Not wanting to wound DiNicola's feelings, Susannah declined to sing it.) In New York, Susannah said she felt like a canary let out of a cage. She took a larger, one-bedroom apartment down the hall from her former one-room studio. A plain place with off-white walls, it had a galley kitchen, a bedroom with room for a double bed, dresser, and closet, and a living room. There, bookshelves lined one wall, a desk and file cabinet crammed with music and phone numbers filled another, and there were a couple of chairs, a long black leather couch, a television and telephone and two cats, always in hiding. And a window that gave her a sliver of a view of Central Park, and photographs everywhere of her friends—inside her kitchen cabinets and closet doors, beside her bed. But very few friends were allowed in. "She seemed to live entirely without pretension or clutter," remarked one of the few who did see it. Susannah was well aware that hers was not the apartment of a diva.

From the end of May into June 1997, Susannah presented her new show, "Darkness and Light: Irving Berlin," at the Oak Room, a show built around not only her album of Berlin songs but some discoveries she'd made about the composer while researching her article about him. Drawn to the darker side of Berlin's character, she had already found herself identifying with the subtext of the seemingly unlikely anthem, "There's No Business Like Show Business." "[It] has been one of the most important songs in my life," she wrote, "ever since I discovered the 'secret' song hidden in the more reflective extra lyrics of the old sheet music" ["you're brokenhearted, but you go on"].[3] Here was a man, she thought, who was like her father—brilliant, accomplished, struggling with inner darkness. Like Tom, and like herself.

She and DiNicola had split up before her Algonquin Oak Room show. Now, no longer on the Prozac she'd taken for some seven years, she seemed like an uncaged bird, slightly manic. DiNicola was exhilarated too. He says, "I wanted a place with spirit in it, I wanted it to smell like garlic and oil rather than health food. Health food doesn't smell!" The funny, talkative, incandescent Susannah with the attractive sheen about her had emerged—the Susannah at the start of her "up" cycle, freed of a problematic marriage, freed of tiresome side effects of her medication, and free to look for romance. There was no time to lose—she was 50 now! That summer, life looked good. She put energy into established friendships and made new ones. At a Jackie and Roy concert, she ran into writer James Gavin, whom she had alienated some years before, and set about forming a close friendship with her fellow Upper West Sider; soon, Gavin became one of her few confidantes. David Alpern was a journalist who admired her at a concert she did in the Hamptons, and she often visited other friends in Sag Harbor or Shelter Island. "She was a wonderful guest," Alpern says. "Unlike some others, she was not a diva. She always brought house gifts and helped in the house."

Soon Susannah had a new man in her life: Eric Olson, with whom she had begun an affair in June in Washington, D.C. Olson was a Harvard-trained clinical psychologist and music lover who'd heard Susannah's music and become an instant fan, establishing an e-mail correspondence with her. "She fell madly in love with him," recalls Julie Ben-Susan, a friend from New York and Shelter Island in the 1990s, adding, "Susannah was in love with being in love, and she loved romance. It was a huge thing to her." Writer Francis Davis and his wife, *Fresh Air* radio host Terry Gross, concur. They saw Susannah perform in Philadelphia fairly often, and Susannah interviewed and performed on Gross's show frequently.[4] Shortly after Susannah had begun her affair with Olson, she went to Philadelphia, where Davis and Gross watched her perform her Irving Berlin show at the Hershey Hotel. Afterward, the three got together in Susannah's room. They were, Davis says, uncomfortable with the effusively euphoric side of Susannah they saw that night. "She was very, very thin and very 'happy'— we'd never seen her so up. And she talked nonstop. I'd seen the down side of Susannah, but that seemed fairly normal—a certain hesitancy, especially in women. But I'd never seen the 'up' side before, and it didn't seem either normal or healthy."

For the moment, life seemed to open up for Susannah. Her article about Irving Berlin was published, and there was a new recording to plan for that October, a calendar full of good engagements—"three cities in two weeks," she e-mailed a friend happily. If life was great, she admitted that it was also exhausting: "Performing is like running a marathon." But she was fueled by her love affair—by the energy of her high. In a stunning about-face, she wanted to reveal to the world her hitherto closely guarded bouts with depression—or rather, how she'd conquered depression. In a letter to *Mirabella,* a short-lived stylish magazine for women, Susannah—whose "slightly manic phase" continued on its upward curve—proposed "an article about overcoming depression without drugs." She'd call it "The Upside of Down." Perhaps, she added, she could then expand the idea into a book, "a companion guide to depression," with a menu of alternative treatments that she had found so beneficial, "including acupuncture, Chinese herbs, massage therapy, chiropractic, yoga, weightlifting, self-hypnosis and meditation." And her own positive experience would serve as a kind of guide for other depressed women who didn't want to take drugs. "I have never in my life felt happier than I do now!" she added sunnily.

But the affair with Olson that made her so happy was short-lived. By the end of September, Susannah was confiding with chagrin not only to

Thea and one or two others but to her new friend Jackie Osteen from South Carolina. She had met Jackie along with her husband Hubert at an Oak Room performance. "I can't believe the way I jumped into it, so open and trusting. It was great before I realized how screwed up he was emotionally, but I really crashed from it and am very wary now. I'm such a romantic. I need to be careful! Wish there were something else as good as being involved in a romance."

Susannah was not one to be seen as the rejected party in a relationship. But though she told people that she had "decided to turn things into a friendship," it was Eric Olson, as it had been DiNicola, who ended the romance, though the two stayed friends—another confidante instead of a lover.

The end of the romance, it was soon clear, had devastated Susannah. "She crashed afterward," says Lurie. "She was crying on the phone to me," adds Jackie Osteen, "and she *never* did that." Susannah later explained, "I was so euphoric to be free from Dan's anger and resentment of my New York life, and then so excited about the wonderful romance I had for a couple of months, that I didn't face the period of sadness and the rebuilding of my life as a single person, which just has to be gone through." But as well, she either overlooked or finessed the back-and-forth influence of her biochemical imbalance on her decision-making—and the urgency of the need to find good medication. None of this was known outside her circle of intimates. To the press, to other musicians, Susannah presented her public face, painted brave and reassuringly grown-up. Yes, she had decided to break off a recent romance, but she said, "I continue to expect to find my soulmate by not looking for him at all. Life has so many other pleasures." What could sound more adult, more sane than that?

The euphoria that had begun after she left DiNicola was followed by a great crash after the break-up with Olson, a low that her very close friends worried might be part of an ominous new pattern, a worsening of her manic depression. She would continue to have "grace" periods when she would feel that at last, *at last,* she had found a way to vanquish the serious blues. In her "up" states, she either didn't remember the crashes that had come and surely would come again, or else she chose to wish them away. She intended to write about depression—but in the way of a conqueror, a victor, a happy survivor, someone who sits in a comfortable, stable present. And yet this was the same Susannah who counseled a friend that year, "It's not good for people to know that you have troubles."

Hardly a surprise then, that Susannah's next album, produced in October when she was in the throes of rejection by Olson and her deepening depression, was more ambiguously received than others. *Someone To Watch Over Me,* Susannah's careful blend of lesser-known Gershwin tunes with familiar, was a supremely apt plea. Once again, she showed her great skill and heart in getting to the core of a song—in Rex Reed's wonderful choice of words, "deglazing" what was almost too-familiar material, and serving up its essence. Once again, Susannah demonstrated an uncommon ability to stimulate the intellect as well as the emotions. But if to some listeners, she seemed noticeably more relaxed on the album (possibly because DiNicola wasn't there, in one witness's phrase, "to add to the neurosis"), others heard a rather listless quality to Susannah's voice. "She thought she was singing better, but I wanted so much to suggest a coach I knew for her," says James Gavin, explaining, "It's so often a problem of support and breathing. But I could never find a way to tell her." Roy Schecter was bothered by the elaborate, "finished"-sounding arrangements, the mannered approach he felt that had crept into her singing. "I got up the courage after the Gershwin album to write her and say that on some of those tracks, the arrangements are not for a warm, emotional singer, but a cool one. Why not do a ballad album with just piano or guitar? I suggested. She wrote back to me and said she'd been persuaded to do some of the songs on the album, that the record company didn't want to do a simple ballad album."

The holidays that year were difficult. She who had often dreaded the holiday gatherings of the clan in past year, now missed DiNicola and the boys and their families at Christmas. Being with her mother that Christmas season of 1997 only underlined her sense of aloneness in the world. It had been a very tough period for her, what she later described to Osteen as a "terrible post-divorce year of self-doubt and hopelessness." She had put her heart and soul, she said, into her pretty little house and worked on every corner of it, but without a partner to share it. "And then the happy home I'd dreamed of creating and being in didn't work out anyway." Though she had often complained to DiNicola about the constant stream of visits by his children and their spouses, now that they had split, she wanted to see them more often—a flashpoint for DiNicola, who was as confused—and angered—by her new needs as Susannah herself was about having a family. "I missed Dan's kids so much!" Susannah exclaimed. Despite her firm resolve not to be a mother, from time to time Susannah expressed regret. While a student living in Europe, she had rhapsodized briefly about the *idea* of having children. Later, as an established singer in her prime, she occasionally mourned the loss of a child. Ellen Bollinger, who'd met Susannah in the early 1980s, had a son in the mid-nineties. "Susannah told me more than once she regretted not having a child," she says.

After the difficult holidays of 1997, Susannah pulled herself together. She told Jackie Osteen, "I have now accepted that I just can't get involved with anyone for awhile, maybe a long while, while I make a kind of interior journey out of one place in my life and to another one, as yet unknown (and therefore scary to contemplate). And much as I love good company, it has to be a solitary journey. If I sound a little sad, I am. But this is all just delayed reaction to the end of the marriage. I have been going through a tough time, family problems I don't even want to begin to talk about," she added evasively. In fact, she had finally come to terms with the fact that she had a variant of the disease that ran through her family, conceding to her sister Maggie that, as abhorrent as it might be, she would always need to be on some kind of medication. In New York, she found a new young psychiatrist, Dr. Cristina Brusco, whom she liked and was to see on and off during the late 1990s. But Susannah was very reluctant to try new antidepressants after her experiences with Prozac. Many observed symptoms, from the dry mouth that could make it hard to pronounce certain words to the shaking hands. She complained of an upset stomach. "She had this nasal drip—and sometimes was hyper, as if on drugs," recalls Diana Lang Phillips. Others agreed. "I remember she told me that she didn't like how she felt with some of the pills," recalls Diane Feldman. "They blunted her creative edge, and made her sleepy, or else, as at a party we gave, she seemed very nervous and agitated." Agrees Osteen, "She said she couldn't seem to function."

When Osteen and singer Nancy McGraw went with Susannah in February 1998 to hear a performance by singer K. T. Sullivan, they both noticed her agitation. "When she was seriously listening to music in a club, Susannah would get very intense. She would go into some kind of trance, and her face would twitch in all different directions with a tic," recalls McGraw. Susannah confided during that winter of 1998, Jackie Osteen remembers, that she had been having "terrible ups and downs.

She said she had to pull herself together and pretend feeling confident about herself, and then life would be better. She said she couldn't describe the depth of her despair at times." Getting all dressed up and going out in New York and acting like she was okay took every ounce of effort. But Susannah had learned at her mother's feet that appearances were all-important. And in New York's competitive little worlds of show business, she felt the facade simply had to be kept up.

But it was getting harder. She told Brad Kay she felt as if "terrible poisons were coursing through her system all the time, stubbornly lodged in her unconscious and pulling her down." Yet within weeks, after she had agreed to go on new medication, the results were miraculous—at least, temporarily. She wrote to the Osteens in South Carolina exuberantly. "You can see how much my attitude toward life has changed, thanks to medicine, friends (like you!). I'm so happy in every way now. The change in me is remarkable!" she wrote enthusiastically. "I am in excellent spirits." During this rosy period, Susannah sang superbly, as on radio host Jim Lowe's program, where she sang a moving rendition of "Someone to Watch Over Me." When her spirits climbed too high, the doctor cut back her new medicine. "I have actually had to cut down on my antidepressant twice because I have been nearly manic with excitement and happiness," she wrote Osteen. Having made the decision to stop taking Prozac, Susannah was now entering into dangerous territory in terms of her illness and how to treat it. Cautions James Stout, who wrote a book about arresting his own bipolar disorder, "Little was known [in the late eighties into the early nineties] about the negative effect of most antidepressants on bipolars," an assertion backed by Dr. Kay Redfield Jamison, who warns that antidepressants can also make a manic depressive "dangerously agitated."[5] The terror and fear and loneliness were all pushed down. At 52, Susannah was a sexy, witty single woman—a woman who seemed to defy middle age or, at least, its more obvious ravages, sleek as a cat preening—the reverse, in fact, of the lumpy, awkward Susan of adolescence and young womanhood.

Feeling much better, Susannah went on a mission, reaching out frequently at that time to her younger sister Maggie, from whom she'd drifted apart. "She'd gained some insight and was worried about me," Maggie recalls. "She said to me, 'You're the most like our father,' and she shared some of her experiences with her deep depressions in hopes that I would pay attention to my own health. I was very appreciative of what she'd done and I did take some meds, for dysphasia [a chronic, low feeling]. It was kind of a miracle when we finally found some common ground—the depression that none of us escaped. I'm sure she was appalled at discovering that despite everything she did to take care of herself, she was going to have the illness that my father and my sister had."

Lonely, yes; needy, check. But also, still, a bit hypomanic. What Susannah craved was a man in her life, a lover, although she was determined to stay away from commitment, with its undertow of obsession and depression, for awhile. "She was desperate for a man," Osteen says bluntly. Susannah papered over the sexual aspect: "Someone," she said prettily, donning the white gloves, "across the dinner table. I wish men were not so important to me and I weren't so attracted to them, but they just are." Friends attempted matchmaking: "She was capable of projecting a sexual neediness; she made it clear she was lonely," recalls her Berkeley friend Tom Luddy, co-director of the Telluride Film Festival. "In Washington, I introduced her to a couple of guys I thought she might like, including Leon Wieseltier." Literary editor of the *New Republic,* Wieseltier was "'the kind of guy I go for,' she told me," says Luddy. "But it didn't click; they became friends instead." Long-distance from California, musician Brad Kay, shy but long smitten, courted her with music, and treats such as the "McCorkle Cantata," a song sung in an old movie called *Pot of Gold* he'd discovered. "Well, she loved that!" Kay says. "And I would go to hear her shows, and I admired and respected and was in love with her." Their romance, for the time being, remained a cross-country promise.

While in her shimmering, newly medicated glow, Susannah had made another great new friend in New York while out clubbing with Osteen—entertainer Mark Nadler. They talked about Irving Berlin—a mutual passion—and were smitten: He was "the brother I've never had" and she, presumably, the sister he'd never had. Within days, after singing together in her apartment, the ebullient, high-energy Nadler persuaded Susannah, with the help of a couple of martinis (his favorite cocktail), to get up and sing with him at his Sardi's show, "Broadway Hootenanny." Looking fragile in a latter-day Judy Garland–ish way but in fine, lazy, jazz-inflected voice, Susannah sang solo on "I Thought About You" and "Do Nothing Till You Hear From Me" and with Nadler on "Two Sleepy People."

Nadler lived with his longtime companion, Joe Holloway. Gay male friends were both a respite and a source of embarrassment for Susannah—embarrassment in the sense that she was acutely aware of the possibilities of cliché: the aging, lonely girl singer bereft of romance. But for Susannah, it was a great relief to have an uncomplicated and fun relationship. Nadler and Susannah both liked to kick up their heels, literally; discovering a passion to learn swing-dancing, they signed up for lessons, though their schedules allowed for little continuity and the dance classes lasted only about a month. "I loved her sense of humor and abandon," Nadler says. "After dance class, I'd walk her home, and we would practice dancing on the sidewalks, anywhere, on the pavement outside of her building, without any cares about people passing by—we were having so much fun. She referred to me as her pal. I was her fun respite; she was my intellectual respite. We loved to go shopping for food. Food was a real center of our relationship—chocolate. She was an absolute chocaholic and would put a tiny little bit in her mouth and savor it as if it were the last bite of chocolate on earth. And once, she stayed at my house when I wasn't here, and I came back and a box of chocolates I'd had was gone. She'd eaten the whole thing, and she was very embarrassed. That was exactly how she listened to music also—that tremendous attention."

Throughout the spring, Susannah, at 52, enjoyed the kind of social life she'd never had as a girl—attention to rival Mimi's as Prettiest Girl on Campus more than a half century before. She went out with three men, then four, then five—one for nearly every night of the week. "Dates, flowers, cars to pick me up, undivided attention across a table in a nice restaurant, cuddling in jazz clubs, etc., etc.," she told Osteen. "I have crushes on all the men I spend time with, but feel very liberated to have decided I will not have any love affairs till at least next year. . . . I am constantly inspired, stimulated." She added offhandedly, "Thanks for all your kindness to me in my darkest months, which were really frightening to me."

To her, all that was safely once more in the past. "Onwards and upwards!" was her motto, as she often ended her e-mails to Thea Lurie. In Ann Arbor, Michigan, glowing with her newly recovered *joie de vivre,* she charmed her Concord reps, despite their exhaustion after a long flight, into going to a nearby jazz club called the Bird of Paradise after dinner, where she sang a few tunes with the bop-oriented big band in residence, to everyone's enjoyment. In March, she performed in Florida, a Johnny Mercer concert—and got a standing ovation by the audience of 1,700 in the packed theater. After playing a private party at the Waldorf, she began a project dear to her heart: As part of the Lincoln Center Film Festival's program for young children, she devised a program built around the music of Shirley Temple movies, one of the high points of her year.[6]

But she continued to long for family ties. That included reaching out to the estranged Anne DiNicola in Japan, who responded to Susannah's written overtures with affectionate wariness: "I have to admit that [your] first letter scared me a little. I felt afraid for you because you sounded *too* happy—almost manic. I didn't want you to 'fall.'" Susannah continued to feel that she conquered whatever demons of negativity had been plaguing her; the antidotes were healthy living, good relationships, the right medication, and her work, above all. But Anne's words turned out to be prophetic.

Susannah's relationship with Dan DiNicola, as it turned out, had ended at a particularly vulnerable time in her recording and performing career. Since Carl Jefferson had sold Concord Records in 1995 to Alliance Entertainment, problems had been building for both the label and Alliance. According to Allen Farnham, who was still working part-time in the marketing division as well as recording for Concord, "Alliance pulled Concord down into bankruptcy. It was a middleman thing. They happened to own Concord, but they didn't care. Benign neglect: Spend a lot of money and if you go bankrupt—OK." While Concord was in the financial and legal limbo of bankruptcy proceedings, it couldn't do business with chain stores like Tower Records. "As one example, in 1997 and 1998," Farnham explains, "Tower Records pulled all the Concord records and sent them back. Artists were in limbo—no royalties were paid for a while. Then Alliance successfully restructured, but it didn't help Concord." (The next year, while in bankruptcy, Concord became part of a new company, Act III Communications, a holding company owned by film and television veterans Norman Lear and Hal Gaba.) And not only was Susannah's record company in a mess—there were changes afoot regarding the Algonquin that would have a negative impact on her relationship with the Oak Room. Late in 1997, the Algonquin, which had been owned for ten years by a Japanese company, the Aoki Corporation, was sold to Olympus Real Estate.

By 1998, there was no Dan DiNicola to get bookings for her. "She spoke to me several times about the lack of work she had," says drummer Tim Horner, who worked with her during the late nineties. "She'd say, 'I don't know what I'm going to do.'" The Lincoln Center kids' movie-music programs and her workshops for schoolchildren seemed a natural, but this kind of performance never developed into a steady thing.

However, Susannah's euphoria about her personal life was still unflagging. "Life continues to be absolutely wonderful," she told Jackie Osteen in May. "It will be a long time before I get involved emotionally with someone again. I have too much to work through on my own right now." But there were the old signs that the high was wearing off again. She and singer Eric Comstock had volunteered to perform together for AIDS patients and met to rehearse. Like many other musicians, Comstock admired Susannah but found her tough going. "She could be prickly about performance, which really surprised me, because otherwise she was warm and friendly and encouraging. But when she came to rehearse at my apartment, she drove me crazy. She showed up with this cart on wheels with her amp and her mike. 'It's my instrument,' she explained firmly. For this little benefit gig! And the first thing she said upon entering my apartment was, 'You really ought to let more light into this place—it's depressing.' I was nervous about accompanying Susannah, and I admit I was off—but she has to let me know by snapping out the rhythm! After the gig, I backed off. She was kind but difficult to collaborate with."

To keep her spirits up as spring turned to summer, she continued to do all the right things. "I race-walked, sang scales [several octaves of chromatic scales in the morning, to the displeasure of her neighbors] and just generally relaxed, talked to my friends, read," she reported to Osteen. At her friend's gentle prodding, she was also trying to develop some spiritual discipline. Susannah balked at setting foot in a church or temple. "I was raised a socialist so religion's not for me," she said with irrefutable illogic. But she tried to open her mind. "I'm reading *Conversations With God,*" she reported, "and when I can now, I have Saturday as a Spiritual Day and Sunday as a Day Devoted to Friends." What Susannah seemed to keep the faith in was romance and being a good person. "I do have strong feelings that I want a more spiritual life," she responded to Osteen's gentle prodding in that direction, "less about me and more about what I can do for other people." But it was a solitary journey, and there were lower moments again, the medications less effective again, the black, black blues hovering always on the fringe. "*I talked myself through my periods of doubt and fear,"* she wrote soon after. So utterly alone.

For her Algonquin show in the summer of 1998, Susannah took up the suggestion from a friend, Edward Gallet, that she build a show around two of America's and Brazil's greatest popular composers, Gershwin and Jobim. "Why not a 'Best of the Best' type of program," Gallet suggested in a letter. "The trick here, and your mission should you choose to accept it, is finding songs that mesh both musically and thematically." Which Susannah proceeded to do, pairing such tunes as "I Got Rhythm" with "No More Blues" (for an upbeat note), and "Desafinado" with "Let's Call the Whole Thing Off" (for the ending of relationships). Her show, which ran for five weeks in a redecorated Oak Room, got excellent reviews. Stephen Holden, of the *Times,* singled out her "I Loves You, Porgy": Susannah had turned it into a "sad hypnotic thrall to a dangerous but irresistible dream lover." Then there was her "sultry grouping of Jobim warhorses. . . . Her blend of scholarship and musicality has never appeared more seamless."

Yet despite "wonderful nights at the Algonquin," as Susannah wrote to friends, she complained of suffering from "horrendous treatment by the management." By this she meant her chafing relationship with manager and booker Arthur Pomposello. Though he'd walled off the noisy Blue Bar from the Oak Room, as he promised her he would, Susannah found the new wall ineffective. She wanted a thicker barrier installed and complained as well about loud waiters, sparse advertising, and poor lighting, but found him unsympathetic. Other singers complained about him too, though none as much as Susannah. "Pomposello looked like a handsome maitre d', but he had cotton between the ears," says one singer who often performs at the Oak Room. "He was not very smart; he introduced one singer by saying, 'And now so-and-so—the *antithesis* of the world-famous Oak Room!' Can you imagine?" Without DiNicola running interference, Susannah became a wreck. By the second week of "Gershwin to Jobim," she was beside herself. "I was caught in the crossfire of a business with a lot of problems," she complained of Pomposello to Jackie Osteen, "treated so badly by the Gonk [that] it has made it that much harder on my body and soul, like dragging a hundred pound weight around all these five weeks. I am existentially tired."

But Osteen and other close friends, especially Lurie, who knew her mood swings better than anyone, worried there was a more troubling reason for her exhaustion, namely, that her high spirits were collapsing again into depression. After attending a show, Osteen went on a long walk with Susannah. Osteen was deeply concerned:

"I could tell how unhappy she was, and I wanted something to help her." But what? Susannah did still talk to her psychiatrist, but she found the new medication she was on unsatisfactory once more and was beginning to look seriously into alternative therapies.

She'd taken one long-distance relationship a step further. In the middle of June, she and pianist Brad Kay, one of her most avid admirers, finally got together in New York. Kay lived in Venice, California, and had been too ill to travel because of years of complications and pain resulting from a head injury at birth. But by early summer of 1998, he finally felt well enough to travel cross-country. "I had no idea what to expect—I expected this imperious diva," he says. He invited her to Sardi's for lunch. Lunch turned into a walk in Central Park and stretched into the evening, back at her apartment, where, to his amazement and joy, they spent the evening together, just talking and holding each other. "'You should give cuddling lessons to men,' she told me," Kay recalls. The next day, they saw a matinee of the play *Side,* and Kay went to her Algonquin show that night. The next day, she again invited him back to her apartment. "I wanted most of all to play piano for her and maybe accompany her in a song. . . . We dragged her keyboard out of the closet, and I played obscure Irving Berlin tunes, and then I improvised—what I thought of as healing music. And she loved it." As a lifelong sufferer of chronic nerve pain after a forceps-induced cranial injury, Kay had been forced to endure what he terms the "vacuous, icky pabulum of new-agey stuff"—music played by many physical therapists and doctors as an aid to relaxation. Like other sensitive musical souls, Kay reacted by tensing up rather than relaxing. The then-sketchy improvised music for healing that he played for Susannah that summer of 1998 opened up a new direction in music for both of them. And by the time Kay had to return home to California, he was head over heels in love with Susannah. They became intimate e-mail friends, and he was one of the few to whom she truly confided in depth about her mood swings and psychic pain.

There were still glimpses of the bubbly Susannah that June, such as the sly imp who nailed "They All Laughed" in the "Gershwin to Jobim" show. But Susannah declared that she was at her best with sad songs. "Those songs go to the bottom of my soul. It's wonderful to have a song put you in touch with your feelings, make poetry out of your sadness." She sang a ravishingly unadorned and mournful version of Cole Porter's "Weren't We Fools?" at an appearance at the annual Cabaret Convention in New York that year. It had been a year of mostly sadness and struggle. Her jazz-festival gig in San Jose was nothing short of a disaster, from a missed flight by band members to being drowned out on stage by a nearby rock band. "She asked the audience if she should stop, and they said no! So she kept on," recalls Diana Lang Phillips, who came to see her. "But at that time, she was in a bad way, emotionally shaky. We spent hours walking. She was such a giving person, but talking things out was a way to give back to her, as exhausting as her neediness was." Susannah, though, saw her emotional state while in San Jose very differently indeed: "I didn't let myself get depressed and fall into a tailspin about this, nothing ever goes right for me, etc. etc., as I would have done even a year ago," she told Osteen proudly.

There was one hopeful sign: She was getting along better with her mother. Mimi attended a performance in San Francisco after the San Jose festival, later writing a loving note: "You've done so well, you're so loved, I'm so very proud of you." But Susannah was still troubled by Mimi's drinking, by her fuzzy thinking and memory lapses, and called Maggie to enlist her help. Maggie expressed her own concern, but pointed out that she lived far away and as a single mother with a young child, could not easily leave her job. Perhaps, she told Susannah, she was overreacting: "She always was the drama queen of the family," Maggie later remarked. This led to an argument between the two sisters. "I am deeply frustrated and saddened that I can't have a friendship with any member of my family (not by my standards of what a friendship is, anyway)," Susannah told Osteen, adding furiously that she was having the problem of her mother dumped in her lap, "since one sister isn't capable of it and the other doesn't care. I'm the one to do it because I'm the one able and caring enough to do it. No one else in my family even keeps in touch with her, except when they want something. It's so sad. I am glad to feel peaceful and giving with her now, and she is grateful for my commitment to be there for her. Families are so hard, but old hurts getting mended in families is great! It feels good I am there for her after a lifetime of distance.

"I have felt very up and down this summer," Susannah went on. "Last summer I was just euphoric to be liberated and living in NYC, spending time the way I wanted to and with the people I wanted to be with. This summer it is sadder somehow." She missed DiNicola also. "I have lost my closest male friend of many years." She found herself sinking lower again, though good things were on the horizon, such as the prospect of a romance with Brad Kay. But then a series of concerts in Portugal that she greatly anticipated fell through, and she pulled back.

Singing at a memorial service for someone she'd known for years who had recently died of AIDS, Susannah broke down in sobs. After confiding to Lurie that she feared another bout of the "black black blues," Susannah agreed to see a different kind of therapist, one who had helped Lurie recently to cope with acute flare-ups of sciatic pain. Perhaps this therapist, Stephen Kahan, who specialized in biofeedback techniques as well as talk therapy, could help Susannah with her stress and mood swings. "It involves meditation, affirmations, learning how to calm your mind and spirit," explains Lurie of Kahan's approach. "And he was incredibly intuitive and helpful about her specific triggers of stress, such as fear and anger." Susannah, of course, was already receptive to such an approach, having enthusiastically talked up a menu of alternative therapies in her article proposal, "The Upside of Down". With Kahan, she began one of the most important relationships at that stage of her life. At his suggestion, she tried to see her aloneness as an asset that gave her time for meditation, reading, quiet talks with friends. Yet she was in deep pain and knew it (as did Kahan). "There is a void in my life," she confided in Osteen: "I need to make a radical change in the way I think and see the world and myself in it. The therapist I see thinks that it's crucial to throw off old pain. But the only way out of it is through it, so in sessions really terrible experiences and memories get dredged up and sometimes I cry and cry. Mid-October was one of those times. I was just too exhausted." The music business, she added as an afterthought, "is so hard and so mean."

In the fall of 1998, she tried to regain her emotional balance through a program of biofeedback techniques, diet, and Chinese herbs. She had more faith in these palliatives than in the "meds" that caused unappealing side effects, although Kahan states in no uncertain words that he soon came to feel that "she also had to take prescribed medication for her condition." Susannah reluctantly agreed, at first. But her focus was on changing her attitude. To her race-walking partner Linda Fennimore, she posed the question while they were exercising in the park, "How do you do it—the 'cup is half-full' attitude?" Fennimore had been in a catastrophic car accident in which she fractionally missed paralysis of the spine, yet she had a basically upbeat, cheerful attitude, despite years of pain and suffering and a tremendous amount of rehabilitative work as a violinist. "I tried to tell her we all have our down days, but that I had learned to ask for help and accept it," Fennimore says, adding, "Susannah had surgery on her leg to repair a bad scar, and she was laid up afterward. I offered to help her, but you couldn't help Susannah. She was very independent, and she had to control as much of her environment as possible."

Susannah's next recording, *From Broken Hearts to Blue Skies,* recorded at the end of October 1998, was by far the most autobiographical of her albums. "I decided to face down my demons and embrace singing more than ever," she declared about the record, which "reflects my journey, going from the depths of despair to philosophizing and laughing at life and embracing the cycles people go through in their lives."

*Broken Hearts* is a wish list, from "Laughing at Life," to the implied yearning in her bright-eyed version of "Blue Skies," the starkly felt "Something to Live For," the tender fantasy in "Stop, Time," the faraway optimism of "Look for the Silver Lining," and her lovely Brazilian ballad, "Caminhos Cruzados." "Caminhos" is recorded on the album only in Portuguese: Susannah failed to get permission from the Brazilian publisher to use her poetic new English lyric, "Faint Music." It was an omission she found devastating, although at least her new English version of Django's "Nuages" was included.

Of all the songs on the album, "I Wish I Were in Love Again" was the most autobiographical. How she loved being called a "bruised romantic," as a *People* magazine profile did; she hugged that phrase to her like an Oscar. "She was always saying to me, you gotta stay romantic—it's the only way to go," remembers Roy Schecter. But in the fall of 1998, depressed, nearly 53, with a lifetime of failed romances behind her, most recently with Eric Olson, it would seem Susannah had little reason to expect a great love affair.

*Broken Hearts* was a recording that almost didn't get made. Susannah was thinking, more and more, of quitting as a singer and becoming a music therapist. It was a turn that mystified many of her friends.[7] She told Sigi Schmidt-Joos in an interview for his German radio show, "I thought, I can't make the album, I'm no good, but then I thought, many many people make such an emotional journey." So well did she mask her own severe doubts and despair, however, that none of the musicians and technicians involved in making the album thought that she was deeply depressed; rather, they observed a cool and distant Susannah at work. "She was rather dour and severe and very proper and rather remote," says Josiah Gluck, who worked with Susannah for the first time on *Broken Hearts* as her recording engineer. "It was frustrating for me because I was new working with her for the three days it took to record. She had a certain aura, rather passive-aggressive, of telling people what to do. Not angrily, but devoid of any bedside manner. She didn't seem to have the skill to be cooperative. And she didn't strike me as a sensual woman. If she could have gotten away with it, she would have worn the pillbox hat and the white gloves."

"Maybe a little anger would have helped. I had noticed on earlier records of hers that she was adamant about being far forward of the instrumentalists—what we call having the vocals hot in the mix. Generally, the vocalists are more integrated with the band," explains Gluck, who'd worked with singers of the caliber and range of Chris Connor, Karen Akers, Judy Collins, Patti Austin, and Karrin Allyson. But then Gluck began to understand what Susannah was about. "I came to see that Susannah's reason for pushing herself up in terms of the sound was that she gave an incredibly nuanced performance and the lyrics were of paramount importance. She liked the lyrics loud in the mix—*she was telling herself a story*. And then we worked well together. Afterward, I remember she sent me a nice bottle of wine and a note."

Susannah's listeners were again divided in their enthusiasm for her latest record. Some fans from the earlier years felt that she had become rather mannered, while others who appreciated her sensitive ballads wondered why she also continued singing brassy showstoppers. (On this album, it was the vaudeville blues "I Ain't Gonna Play No Second Fiddle.") But she was choosing to sing what she wanted to sing, after all.

After recording the CD, Susannah performed at a concert in Southampton in the fall, and appeared at Carnegie Hall as the featured singer with Skitch Henderson and the New York Pops Orchestra in a program called "The Brazilian Beat," singing "Wave," "The Waters of March," "One Note Samba," and "Manha de Carnaval." The concert was a great success—"the happiest night of my life," Susannah called it—before she went on the road for three more performances with Henderson and the orchestra.

And Susannah was feeling more hopeful as the 1998 holidays came around. At Christmas, she wrote Jackie Osteen, "I can really feel myself emerging from [the depression] in a good way, more hopeful for the future and in a better more solid way than I've ever been." She postponed a visit to California to see Mimi—too depressing—and turned to her new best friend, Mark Nadler, in whom she'd finally found the perfect Christmas cookie-making partner. Keith Ingham had simply shrugged when she was into her cookie-baking and -painting extravaganzas; Richard Rodney Bennett, in whose apartment she made the cookies after she split up with Ingham, found the whole idea "ghastly, all these cookies painted in ugly colors that you threw away and all these people invited to make them who weren't at ease"; and Dan DiNicola had found the whole occasion "out of control," with special trips downtown to SoHo for special cookie paints. But for Nadler, it was a chance to be a kid again. "Mainly what we did was laugh." When a painted snowwoman broke in half, they ended up making what they called "sick cookies"—cookie amputees and so on. And laughed the harder.

But there was still, for Susannah, the hurdle of New Year's to get through. She traveled out to Shelter Island, where she spent New Year's Eve with her friends the Ben-Susans, who hosted a small gathering every year at their place, where Susannah liked to go to escape the city. She was back on medication and felt better, on an upswing. In a holiday card to Chris Ellis in London, she wrote that January 1 of 1999, "I'm a happy canary, it's a very happy birthday this time. I went walking with people, good people. I never felt so good starting a New Year." She liked Julie and Paul Ben-Susan, he a high-level financial planner, who had given Susannah hours of free financial advice when she requested it over the past several years—and she liked the tall, dark, interesting man she met at the party, Daniel Moran, a dentist who also wrote poetry and had attended her fall concert in Southampton. But the Ben-Susans remember a Susannah still struggling with her emotions. "We were not close friends, but we knew about her concern with the depression," says Julie Ben-Susan. "She had an obsession with looking gorgeous and staying healthy, but I knew she was tortured. She'd call and say, 'I'm going through a depression—just leave me alone until I resurface.'" That New Year's Eve seemed even harder for her to cope with others they'd shared. "She hated the thought of another year, every year," says Paul Ben-Susan. "She wouldn't come out of her room for a dinner for 21 people, though finally she did."

Several days later, Susannah flew out to spend time with Mimi. Returning to New York in mid-January, she wrote Osteen that it had been a tough visit. Mimi, she said, was depressed, and why wouldn't she be, "having to deal with Katie and Carlos, Katie's hot-tempered, lazy, sponging son." Susannah played mom, and Mimi let her. "I just pampered her and spent money on her till she responded to it. She drank less and less during the visit as I got her more things to make her life better and easier. I kept up my positive feelings," Susannah reported. "And I am fine, never better! Yes, you are actually seeing those words. It's a combination of therapy, meditation, medicine (which I just had to cut in half because I was getting too wired and happy!), friends, and some good breaks professionally."

But in fact, her singing work appeared to be drying up—she still had no manager or regular booking agent, though publicist Bryan Utman stepped in at times. Susannah was drawn back, more and more, to the idea of writing long, absorbing stories, perhaps a book. In the meantime, *American Heritage* accepted her proposal to do an article that would highlight entertainer Mae West's little-known importance as a singer, a plan she abandoned after she'd delved further into West's autobiography. If not a really notable singer, however, West was a female character to admire, Susannah surmised.

But she also had another project in mind, far bigger than Mae West. While sorting through some boxes she'd brought with her from Schenectady that year, Susannah came across a bundle of a dozen dusty old notebooks filled with her accounts of living in Rome from 1970 to 1972. Reading them for the first time after all those years, Susannah felt a growing excitement. There were wonderful anecdotes, vividly drawn characters at the time she had launched herself as both a singer and a woman having her first serious love affairs. She would transcribe them, she decided, then polish them and talk to her agent: This might be the book she'd been circling for years. Susannah thought her coming-of-age story would be compelling to both young women struggling to find themselves and especially to others of her generation, who would relate to it out of their own experience. She began typing the handwritten journal entries into her computer but soon found that she couldn't work at home—this time there was loud noise from construction outside, and a neighbor "who played loud, terrible music all the time," she complained in an e-mail to Osteen. So she was very receptive to Mark Nadler's suggestion that she make the third-floor aerie of his charming, narrow old house in nearby Riverdale her office. She had what amounted to an entire apartment to herself—a study with a view of shade trees, bedroom, bath, and kitchenette. "She would work up there for hours, days," Nadler recalls.

Once she'd transcribed and polished the diaries, she sent the manuscript to her agent, Gail Hochman, to look at. Hochman was measured in her response, telling Susannah she had a wonderful eye, wry and observant. Added to which she had rich material. But, the agent cautioned, the manuscript was far from ready to show to publishers. "I said that very few journals are that interesting, and hers was filled with a lot of unnecessary detail. Then there was its tone. Cornelia Otis Skinner wrote a book about going to Europe, *Our Hearts Were Young and Gay,* about being young, on her own, happy. Well, Susannah's journals were not transcendent like that. Yes, there were wonderful descriptions of her Roman neighborhood, but there was also all the unhappiness. She sounded like a scared young girl in a woman's body, putting up with all these creepy guys. Not perverse, but sad." True: Though *Secrets in Piazza Navona* contains funny and joyous passages, there are as well many depictions of a deeply unhappy, depressed Susannah in her 20s, including several scenes in which she contemplates suicide. Last but not least, Hochman added, the current publishing market was tough—the book might be difficult to place.

Susannah responded with dejection. "I've always suffered from lack of confidence," she explained to Diana Lang Phillips. "And now, everything's getting turned down." In addition, revisiting the past was harder than she'd expected: There'd been a great deal of pain, even trauma, that she'd put aside in ensuing years. "It was painful, scary, though a cathartic experience for her, those journals from when she was starting out as a jazz singer in Rome," Phillips recalls. But Susannah willed herself to go on with the book. She settled on a theme—the search for love and meaning in her life at a time of great social and political change in both America and Europe—and began eliminating anecdotes that were amusing but basically irrelevant. She wrote of the darkness that periodically enclosed her, that forced her into darkened rooms, into dark corners of her psyche, but also of her zest for beautiful surroundings and adventure and colorful companions, of meeting her closest friend during those years in Rome, of falling in love with music, and, finally, of finding one of the great loves of her life.

Energized by the book project, Susannah began to feel better again and was more than ready to meet attractive men after having kept her distance. Jackie Osteen had tried to play Cupid: Falling into conversation with a man on a plane, she discovered he was a music buff—and a fan of Susannah's. Was Susannah interested in corresponding with him? Maybe. "Is he tall?" she wrote in a joking e-mail. "You know I like big men." They exchanged e-mails, but she was put off when she found that the man, John Hewett, had been a Protestant minister before becoming a fund-raiser for fine-arts programs. "Religion is just not an answer to me—spirituality, yes, religion no," she told him after some back and forth. When Hewett learned that Susannah's father had died by his own hand four years before, he sent her a copy of his book, *After Suicide,* written for friends and family of the deceased. But Susannah let the correspondence drop. "She gave Hewett's book back to me," says Osteen, "saying she hadn't read it."

In March, the man she'd met and liked at the Ben-Susan's New Year's party on Shelter Island called her. Dr. Daniel Moran was a tall, dark, intense man passionate about the arts and with children from previous marriages—not unlike the previous Dan. Also like Dan DiNicola, he was in the process of finalizing his second divorce—and extricating himself from a messy rebound relationship. Paul Ben-Susan and Dan Moran were very close. "It was almost a father-son thing between them. They spoke every day," says Julie Ben-Susan, "mostly about Dan, who was torn between being a dentist and a poet."

Moran had tickets for a Carnegie Hall concert on St. Patrick's Day. "I called Susannah and she was happy to go," he says. "We had dinner and went to the concert and then I walked her back to her apartment. Afterward, she told Gary and Phyllis Gates [other Manhattan–Shelter Island friends] that she was immediately smitten. She didn't tell me that, although she did say she'd had a fabulous time. But when I asked her out again, she was busy. Then, two weeks later, she called me."

That was the start of their affair, these two romantics pressing daffodils in a book, writing poems, and singing songs to each other. "When I wasn't looking, I met somebody who's perfect for me! He is so friendly and kind that everyone likes him," Susannah enthused. "I've been incredibly busy and it's a wonder and a good sign that Daniel and I made it through." Euphoric, she called old friends, including her old therapist, Roberta Todras, to tell her she was happy at last. "I tried to be supportive," Todras says. "She was idealistic—that was her strength and her vulnerability."

Says Moran, "I loved her. We talked about getting married." But privately, others wondered about the relationship: he so recently divorced, Susannah typically effervescently over-the-top In Love. There was an aura of puppy love around this middle-aged couple. "She instantly became like a child about him—it was amazing to me," observes Julie Ben-Susan. Susan Monserud and Ric Sonder, whom the new couple visited in Roxbury, agree. "Each conspired to be in love, I think," Monserud says. Adds Sonder, "They sat on our couch cuddling. He was possessive, infatuated with Susannah. And she said, 'I *think* I'm in love.'" Says Rex Reed, whom they also visited nearby, with a wave of his hand, "He was a dentist who really wanted to be a poet, very emotionally needy and not her type—she liked tweedy men."

Meanwhile, her divorce from Dan DiNicola was finalized, with Susannah receiving half of the value of the Schenectady house.[8] "And then she wanted money for the furniture and effort she'd put into it," DiNicola adds. "I went along, although my lawyer thought I was crazy." But there was little acrimony between them—rather, a sense of deep regret and of unresolved matters. "We always knew that we were forever best friends," DiNicola says. "We never lost our love for each other." Thea Lurie agrees: DiNicola was the love of Susannah's life.

Despite her divorce settlement, she was still worried about money, specifically about her lack of income from singing work. She had fewer bookings. But in the spring, still up and high on her new romance, Susannah felt far more generous than fearful. She did a benefit concert for the Eye Bank, in gratitude for its help with her wandering eye problem. And she decided to become active in breast-cancer workshops to help other women who had the disease. "Now it's not just about me, me, me, all the time," she wrote happily. But her singing career still mattered greatly, too. "I won a MAC award [a cabaret organization] for the best jazz or swing CD tonight!" she wrote Osteen. "Mark won too. We were really soaring from such a happy night." She joined Mark Nadler and Joe Holloway for dinner at Easter, before the director-choreographer-producer died after a lengthy illness in May. "She was the last witness of Joe and me," Nadler says.

Notwithstanding Susannah's worries about less work, the late spring was a productive time for Susannah. She played one of her favorite clubs, Blues Alley, in Washington, D.C., then Boston in June, and prepared for her latest Algonquin show opening a month later (but without the higher salary and percentage that she'd prodded Pomposello for). The show, "From Broken Hearts to Blue Skies: A Single Woman in Manhattan," built on the album's theme of a single woman's experiences in New York, was pure autobiography. It was one of Susannah's more successful programs. Though long, with 18 songs, the performance was well paced, well rehearsed, with the clever, on-point commentary that Susannah, sleek and purring like a cat, had mastered. Gone now were the awkward, schoolmarm mannerisms. This Susannah was still believably sensual and smart, warm and yearning, but controlled, smooth. And the songs were mostly marvelous, framing the "story" of a long love affair, from an upbeat beginning, "Blue Skies," to its end, "Bye Bye Blues." The first half centered on recovering from heartbreak, though the plot did at times veer, as when for no apparent reason she sang Dave Frishberg's "I Wanna Be a Sideman." The second half was about finding a new love. "It was about us, about falling in love," Moran declares. "It was a real thrill to be there and to hear her sing about me!" "During that time she was with Daniel, she seemed so happy," concurs Lisa Popa of the Algonquin. "Enjoying things—sometimes she'd even sit down and talk after a show at the Algonquin. It was unheard of for her to hang out—she didn't do it! But I remember one night in 1999 after a performance, she sat in the lobby and talked until 2:00 A.M. with a bunch of people including Andrea Marcovicci."

For Susannah, performing in 1999 was "a time of really great closeness with my audiences." "Seeing as many of her performances as I did over the years, these were supremely honest performances," says her longtime friend Andy Lipman. "Susannah didn't pander to the audience, and because she'd never dumb it down, her product wasn't accessible to large audiences." Yet despite the show's excellent reviews and response, despite her protestations that her personal life was happier than it had been in ages, the old ominous signs of a crash were creeping in again. "I have been feeling very fragmented for weeks, feeling I just wasn't doing a good job at anything (including looking after myself), am tired and frazzled," she wrote Osteen. And her friends and fans noticed telling details that summer at the Gonk. "There was something about Susannah that always seemed a little tied up, even when she was performing—her very clenched jaw that gave her that very specific and wonderful way of speaking. Her laughter—she would always laugh as if she was trying not to," Nadler notes. "She looked gorgeous and younger than she was," singer Carol Fredette observes, "and she had great posture. But she looked so stiff she could break; there was a fragility there at the same time she was holding it together—this *tight-ness*. I had a vision of her crumbling."

"We were at the Oak Room that summer," Ric Sonder remembers. "Before the show, on my way back from the men's room, I saw Susannah standing in a little curtained vestibule I had to pass. I touched her arm and said hello. She looked at me as if I were a foreign object." Bassist Bill Moring, who played several of her Algonquin shows, had a similar experience. "Susannah working was very uptight—her face would be twitching before a show. One night, right before an opening, I went up and impulsively gave her a hug. Wrong move. She was shat-tered by this. But after a gig," he adds, "she would be all relaxed and bubbly."

Says Moran, "She was extremely, pathologically private, and she was a master at acting a part. There were three of her: the person on stage; the person with friends and family; and finally, the incredibly tortured, wounded little girl. I saw her go from a human puddle to getting into a sequined gown and going on stage. Her public image was terribly important to her—every bit of that image. And it was all different from the private. Her emotional self wasn't sane—it was unpredictable and bizarre. So I had very mixed feelings."

That needy, sad, observant, *determined* little girl telling her mother, "Someday I am going to be bigger than you." (And she was! her elderly mother had exclaimed, all those years later.) The complex, layered, and compartmentalized way of living, begun as a child. The stories she wrote, all about Susannah playing parts—forbidden or shameful or exciting. The appraising onlooker, the voyeur, including of scripted sexual scenarios. (Those tawdry sexual incidents recalled by Keith Ing-ham are more disturbing because they appear so out of synch with the white-gloved romantic with a capital "R," good girl Susannah.) The many passages in which the female protagonist considers or even plans suicide—and in several cases, characters who go further than planning it. And then the droll Susannah, laughing at life and herself, the Sun-shine Susannah, the acute intelligence, the deep sensitivity to a lyric.

At this stage of Susannah's life, a number of her friends—Rick McKay, Eric Olson, Gary Gates—stumbled onto other bits and pieces of the puzzle that was her personality. When they called her on the tele-phone, they were taken aback to hear her pretending to be a personal assistant named Anne Jeffreys. (Susannah also printed up stationery in Jeffreys' name for her business correspondence.) "She didn't like to admit she didn't have an actual message-taker, and she very much wanted to screen her calls," Gates says, "hence, the ploy of the secretary." "But," adds Olson, "she was embarrassed when I caught her at it. It was a kind of doubling or splitting, I think. And, she felt shame about this person—herself—who was not the hopeful persona of 'The Waters of March.'" There was also the Susannah who trolled the Internet under several pseudonyms, posting a description of herself on at least one online dating service, though she then backed away from a date. The doubling, of course, went way back. Another example had been early in her New York recording career, when she wrote interesting liner notes about the Hollywood lyricist Leo Robin for her album tribute to him, as well as notes about herself for "How Do You Keep the Music Playing?"—but both under the pseudonym "R. Nicholson."

In August, Susannah headed for California, where she had finally landed another booking at the recently enlarged jazz club Yoshi's in Oakland's Jack London Square. Getting that gig spoke volumes about the way the music industry viewed Susannah, then at the peak of her artistic powers. On the one hand, the club wanted her; on the other, they wouldn't take her without a jazz "name" to draw a crowd. So, says Allen Farnham, they brought in guitarist Charlie Byrd, whose simple accompaniment worked beautifully for Susannah—and drew a sold-out audience. Ironically, Susannah got a rapturous review: Her voice was called "luscious." But the positive outcome at Yoshi's was not enough to quell Susannah's demons of insecurity. *I can never believe anyone is going to come see me,* she confided later back in New York.

There were other demons at work for her there. While in Oakland, Susannah naturally visited her mother, alone. "She wanted me to go out to California with her, but I couldn't," says Dan Moran. Things did not go well with Mimi; more to the point, Susannah was cycling down into a depression. "When she came back, she was an absolute mess—she hated it out there," Moran recalls. He and Susannah thought it would be better for their relationship if he bought a house, as he'd been planning to do eventually. "He'd been living in these post-divorce, temporary cabin quarters, not acceptable to her, and he wanted a house anyway," says Julie Ben-Susan. "So he bought one, and he was converting the living room into a study for Susannah to write in. But then she said she couldn't work there—she found it stifling. He didn't understand that she needed space and time alone, although he didn't want her to leave her city world completely."

Susannah feared a repeat of Schenectady and couldn't imagine spending the bulk of her time on a small island with a limited number of diversions. "She said she thought her career had almost tanked because of living in Schenectady," Phyllis Gates says. In early September, Moran went to dinner with his longtime confidant, Paul Ben-Susan. "He wanted to talk. He was in anguish," Julie says.

"Then came the hot button," Paul Ben-Susan recalls. "Dan asked me if I thought the relationship would work long-term, and I told him I didn't think so. The relationship was oil and water. I had seen Susannah with Dan DiNicola, too, which is how we met Susannah. Both the Dans have big egos, the same sort of edge about their own self-worth, this in-your-face attitude. And I thought Susannah had a great deal of ego as well." He was concerned as well about their age difference. Susannah had never mentioned her age, and Moran hadn't asked. But now Ben-Susan brought it up. "I asked Dan Moran, who was then 42, 'How old do you think she is?' He certainly didn't think that Susannah was 53."

"The fact that he was a lot younger bothered *her* a lot," emphasizes Susan Monserud. Julie Ben-Susan recalls that Susannah found out that Paul, citing concern about the relationship, had told Moran her age. "She exploded. I had never seen that side of her. She was furious and lambasted Paul when she called," says Julie Ben-Susan. The long friendship between Moran and Paul Ben-Susan ended, and the friendship between Susannah and the Ben-Susans hung by a thread.

Her relationship with Moran crumbling, unable to concentrate, Susannah postponed her next recording date, which had been scheduled for October, to March of the following year. Instead, that October, Moran accompanied Susannah to upstate New York, where she did a "Broken Hearts" show in Kinderhook and he wrote a poem he titled "Austerlitz at October's Ending," containing the line, "Deny the coming of bareness and numbing." Says Moran, "It was hard to deny when the end did come, soon after."

The parting occurred when Susannah was on the verge of moving in with him to his new house on Shelter Island. "It was then that I realized I was going down into a black hole if I stayed with her," Moran says. "It would have been a disaster. I was way too concerned about her emotional state. In early November, I ended the relationship. She was really surprised. She asked, 'Do you really think we have to end it now?' It shook her up. I said yes, or else it will be on-again, off-again." Susannah went off by herself, seeing no one, crushed. "She was terrified of rejection by anyone on any level; she made the breakup into a mutual thing. That's what she told people we knew."

"It was not a pleasant breakup; there was no cordiality involved," adds Lorraine Ruggieri, Susannah's dressmaker and a confidante. Very good at having the last word, Susannah told Mark Nadler, "He wasn't in love with me—he wanted me to be something that wasn't me." She added, dismissively, "He was a dentist who wants to be a poet."

Keith Ingham had found another woman, then terminated their professional relationship; Dan DiNicola had rejected her idea of a trial separation, opting for divorce, and he also found another woman, who subsequently moved into the Schenectady house. And now there was Dan Moran, who would prove to be the last man to shut the door on her dream of love. But she was not going to let people see how much she had been hurt by these experiences, or that she had been rejected. With her intense and obsessive need to shape and protect her public self-image, Susannah characterized these breakups as initiated by her.

As she had always done, Susannah put on her public face, the cheery and slightly heroic survivor: "Still resting from romance after my last one," she wrote in a Christmas letter to Roy Schecter, "when I almost got married to another controlling and angry man who was excited to have a girl friend who was an artist but wanted to turn her into a housewife and fence her in. Life is good but I want more!" she concluded.

She turned to friends for solace. Nadler was hugely supportive, especially now. "Our friendship didn't really deepen until after Joe died— because it's different when you're three." And Brad Kay, who visited early in December, recalls how very sad she was at dinner. "I told her he didn't deserve her and gave her a book, *The Courage to Create,* by Rollo May. It was the beginning of our intimate friendship; though still reticent, she told me things."

Indeed, her friendships were hugely important to her that Christmas of 1999, particularly after an article that month in *Time,* lauding the "aristocracy of the cabaret world," made no mention of her, which cut deep. She celebrated Christmas with Lurie, as Nadler was still in mourning for his companion. She consoled Schecter after learning his father had committed suicide, adding, "I have vowed to myself to write a book. I am scaring myself into doing it—no bookings until March. And I'll be recording in March too."

There was no man in her life now, and it seemed less and less likely that there would be someone to fulfill her dream of romantic love. "You know the song 'Falling in Love With Love'?" asks Nadler rhetorically. "That was Susannah. She was never really in love with the men she thought she was in love with. There seemed to me nothing wrong with her relationship with Dan DiNicola in real life, the way we are on this planet. But it didn't begin to measure up to the songs, the lyrics. And with Daniel Moran, it looked really good in the beginning. He was attentive, he was interesting, he seemed very much in love with her. She had such clear pictures in her mind of when she would finally be really in love. And of course that's not how it works. And I think because these relationships never lived up to what was in her mind, she idealized 'love' in her mind's eye. She would sing these songs and want her life to *be* these songs. And it was absolutely not possible that her life could ever be that way."

Two days before 1999 ended, after thanking Brad Kay for his "kindness and compassion at this very hard time in my life," she wrote him the following letter:

> Sometimes when I'm so down I can hardly bear to go out. I make myself go out anyway and in my pained state I feel the pain of other people in the streets so intensely that it is at once impossible to bear and beautiful to bear. And then when I sing a sad song, the pain I have known flows out of me and comforts people. At least, I hope so . . .
>
> I think one of the saddest things for me is that I hardly listen to music when I am down. . . . The music that inspired me to become a singer isn't what I want to hear now. I feel too beaten up by the music business. I think I'm just burnt out. I am so tired of fighting to keep alive and make a living in music that I am deadened by it. I'm even feeling I can't sing any more.

Or maintain a love affair anymore. Susannah contemplated getting in touch with Francesco Forti. He'd written to her several times over the years, but she'd felt it was better not to see him: "He was a figure from the past." But now that her romantic dream with Moran had shattered, she found she was reliving the precious feelings she'd shared with Forti again as she reread the diaries that chronicled her coming of age in Italy and England a quarter century before. Now she wanted to reach out to her first love, to tell him that she at last realized just how important their relationship had been to her. But before she could do so, she was stunned to receive a letter from—of all people—Francesco's wife, Donatella. She was writing to tell Susannah that Francesco had died of cancer the previous February. "I know how important Francesco was in your life," she said. "It is stupid to ask if we would have been any happier if things had gone differently. Maybe yes, maybe no—life is so mysterious, not to speak of death."

For Susannah, Donatella's letter yanked open a door to the past. "I knew that this wasn't all just a coincidence—it was a sign." A portent that revived the memory of what, as she told her mother then for the first time, "had been the greatest love of my life"—and, as she learned now from Donatella, she had been so for him. Well, if she couldn't have romance one way, then she'd find it another. With renewed intensity, Susannah vowed to focus on the past and began to reshape the diaries into a book.

# Stop, Time

I cannot live without love and affection and without loving people, and I *must* be around people even though I admit some of
them, even most of them, are disappointing.
>—Susannah, journal entry, 1970 in Rome

As she turned 54, Susannah turned often to Brad Kay as a confidant. Of
course she confided in others, in Mark Nadler and Jackie Osteen and
old friends she saw less often, and above all in Thea Lurie. But Kay,
who adored her, was an amusing and sympathetic correspondent, a
musician who knew a lot about pain from his own experience. And,
most importantly, he was far away. She could safely send him dis-
patches about her unhappiness. "This will be our secret conversation,"
she told him in early January 2000. "I have friends, I am blessed with
friends, but sometimes I just can't reach out to anyone. No one would
believe how scared of the future I am and I don't want to scare them
about me, or come across as a person in crisis or a depressed (and therefore depressing) person." She was still mostly successful in keeping the
image intact. The polite smile and bread-and-butter notes to generous
friends and fans continued to the end. But inside, she now waged an
ever-fiercer battle against the negativity that threatened to engulf her
completely. She kept up the health-food diet, the race-walking, the visits to biofeedback therapist Stephen Kahan, to help "stop the chatter,"
as he puts it. To "stay positive," as Susannah said. She also took yet
another new prescription dispensed by Dr. Brusco, though reluctantly.
This, recalls Kahan, was "little bits of Clonopin, which is like a stronger
Valium."[1] "But she would not take a mood stabilizer—she didn't want
the side effects she saw in her nephew and others."

The hope was that this medication would help level the mood

swings to some extent; instead, the general tenor of Susannah's life from then on was a seesaw from despair to hope back to despair; furthermore, the "cycling," as it is called, was, her closest friends observed, both more rapid and extreme as the year 2000 continued.

Yet she did rally—for, of course, Susannah was a trouper as well as a tragedienne. New projects gave her inspiration—Kay's "music for healing" encouraged her to explore seriously the idea of becoming a music therapist or, perhaps, to collaborate with him. She told him, "I am finding my way out of this strange transitional time in my life and feeling less alone than ever in my journey!" The positive note may have been partly due to having completed her Mae West article; she described herself as being "elated" with the 10,000-word piece. (Though not for long. She was soon told it had to be cut *by half,* a loathed task that took her months.)[2]

Meanwhile, Susannah prepared for her next recording session at the end of March. The CD, to be called *Hearts and Minds,* was the basis for her next Algonquin show, for which she would expand both the number of songs, and the title, to "Hearts and Minds: Life in Manhattan as a Hopeless Romantic." As "Broken Hearts and Blue Skies" had been, so too was *Hearts and Minds* deeply autobiographical, about a single woman in middle age, still longing for romance and companionship. The album had the usual cluster of beautiful songs of longing: "I Can Dream, Can't I?" "For All We Know," "Love Look Away," and a gorgeous version of "I Don't Want to Set the World on Fire." And there were also songs that expressed her fragile mental and emotional condition: "Haunted Heart" and "Scars" and "Down," the latter a chillingly accurate reading of depression, by the witty but mordant lyricist Fran Landesman. "Susannah would always get songs from people," recalls pianist-arranger Allen Farnham. "Landesman came to a show at the Algonquin, and Susannah wanted to develop a relationship with her. She sang her 'Feet Do Your Stuff,' and she loved 'Scars,' sang it two years in a row." An album and show by Susannah were also never complete without something by Dave Frishberg—here, "My Attorney Bernie" and "Do You Miss New York?"—and something from Brazil, in this case, Ivan Lins's ballad "Evolution" and, on Farnham's recommendation, Susannah's lyric to a catchy Brazilian melody for which she'd written an English translation as "The Computer Age."

For the CD, producer Nick Phillips again brought in Josiah Gluck, as both the recording and the mixing engineer. "I'm not only the chef that buys the provisions—I get to cook it too," he says. Gluck's "cooking" included tweaking and fine-tuning around Susannah's sometimes wavering pitch and subsequent tendency to colorlessness. But the final product on the CD is hers, a voice roughened by time and use (something to which Susannah did not at all object) but, at the same time, with a rather lighter timbre than usual on her recordings—what *Times* reviewer Stephen Holden described admiringly as her "undercurrent of swinging enthusiasm" and one listener called "a thrilling mixture of girlishness and maturity." "It took two ten-hour days," Gluck recalls of the recording. "She took it very seriously." As with her *Broken Hearts* CD, Susannah wanted the sound of the vocal to dominate, with the piano and drums way back—"the singer apart from the band," Farnham says she told him, adding, "It was the sound she'd fallen in love with in Paris and Rome." And this old-fashioned mix, they all agreed, worked for her. "I feel it's going to be my best CD ever!" she wrote Mark Nadler enthusiastically. It was also to be her last.

*Hearts and Minds* behind her, Susannah accepted an invitation to visit Jackie and Hubert Osteen's beach house in South Carolina. But with the focus off her work and back on herself, Susannah's mood swung low again. "I could tell she was down on herself when she arrived," Jackie Osteen says. "I knew Susannah loved peace and solitude, gardens and flowers, so that's the kind of visit we arranged." Depression also made Susannah irritable. When Osteen, to whom she had often confided about her longing for romance, suggested she date a certain musician, Susannah snapped. "She said, 'You've brought up my looking for a man several times in front of others!' I was hurt, and it was a tense evening. But the next morning, I brought her orange juice, and she just put her arms around me and hugged me. And then it was all right again."

But things were not all right with Susannah. "It isn't going well," she told Mark Nadler about her state of mind on her return to New York. She was determined to finish editing her Mae West piece, but, above all, she wanted to complete and publish her book, an accomplishment that would give her much-needed validation as a writer. She had now come full-circle, it seemed, back to the late 1960s in Europe, when she had done an about-face and decided to become a singer and keep writing on the side. "Singing work was diminishing," says James Gavin. "She knew editing the diaries was a good idea and was applying the old drive, but was wracked by a lack of confidence." While she did have some singing work coming up—workshops in New York City high schools with Farnham and bassist Bill Moring in the spring and several other engagements—Susannah still could not find an agent to take on the endless work of promotion and marketing, and though she had worked intensely, and some would say rather ruthlessly, at promoting herself earlier in her career, by this stage of the game, as Dan DiNicola puts it, she was "not a schmoozer." It had become too much of an effort for too few results.

"How I wish that someone would encourage me in what I'm doing," Susannah told her dressmaker, Lorraine Ruggieri, in the spring of 2000. She no longer went up to Nadler's. When he needed to rent out her third-floor aerie as a separate apartment, he offered her a bedroom downstairs and a desk in his living room to work on, but she'd lost the privacy she cherished, and she and the new tenant upstairs did not get along. "She vocalized early in the morning, and it drove him crazy," Nadler says. So, instead, every day that she could bring herself to do it, Susannah would lug her laptop across the park to the quiet of the private New York Society Library on Manhattan's Upper East Side. There, she'd work for hours on her book or, sometimes, write *about* writing in her "library notes." Her lack of confidence persisted. "I'm glad I have so many resources for pulling myself up, but sometimes they just can't lift me that extra inch over the line between hope and despair," she wrote.

In June, she felt better. "She said she had an important breakthrough about her book and was feeling good writing instead of hating everything she did," recalls Nadler, "and she planned to work on the book all summer." And then down again, into the well-worn psychological grooves of her constant battle with self. When it was bad—and it was usually bad—her money fears tightened, and her ability to deal with life's aches and pains dissolved. At a session with "SK," as she referred to Stephen Kahan in her diary, she told him she couldn't afford to see him regularly—biofeedback therapy was not reimbursable through her medical insurance—though the day before, she expressed gratitude that she had a "nest egg" to see her through the next year so she could concentrate on her book. An orthopedist had told her she had to stop race-walking until a painful foot condition improved, but she continued, getting wraps and heel lifts, and she shouted at Kahan when "he suggested that my feeling of being ungrounded in life is reflected in my foot pain." Later, she realized she had misconstrued the therapist's remarks, but she told him she was still angry—and terrified of what she called "sinking financially."

Yet somehow, as she'd always managed to do, Susannah back-burnered her fear and black moods and worked hard, that summer of 2000, on getting her book finished or, at least, finished enough to show her agent. It was a season that seemed to move in slow motion. "I'm enjoying a quiet summer," she said, "feeling calm and purposeful." Friends to whom she read out passages were entranced. In July, she took the manuscript up to Roxbury to Susan Monserud and Ric Sonder's house. "We were so taken by her ability to create the moment in words," Monserud says. Heartened by their enthusiasm, Susannah took her laptop later that month out to her friend Pam Berlin's farmhouse in New Jersey. Work, she'd decided, was *the* antidote to the low moods. She and Berlin, a director, worked on their projects, then had long walks and conversation. "I'm successfully hiding from romantic entanglements," Susannah joked. "There is so much that is positive and constructive about me—I am fighting the dark side much harder than I ever have before in every healthy way I know how."

There were very occasional interludes of music-making, too, during that literary summer, such as a session with Marian McPartland on her popular *Piano Jazz* radio program. It was an all–Alec Wilder date, with Susannah singing, beautifully, six of his songs. After she'd finished the mournful, complex lament "Who Can I Turn To?", a song pervaded with loneliness, Susannah complimented McPartland on her playing. "You really brought out the sadness in the song," she told her. McPartland returned the compliment, then laughingly added, eerily in retrospect, "As long as nobody throws herself out of a window!" This program, broadcast six months later, the day after Christmas, is one of the very last recordings of Susannah singing.

Mostly, the summer of 2000 was a time of intense reflection for Susannah through her writing, a season that she seemed to live almost in slow motion. But by the end of August, she had an impressive number of pages to show Gail Hochman: a proposal, outline, prologue, and 270 pages of the work she now called *Secrets in Piazza Navona*. "I *burn* to write this book! I am completely committed to it!" she wrote Hochman in a cover letter. But the agent's considered response was sprinkled cool water over the fire: She saw a lot more work ahead before they could think of sending *Secrets* around to publishers, a lot of cutting and rewriting. Susannah was crushed by Hochman's reservations. "Everything's getting turned down," she told a friend sadly. "She felt really bad about her writing," James Gavin explains. "She had no confidence in it." For some time, she couldn't face returning to work on *Secrets*. Another period of the "terrible black black blues" was gathering on her psychic horizon.

Although Susannah remained careful to a fault about how she appeared to others, especially on stage, people who lived in her neighborhood often saw a quite different person than the groomed and luminous performer. "She always looked sad, and sometimes *really* sad," says writer Peter Keepnews, who lived nearby. More chilling is a memory of Susannah by her by-then-estranged friend, Richard Rodney Bennett. "The last time I saw her, in late September of 2000, I was walking down Columbus Avenue [on Manhattan's Upper West Side, near Susannah's apartment building] quite late, coming back from dinner. I was with my dearest friend in the world, who also knew her. Coming towards us, at first I thought I saw a boy with a close blonde haircut and wearing a black pantsuit. She had a strange sort of half-smile, and was looking up at the sky—you know that expression on some of her albums? She walked past without looking in our direction, and I thought, 'She's *mad.*'"

In fact, it was right at that time, in late September, that Susannah decided to stop taking her medications, over Stephen Kahan's objections: Bennett may well have been witnessing a woman just freed of the unpleasant side effects of her meds, free-floating into a hypomanic state. Explains bipolar-disorder expert Kay Redfield Jamison: "Artists stop taking their medications because they miss the highs or the emotional intensity associated with their illness or because they feel that drug side effects interfere with the clarity and rapidity of their thought or diminish their levels of enthusiasm, emotion, and energy." To her sister Maggie, Susannah said, "I've had to try different medications with all sorts of terrible side effects. I can only tolerate small doses." Says Kahan, "She told me she was going to stop her meds before her fall Algonquin show because her hands shook, and she wanted to sign autographs. I don't push medication," adds this longtime advocate of alternative therapies, "but she *needed* to be on medicine all her life. And she promised to go back on it afterward."

As Susannah prepared to open her new month-long show at the Algonquin in late October, she was in a soaring, happy frame of mind. "I have great clarity, am super-efficient at carrying out the tasks I have to do, have intense and inspiring and comforting conversations and am not depressed in one single cell of my body!!" she announced, the by-now familiar proclamation of liberation from depression that she had made countless times before and that seemed each time to usher in a return of hypomania. But her mood, seesawing more quickly now between highs and lows, could easily turn. "I had such a terrible time with the hotel and getting settled in a room that I was totally stressed out and crying at 7:00 P.M.," she told David Alpern about her "faux" opening the night before the "real" one. She'd arrived early for her room (although she lived a 10- or 15-minute cab ride away from the hotel, she used the room for resting, dressing, and decompressing), but, then-maitre d' Arthur Pomposello recalls, the room was late to be made up. "She sat there in the lobby and then started bullying this young room clerk. I got a call that Susannah was furious." Pomposello arranged for her to be given the much more spacious Bodne suite. "And she loved that."

Indeed. She wrapped herself in the literary ghosts of the Algonquin's tenth floor, once the longtime owners' New York home, with huge windows and a library full of autographed biographies of the famous and the famously interesting (the next year the suite was chopped up into rooms for paying guests). "I love my old beat up suite at the Gonk," Susannah confessed to Jackie Osteen. "I go through Mrs. Bodne's for-ties-to-fifties library and sit up late feeling so happy I almost cry after my shows, which are going really well! There is a semi-broken microwave and a small refrig there, and I have brought in a humidifier and a small electronic radio–cassette player–soothing sounds machine. I meditate to the babbling brook sound after my truly thrilling and fulfilling performances." Staying in the commodious, romantic old set of rooms of the former owners and having a powerful opening night, swung Susannah's mood back up again. "For the first time I can remember," Pomposello recalls, "she acted affectionate to me. She had never given me a hug before, now she did and more than once."

Like the show "Broken Hearts and Blue Skies" in 1999, her perfor-mance of "Hearts and Minds" consisted of urbane, wry commentary about the difficulty of finding love and meaning in everyday life. Com-pletely scripted, it was a long performance that she slashed by nearly 20 minutes after the opening. "Her show was cabaret, completely autobio-graphical, like she was using the audience for therapy," Farnham notes. Though she had intonation problems, he recalls, either Susannah didn't notice or else was able to rise above them, for her mood stayed upbeat onstage. "This is such a happy, productive, creative, fertile, fulfilling time for me, my brain is cooking with even more creativity," she wrote Brad Kay in November. One afternoon, she performed on television, where she'd appeared before several times, on the Oxygen network.[3] "I wore a sparkly red diva gown, sang 'Love Is Here to Stay' and felt grrrrrrreat!"

Susannah had a solid base of fans who followed her every show with enthusiasm, and the critic who most counted in cabaret, the *Times'* Stephen Holden, gave the "Hearts and Minds" show an excellent review, singling out "Scars," a song, he said, that just about summed up Susannah in performance, in which she "wear[s] [her] emotional wounds like battle ribbons"—a stance, though, that made at least some of her audience uncomfortable by then. "I had a discussion with her: 'Can't you lighten it up? It's too depressing!'" says Andy Lipman, who had known Susannah since the early eighties. "She said, 'What's the purpose of art if not to share one's suffering?' I countered, 'To uplift, to entertain.' Such an attitude limits your audience."

"A more subdued sound, I thought, in her last performances," agrees her friend David Alpern. Says James Gavin, "She seemed to be singing to herself. She'd do the whole show to a spot on the wall." Singers Eric Comstock and Paula West concur. "We sat right in the front," says Comstock of the "Hearts and Minds" show. "Susannah was physically awkward at the show we saw, but then, she always was on stage. That didn't really matter, but this time she had a wild look in her eyes. Paula said it was a Norma Desmond–like stare." "A lot of people," comments singer Carol Fredette, who also attended a performance, "saw the madness in her."

Yet in a business where the important thing was to fill the chairs, Susannah was doing so, and most of her audience was charmed and delighted by her show. With a successful run behind her, Susannah was booked by Pomposello to return the following autumn. Fresh from the Oak Room, Susannah went to Feinstein's at the Regency on November 27, to do a benefit with her trio: Allen Farnham, Steve Gilmore on bass, and Tim Horner on drums, opening for Rosemary Clooney, who was presenting her "White Christmas" show through December 3. "We did this big medley from the Algonquin show, songs about New York, which we'd not done before with drums," Farnham says. As it turned out, the benefit performance at Feinstein's was to be the last time Susannah performed in public.

Though Kahan kept urging Susannah to go back to Dr. Cristina Brusco, the psychiatrist she'd seen on and off since the late nineties, and obtain a prescription for new medications now that she was finished at the Algonquin, Susannah hesitated. She was attracted to what homeopathy describes as its "gentle, non-toxic" remedies. Following the principle of "like cures like," or "the law of similars," homeopathy utilizes trace amounts of substances to help activate a person's self-healing powers. They seemed to offer a welcome alternative to side effects of Prozac and other medications she'd taken. Now, after dabbling in homeopathy on her own, she was seeing Ronald Dushkin, a general-practice physician who specializes in homeopathic medicine. She wanted, Susannah told Kahan, to give Dr. Dushkin's prescribed treatments time to "work." "The doc," she said in early December, "has me off all vitamin and herbal supplements except a multivitamin, and on 1/3 of the smallest daily dose of homeopathic remedy." But Susannah, whether as a side effect of that or for other reasons, suffered from incontinence and increasing nervousness, Kahan recalls.

However, her mood was on an upswing that late fall of 2000. "I refuse to live life depressed anymore," she told Mark Nadler. "If I get down, I ask myself: Am I seriously ill? Am I completely out of money? Am I without a friend in the world? If the answer to any of these is no, I pronounce myself undepressed and I go out and race-walk, eat chocolate or have a good conversation with a pal, or curl up with the cats and watch old movies. Onward, onward, onward." And to Brad Kay she added, "I love my interesting and varied New York City single life."

As a boost to her spirits, she had decided at last to decorate her apartment, eliminating the drab, worn colors and furniture she'd simply put up with for years, making it a place she'd feel good about inviting people to. Many good friends, like Rex Reed, never even saw Susannah's apartment. "She was afraid they'd see it wasn't glamorous," says her friend Rick McKay. Susannah explained to her London friend Frances Bendixson, "I had no spirit left over to fix it up here when my attempt at making a happy pretty home (albeit with the wrong man!) failed. I'm finally feeling less scared about money and am putting some into my apartment." Typically, Susannah thought through every bit of the plan, choosing shades of blues and greens and red for living room and bedroom. "I've put together a fat fat file of apt. stuff. . . . Wow I am happy about this. I just needed to feel brave enough to spend the money," she informed Nadler, who was helping her. She bought a "floating fish bottom drinking glass and soap dispenser, a little plastic chest of drawers. And how about a bright red rag rug from Ikea? Looking forward to having more painting done, covers made, rugs woven, etc. *Très contente ici.*" All this and another checkup at her doctor to confirm that she was, after eleven years, still cancer-free.

Then a family emergency arose. Mimi, in her late seventies, had a heart attack and a series of strokes. This was the scenario that Susannah had long feared: her mother's decline and decrepitude, and Susannah's consequent crushing responsibility. (It seemed not to matter that both her sisters also rallied to help: Maggie would come to stay with Mimi over Christmas, and Katie was to come the week after that, but Susannah still felt responsible.) Immediately, she booked a December 6 flight to California, planning to stay with Mimi for a week. She was still "up," still projecting her sunny, competent image. She was also back to her writing, buoyed by encouragement she'd gotten from a new literary agent; after Susannah described *Secrets in Piazza Navona,* the agent asked to look at it. "I'm quite on top of the world now—I have plenty to give!" she enthused to Nadler. "Had a great reaction to my book ms. too! I'll get back to it in January. I have even taken on the care of my mother and cheerfully." "I sure feel like doing some laughing," she went on in the same bubbly fashion, "and I don't mean hearing my mother say vodka when she means yoghurt!" Then she turned serious. "I tried so hard to be patient. I felt needed, for the first time. It is still me, definitely me, a happier, more peaceful, more hopeful me than I've ever known before!!"

But few believed she would stay "up" for long And her "up" was even more noticeable to some. "For the first time, I thought *she* was manic, too," Maggie comments, "and I understood some earlier episodes with her in the light of that. And she'd gone off her meds. We'd talked about the meds over the last few years—and I believe going off them is part of the disease. She was manic, really aggressive; she and Mom shouted at each other—for example, she made a crack about putting Mother in a 'rest home.' Maybe she was being sarcastic—I don't know. But it upset Mimi terribly. Of course, Mother was difficult. Everything had to be done just so, as she would have done it. And her speech was still garbled, so it could be hard to understand her. But I was really concerned to see Susannah at Mother's." In fact, far from being grateful at having her life rearranged for her, Mimi was furious at the limitations that she felt Susannah was imposing, or trying to. "She left a five-page note of instructions for me when I came to take care of Mother after she left!" Maggie says. "She made all these lists; she was trying to organize everything, even what didn't need organizing."

The crash inevitably loomed, and glimpses of it came soon, back in New York. On December 14, Allen Farnham dropped by her apartment, to ask her to autograph some CDs he was taking to Japan for a promoter. "When I arrived, music was blaring—Brazilian—and Susannah was crying. When I asked her what was wrong, she said, 'I'm OK—I'm having trouble with my mother is all.' And she signed the CDs."

Her visit to Mimi continued to prey upon her. The next day, she wrote Jeff DiNicola. "It is incredibly painful for me to have her misunderstanding the situation and shouting at me. I feel sane and stable, thanks to all the non-medical wellness stuff I have been doing, meditation, biofeedback, homeopathic medicine, and to friends and to music and to reading. But I am devastated, horrified, depleted. Cried only a few times out there, but burst into hysterical sobs the moment I got into my apt building lobby. Lovely building staff and neighbors helped me upstairs and then, home at last and back to my own, healthy life." (She'd also had a shouting argument with Dan DiNicola, she added, over an overdue cell-phone bill. She was sorry about that.) She ended her letter by papering over her extreme reaction. Her feelings, she said, were "traumatic, yet productive." She intended to go back to California in January. "She has heart disease and early dementia. I am overwhelmed," she said. Thea Lurie's and Lorraine Ruggieri's mothers had both had Alzheimer's, and Susannah knew how difficult their care had been; she presumed that she would be shouldering such a burden now. "The hardest part is being made to feel bad about myself when I am working so hard to help her. Sometimes she is grateful, other times paranoid."

What kept Susannah going was her book. "I won't feel good about my life unless I write this book," she'd confided to Osteen the previous spring. "I have to have faith in this book, in myself. I am gambling my life on it." Now, more than ever. After her trip to California, she plunged back into it, deciding to flesh out the narrative with much more detail about her childhood. On the day before Christmas Eve of 2000, she worked prodigiously, outlining her new chapter and then writing page after page of notes in longhand—sixteen pages of mostly painful memories, many of them leading back to her mother. She jotted sentences about Mimi's frequent starvation diets, "consisting of black coffee and chain-smoking," and the huge fight between her parents after Mimi caught Tom kissing "Hurricane Ann," as well as a sad passage about a "sweet sixteen" party that Mimi threw for her: "A big cheerful party and I am aware that I am alone, alone, alone."

She finished her writing by circling back to Christmases past: Her first December in London, in 1972, when she was all alone and broke and scared, but decided to visit a senior citizens' center and sing Christmas carols; there, she recalled, a young blind pianist had suddenly shown up to accompany her. She wrote about her first ecstatic Christmas in her new house in Schenectady with DiNicola. About her beloved holiday rituals, the tree trimming and the cookie baking and the carols. ("I'll Be Home for Christmas" was her favorite; she loved what she called "the sweet sadness of the lyric.")[4]

She spent Christmas 2000 not alone but with Mark Nadler at his house in Riverdale. They decorated a tree, listened to Christmas albums, made dinner, and watched *The Man Who Came to Dinner,* an annual Nadler movie ritual. They toasted the holiday with cocktails. "At midnight, we fell asleep halfway through the movie, and she went to bed. Walking by her door, I heard her crying—no, weeping. I can't stress enough how sunny Susannah always was around me. I had never heard her crying, so I knocked on her door and asked to come in. I held her, and she wept on my shoulder. 'She's just so mean, Mimi's just so mean. She's being vicious and nasty, and all I'm trying to do is help her and make her life pleasant. I feel so much pain from childhood.' She said she always wanted to please her mother but could never do so."

Commenting on Susannah's portrait of Mimi as the wicked witch, psychotherapist Donna Marshall, who admired Susannah and knew her slightly, asks, "Was the mother cruel? It is so complex—a *Rashomon* thing." Certainly Mimi was blunt, if not tactless at times and unforgiving of physical imperfections. But Mimi was not always overtly cruel, as this letter she wrote to Susannah during the 2000 Thanksgiving holidays attests: "Susannah, you are beautiful and talented and brilliant. I don't believe you have Tom's disease [i.e., bipolar disorder]. You photograph well. You could do anything. I love you." Susannah's Berkeley friend Tom Luddy recalls Mimi attending several performances in California and beaming with pride. "But Susannah felt her mother was incapable of showing real pride in her," he adds. "Mother *was* very, very proud of Susannah," confirms her sister Maggie, "but I think Susannah probably didn't feel that at all, because of her complex personality." Points out Marshall, "One of the ways to hold onto a parent you need is by hanging onto the negative."

Certainly, Mimi was unpredictable and, when drinking, increasingly less able to "handle herself." And certainly, a number of people who witnessed the effects of her drinking thought she had a problem. Mimi herself wrote a letter to Susannah shortly before she had her heart attack and stroke in early December 2000 that illustrates her brand of defiance of the conventions. In a shaky hand, she told of being in a supermarket checkout line, behind "a sharp and smart-looking old lady. She was carrying only a liter bottle of vodka. I couldn't resist. I said: 'I'd like a picture of you like that,' and I patted the bottle, and she said, 'Will you join me?' We both laughed and parted. That is how life should be." Mimi went on, "The hell with the changes that happen to you as you get old. I think it's my responsibility to keep happy and that helps me. I don't have much otherwise. I am able to do only little things for the persons I love. But I fight to be happy and interested in life." As Susannah grew older and as her bipolar disorder worsened, friends noticed that *she* appeared to need a drink during social occasions. Diane Feldman was a friend since the early 1980s. In her opinion, "She'd get anxious at cocktail hour if the drinks weren't served promptly—and yes, she had more than one. And they helped her relax. I remember in 1998, during the July 4th weekend, she came out to our beach house, and when cocktail hour came, there was an edge to her. I think she had a problem on a *coping* level. Maybe it was hard to live up to this lovely woman she was." When she was alone, she told both Gary Gates and Stephen Kahan, instead of using sleeping pills to sleep, she'd take a little vodka. But sometimes, if she had more than "a little," she became distraught, as at Christmas Eve at Mark Nadler's. In June 2000, she confided in an e-mail to Brad Kay: "For me alcohol is a terrible depressant. I don't even drink at all any more. I miss it a lot, but not enough to feel as bad as I do physically and mentally the next day after even one drink." Psychiatrist Dr. Paul Fox states flatly, "Even *one drink* for a bipolar person tends to put them over the edge. They cannot drink."

Christmas Day was not much of an improvement over Christmas Eve, though she tried. She and Nadler opened presents to each other and toasted the season, again. Though it was Christmas, Nadler was booked to do a matinee. "So she left, and we both came back to the house that evening, when I cooked a rich Christmas dinner of goose and all sort of things. I'd been drinking all day, and I got very sick, and some of my friends were there whom she didn't much like. So Susannah left unhappy. That was her last Christmas."

True to form, Susannah donned her metaphorical white gloves immediately, writing Nadler a bread-and-butter e-mail thank-you, then turning to the events of the night before: "I can't believe how I cried in your house. I realize now it was because I had finally relaxed. I felt safe in my soul to let go and weep and I knew that my cries would be heard."

She was abstemious on her next outing on New Year's Day to David Alpern's annual party—her 55th birthday as well. As she always did, she brought her own food to the party and sipped only mineral water throughout.

And then Susannah booked a ticket to California for a two-week visit to help with Mimi's aftercare. "I need a three to four day sanctuary—when I can find the time to do it," she e-mailed Brad Kay, politely turning down his offer to come stay at his house in Venice after dealing with Mimi. "However, first another hell week with my mother (I'll stay in a hotel this time, for my sanity) in Oakland."

This second trip to care for Mimi began badly. Mimi was the old lioness defending her lair, still seething at what she perceived as her daughters' efforts to "imprison" her by making her give up driving her car, her house, and alcohol—in Mimi's mind, her independence and what made life worth living! Not long before, Mimi had had a car wreck when she mistook the accelerator for the brake; reluctantly, she agreed to give up driving. "She thought I had a drinking problem," Mimi related the following year, shaking her head "no." In January, Mimi stopped taking the painkillers prescribed in the hospital and became much more lucid. Still, "Susan and Maggie thought I would be safer in those old ladies' homes—a nursing home. That would be a relief to them. Susan went to my lawyer and got papers about how to sell my house against my wishes. She asked for my power of attorney and wanted me to sign these two pages of documents letting her sell the house. I wouldn't sign it." Instead, Mimi proposed that she rent a room to a student or single teacher from the university who would "pay" by checking on her and running light errands. "Just check on me and see if I were still alive. That's all. So the girls agreed," Mimi recalled in 2002 of that difficult time.

Resolving all of this entailed a good deal of shouting and arguing back and forth. "Susannah was very stressed out," Tom Luddy remembers. "We had dinner, and all the issues came up. Her mother was the huge issue in her life. Susannah was so angry at her I couldn't believe it." Diana Lang Phillips, who stopped to visit Susannah at Mimi's house, had a similar experience: "She said her mother was not capable of managing her finances, that she was irresponsible financially. Later, she wanted to go out to dinner, but I was wiped out—Susannah could be really exhausting sometimes. So I made some excuse and left." Still, by the following week, Susannah and Mimi resolved the problem of the house—Mimi arranging to have a companion-driver live in—and the tension abated. "Things are going much better this time," Susannah e-mailed Nadler. She even attempted heart-to-heart talks with her mother. "There's much she didn't tell me over the years," Mimi said. "I never thought that I really knew her. I knew she was in love when she was in Europe, but that was just instinct. But she told me all about it then and the book she was writing."

Now that they had arrived at an accommodation, Susannah returned to New York determined to get back to work on her book and finish decorating her apartment. She continued to put the best face on her emotional condition. "This homeopathic medicine is really doing it for me," she told worried friends when she finally finished a dreary five-week stint on jury duty, though she promised Stephen Kahan that yes, she would go back to her psychiatrist for a new prescription—soon. Meanwhile, she was busy with plans, including her new album.[5] "In late February, she called to ask if we could get together and go over some music for the recording," Farnham says. It would be, she had earlier told an interviewer, "all love songs in several languages": English, and something in French, Spanish, Portuguese of course, and even one in German.[6] But privately, Susannah was far less sanguine. "How am I going to make a record? I'm so depressed." Farnham was touring and unable to meet with her. When he finished the tour in March, he left her an answering-machine message about getting together. Susannah did not respond.

She had faced the "black black blues" before and won. Now, as a hopeful sign, she began to plan her wardrobe for her Algonquin show in September 2001. Looking good was essential to her peace of mind. "I want to be known for my elegant long gowns," she told Lorraine Ruggieri, her dressmaker and confidante. Some fans thought Susannah had never looked better—certainly never thinner—than in those last years, in her signature glittery gowns, many of them sleeveless, and with whimsical names: Pearlie Sue, Big Red, Green Goddess. For her next show, Ruggieri recalls, Susannah had decided on a black velvet gown. And a little jacket in gold. "We went shopping together and found this beautiful, delicately encrusted sheer gold—the *most* expensive—fabric. She bought it. Then, coming back from the shop, she said, 'I don't believe I just spent that much!' I reassured her." What Susannah saw as elegance, however, some saw as gaudiness. "Why," wonders one, "didn't she just go and get a simply cut, good dress from Bergdorf's?" (And why that dark businesslike pants-suit for the cover of her *Hearts and Minds* CD? "She was the one who chose her outfits," responds her photographer, Carlos Spaventa.)

Yet most people agreed that in her mid-fifties, a made-up Susannah looked better than ever. On stage, in public, on a date, at a dinner party, she was smart and sexy. Gone were the big thighs and the oversize breasts, banished were the dowdy dresses and girdles and pageboys. Expert help with hair and makeup showed her features to best advantage. She even had a brief affair with a man 20 years younger, a male nurse who was the son of longtime fans. "And she had a young spirit," observes James Gavin. However, keeping that image up was an exacting task. Staying thin—not just average-sized but model-thin—was a constant effort.

Concerned about the paucity of singing jobs, Susannah tried to get an agent. "I told her about a big agency, Joel Kriss, and she contacted them," remembers bassist Steve Gilmore. "But they weren't interested." She contacted the music department at U.C. Berkeley when she was out there in January about joining the faculty to teach jazz singing, but nothing came of it. "She gave up that idea," Mimi said. She had more success applying some of the biofeedback exercises she'd learned from Stephen Kahan to a budding practice as a relaxation therapist. "What she generates in her sessions is an extraordinarily artful and powerful form of prayer—one that you can literally feel vibrate around you.... I recommend Susannah as a spiritual partner," wrote one client, a cancer patient. Yet though she discreetly advertised her "meditation therapy for carefully screened patients," Susannah was of two minds about it: She simply found working with ill patients too depressing. What really interested her was becoming involved with music as sound therapy, especially after hearing Kay's jazz-based therapeutic music. Encouraged by Susannah to develop an entire album, Kay began sending Susannah more of his music that winter and spring, and they wrote back and forth about it frequently. In his words, "She road-tested the stuff. She especially loved 'From Blue to Sweet.'" Susannah also volunteered to write up his life story for the liner notes, though that didn't happen.[7] "Susannah also was busy researching and networking with doctors and therapists, to find out what was going on in the field of music therapy, and how she could develop it as a new career."

All these activities—and of course, her writing—were solitary pursuits, however. More than anything, Susannah yearned for what had drawn her to music in the first place—the sense of family, of belonging, of acceptance. As she told Osteen that winter, "I feel a great great need to have a spiritual center, and to feel a part of a larger community." Says Nadler, "Rex Reed told me that he was so grateful to me because she felt so cast out of the cabaret community and I let her in, though the people who knew her felt the same way I did—that she was a treasure." A treasure, though, is something to be admired rather than a confidante or pal, and Susannah's habit of keeping people at arm's length contributed to her sense of isolation.

She and Dan DiNicola flirted over the phone with the idea of seeing each other again. In January 2001, when Susannah learned that he had had open-heart surgery to replace a valve, she called him, eager to come and help take care of him; DiNicola, who had a live-in girlfriend, demurred but said he'd see her when he was better. In late February, after splitting up with his girlfriend, he came to Manhattan on business and called her. "I said, 'I'm here if you want to see me.' The future seemed open-ended. We talked about how I might use her apartment when she wasn't there. But Susannah didn't want to get together then. In March, we talked for a long time on the phone. She said she had had some kind of epiphany. She was often having these epiphanies. She talked about this fantasy of having a little cottage together when we grew old. She told me I was the only man who really cared, who was there for her. But we never got closer again."

If Susannah and DiNicola were "forever best friends," as he put it (and certainly she continued to care for him, making him one of her beneficiaries in her will), she still made many negative comments about him, such as when she cited "my exhausting years with a workaholic." Even four days before she died, on her last race-walk with Linda Fennimore, she talked about DiNicola: "Whenever Dan calls, it always puts me in a downer. *Always.*" Perhaps in part this was because when Susannah mentioned their living together in a "country cottage" during their last talk, DiNicola had not responded enthusiastically.

Sometime in late winter, Susannah took the train to Washington, where she visited her friend Leon Wieseltier and his wife, and spent a day with Eric Olson. "We went to the National Gallery and had our last conversation," Olson remembers. Despite her deepening anguish, he notes, "She hid her despair—I should have paid greater attention to her state of mind, but you had to be tough and insistent to get her to talk about herself. And right then I was in a weird period." Olson had been prodding the government for years to investigate his father Frank Olson's death. In an eerie parallel to Susannah's death, the older Olson had fallen from a Manhattan window in 1953. But his son became convinced that it had been a CIA-orchestrated hit, to keep Frank from revealing a nerve gas experiment he was working on. In 2000, Eric learned the case was being held up. "The lawsuit," he explains, "was stalled because the D.A. had succumbed to political pressure. Susannah was characteristically supportive and empathetic."

In that dreary gray season in Manhattan at the end of February, she was still fighting her depression, yet she did have projects to look forward to: her book, of course, on which she hoped to resume serious work; exploring a career in music therapy; her new recording; her next Algonquin show; and some other possible singing jobs. "I am up for a wonderful concert series in Boston," she wrote to Jeff DiNicola that day. Singing before a live audience, of course, provided a connection that was crucial for Susannah.

Then, on March 2, Susannah got the first of three devastating phone calls she received that month. She thought she'd be discussing her new CD with Nick Phillips. Instead, a conference call had been arranged with new Concord president Glen Barros, executive vice president John Burk, and Phillips, as her producer, to inform her that not only would there not be a new recording, but her contract would not be renewed. They cited her recent albums' comparatively poor sales. Susannah was not the only artist that the reorganized company let go in 2001; so were Ken Peplowski, Carol Sloane, and a number of others, some of whom had long been with the label. But this was cold comfort to Susannah. "During that conference call," Phillips says, "we did say that we thought a compilation of her songs would be something that would work for all of us. With a compilation, she would have, for all intents and purposes, a 'new' CD out on the Concord label that we would promote. She was very calm about the decision and seemed OK, and we worked on the *Most Requested Songs* collection throughout March into the beginning of April."

Susannah did her show-biz best, masking her huge disappointment by telling Phillips about an in-concert DVD that a company planned to produce. She polled friends to nominate their three favorite songs from her albums for the compilation CD. "I suggested she write the liner notes, and she did," James Gavin says. "But she never told me the Concord contract was over." *Most Requested Songs,* released posthumously, was her best-selling record, leading quickly to a second compilation called *Ballads* that also did well.

Hardly had Susannah received the bad news from Concord when, about a week later, she had her second major rejection. Her September–October Algonquin performance, she was informed, was canceled; the younger jazz-based singers Jane Monheit and the more seasoned Paula West would replace her (Monheit appeared for the first part of what would have been Susannah's run and West for the latter). The heavily promoted Monheit was the jazz flavor of the month. She had pronounced Susannah's *Hearts and Minds* show "awesome" and was to include a cover of Susannah's signature song, "The Waters of March" on her *Come Dream With Me* CD, which topped *Billboard*'s jazz chart in May 2001, the same month Susannah died. However, many in the jazz world were less than ecstatic about Monheit's talent; her "Waters of March" was "almost robotic," one reviewer complained. West, on the other hand, has built a following as a talent who can handle cabaret or jazz with aplomb.

Susannah had built a loyal audience, too; her Algonquin shows were not only critical successes but moneymakers, so much so that Oak Room manager Arthur Pomposello was later to say, "She was exactly what was needed—she made me look like Ziegfeld."[8] But there were factors working against her. The hotel was in the process of being sold again. Olympus Real Estate had owned it since 1997, but a Denver-based company with the stark moniker of Miller-Global Fund IV was in the process of buying the slightly shabby gem and was bringing in new management that meant, inevitably, changes, including closer scrutiny of the numbers; and, says Pomposello, "They saw that Susannah's had dropped off a little in the last two years."

Still, Susannah was a class act, and she filled chairs—and Pomposello understood this. Although there was friction between them, the Oak Room manager and the performer had accommodated to each other—and, in another sad irony in Susannah's life, she'd even taken pains to be affectionate with this key player in her career, notably during her "Hearts and Minds" run. But with the latest turnover in hotel ownership and management, the pressure was on to increase profits, bring in fresh talent. Pomposello saw a new crop of up-and- coming singers he could get for less money than established talent and, he hoped, would parallel the success of the likes of Diana Krall and Harry Connick Jr., who had played the Oak Room before they became stars. But, despite the pressure he was under to drop Susannah (the *grande dame* of cabaret, Julie Wilson, had already been axed over his objections), Pomposello says he refused. Instead he decided to circumvent management—"I did this all the time; I was constantly at odds with management"—by creating a summer jazz festival with Susannah as the star. "I called her about it. I didn't tell her they didn't want her back—that I couldn't do. Instead, I said this would be a great move for her, and that she'd be sensational." DiNicola feels certain, though, that Susannah would have viewed such an offer, with the fee based on how well she drew customers, as a comedown: "What would come of her career after a summer gig? What kind of money could you make then? Nothing!" Indeed, Susannah was terrified that she'd end up simply working for the door—a has-been, no longer a serious contender—and Pomposello's offer of the summer time slot underlined her fears. Adds Allen Farnham, "I imagine she didn't like the Gonk jerking her around." She saved face by telling Pomposello she couldn't do it because of commitments to sing at jazz festivals.[9] "She said especially festivals abroad," he remembers. But there were no jazz festivals, no abroad—though not for want of trying. Sigi Schmidt-Joos, a well- connected Berlin jazz journalist, had recommended Susannah for German festivals, for one thing, but was told she was not cutting-edge enough for their audiences.

For Susannah, losing her one really lucrative, prestigious gig was heartbreaking and the news that newcomer Jane Monheit was booked in part of "her" fall slot only made the cancellation worse. "Thank God for beautiful songs about feeling despair when you yourself are in despair," she once remarked to a friend. "They really get us through, don't they?" Not anymore. "She *lived* for the Algonquin job," says bassist Steve Gilmore. "She loved it. And she made good money. She sold tons of CDs there, too. That was her yearly financial and emotional nut. And," he adds, "she was a lot cheaper than some of the other acts."

Then—diabolically—came the third strike, in many ways the most devastating. Since coming back from Oakland in January, Susannah had been talking to Mimi regularly. "In March," Mimi said, "she asked if she could come back to California again to visit and check up on me. And she said she might be coming back here to stay. I told her no—the medicine made me sleepy and I was too sick. I couldn't have borne it. She wouldn't have helped me—she was going to control how I lived, to imprison me." Several days later, Susannah called again. "This time she asked if she could borrow $20,000 to live on, and she'd pay it back the next year. Earlier, she had told me she had $80,000—then, within several months, she had none? I didn't believe her. I said I couldn't afford it."

In fact, both Mimi and Susannah had a fair amount of money put away—not a munificent amount but more than adequate for their needs. "My mother was very, very funny about money; she always was thrifty in odd ways," Maggie explains. "As she got older, she got funnier about it." Mimi had her Social Security benefits and still some savings and income from investments, and she had her house. But she didn't have much cash on hand. Susannah's $20,000 request represented about half of what Mimi had in her account—at the same time that she, herself, faced the vicissitudes of old age. "When Susannah had come out in January," Maggie says, "Mother had noticed that she spent a lot of money she gave her, about $2,000. Well, she didn't view that as a good sign. You see, she wanted to stay independent—she didn't want any of us to have to take care of her. So she declined to give any more to Susannah."

But Mimi, relenting somewhat, thought more about Susannah's request and called her back. "I told her I did want her to come out here, but not to stay with me. She would just upset my house, which was running perfectly then; I had someone to stay there and do errands for me. Instead, I'd put her up in a house nearby and get her a little car, and she could write that novel she'd told me she was writing," Mimi said. "But that arrangement didn't suit her. 'I'll have to think of something else,' was all she told me." Replies Maggie, "Her suggestion that Susannah come out to live more cheaply in California would have been a fate worse than death for Susannah. She'd never want to give up her New York apartment and life."

Susannah, of course, modeled her attitudes toward independence and money on Mimi's. "She would always talk about her nest egg and that she didn't want to touch it because it was for her security, her retirement," Mark Nadler says—yet he had no idea of the real amount in that "nest egg." Explains her stepson Roy, a financial planner who had helped her invest her money in the mid-nineties, along with Paul Ben-Susan after that, "Half her money was put in a very stable account of tax-free New York State bonds. It was like a savings account; she'd add and withdraw from it from time to time. The other half was her 'long-term portfolio,' spread across stock mutual funds. By 1999, she was saying to me, 'Roy, I have more money now than I've ever dreamed of.' Her investments were in fine shape; the market was just starting to come down when she died. So I cannot understand why she was asking Mimi for $20,000." It would astonish all her other friends, even Thea Lurie, to find out just how much of a cushion Susannah did have, given her frequent comments about the need to be extremely frugal. Lurie figured that Susannah had around $50,000: In point of fact, when Susannah died, she had nearly $250,000 in various mutual-fund accounts.

Clearly, in Susannah's rapid cycling states of manic depression in 2000 and 2001, her fear of financial insecurity had mushroomed into a near-panic state so that in her mind she *needed* that $20,000 from her mother. Coupled with that fear was her feeling, as many who knew her believe, that Mimi's refusal to grant her request represented the with-holding of the love that Susannah had always yearned for. Explains Lurie, "She saw it as a final rejection of *her*—and a final failure of her attempt to repair the broken relationship with her mother. Susannah felt like she had been given nothing—that her mean older sister had gotten huge amounts and the younger sister had gotten money for a house. This was also behind her feelings of rejection and anger." Of course, Mimi would have seen the situation quite differently: She had supported Susannah in Europe and for years afterward, and had given her a substantial amount for the down payment on her Schenectady house.

For Susannah, Mimi's "no" echoed all the "no's" that Susannah had stored up, all the times she'd wanted acceptance from her mother but had instead received criticism, anger, envy. Poignantly, she once told her stepdaughter Anne, "You're really lucky: You're really loved. You never get over not being loved."

Their history of hurts and resentments swamped both Mimi and Susannah. They never saw each other again.

Even before all these rejections had struck, Susannah contacted the lawyer she'd found through Lisa Popa in January. Lana Cantrell, an Australia-born singer who became an attorney, counts among her clients a number of entertainers. She met with Susannah for the first time in the second week of March. "She wanted to look into her contracts and make sure everything was up to date, as well as to draw up her will," says Cantrell, who also remembers Susannah mentioning that she would not be performing at the Algonquin. "She talked about that in a matter-of-fact tone, as well as about how the entertainment business was getting more and more difficult. She said she planned on teaching and was working on a book." Their initial meeting was followed quickly by a second, in which the will was signed and witnessed. Immediately afterward, Susannah had a dress fitting at Lorraine Ruggieri's. "Susannah said cheerfully, 'I've done my will. It's taken care of—you're in it.'" Soon after, Susannah e-mailed friends and family to tell them she had "put her things in order." "She just mentioned it casually, along with other things," says Roy DiNicola. Jeff DiNicola agrees: No alarm bells went off.

However, there were other warning signs. Ruggieri, who saw her often for dress fittings, worried about her physical condition. "She had become terribly thin—she looked anorexic—and it scared me. I knew she was going to a homeopathic doctor. She said she felt good about whatever she was taking because he was treating her *naturally*. But she was having a lot of trouble keeping food down." Therapist Stephen Kahan concurs: Susannah was suffering from frequent diarrhea and incontinence. Ruggieri, who loves to cook, had helped Susannah through her previous bout of deep depression in 1998, bringing her meals and urging her to see a nutritionist, who advised her to add smoked fish to her diet for protein; that and the vegetarian fare Ruggieri prepared helped her gain weight. "But this time, when I offered to cook anything she wanted and bring it to her, she became offended."

People kept noticing noticed how frail and out-of-balance Susannah looked. Lorna Sass, an acquaintance, ran into her in Central Park. "It was the end of winter, a very cold day, and there was snow on the ground," she says. "She was wearing a tired red parka and looked positively awful. I remember thinking that her skin tone was sickly and wondered if she was ill. I could tell she didn't want to talk, so we just exchanged hellos and went our way." When she had to drop off some music to bassist Chris Berger, she could barely stand still or talk to him at the gig where he was working. Berger says, "She seemed totally ill at ease, like it was a social situation she couldn't control. She didn't look good." Thea Lurie's second husband Joel Kaye remarked after having dinner with Susannah one night that she looked "frozen." Even such a close friend as Rex Reed caught glimpses of a Susannah he'd never seen: "I saw her in the street one day, talking to herself, clutching her coat and looking around—very odd behavior." So changed was she at times, says Keith Ingham, that he didn't always recognize her that last year when he occasionally ran into her in the street or the lobby of their apartment building. "Her hair had changed, and her weight was different." Ingham adds chillingly, "I read somewhere that suicides can 'lose their identity.' I wonder if she lost hers."

"She said that life had been very hectic in a bad way, that she was relying on old movies and homeopathy to keep her balance," recalls Brad Kay of a conversation they had in April. "And she wasn't into music—she said it took her into herself and she needed to get outside herself." While her friends and acquaintances were occupied with work, families, the usual obligations, she became more and more isolated in her despair. Occasionally, she did get out. "I miss you so much," she e-mailed Lurie, who found time in a hectic work schedule to go to the movies with her (*Heartbreakers*: Susannah suspected she'd hate it but agreed to go because it featured her recording of "The Waters of March"). A week later, she e-mailed Kay. "It's hard to keep my spirits up." She added that she knew that she "must" accept her aloneness, but the lack of a soul mate, she admitted, sometimes made her despair. "No one to cheer on. No one to hold. No one to cheer me on. No one to hold me. I am so alone in the world." And for her, the hardest thing now was to will herself to go on.

After making a rare public appearance, presenting awards at a Cabaret Convention event early in April, Susannah began hinting that she had lost her Algonquin anchor. "I am in hibernation mode now, working hard on [*Secrets in Piazza Navona*], usually feeling terrible about it. . . . I never realized what an obsession it would become or how it would take over my life." The book became her entire focus. On April 5, she e-mailed Diana Phillips. "It's a hard time for me. But I'm still standing. I'm putting all my energy and hope into my book—working hours a day at a private library. This has got to work! I'm grateful for what I do have."

Gail Hochman, her literary agent, had suggested months before that Susannah further develop the love story between the singer and the

Italian saxophonist and keep pruning extraneous material, but Susannah sensed that, even with these changes, Hochman remained only guardedly optimistic about finding a publisher. Then the new enthusiastic literary agent she'd met that winter sent back the manuscript. "The agent was curt and not too encouraging about it," Lurie says. "Susannah saw it as yet another rejection." Still, in early spring of 2001, Susannah went back to *Secrets,* working on the passages about Francesco Forti and getting as far as the moment, in 1971, when the young Susannah was about to embark on an affair with this married and conflicted man with his many children and his unstable second wife, this man who loved music—and Susannah, he said—more than anything else. She already knew the end of the story—it was an opera and they were doomed lovers. But oh, to relive that moment in the gold and ochre light of the Roman piazza, when she was about to set out to make a new life for herself—a new identity. Oh, to relive the moment when she could believe in romance and passion and live it, too.

Yet even as she worked, usually at the New York Society Library on her laptop, she had the sense that the writing was not going well. She told Kay in April: "I don't feel at all good about the book, I feel I have a good story to tell but am not telling it well." The solitariness of writing, of real writing—one writer refers to a morning at his desk as feeling like he's been breaking rocks—was exhausting and depleting her, and, above all, was a lonely job. She pushed herself, adding to Kay, "I will never forgive myself if I don't do this book!!!!!" She meant it.

Susannah was in dire depression at this point, but even so, she retained her ability to care for others—an admirable quality but one that also enabled her to continue to deflect attention from herself. She sent her friend Rick McKay, a filmmaker who helped her with her computer, a letter containing tickets to a movie they'd planned to go to. Invite another friend, she urged, explaining that she needed to be alone for a while. To Kay, she wrote, "I'm sending you extra extra friendship and support and thinking of you," and she asked if he would come out to New York soon. "Boy, did I want to see her," says Kay, then recovering from surgery. "But I was in no condition to travel then, so I reserved a flight to New York for June." As April turned to May, Susannah, who had always drawn people to her—especially in the "up" states of her biochemistry, found it harder and harder to be with others.

She ventured out more rarely, though she continued to talk or write to close friends—Nadler, Kay, Marion Roach Smith, Rex Reed, Jackie

Osteen, and a few others, and of course, Thea Lurie. But it was difficult for Lurie to find time to connect with Susannah that spring. "Normally I called her every day, but the last few months of her life, I didn't," she says. "I was preoccupied with work and family, the daily things that seemed very unimportant after she died." Susannah's "brother"—Mark Nadler—was very busy working as well. On April 13, she e-mailed him: "I'm going away for Easter weekend . . . maybe we can have a little walk in the park? . . . It makes me very happy to think that you are in a good show and good relationship and that your dogs aren't eating the staircase carpet."

She spent Easter with Marion Roach Smith and her husband in Troy, e-mailing Kay afterward (she rarely picked up the telephone anymore) about how much she'd enjoyed dyeing Easter eggs. "But heading home on the bus, a trip I made hundreds of times over 13 years, I was surprised how sad I was to be there and think of all the times I'd arrived there full of hope for my marriage and my own home." When she got home, she had to go straight to bed and added, "I really have been reflecting on my own past too much lately. This is what happens when an artist is inactive creatively. Time for me to plunge back into writing my book, scared of rejection or not!!"

Her downward-cycling depression was increasingly immobilizing her, but she was still reluctant, Kahan says, to go back to a psychiatrist to get new medication, and have to endure, once more, the side effects, while waiting for a chemically produced relief she no longer believed in. But she kept pasting on her social face, e-mailing Nadler on April 20, "Nothing like talking to friends, always! But I am in slug mode. It's a rough time right now, so inwardly turned on this book of mine, so worried it won't work and of course the music business is a killer, worse than ever." Maybe, she suggested separately to Nadler and to Lurie, they could go to lunch or the movies? But both were busy at the moment. She was still hopeful she could develop a new career in therapy—and wrote that day to a psychiatrist she had recently met about her "serious research into Sound Therapy and Meditation Therapy." She very much wanted, she told him, to work in these fields, adding, "Artists must constantly be self-absorbed. I want to use my life experience and abilities to turn outward now and be useful to society."

But by the weekend, she was in a terrible state once again. "I am going through a rough patch, and feel as if I am screwing up all the time," she told Nadler. "I am not good company for you. I am really feeling stuck in life. I want to wait to see you till I feel better about things." She asked him to keep in touch, adding that she was always interested in her friends' lives "and never more so than when I am trying to figure out what's going on in mine!" She pulled herself together enough to get on a bus for Roxbury, for a visit first with Ric Sonder and Susan Monserud, then with Rex Reed. "She was very depressed all weekend," Monserud recalls. "She asked if I'd go on a walk with her— a mutual passion of ours. I was busy fixing things in the kitchen for a big party and said perhaps later. But I remember looking out my kitchen window where I could see Susannah's bent head and drooping body walking down the drive, toward the road." Adds Sonder, "She was consumed by her disappointments that last visit, and by being let down by people, professionally and personally. When she said her good-byes, she apologized for being so down. She said she knew she couldn't count on the jazz career as she had in the past."

Despite the terrific drag of her illness, by the end of April Susannah had been able to pare by half her article about Mae West and was ready to send it in to *American Heritage.* And in early May, she finally called Allen Farnham to tell him about the canceled Algonquin gig. "She said it *might* not happen in the fall and to go ahead and take other work," Farnham remembers. "I thanked her for letting me know. She sounded dark. That was as close as Susannah ever came to telling me the gig was off. And that was the last time I spoke to her."

She still socialized, though, occasionally. When Lisa Popa was anxious about a somewhat painful medical procedure she had to have, Susannah accompanied her to the doctor's. "She was there for me constantly," Popa says. "She was helpful. But she held her emotions tightly inside. That last time I saw her, she was just the same; she was always concerned about *you.*" Concealing her true feelings, said her friends later, was one of Susannah's major talents. Says Eric Olson, "We were very close. She trusted me and confided in me, and I think Susannah was groping toward being more open. But she was so successful at transforming herself into the *singer* Susannah McCorkle—she *willed* it—that it was hard for her to dismantle this self-construction so others could know her. She had an insistent quality about maintaining this facade, and it became a problem more and more in our friendship; but at the same time, there was a desire to speak, to open up. Now, looking back, after she'd died, I think I and other people colluded in the defense she had."

After composing letters on May 3 about how she wanted her effects distributed and her body disposed of (cremation) after she had died, Susannah went for a visit to Rex Reed's Roxbury farm. Says Reed, "She stayed at my place in the country a lot. Toward the end, she was coming here on many weekends to fall asleep, then I'd cook, then she'd fall asleep again. I said, I can't cook for you—you only want to eat vegetables. She used to lie on my couch with her eyes closed and listen to music. But the last couple of times she came, she didn't even want to listen—a bad sign. And though she'd brought along her writing, she did not work. That last visit, she told me all her problems, and I commiserated. But I was frustrated. She said, 'I don't have Dan to do the dirty work for me.' I said, 'Well, call Dan, perhaps he will do it for you,' but she said they'd had words. She was very unhappy with everything. I said, 'What's the alternative—throw yourself out the window?' And she looked *extremely* startled. I told her *I* wouldn't do that, that I'd be afraid I'd miss something. But Susannah was noncommittal about it. She was filled with sadness and loss." She had discussed Eric Olson's father's death being thrown from, or throwing oneself from, a window, just weeks before during her visit with Olson in Washington, and she mentioned suicide occasionally to two or three others. But with most people she knew, Susannah never discussed it.

By then, few people were able to get through to talk to her. "Where are you?" Nadler wrote. "I'm a little worried about you but I don't want to pry or be a pest. If everything's okay, please let me know. If it's not, please let me know as much as you care to. Your silence is alarming me." On May 5, she responded gently, "Yes, yes, I know I'm avoiding anything about myself. I am just not good company now. Thanks for making me feel loved and wanted at this tough time." Same thing with James Gavin, who—finally—heard from her, nine days before she died. "When her spirits were better and she 'felt worthy of my lovely company,' she e-mailed me, she'd give me a call."

To Brad Kay she confessed "total loss of confidence in self, book, music, etc., not that I've ever had much, I just always had a powerful creative drive. Feeling totally immobilized. Can't even listen to music." She was concerned, she added, that word would get around of her sorry state if she saw people so she was avoiding them. "I am getting help," she added, "but it isn't working yet." But she was still relying on her homeopathy and, as it turned out, never began her new antidepressant prescription. "I was terribly concerned," Kay says. "'You have extravagant, exquisite gifts,' I told her."

"After her last visit," Reed says, "she sent me an e-mail." It was the same message she was sending everyone. "'I'm not worthy of your company. I shouldn't have unburdened myself.' I e-mailed back, telling her not to be absurd. And then, on May 16, I got her very last e-mail: 'I'm going through a very difficult time, and I've decided to be alone for a few days, and I'll contact you later.'" (She sent essentially the same message to a number of people.) Concerned, Reed called and left a message on her answering machine. "'Let's go out,' I said. But I did not hear back."

"We'd agreed that she would see a psychiatrist to get back on meds in January of 2001," confides Kahan, who Susannah continued to see for biofeedback therapy, though less often after March. "There were so many things going on," he adds. "She continued to have problems with incontinence, and she was worried about growing older. By April, I saw that things were not good *at all*. I called her psychiatrist, [Cristina] Brusco, who had been her doctor and knew the meds. And Dr. Brusco said something like, 'You know Susannah is a very difficult patient— she calls a lot. And I've just had a baby.' I asked her, 'Are you going to work with her?' And she said, 'No, I think it would be better with someone else.' Given the gravity of Susannah's condition," Kahan says, "I was *shocked*."

Brusco, says Kahan, then gave him the name of someone else Susannah could call, but it would be weeks, said the new psychiatrist, Christine Macmillan, before she could meet with Susannah. "Weeks!" Kahan emphasizes. "But Susannah would only go to a new psychiatrist through a recommendation. She was very particular. She wanted quality care." Kahan was so concerned about the wait to see the new doctor that he urged Susannah to consider visiting a well-regarded psychiatric center at Columbia University. She declined. "She was concerned she might be seen by just a resident," says Kahan, who found the situation deeply frustrating: "I couldn't get doctors to see her, nor could I get her to see doctors!" Meanwhile, Susannah, increasingly anxious— unjustifiably so—about running out of money, saw Kahan infrequently, reluctant to pay out-of-pocket for the biofeedback sessions not covered by her medical insurance plan.

Susannah cracked open the door to her inner agony to a few other good friends: "I have opened up to you about my incredibly frightening bouts of depression because I know you have gone through your own," her transcontinental friend Brad Kay recalls. "Susannah said she told very very few people about it and didn't want people to know. She kept hoping to find the right combination of medication and way to live her life so she wouldn't get what she called these 'attacks-from-within' again."

Susannah's condition was so dire now (if still disguised) that she agreed at last that she could no longer refuse medication. "Some of us are born with a chemical imbalance," she told Brad Kay. "We might be okay some of the time but much of the time we need something to help us balance." What she found so hard to take was the period of testing different medications. Yet despite her deep distress she had to hold on. She could not get an appointment until May 9 with the new psychiatrist, Dr. Macmillan, who Susannah felt was the only one to prescribe new medication for her. Meanwhile, she still clung to the hope that Ronald Dushkin, her homeopathic/holistic M.D., might be able to help her. She saw Dushkin on April 27, her gynecologist on May 2, and then Kahan again on May 8. Kahan knew her homeopathic doctor. "I called Ron Dushkin when I saw her that day. I said, 'I'm not liking it. I think she needs to go on meds right away.' Dushkin said, 'Give me one more week.'" Kahan pressed him. "I said, 'Are you sure?' He was, and Susannah told me, 'I want to work with Dushkin.'"(Dr. Dushkin declined to say what homeopathic remedies Susannah was taking under his care.) But Kahan insisted that she keep her appointment with the psychiatrist, Macmillan, who had reviewed her file, sent on by Brusco, and who immediately wrote her a new prescription on May 10 for Trileptol, or oxycarbamazepine, after their initial visit. "I found out later that she never took the medication. But at the time she was trying to reassure people about how she felt, hiding how serious her depression was," says Thea Lurie, who adds that Dr. Macmillan told her afterwards Susannah had come clean to Macmillan about her thoughts of suicide. Macmillan, Lurie adds, "also said Susannah didn't think medication would help her, because she felt she had already tried everything."

Indeed, Susannah had by then tried Prozac, Lithium, Clonopin, and probably other drugs, which had alleviated her bouts of depression to varying degrees. But all had hard-to-take side effects. Yet new and possibly more effective drugs continued to be offered. Her latest untried prescription, Trileptol, for example, is touted as an "improved" version of Tegretol, to be taken, among other indications, by people with bipolar disorder who cannot tolerate lithium and certain other medicines.

A month after Susannah died, *Down Beat* published an interview with her done months before in which she chose her five "desert island discs," the music she'd want to have if marooned alone. First choice was the music that had got her started, Billie Holiday's classic 1939–44 Commodore Records sessions. Other favorites were Antonio Carlos Jobim's *Stone Flower,* Stan Getz's *Focus,* an album of music from the Amazon, and Paul Robeson's *A Lonesome Road.* "When I'm in deep pain," she said of the great African American bass-baritone, "there's no more comforting voice than his." But it was a sad irony that in the end, Susannah, who loved and was soothed so much by music, could no longer listen to it, no longer take comfort from it—or from anything. As she lay for hours curled on her couch, watching old movies on television, the memory of her deeply depressed father when she was a teenager, as he lay staring at the tube for hours in the sixties, was surely with her. She had long feared becoming like him, this man bursting with energy, ambition, and intelligence who had come to a sorry end. She'd outshone him, she'd won prizes, but she seemed to be ending in the same place. A place where it didn't matter anymore.

Her friends' advice and love and concern seemed to bounce off the facade of optimism and hope Susannah had built with the same skill she brought to her storytelling in words and song. This was a woman, a survivor, who had practically made a cottage industry out of recycling hope back into her life. A typical pronouncement, to critic Don Heckman of the *Los Angeles Times:* "The truth is that—even with everything I've gone through—I still have a basic optimism about life. And my belief in [the various songwriters] has given me a real sense of mission, as well as a creative way to express that optimism."

She continued to gloss over her terror and despair. After accepting a dinner invitation to a fan's nearby apartment on May 9 and talking about the difficulties of finding work now, she sent her hostess, Meryl Gordon, a thank-you note that managed to be charming and to deflect closer scrutiny: "Everyone goes through incredibly hard stuff in NYC, survives and feels better again. We are a hardy bunch." When Berlin journalists Sigi Schmidt-Joos and Kathrin Brigl came to New York in May for their annual visit to theaters and clubs, they saw Susannah several times during the last week of her life. "We found her depressed," Schmidt-Joos says. "Above all, she said she'd lost her talent for writing. But she said she was in therapy, then—'Let's not talk about me'—and she asked about others." Adds Brigl, "The last day, she was with us when we had to get a taxi for the airport, and she looked at Sigi with such a long look. I wondered what was going on in her head, but I was afraid to ask. I turned and waved in the taxi, and she looked so sad, waving back. So sad. She was always singing the other side of the moon—that's what had interested us so in her singing."

Her old college friend Jon Carroll notes, "Every time I talked to her, things were bad, she said, but now they were going to be better." She was destined, it seemed, to perennially wrest hard-won insights from each recent crisis; always, says a friend, "Susannah would exclaim, 'Now I understand, now I really understand this.'" A coping mechanism, to help her go on? A manner of deception, to keep her demons secret? Whatever it was, it worked for decades—until the illusion that there was hope, progress, a better future, could no longer be kept up and she felt there was nothing to replace it, nothing to hold onto.

Unmedicated, Susannah dragged on, seeing her eye doctor on May 11, a Friday, where she ran into Thea Lurie, there to see the doctor as well. Lurie recalls that Susannah was smiling and seemed receptive to Lurie's suggestion that they plan a trip to Rome together. "She seemed a bit depressed," notes Lurie, "but I had seen her come through so many depressions before. I didn't realize just how bad it was this time."

Susannah was still making a heroic effort to appear okay, following up her encounter with Lurie the following Monday, May 14, with a casual, cheery letter, ending with "Here's some routine information I should have sent you months ago about my will, just for your records, since you are an executor and a beneficiary." Incredibly—she was always organized about bill-paying—she also assembled some half-dozen different medical bills and receipts along with a polite, neatly typed letter to her medical insurer for reimbursement, dated May 14. The next day, she saw Kahan. "I said to her, 'You're going to take your meds, right?' She said yes. I walked her to the door—I don't usually do that—and we hugged. She knew she could call me anytime, and I trusted that she wanted to live. But I was hesitant; I saw her sadness and loneliness. It was thick. I was leaving on a vacation, and I called Thea. I told her that Susannah was lonely and it would be great to make a date with her. And they did have a lunch date for Saturday."

In her datebook, Susannah entered the Saturday, May 19, lunch date with Lurie. It was one of few future appointments on her calendar.

In truth, by the last months of her life, Susannah, though unbearably lonely, could hardly bear to be around anyone. "She was very careful and conscious about not having her personal problems known," says Linda Fennimore, who saw her for a race-walk session on May 16. "She was very private about everything. She had an invisible wall up. She did say to me, '*I can't seem to pull out of this one.*'"

No one could quite divine the depth of her last deep depression, what Susannah called "attacks of the horrors," "the black pit," "the demons," and "the black black blues." They had some sense of her pain, of course they did, her inner circle, but they knew her as a fighter who always got through her periods of the "horrors" and moved on.

Despite Susannah's sunny notes, her fiction had often turned to the theme of suicide. One of her earliest short stories, "Turning Point," was written at 13 about an unhappy young girl musing about a troubling event that has just occurred. "If I had been older and more mature at the time, I might have committed suicide or something," Susan had penned. (She got an A+ on the story.) In 1970, there was this entry in her diary while living in Rome:

> On the brink of suicide many times in those years, I always man-aged to pull back in time, deciding I couldn't "go" before I'd chron-icled some of the people and things that happened almost daily. Time was unimportant in Rome in those years.

But the prospect of suicide as a viable choice was never more horrifically evoked than in her 1977 story "My Lover's Wife." Here, the unnamed female protagonist has just been told by her lover that they must end their affair. Her reaction chillingly predicts Susannah's even-tual end:

> I hung up the phone and walked around my apartment. Suddenly everything in it looked unbearably grimy and I compulsively washed every single dish, even the ones put away in the cupboard. . . . I lay in bed for a day and a night, sobbing and hallucinating. I saw myself leaping from my roof to the busy street six storeys below, stuffing the cracks around the bedroom windows and under the door with rags and turning on the gas heater without lighting it, swallowing every pill I had in the bathroom cabinet and lying down waiting to die.

Then there were the notes of farewell that Susannah wrote but put away at the back of a drawer.

If she did write privately about suicide, it was usually as fiction. Very occasionally, very selectively, she also talked about it. During her marriage with DiNicola, for example. "Once she said she wished the plane we were in would crash," Dan DiNicola recalls. "Another time, she talked of it, but said she wouldn't want to leave me." With Lorraine Ruggieri, who was involved with support groups for caregivers of Alzheimer's patients, she talked in the later nineties of how she would end her life if she suffered from Alzheimer's. "She would definitely kill herself," Ruggieri recalls. "She believed in it as an alternative. We discussed end-of-life decisions—healthcare proxies and so on. We were comfortable talking about it." Explains Lurie, "There are people who never think of suicide and there are people for whom suicide is always an option. Susannah was someone who throughout her life saw suicide as an option."

Susannah also knew, firsthand, how devastating a loved one's suicide can be: She'd comforted a number of friends who had gone through the experience of losing loved ones that way, and of course she had lost her father and her aunt to suicide.[10] But though she reached out to others, she hinted that the release of suicide could be a good thing. Friends who survived loved ones' deaths responded vehemently. Christine MacDonald, for instance, told her she was being defiant in not taking medicine to help with her depressions. "I lost two sisters to suicide, one of whom jumped from a building," MacDonald explains, "and I let her know." And when she brought up the topic while walking in a garden with Mark Nadler in 2000, he erupted. "Having had experience with a person close to me attempting suicide, I told Susannah that I thought suicide was *not* acceptable. I told her that it is the most violent, the cruelest act to another person, the most aggressive act imaginable. Now, in hindsight, I suspect that she allowed me to get close to her because maybe I could convince her not to go ahead with it."

Nevertheless, Susannah was also long skilled at concealing the degree to which she suffered. Psychiatrists call the planning that precedes killing oneself "suicidal ideation," and Susannah apparently plotted hers as painstakingly and well as any Oak Room performance. For her, the notion of killing oneself had been a familiar concept since childhood; it had been a fantasy with comfort in it—the relief she sought from acute, chronic psychic pain. Anyone who's been depressed knows how at such times life can feel like a prison sentence, with all the joy bleached out, replaced by a dull, feverish lack of *savor* as one plods on; but more than that, there is a constant, hammering psychic pain to endure as well. For a chronic, deteriorating, manic depressive, it is a "long, lacerating, black, suicidal depression," writes Kay Redfield Jamison, describing her own untreated state. "My memory always took the black line of the mind's underground system. . . . You are enmeshed totally in the blackest caves of the mind. You never knew those caves were there. It will never end, for madness carves its own reality."[11]

It is at once tragic and instructive to reconstruct the path that Susannah was taking, to see, in retrospect, how she sprinkled clues about her dire state of mind, like some Hansel-and-Gretel child lost in the dark woods tossing bread crumbs behind her in a vain attempt to be rescued. And at the same time, like the birds swooping down to eat the crumbs, she covered up the clues. There was a practical side to this concealment—she was convinced that, were her illness known, it would be devastating to her professionally. This is, of course, an apprehension shared by many, including people at the top levels in business and the professions. A year after Susannah's death, a *Wall Street Journal* article addressed the tragic ends of executives suffering in secret from clinical depression: "At the highest reaches of the business world, battles with anxiety and depression typically remain secret. . . . Often, the illness comes to light only after a person takes his or her own life. The refrain after such an event is unvarying: No one saw it coming. The near-absence of clues is explained by the fact that executives grappling with depression become remarkably adept at one thing: hiding their illness. Indeed, many spend more time concealing the disease than they do seeking help."[12]

For Susannah, that concealment of the unimaginable dark turbulence within even extended to her living quarters. "She used to have stacks of stuff all over her apartment," her stepson Roy remembers, "but when she died, it was all neat as a pin. She got everything in order before she died." She said her good-byes, in a few letters and mostly e-mails. On May 15, she hugged Stephen Kahan before he left town for a short vacation. Over the next three days, she e-mailed a host of family and friends. She wrote her stepson Jeff in her usual bread-and-butter polite way, informing him of her will. "You are all in it (including Dan, if he survives me). . . . I feel better knowing you have this information." And then, "I miss all of you so much, and treasure my pics of you inside my kitchen cabinets. . . . Much love to everyone." She dropped a note to thank Helen Manfull for sending her newest book about women directors.[13] "I love it, the book, and I'm thinking of you," she wrote. She e-mailed the Osteens on May 17 that she looked forward to seeing them in the fall. On the following evening, a Friday night, she continued dotting her "I's," e-mailing Gary and Phyllis Gates at 8:30 to say she was going to send back some jazz videotapes they'd lent her. "And she thanked us," Gary adds, "for offering to let her house-sit at Shelter Island that summer." Then she e-mailed Brad Kay: "I know I'll be okay—thanks so much for your offer of support and help. Take care of yourself! I'll get through. I always do. Love, Susannah."

Susannah also took care of the last bits of her singing-career business. She wrote a check and mailed it to Wisconsin Lutheran College, returning an advance against a performance scheduled in August. That, and a concert at North Point Center for the Arts in Kinderhook, New York, in November, were her only solid bookings, although there were some prospects: A jazz promoter she'd met through Kahan, Jimmer Bolden, was in the process of setting up an engagement for her at AspenJazz in the fall; a DVD company was planning to film one of her performances; and a Brazilian fan was working to bring her to Bourbon Street, a well-known jazz club in São Paulo.

Sometime before or during the evening of May 18, Susannah wrote down Lana Cantrell's, Thea Lurie's, and Dan DiNicola's names and phone numbers on the back of one of her business cards, tucking it into the pocket of the green sweats she'd put on. She placed a copy of her will and a sealed letter with detailed instructions about disposition of her estate and belongings (including her beloved two cats) on her desk, along with a suicide letter.

"She left behind a detailed note. She would. That figures. She was always trying to be a good girl," her friend Jon Carroll was to write sadly in his May 24 obituary in the *San Francisco Chronicle*. "She was always trying to please. 'I'm really interested in how you're doing.' Always so polite. I didn't really want polite. 'Your daughters sound so wonderful. I hope I can meet them someday,' she would say. But she didn't. She won't."

"[I]n a real dark night of the soul it is always three o'clock in the morning, day after day," wrote F. Scott Fitzgerald in 1936 in *The Crack-Up;* he was chronicling his own depression. Dark, lonely, cold: "A suicidal depression is a kind of spiritual winter, frozen, sterile, unmoving," writes A. Alvarez, who suffered such a bout himself.[14] Hell, in other words. Cut off by now from the outside, Susannah had entered a dark psychic tunnel, a kind of mental constriction in which the ties to memory and loved ones are tenuous.

Nearly 30 years after writing "Ramona by the Sea," the story that depicted so well the bitter, arid familial landscape in which the young Susannah-like protagonist wandered, Susannah's tortured imagination made the leap away from an unbearable existence, and her body followed. It was around three o'clock in the morning on Saturday, May 19, 2001, when Susannah opened wide her 16th-floor window that overlooked 86th Street and pushed herself forward, out the window. Did she cry out? No sound was reported in that densely populated building, but after all, this was New York City, where screams in the night are not unknown.

Death was nearly instantaneous. Her body fell not far from her window, striking a low iron grille close to the curb before landing near the curb in the wide, empty street in the middle of the night. But New York City streets are seldom really empty. Soon a man drove by looking for a parking space, saw the mangled body, and ran inside the building for the doorman; then both went outside and looked at the still and broken form before the doorman called first 911 and then the building manager. (Both the doorman and manager knew Susannah and were devastated.) Efficiently, routinely, the city's machinery took over—the EMTs, the detectives. There was nothing suspicious or mysterious about this one: Susannah had seen to that. There was the card in her pocket and the orderly apartment. The police report, leaving no doubt that Susannah had jumped to her death, added with a slight air of wonder, "Some of the information was spelled out in great detail as to her possessions, the two cats, even down to her ashes being spread around Central Park."

After they had examined the apartment, the police phoned lawyer Lana Cantrell. It was now around 4:30 A.M. Then they called Thea Lurie, duly noting her comments in their report: "The deceased was always depressed and on medication for it and the victim's father had depression problems . . . [and] a record company and a nightclub where she had worked had ended her contract." Dan DiNicola was called. "The police officer said, 'There's been an accident with Susannah McCorkle. It appears she's dead.' My mind immediately went to a car crash. I saw a street, an accident. 'No,' said the officer, 'it appears to be suicide.' I had an image of her lying in bed in the apartment. Then he

told me she jumped. I said, 'No!' I protested loudly, I demanded, 'v.
was she with?' I told him, 'Susannah would not have done that! She
was consumed with always looking right. She would not have wanted
people seeing her in that state. Somebody had to have pushed her.'
Then the officer said, 'There's a note.'" DiNicola left Schenectady to
drive to New York immediately.

At 6:30 A.M., Joel Kaye, Lurie's husband, arrived and confirmed that
a Polaroid picture taken of the body was indeed Susannah McCorkle
and then, because someone had to do it, went down to the city morgue
where EMS had taken the body, to make the identification. "I was planning to go down to the morgue also, but he told me, 'No, don't go
through that,'" DiNicola adds. Within hours, an autopsy was performed, confirming that she had died from the massive injuries from
the fall, and confirming that no drugs of any kind were detected in her
system. In Susannah's medicine cabinet, her prescription for the Trileptol had been found, the bottle unopened. As Kay Redfield Jamison has
written, "No pill can help with the problem of not wanting to take
pills."

The story hit the newspapers on the weekend. Stephen Holden's
*New York Times* obituary was the first of an outpouring of remembrances by writers such as Leon Wieseltier, Jon Carroll, and others,
including another *Times* article several days later. Susannah was
famous in death as she had never been in life. Friends and fans visited
Susannah's building; someone lit a candle and placed it under a tree in
front of the apartment house.

In her last extended piece of writing, an admiring critique of Mae
West, Susannah had quoted from West's autobiography: "Her fans
don't want Mae West to have problems 'n' have to struggle. Mae West
always triumphs."[15] By her suicide, had Susannah, in her own mind,
stopped time, leaving the world with an indelible image of a sophisticated, still-beautiful songbird? Was this her version of a triumph? Yet
this divided soul had always strived to overcome obstacles, to get past
them. "It's the worst times of your life that make you the person that
you are if you get through them and survive them," she'd said, just a
year before. This last time, however, was a confluence of too many
tragic events, too many obstacles to get through.

"I feel very guilty," said Mimi McCorkle, a year later. "I'd had a fight
with her, and I had a hard time with her death because of that—I
talked to two psychiatrists. She must have been very unhappy in a way

she couldn't tell me. I blame myself about it for not knowing what killed her, what decided her to die. But she had such a strong heart. I thought she'd never give up."

Some blamed Susannah's mother. One old Berkeley Hills neighbor, Ethel Hanson, called Susannah's sister Maggie, criticizing Mimi as a parent. After Jon Carroll wrote a eulogy to Susannah in his column in the *San Francisco Chronicle,* "There was," he says "a distinctly large outpouring of people who wanted to get it off their chests how awful they thought Mom was—that if you've got a mom telling you that you're never going to be good enough, you're going to tend to believe it."

Though she was invited, Mimi McCorkle did not go to Susannah's memorial service in New York. "She was certain Susannah had turned her New York friends against her," explains Maggie. In fact, no one from Susannah's immediate family was present at the event at St. Peter's Church. Instead, Mimi, Susannah's sister Maggie and Susannah's niece Alice, her sister Katie, and Susannah's nephew Carlos gathered along with several old family friends in Berkeley for a picnic remembrance. Mimi McCorkle passed away peacefully in her sleep at the age of 86 on May 21, 2003, two years and two days after Susannah's death. Adds Maggie, "Mother's friends at *her* memorial service thought she was a 'great lady.' And she was—but maybe not a 'great parent.'" After Susannah's death, the mother she could never feel close to had mourned, "Susannah didn't say good-bye."

# The Song Is Ended

You don't become a jazz legend by growing old.
—Susannah McCorkle, "The Mother of Us All—Ethel Waters"

In the aftermath of Susannah's death, as the dark shadow cast by her suicide put the lie to the bright illusion, many of her friends struggled to reconcile the picture of a tortured Susannah with the captivating friend and performer they'd loved. Her suicide became a media event, and for the survivors, the achingly sad difficulty of coming to terms with their loss was exacerbated by the very public examination of Susannah's life and psyche. "I was astonished at what happened with the memorial," Mark Nadler says. "It became the place to be and be seen. People were there who had never attended a performance of Susannah's. I was told it was going to be a pretty private affair. I got calls. People would say, 'Why wasn't I invited? I need to go.'" It ended up as a crowd. There were those who mourned a beloved friend; there were the curious, and perhaps the morbidly curious; there were those who came to be seen; and there were those who felt the need to attend. Even people she'd fallen out with were there. Everyone, that is, except her mother and close relations. For all, surely, the mystery of who Susannah really was deepened that afternoon.

Many who had been close to her, as they thought, discovered there were important parts of her life they knew nothing about. "She had all her friends in little boxes and nobody knew each other," says writer Gary Gates. A sculptor, who had befriended her, only learned that she was a singer after she died, and many longtime friends discovered she had other lengthy friendships they'd never heard of—Susannah had never once mentioned Thea Lurie to Rex Reed, though she'd known both of them for decades. He comments, "She went from friend to friend, looking for the key to the Secret Garden. She wrote a strange, complicated scenario."[1] When Dan DiNicola declared, "The only ones who really knew her were Thea and myself," he was mostly right: No one had been as privy for as long as these two to what DiNicola terms her "tortured soul." Even so, after they parted in 1997, Susannah and DiNicola spent little time together. And her closest confidante, Thea Lurie, was unaware of the depths of Susannah's despair at the end.

A suicide is a catastrophe that cannot by its nature be mourned like other deaths, even other tragic and unexpected deaths, for suicide leaves behind not only the bereaved—who must find a way to cope with loss—but exacts extraordinary suffering in those who are alive and very often feel a heavy burden of guilt, anger, and betrayal. The guilt: Her family, of course, above all, Mimi. "I know that Katie was very upset about Susannah's death, and she probably feels a lot of guilt," says Maggie, who was quiet and careful about her own feelings. "She's aware she wasn't the easiest sister to get along with." Susannah's circles of friends talked about the walks they didn't take with her, the movie dates and the lunch dates they had to cancel, postponing for a more opportune time. Says Lurie, who had planned to see Susannah for lunch on Saturday, the day when Susannah killed herself in the pre-dawn hours, "She had so many talents. She loved life. I did not get signs that what she was going through was so much worse than her previous depressions." Dan DiNicola recalls he had to reschedule her planned trip to visit him in Schenectady to retrieve one of her paintings. And finally, there were the reactions of the psychiatric and medical community. Says Stephen Kahan, "I remember I had a call from [homeopath Ronald] Dushkin on my answering machine the day after her death, not more than a few words: 'Susannah McCorkle killed herself.' So callous and cold." Even Kahan, the therapist she was closest to, who'd urged and prodded Susannah to get back into therapy, to try a new kind of medication, was out of town the last week of Susannah's life; he was on vacation when he received the news of her death. Everyone that Susannah knew had a *life,* was busy with the normal press of work and family and social obligations. What they didn't realize was how little Susannah had of her own life by the end of it.

There was the anger at what Susannah had done, and how. The anger of betrayal cut some deeply. Mark Nadler says, "I've screamed at her, 'If you were such a private person and you wanted to be left alone and not talked about and gossiped about, why did you do this?'" The means of suicide is a form of control, says suicidologist Herbert Hendin, and the method must be "in keeping with their personalities." For those who choose to throw themselves from high places, he adds, "the grotesque, grim wish to make a splash by jumping to a notorious death." Exclaimed *Fresh Air* radio host Terry Gross, who had interviewed Susannah many times, "It was such a punishing way of killing herself." When she pushed herself forward from the high ledge of her apartment window, Susannah had found a way to literally *let go,* to end the too-painful performance of life—with a smashing last act. But in doing so, it was as if a psychic bomb had exploded, with painful bits of emotional shrapnel exploding afterward, causing survivor injury. Her public form of destruction, of blotting out herself on the street, caused many to recoil. When Dan DiNicola was notified of Susannah's death by the police, he found himself initially unable to accept that someone who had been so meticulous about her appearance could have thrown herself out of a window onto a public street. Many reacted to the rage expressed by such an act with their own anger. "What kind of a death is that, what kind of anger, to throw yourself out of a window and leave all the awful remains for some poor guy to come along and discover?" asks a musician who worked with her.[2] "Though she was still kind and thoughtful, it's the same kind of anger I saw when she had cancer," DNicola remarks. "She must have been angry, a 'Fuck you, look at how I tried to do everything, tried and tried.'" Agrees therapist Stephen Kahan, "She had so much love to give, but she was filled with rage." "I also think she was being defiant," Christine MacDonald asserts: "115 in 1,000 manic depressives kill themselves. I know—I researched it."

Her suicide note, dated Wednesday, May 16—three days before she acted—says much about her, a neatly handwritten, polite, and oddly solicitous letter that begins with the word "please" and ends with the word "love." "Please believe that I do this because I am convinced that my illness cannot be helped for any length of time and I cannot bear to be a burden on anyone any longer. Please convey my love to everyone I leave behind. I just can't keep fighting myself and my own biochemistry any longer."[3]

It was typical of Susannah—neat, thoughtful, organized, the "good girl." In the good times, when she was not despairing, Susannah could be incandescent and witty, a caring companion and a lot of fun. From Thea's point of view, Susannah had always been there for her. "Susannah and I always supported each other emotionally; it was a two-way street," she says. Still, although many people comment about how much Susannah gave to them, clearly this was a deeply divided soul. Suicidologists note that a "you are not to blame" type of suicide letter can mean the opposite.[4]

The urgent and unbearable question remains: *why did she kill herself?* Countless people undergo depressions, despair, immense suffering, as indeed Susannah did. To kill oneself, something else must take place. Observes suicidologist Edwin Shneidman, "There is at least a touch of schizophrenia or insanity in every suicide in the sense that, in suicide, there is some disconnection between thoughts and feelings."[5] For Susannah, suffering from bipolar disorder, the touch of insanity, the disconnect, was built into her biochemistry. She had written about this condition from her teens. Fellow bipolar sufferer James Stout writes, "Daily my surroundings took on *a strange sense of unreality,* as if I was an actor in a play and at the same time, a spectator watching myself perform. Sadness shrouded me like rain clouds blotting out the sun. . . . I was turning into a different person. . . . I secluded myself. . . . I felt my life was spinning out of control . . . anxiety and self-blame kept me from coming up with a positive way to deal with [a situation]. . . . Thoughts of suicide invaded all my thinking. I couldn't outrun them. It panicked me to think of what the future might bring."[6] Though Susannah didn't write that, she might as well have. But a crucial difference between her and Stout was the kind of support systems each had. Stout had consistent help and regular visits to psychiatrists with closely monitored medication. Susannah had a number of stop-and-start therapists and psychiatrists, was off and on medication with long gaps between treatments. Left largely to herself in a deepening psychic crisis that clouded her perspective and judgment, Susannah continued to rely, as she always had done, on her own inner resources, her own intelligence, her own willpower to get better. "She thought you could intellectualize any problem, rationalize it," mourns James Gavin. "You see, she had come so far that way in her career, with the careful, thoughtful planning." But she was wrung out, unable to escape the pain. "Most of us can pull out of depression. We just assume others can, too. I felt as if I were her husband again, that I should have done something," DiNicola says. But Susannah saw no way out of her suffering except to kill herself.

In the months before her death, Susannah was moving towards what she believed was checkmate. When she could, she worked in the spring of 2001 on *Secrets in Piazza Navona,* ending a freshly written prologue with an enigmatic reference to "a secret that had jumped out" from the pages of her original notebooks. "But did *you* know it?" she wrote, adding, "I've lost my chance to tell you face to face." The "you" she addressed was Francesco Forti, her lover in Rome, whom she'd recently learned had died. He had been the one who awakened her to music, and his death meant the death of that dream of love and art; they were impossible any longer. At 55, Susannah felt she was doomed: no singing, no career, about to run out of money, no support from her mother, losing her allure, and worst of all, condemned to be alone, without a lover.

Singing had been vital, a way to connect her to the world, to people. Jazz music and musicians, she'd said long before, when she moved to London to embark on her singing career, had become her "tribe," the family she longed for. But the music community was as divided about Susannah in death as it had been in life. When the poet Sylvia Plath killed herself, another woman poet had remarked that her suicide was "a good career move." Similarly, under the cloak of anonymity of an Internet chat room for vocalists, certain of Susannah's detractors let it rip. "Well, she'd got her 15 minutes of fame now!" typed one. Another replied by e-mail that Susannah was now "getting attention. Lots of it. Immediately after her death, she achieves a position near the other music and literature greats whose romantic auras include unbecoming deaths.... I'd venture that this, more than anything else, was what triggered her behavior."

But while a good many singers have lived self-destructive lives, overt suicides have been rare in the jazz community. There have been very few among vocalists: Beverly Kenney, a very good though little-known singer and poet in the fifties, and Joy Marshall, an English singer of West Indian descent, are two who come to mind. Eerily, Susannah's death most closely parallels that of Chet Baker, a singer as well as a trumpet player; Susannah recorded tributes to Baker's earlier versions of "My Buddy" and "Look for the Silver Lining." Baker fell to his death from a hotel window about eleven years before Susannah killed herself. His biographer, James Gavin, says Baker jumped, disputing a widespread notion that he was pushed. In his death, Baker became a symbol of the haunted jazz life.[7] And Susannah, says Rex Reed, "wanted to be an icon like Billie Holiday." Yet despite her detractors' cynicism, by the time Susannah put her suicide plan into action, she had little illusion left that her life—or death—would give her the kind of fame Baker or especially Holiday had. She felt unsupported, ignored by the jazz community. Bassist Sean Smith tells a sad story. "A few days before she died, Susannah asked a singer I know, 'Why don't other singers like me?'" Adds Smith, who had played with Susannah years before, "None of us in the jazz community knew what she was going through."

It was as a writer that Susannah had a clutch of compelling, tragic role models: Virginia Woolf slowly wading into the water to drown, her pockets weighted with stones; poet Anne Sexton, orderly arranging her death by first lunching with a close friend, then turning on her car engine in a closed garage; Marilyn Monroe going out on pills. And then male writers like Hemingway, who shot himself, Malcolm Lowry, who overdosed on pills, John Berryman, who threw himself off a bridge (and like Susannah, had a parent who committed suicide), and Hart Crane, who threw himself over the side of a ship. But above all, there was the example of Sylvia Plath, who put her head in a gas oven at 30. Susannah had read Plath's diaries and knew well what a Plath biographer described as the poet's "inner scape: a world of dread and meaninglessness. Even as [she] hopefully formed dreams, they had already been dismissed by her implacable deeper self."[8]

Susannah's will was characteristically well thought-out. She had divided her assets into four parts. One quarter, as well as all of her "tangible personal property," was left to Thea Lurie; in addition, Lurie was named executor of Susannah's estate. Another quarter went to her sister Maggie; a third quarter went to Dan, Roy, Jeff, and Anne DiNicola; and the final fourth was divided among friends, their charities, and her favorite institutions: 5 percent to Mark Nadler (or the Gay Men's Health Crisis); 5 percent to Lorraine Ruggieri (Women Against Violence); 5 percent to Theodora Skipitares (Women in Need); and 10 percent divided among Yaddo, the MacDowell Colony, the New York Public Library, the Society of Singers, and the National Abortion Rights Action League. Left out of the will was her older sister Katie, who seemed resigned at first. "Katie called soon after Susannah died and thanked me for being such a good friend to Susannah," Lurie says. Later, Katie did ask for money from the will for her son Carlos, who came to New York from California and attempted unsuccessfully to get into Susannah's apartment to remove some of her things.

Wills often contain surprises. The fear of impoverishment that Susannah had expressed time and again, by implying that she had only modest savings, the frantic final request from her aged mother for a $20,000 loan to see her through a bleak period—all this was revealed as bogus: she had close to a quarter of a million dollars in various accounts. Posthumously, Susannah's estate has grown. When the compilation CD *Most Requested Songs* came out four months after her death, it soon became her best-selling album. Lawyer Lana Cantrell says royalties distributed to her beneficiaries doubled and tripled after her death. "It's always the way when an artist dies," she adds.

In the struggle to come to terms with the shock of a dear friend's suicide, many found understanding in metaphor. "Maybe she felt she was flying like a bird when she jumped, out toward the park," says Nadler, who had helped her to paint her "blue skies" bedroom walls with sky and clouds in the apartment that gave her a sliver of what she called a "Cole Porter view" of Manhattan. Maybe: "Skylark" was one of her nicknames, as were "canary" and "songbird." "She was born to sing— she was only really happy when she sang," says Dan DiNicola. Some have had dreams of Susannah—the photographer Carlos Spaventa, her old friend Roy Schecter, her therapist Stephen Kahan. In Kahan's dream, "She was in a university hallway, there was gold everywhere, and she was kneeling. She was wearing a fun hat and she had books in her hands, and I realized it was the University of God. She said to me, 'I'm finally there, Stephen. I've gotten it.' Then I woke up."

Susannah has not been forgotten. She loved flowers, and on the first anniversary of her death, a group of intimates met in Central Park's beautiful Conservatory Garden. There they paid their respects to her and then scattered her ashes. "It was," Lurie says, "her secret garden." Moving and eloquent tributes appeared in print, including a beautifully wrought piece in the *New Yorker* by Leon Wieseltier. Wrote Sheridan Morley in the *London Spectator*, "She was one of the great jazz singers of our time, and one of the few who understood that a great song doesn't need scat or improvisation or any kind of vocal tricks. She just sang the lyrics straight and simple and true as they had been written. And for that she will be ever missed."

"My albums," Susannah once said, "are like children. For me they're what I'll leave behind in the world when I go." And she was right about that. Because of her suicide, Susannah will always be something of an enigma. "There is no one to whom one so yearns to connect," says

Edwin Schneidman, "as a person who has committed suicide."[9] But there remains her art. Susannah's sweet but sophisticated voice, so literate and so sympathetic to the American songbook, so capable of communicating deep despair and child-like joy, has not been silenced. Those who loved her have her recorded legacy. The melody lingers on.

# Notes

*Acknowledgments*

   1. Susannah recorded "Haunted Heart" on her last album, the CD *Hearts and Minds.*


*Careless Love*

   1. Letter from a woman identified as "A.D.," in Susannah's files, in 1989. The letter had originally been sent to columnist Jon Carroll of the *San Francisco Chronicle.*
   2. Susannah McCorkle, "Just Me and My Radio," *Listen,* April 1982.
   3. To Roy Schecter in unpublished interview circa 1981.
   4. "The Bearer," *Woman's Journal,* 1978.
   5. *Fajardo's People: Cultural Adjustment in Venezuela,* Latin American Center at the University of California, Los Angeles, Latin American Studies, vol. 1 (Caracas: Editorial Sucre, 1965).
   6. H. Thomas McCorkle Jr., "Cultural Change and the Iowa Amish," in 1956, and "Chiropractic: A Deviant Theory of Disease and Therapy" in *Human Organization* 20 (1961): 20–22.
   7. Interview by Leonard Feather in *Jazz Times,* September 1994.
   8. She called it *Secrets in Piazza Navona.*
   9. Interview by Siegfried "Sigi" Schmidt-Joos and Kathrin Brigl on the Radio Free Berlin program *Showtime.* Interviews were conducted in 1993, 1995, 1996, 1997, 1998, 1999, and 2000.
   10. Ibid.
   11. Ibid.


*Susan Savage*

   1. Francis Davis, "A Champion of Song," *High Fidelity,* 1988.
   2. Jon Carroll, "In Other Words, Hold My Hand," *San Francisco Chronicle,* obituary for Susannah, May 24, 2001.

3. W. J. Rorabaugh, *Berkeley at War: The 1960s* (Oxford University Press, 1989).

4. Chris Albertson, *Stereo Review,* March 1984.

5. John Keats, *You Might as Well Live: The Life and Times of Dorothy Parker* (Simon and Schuster, 1970).

6. Tom Collins, "Peliboy, the Great American Lie," *Daily Californian,* May 11, 1966. Article about the *Pelican*'s satire on *Playboy* magazine.

7. Per correspondence with medical insurers about Tom McCorkle's psychiatric records, in Mimi McCorkle's private papers.


*La Signorina Scontenta*

1. Stephen Holden, *New York Times,* 1985.

2. From her "Rome diaries," later called *Secrets in Piazza Navona.*

3. Susannah McCorkle, "I Was a Compulsive Overeater," 1978.

4. To Chris Albertson, *Stereo Review,* March 1984.


*Gateway to Jazz*

1. And the letter did end up in a file retrieved by Susannah's biographer!

2. To Roy Schecter, unpublished interview, 1981.

3. In *Jazz Singing: America's Great Voices From Bessie Smith to Bebop and Beyond* (Scribner's, 1990).

4. Unpublished interview by Roy Schecter, 1981.

5. Sigi Schmidt-Joos, *Showtime* radio program, Radio Free Berlin, 1998.

6. To Terry Gross, *Fresh Air,* NPR radio, April 12, 1991.

7. Susannah McCorkle and Keith Ingham, interview by Stan Britt for a BBC radio program, London, March 7, 1979.

8. She also included descriptions of her life pre-Rome, in Mexico, in Paris, a difficult trip to California, and eventually, her first months in London.

9. "I Was a Compulsive Overeater."

10. "French Lessons."

11. From *Secrets in Piazza Navona.*

12. Ibid.

13. Ibid.


*Foggy Day*

1. Interview by Stan Britt, 1979.

2. Liner notes to *1975: The Beginning,* Susannah's debut recording, a demo, posthumously released.

3. Letter to Thea Lurie, August 11, 1974.

4. Ibid., August 29, 1973.

5. Ibid., June 1975. She said she felt compelled to write about such episodes, so as to shed psychological light on them. Susannah was fascinated by Thomas Mann's story *Tonio Kroger,* dramatizing the conflict between the artist-observer and the participant in life.

6. Ibid., August 11, 1974.

7. Also on the date: Sudhalter, cornet; Keith Nichols, trombone; Paul Nossiter, clarinet; Peter Ind, bass; and John Cox, drums. Private collection.

8. The Edinburgh date is on a tape in the BBC archive in London, as is a program called "Leaving on a Jet Plane," number 13 in a series called *The American Popular Song.*

9. Letter to Thea Lurie, May 21, 1974.

10. With Don Coates on piano, Frank Tate, bass, and Jules Moss, drums.

11. To Marian McPartland, summer 2000, Piano Jazz session on Alec Wilder and his music.

12. *Intimate Nights: The Golden Age of New York Cabaret* (Grove Weidenfeld, 1991).


*The Hungry Years*

1. In *Woman,* a popular "women's" magazine in England.

2. Susannah appeared at various times on BBC broadcasts, including on February 8, 1975, with the Keith Ingham Trio at Traverse Theatre, Edinburgh; March 8, 1979, in a program called "You and the Night and the Music"; a February 26, 1979, program called "Round Midnight"; a Stan Britt interview on March 7, 1979; and a March 16, 1980, *BBC Jazz Club* show, "Leaving on a Jet Plane," episode 13.

3. Per reports and questionnaires that Tom McCorkle completed for reimbursement of certain claims (for psychiatric counseling) from his medical insurers, in Mimi McCorkle papers.

4. For a complete list, see bibliography.

5. She also sang "I've Got Your Number" and "Bye Bye Baby."

6. The program included Ginger Rogers's "Let Yourself Go" and "A Fine Romance"; Mae West's "My Old Flame" and "A Guy Who Takes His Time"; Marlene Dietrich's "Falling in Love Again"; Joan Blondell's "With Plenty of Money and You" and "Remember My Forgotten Man"; Alice Faye's "Wake Up and Live" and "No Love, No Nothing"; Bette Davis's "They're Either Too Young or Too Old"; Betty Grable's "I Wish I Knew"; Betty Hutton's "I Got the Sun in the Morning," "They Say It's Wonderful, and "Arthur Murray Taught Me Dancing in a Hurry"; Jane Powell's "It's a Most Unusual Day"; Doris Day's "Ten Cents a Dance"; and Marilyn Monroe's "Diamonds Are a Girl's Best Friend," "I'm Through With Love," and "Bye Bye Baby."

7. *Jazztimes,* September 1992.

8. Susannah's two appearances on *Piano Jazz* were first aired in 1994, and on December 26, 2000.

9. Letter to Ken Pitt.

10. September 12, 1983.

11. Per tapes by Roy Schecter of 1982–84 performances.

12. Interview by Stan Britt, 1979.


## I'll Take Romance

1. On the Madison Square Garden cable channel. Susannah appeared a number of times also on his WNEW-AM radio show, *New York Tonight,* including in September 1984, November 1984, June 1985, and October 1985. In the 1990s, she sang on his radio show on WQEW-AM, including his annual Christmas show in December 1995.

2. Susannah sang at Rainbow and Stars in June 1992 with Jonathan Schwartz. After Schwartz sang a number of standards (including his father's composition, the lovely "Haunted Heart"), Susannah sang seven songs. They finished the program in duets on "You Took Advantage of Me," "It's a Grand Night for Singing," and "Hit the Road to Dreamland." They were accompanied by Tony Monte on piano, Steve LaSpina, bass, and Joe Cocuzzo, drums.

3. Personal papers.

4. Proposal to Susannah's literary agent for a memoir to be called *A Singing Life,* 1994. The book did not materialize.

5. According to Roy Schecter, a superior rendition of "How Insensitive," recorded at the session with bassist Steve LaSpina doing delicate bow-work behind Susannah, was not included in the LP or the subsequent CD. "It was a thing of melancholy beauty," Schecter remembers.

6. Gerald Nachman, *San Francisco Chronicle,* September 10, 1987.

7. Three pounds of flesh had been removed, she told her London friend Frances Bendixson.

8. Proposal for *A Singing Life,* September 14, 1994. The project did not go forward.


## Sunshine Susannah

1. *Jazztimes,* 1994.

2. In 1999 interview with Siegfried "Sigi" Schmidt-Joos and Kathrin Brigl on the Radio Free Berlin program *Showtime.* Other interviews were conducted in 1993, 1995, 1996, 1997, 1998, and 2000.

3. Interview with Terry Gross on her *Fresh Air* radio program, 1996.

4. By National Public Radio reviewer Karen Michil McPerson, 1990.

5. On *DiNicola's World* on the PBS affiliate, WRGB, 1990. The show won an Emmy.

6. In *Bossa Nova, the Story of the Brazilian Music That Seduced the World,* author Ruy Castro says Jobim perenially lacked a first-class lyricist in English.

7. "Mae West, Why She's a Bigger Presence Now Than Ever," *American Heritage,* September 2001.

8. Richard Cook and Brian Morton, *The Penguin Guide to Jazz,* 1998.

9. To Terry Gross, *Fresh Air* radio program, May 1996.

10. On *Showtime* radio program, Berlin, 1995.

11. Kay Redfield Jamison, *Touched with Fire: Manic Depressive Illness and the Artistic Temperament* (Free Press, 1993).

12. Neva Chonin, "Susannah McCorkle Sings Like a Satin Doll at Yoshi's," *San Francisco Chronicle,* 1999.

13. For a low-fat frozen dinner commercial, she sang a snippet of "You'd Be So Nice to Come Home To."

14. Leonard Feather, *Jazztimes,* 1994.

15. Letter to Roy Schecter, January 5, 1996.


*Faint Music*

1. Paul Solotaroff, *Group: Six People in Search of a Life* (Allen Lane, 2000).

2. According to William Bastone in "The Charlatans," *Village Voice,* October 13–19, 1999.

3. "Always: A Singer's Journey through the Life of Irving Berlin," *American Heritage,* November 1998.

4. Susannah McCorkle appeared on NPR's *Fresh Air with Terry Gross* in July 1987, December 1988 (Christmas concert), April 1991, July 1996 (featured performer at the annual National Public Radio Conference in Washington, D.C., with Cliff Korman, piano). Also on NPR's *All Things Considered,* June 3, 1999, "The Career of Singer Susannah McCorkle." A live broadcast of Susannah singing "If I Only Had a Heart" from a *Fresh Air* program was included in a CD compilation released in 2003, *Fresh Air in Concert.*

5. Jamison, *Touched with Fire;* James T. Stout, *Bipolar Disorder: Rebuilding Your Life* (Cypress House, 2002).

6. The March performance at the Walter Reade Theater at Lincoln Center. Susannah, with Allen Farnham and Chris Berger on bass, was billed as "Curly Top on Broadway," and featured Temple's 1938 film *Little Miss Broadway,* along with her songs from the movie, including "Be Optimistic" and "Happy Ending." On December 19, 1998, in "A Shirley Temple Christmas," Susannah sang the Temple song "You Gotta Smile to Be Happy." After the movie *Heidi* was aired, Susannah performed other Temple-associated songs: "That's What I Want for Christmas," "You Gotta Smile" (again), "How Can I Thank You," and a medley of Christmas songs with audience participation, including "Rudolf the Red-Nosed Reindeer" and "We Wish You a Merry Christmas."

7. *Denver Post,* April 25, 1999.

8. The divorce was finalized in New York on May 4, 2000.

*Stop, Time*

1. Clonopin (the generic is clonazepam), prescribed by Dr. Cristina Brusco.

2. Her Mae West article appeared in *American Heritage,* September–October 2001.

3. *CBS This Morning,* December 18, 1990, singing "The Christmas Song"; *Live at Five,* local New York City affiliate, December 20, 1990; CBS *Sunday Morning,* July 14, 1991, a profile of Susannah hosted by Billy Taylor. Also appearances on talk-show host Joe Franklin's late-night New York television program.

4. She sang this song on Jonathan Schwartz's Christmas radio show in December 1995.

5. She also had titles for future shows—"Thank You, Billie Holiday" was one; another, surprisingly, was "Mamas & Papas." Nothing else has turned up about these shows, though it is intriguing to think of a Susannah McCorkle version of, say, "California Dreamin'."

6. Matthias Kirsch, *Jazz Lounge,* on *Jazzradio,* Berlin, 2000/01 (jazzradio.net musicarchive/SusannahMcCorkle.html). Susannah had appeared at a concert at Alice Tully Hall at Lincoln Center in New York in 1996, where she sang "Falling in Love Again" (from *The Blue Angel,* the 1930 film with Marlene Dietrich), in English and in German.

7. In 2002, *Healing Time* was released as CD Superbatone 737. Solo pianist Brad Kay describes the album thus: "Jazz compositions designed for relaxation, recuperation or meditation. . . . Album concept, creative consultant and test driver: Susannah McCorkle." "I did the album to help *me* heal," Kay adds.

8. Susannah's important Manhattan cabaret shows include: (1) November 27–December 31, 1989: Oak Room at the Algonquin, "Men, Women and the Old Devil Called Love"; (2) November 27–January 5, 1990: Algonquin, "The Politically Correct Chanteuse"; (3) September 24–October 19, 1991: Algonquin, "Autumn in New York: A Celebration of the Great Singers and Songs of Manhattan"; (4) September 8–October 10, 1992: Algonquin, "I'll Take Romance: Love Songs for People Who Love Songs"; (5) March 30–April 3 and April 6–10, 1993: Tavern on the Green, "From Bessie to Brazil—60 Years of Great Songs, Songs of Survival and Hope" (this show introduced "Os Aguas de Março/The Waters of March"); (6) March 7–26, 1994: Rainbow and Stars, an untitled show (*New York Times* reviewer Stephen Holden thought it should be called "The Making of a Modern Pop-Jazz Singer"); (7) June 4–29, 1996: Algonquin, "The Passionate Cole Porter"; (8) May 6–June 3, 1997: Algonquin, "The Passionate Irving Berlin" (aka, "Irving Berlin: Darkness and Light"); (9) June 8–July 4, 1998: Algonquin, "Gershwin and Jobim"; (10) June 22–July 23, 1999: Algonquin, "From Broken Hearts to Blue Skies: A

Single Woman in Manhattan"; (11) October 27–November 25, 2000: Algonquin, "Hearts and Minds: Life in Manhattan as a Hopeless Romantic."

9. Arthur Pomposello departed his job at the Oak Room by the end of 2001.

10. Children of a parent who committed suicide are six times as likely to try to kill themselves, according to a 2002 study in the *Archives of General Psychiatry*.

11. Kay Redfield Jamison, *An Unquiet Mind: A Memoir of Moods and Madness* (Knopf, 1995).

12. Article in the *Wall Street Journal*, June 26, 2002.

13. Helen Manfull, *Taking Stage: Women Directors on Directing* (Metheun, 1999).

14. A. Alvarez, *The Savage God: A Study of Suicide* (Random House, 1972).

15. This quote was deleted from the heavily cut published version in *American Heritage*.


*The Song Is Ended*

1. Besides Reed's remarks at the service, there were eulogies by Thea Lurie and Dan DiNicola, by *American Heritage* editor Frederick Allen, by Concord Records producer Nick Phillips, by *New York Times* writer Margo Jefferson, and by Susannah's stepsons Roy and Jeff DiNicola. Allen Farnham, with bassist Bill Moring, drummer Tim Horner, and guitarist Howard Alden, played "The Waters of March" in her honor.

2. He asked to remain anonymous.

3. As published in Gwenda Blair, "The Melody Lingers," *New York* magazine, June 3, 2002.

4. Herbert Hendin, in *Suicide in America* (Norton, 1995).

5. Shneidman, *The Suicidal Mind* (Oxford University Press, 1996).

6. Stout, *Bipolar Disorder*.

7. James Gavin, *Deep in a Dream: The Long Night of Chet Baker* (Knopf, 2002).

8. Anne Stevenson, *Bitter Fame: A Life of Sylvia Plath* (Houghton Mifflin, 1989).

9. Schneidman, *The Suicidal Mind*.

# Selected Discography

Waiting for Susannah's latest record, a fan once said, was "like reading the latest installment in a favorite author's series."

**July 28 and August 21, 1974:** *Songs of Cole Porter,* Warner Bros CD CP1; as *Cole,* EMC LP 3049; as *A Musical Tribute to Cole Porter,* Stanyan LP 10136. With Keith Ingham, musical director, piano, and session musicians on "I'm in Love Again," "Don't Look at Me That Way," "You'd Be So Nice to Come Home To," and "Let's Do It," one verse (other verses by Ian Carmichael, Elaine Stritch, Patricia Routledge, the Mike Sammes Singers). London.

**August 27, 1975:** *Susannah McCorkle with Keith Ingham: The Beginning 1975.* Challenge CD AL 73233 (Holland). Demo recording. 22 selections. London.

**May 27 and June 10, 1976:** *The Music of Richard Rodgers.* EMI SH236. On "A Lady Must Live" and "This Funny World" with Keith Ingham, piano. London (LP only).

**August 23 and 29, 1976:** *The Music of Harry Warren.* World Records WRS 1001 and Inner City LP IC 1141. (IC LP includes substitute 1981 recordings of "Forty-Second Street" and "Chattanooga Choo-Choo.") Keith Ingham, piano, Bruce Turner, alto sax/clarinet, Len Skeat, bass, Johnny Richardson, drums. London (LP only).

**March 15 and 16, 1977:** *Keith Ingham Plays the Music of Jerome Kern.* EMI WRS 1003. On "Why Was I Born?" and "Nobody Else but Me." London (LP only).

**September 19 and 21 and October 3, 1977:** *The Songs of Johnny Mercer,* Jazz Alliance CD TJA-10031/Concord; and as *The Quality of Mercer,* Black Lion BLP 12169 and Inner City LP 1101. Keith Ingham, musical director, piano, Ron Rubin, bass, Derek Hogg, drums, Danny Moss, tenor sax and clarinet, Digby Fairweather, trumpet and cornet, Duncan Lamont, tenor sax and flute. London. "How Little We Know" from *Mercer* included on *The Classic Hoagy Carmichael,* Smithsonian Collection CD038, 3 CDs, vol. 3, and LP R38, and Indiana Historical Society HIS C1002. "One for My Baby" from *Mercer* included on Rhino 5-CD boxed set, *Great American Songwriters,* vol. 2.

---

All recordings are U.S. unless otherwise indicated.

**1979:** Untitled demo from BBC radio broadcast. With Keith Ingham Trio. Includes "The Lady's in Love With You," "Bridges," "Too Close for Comfort," "I'm All Smiles," "The Joint Is Jumpin,'" "Talk to Me Baby," "Just the Way You Are," "Big City's for Me." London (LP only).

**January 11 and February 19, 1980:** *Over the Rainbow: The Songs of E. Y. "Yip" Harburg.* Jazz Alliance CD TJA-10033/Concord and Inner City LP IC 1131. Keith Ingham, musical director, piano, Jack Six, bass, Ronnie Bedford, drums. "The Begat" from *Over the Rainbow* included on *American Songbook Series: E. Y. Harburg.*

**November 16 and 18, 1981:** *The People That You Never Get to Love.* Jazz Alliance CD TJA-10034 and Inner City LP 1151. Keith Ingham, musical director, piano, Al Gafa, guitar, Steve LaSpina, bass, Joe Cocuzzo, drums.

**December 1983, January 1984:** *Thanks for the Memory: Songs of Leo Robin.* Jazz Alliance CD TJA-10035 and Pausa CD PAUSA PCD 7195 and LP7175. Keith Ingham, musical director, piano, Steve La Spina, bass, Joe Cocuzzo, drums, Phil Bodner, clarinet, alto sax, and flute, Chris Flory, guitar, Al Klink, tenor sax.

**June 1985:** *How Do You Keep the Music Playing?* Jazz Alliance CD TJA-10036 and Pausa Records (LP) PR7195. Ben Aronov, piano, Steve LaSpina, bass, Joe Cocuzzo, drums, Al Cohn, tenor saxophone, Gene Bertoncini, guitar.

**October 4–5, 1986:** *As Time Goes By.* CBS/Sony CD 32DP 685 and CBS/SONY LP 28AP 3315. Billy Taylor, piano, Victor Gaskin, bass, Tony Reedus, drums, Ted Dunbar, guitar, Jimmy Heath, tenor saxophone.

**December 9–10, 1986:** *Dream.* Jazz Alliance CD TJA-10037 and Pausa LP 7208. Ben Aronov, piano, Frank Wess, tenor saxophone, Gene Bertoncini, guitar.

**October 1988:** *No More Blues.* Concord CD 4370 and Concord LP 370. Ken Peplowski, musical director, clarinet, and tenor saxophone, Emily Remler, guitar (certain selections), Bucky Pizzarelli, guitar (certain selections), Dave Frishberg, piano, John Goldsby, bass, Terry Clarke, drums. "Breezin' Along With the Breeze" from *No More Blues* included on *American Songbook Series: Richard Whiting,* Smithsonian Collection CD. "Fascinating Rhythm" from *No More Blues* included on *Great American Songwriters,* vol. l, Rhino CD.

**February 1990:** *Sabia.* Concord CD 4418. Lee Musiker, piano, musical director and arranger, Scott Hamilton, tenor saxophone, Emily Remler, guitar, Dennis Irwin, bass, Duduka Fonseca, drums, Café, percussion.

**September 15–17, 1991:** *I'll Take Romance.* Concord CD 4491. Hank Jones, piano, on "I'll Take Romance," Allen Farnham, musical director, piano, on all others, Frank Wess, tenor saxophone and flute, Howard Alden, guitar, Dennis Irwin, bass, Keith Copeland, drums.

**February 1–3, 1993:** *From Bessie to Brazil.* Concord CD 4547. Allen Farnham, musical director, piano, Howard Alden, guitar, Kiyoshi Kitagawa, bass, Chuck Redd, drums, Randy Sandke, trumpet and flügelhorn, Dick Oatts, alto saxophone and flute, Ken Peplowski, tenor saxophone and clarinet, Robert Trowers, trombone. "Aguas de Março/The Waters of March" from *Bessie* included on soundtrack to film *Heartbreakers,* RCA CD 63770.

**April 20–22, 1994:** *From Broadway to Bebop.* Concord CD 4615. Allen Farnham, piano, Kiyoshi Kitagawa, bass, Richard DeRosa, drums, Frank Vignola, guitar, Randy Sandke, trumpet and flügelhorn, Ken Peplowski, clarinet and tenor saxophone, Dick Oatts, alto and soprano saxophones and flute, Robert Trowers, trombone.

**May 18, 1994:** *Concord Jazz Christmas.* Concord CD 4613. On "The Secret of Christmas" with Allen Farnham, piano.

**July 8, 1995:** *Jazz Celebration: A Tribute to Carl Jefferson.* Concord CCD-7005. On "They Can't Take That Away From Me" with Allen Farnham, piano, Michael Moore, bass, Akira Tana, drums.

**September 6–8, 1995:** *Easy to Love: The Songs of Cole Porter.* Concord CD 4696. Allen Farnham, musical director and piano, Howard Alden, guitar, Steve Gilmore, bass, Rich DeRosa, drums, Randy Sandke, trumpet, and on selected tracks, Chris Potter, alto saxophone, Robert Trowers, trombone, Ken Peplowski, tenor saxophone and clarinet.

**October 28–30, 1996:** *Let's Face the Music: The Songs of Irving Berlin.* Concord CD 4759. Allen Farnham, musical director and piano, Al Gafa, acoustic and electric guitars, Rich DeRosa, drums and synthesizer, Steve Gilmore, bass, Jerry Dodgion, alto saxophone and flute, Gregory Gisbert, trumpet and flügelhorn, Conrad Herwig, trombone, Chris Potter, tenor saxophone, clarinet, and alto flute.

**October 21, 22, and 24, 1997:** *Someone to Watch Over Me: The Songs of George Gershwin.* Concord CD 4798. Allen Farnham, music director and piano, Chris Potter, tenor saxophone and alto flute, Howard Alden, guitar, Randy Sandke, trumpet and flügelhorn, Conrad Herwig, trombone, Jerry Dodgion, alto sax and alto flute, Rich DeRosa, drums, Steve Gilmore, bass, Dick Sarpola, bass.

**October 27–29, 1998:** *From Broken Hearts to Blue Skies.* Concord CD 4857. Allen Farnham, musical director and piano, Al Gafa, guitar, Steve Gilmore, bass, Rich DeRosa, drums, Dick Oatts, tenor and soprano saxophones and alto flute, Jon Gordon, alto saxophone and flute, Greg Gisbert, trumpet and flügelhorn, John Fedchock, trombone.

**March 28–30, 2000:** *Hearts and Minds.* Concord CD 4897. Allen Farnham, musical director and piano, Paul Meyers, electric and acoustic guitars, Steve Gilmore, bass, Dennis Irwin, bass, Tim Horner and Vanderlei Pereira, drums, Thiago DeMello, percussion, Dick Oatts, tenor saxophone.

*Compilations*

Susannah McCorkle's recorded work has appeared on a number of compilations, including, but not limited to, the following:

*Ballad Essentials.* Concord CD 2129. Compilation of her recorded songs with various instrumentalists from 1983 to 2000.

*From Pearl Harbor to VJ Day.* Concord CD 4959.

*Jazz Moods: Brazilian Romance.* Concord CD 5200–2.

*Jazz Moods: Jazz at Love's End.* Concord CD 5207–2.

*Concord Jazz Christmas.* Concord CD 4613. On "The Secret Christmas."

*Most Requested Songs.* Concord CD 4976. Compilation of recorded songs with various instrumentalists from 1977 to 2000.

*Playboy: Jazz After Dark.* Playboy/Concord CD 2–7507–2.

*S'Wonderful: Concord Jazz Salutes Ira Gershwin.* Concord CD 4741.

*Women in Jazz.* Concord CD 4957.

# Bibliography

*Short Fiction and Nonfiction by Susannah McCorkle*

"The Dog." Nonfiction. *American Girl* (the Girl Scouts Magazine) award, October 1959.

Numerous articles (as Susan Savage) as contributing editor to the *Pelican,* satirical magazine of the University of California at Berkeley, 1963–68.

"A Good Man Is Hard to Find" (as Susanna Glenn). Unpublished, 1969.

"The Decline of American Femininity." Unpublished, March 1969.

"Cordelia" (as Susanna Glenn). *Mademoiselle* college issue prize-winning story, August 1969.

"Ramona in Southland." 1970. Revised as "Ramona by the Sea." *Mademoiselle* (winner, College Fiction Competition), October 1973, and in *Prize Stories 1975, The O. Henry Awards.*

"Rides." Unpublished short story, 1971.

"An Episode" (condensation of "The Lover Who Got Locked Out of the Garden"). *New Idea* (Australia), April 1974.

"The Lover Who Got Locked Out of the Garden." *Woman's Journal* (U.K.), August 1977.

"The Bearer." *Woman's Journal* (U.K.), *Good Housekeeping* (U.K.), *Fair Lady* (South Africa), *Margriet* (Holland), *Allers Famalie Journal* (Norway), 1978.

"The Woman in 2B." *Woman* (U.K.), *Fair Lady* (South Africa), *Anna* (Finland), *Svensk Damtidning* (Sweden), June 3, 1978.

"The Woman Across the Room." *Woman's Journal* (U.K.), *Good Housekeeping* (U.K.), *Female* (Singapore), *Fair Lady* (South Africa), *Svensk Damtidning* (Sweden), *New Idea* (Australia), *Margriet* (Holland), 1979.

"George, Mary and the Babysitter." *Woman's Journal, New Idea* (Australia), *Female* (Singapore), 1978–79.

"My Lover's Wife." *Woman's Journal* (U.K.), *Svensk Damtidning* (Sweden), *Fair Lady* (South Africa), *Alt For Damerne* (Denmark), *Female* (Singapore), 1977–78.

"I Was a Compulsive Overeater." 1978. *Huisgemoot* (South Africa), *Ladies' Home Journal,* 1982.

"Love in a Department Store." Unpublished story, July 1979.

"Mr. Dunphy." *New York,* October 15, 1979.

"Caroline's Mother." Unpublished story, 1979.

"French Lessons." *Sarie* (South Africa, Afrikaans magazine under mandatory Afrikaans pseudonym: Susan Kruger), November 1979.

"At the Keyhole Club." Unpublished story, 1979–82.

"The Kid Who Loved the Marx Brothers." Unpublished article about lyricist Dick Vosburgh, 1980.

"George LeMoine." Unpublished article, 1980.

"Barney Beck, Beekeeper." Unpublished article, 1980.

"The Little Girl Who Got Bored." Unpublished story, 1980.

"Theodora Skipitares." Unpublished article, 1980.

"Assault in Central Park." Unpublished article, October 1980.

"Diary of a Chorus Girl." Commissioned for *Cosmopolitan* but unpublished, 1981.

"Harry's Wives." *Margriet* (Holland) and *Female* (Singapore), June 1982.

"Good Night." *Female* (Singapore), *Margriet* (Holland), October 1982.

"The Prisoner of Plato's Retreat, A Modern Morality Tale." Unpublished story, 1982.

"Fellow Travelers." Formerly "Leonard's World." *Newsday,* April 14, 1983.

"Waiting." *Cosmopolitan, Woman* (U.K.), *Fair Lady* (South Africa), *Svensk Damtidning* (Sweden), *Margriet* (Holland), October 1983.

"Without Him." *Woman's Journal* (U.K.), 1983.

"Taking a Vacation With a Type-A Man." Unpublished article, 1990.

Paragraph in "Metropolitan Diary" about a woman buying apples on the street: "a dead ringer for a Frans Hals." *New York Times,* October 16, 1991.

"I Swear I Won't Call No Copper." *New York Times Magazine,* January 9, 1994.

"The Mother of Us All—Ethel Waters." *American Heritage,* February–March 1994.

"Back to Bessie." *American Heritage,* November 1997.

"Always: A Singer's Journey Through the Life of Irving Berlin." *American Heritage,* November 1998.

"Mae West, Why She's a Bigger Presence Now than Ever." *American Heritage,* September–October 2001.


*Unfinished Longer Works by Susannah McCorkle*

*The Quitter.* 1970–71. A mystery "about my short and unsuccessful life." A new tenant of a bell-tower apartment in Rome begins to seek clues about the mysteriously vanished previous tenant, and gradually comes to realize that they are the same person.

*Closer to Home.* Two versions, 1980 and 1985. A mystery about a woman's failing marriage and her affair with Henry Rosenbaum, "a cruel coin dealer." Said McCorkle, "It is a book about contemporary relationships—It has one character in it who's a magician, but it's mainly about single adults in New York."

*A Singing Life/Because of Billie.* 1994–95. A proposal for a "book about my life as a singer," said McCorkle, "but I would really love to do a book about the singers and songs of the 20s, 30s and 40s."

*The Listening Room.* 1996. McCorkle described this as a "two-character play about a singer's private life."

*The Upside of Down, a Companion Guide to Depression.* 1998–99. An article idea, then a book proposal, in which Susannah suggested including a CD of her recordings on the theme of overcoming depression, e.g., "Blue Skies" and "Down."

*Secrets in Piazza Navona.* 1999–2001. A memoir based on diaries written in 1970–72 when Susannah lived in Rome and fell in love with Billie Holiday's singing, thirties jazz, and a musician. Includes a prologue and thirteen chapters.

*Selected Readings about Depression, Suicide, and Afflicted Artists*

Alvarez, A. *The Savage God: A Study of Suicide.* Norton, 1990.

Blauner, Susan Rose. *How I Stayed Alive When My Brain Was Trying to Kill Me.* William Morrow, 2002.

Colt, George Howe. *The Enigma of Suicide.* Simon and Schuster, 1991.

DeSalvo, Louise A. *Virginia Woolf.* Beacon Press, 1989.

Fine, Carla. *No Time to Say Goodbye: Surviving the Suicide of a Loved One.* Broadway Books, 2002.

Fitzgerald, F. Scott *The Crack-Up.* Reissue ed. New Directions, 1993.

Hendin, Herbert. *Suicide in America.* Norton, 1995.

Hewett, John H. *After Suicide.* Westminster John Knox Press, 1980.

Heyman, Ronald. *The Death and Life of Sylvia Plath.* William Heinemann, 1991.

Jackson-Triche, Maga, Kenneth B. Wells, and Katherine Minnium. *Beating Depression, the Journey to Hope.* McGraw-Hill, 2002.

Jamison, Kay Redfield. *Night Falls Fast: Understanding Suicide.* Knopf, 1999.

———. *Touched with Fire: Manic Depressive Illness and the Artistic Temperament.* Free Press, 1993.

———. *An Unquiet Mind: A Memoir of Moods and Madness.* Knopf, 1995.

Kaysen, Susanna. *Girl, Interrupted.* Random House, 1995.

Koplewicz, Harold S. *More than Moody: Recognizing and Treating Adolescent Depression.* G. P. Putnam's Sons, 2002.

Kushner, Howard L. *Self-Destruction in the Promised Land.* Rutgers University Press, 1989.

Middlebrook, Diane Wood. *Anne Sexton: A Biography.* Houghton Mifflin, 1991.

Shneidman, Edwin S. *The Suicidal Mind.* Oxford University Press, 1996.

Smith, Judie. *Coping With Suicide.* Rosen Publishing Group, 1989.

Solomon, Andrew. *The Noonday Demon: An Atlas of Depression.* Scribner's, 2001.

Stevenson, Anne. *Bitter Fame: A Biography of Sylvia Plath.* Gardners Books, 1991.

Stout, James T. *Bipolar Disorder: Rebuilding Your Life.* Cypress House, 2002.

Styron, William. *Darkness Visible: A Memoir of Madness.* Random House, 1990.

Torrey, E. Fuller. *Out of the Shadows: Confronting America's Mental Illness Crisis.* John Wiley and Sons, 1996.

# *Index*

Quotation marks enclose: titles of concerts and songs. Titles of books, journals, movies, musicals, newspapers, and recordings (record, CD, etc.) are in italics.

McCorkle, Susannah (*continued*)
299; *Most Requested Songs,* 260,
287; *The Music of Harry Warren,*
113, 297; *The Music of Jerome
Kern,* 117; *The Music of Richard
Rodgers,* 113, 297; *New York Songs,*
189; *No More Blues,* 172; *Over the
Rainbow: The Songs of E. Y. "Yip"
Harburg,* 130; *The People That You
Never Get to Love,* 143, 144, 155,
158, 159; *Someone to Watch Over
Me,* 217; *The Songs of Mercer,* 118;
*Thanks for the Memory,* 152, 159;
*Thanks for the Memory: Songs of
Leo Robin,* 159, 298

songs: "All of Me," 171; "Alone Too
Long," 126; "Anything Goes," 205;
"As Time Goes By," 158; "At the
Jazz Band Ball," 118; "Autumn in
New York," 158; "Baby Won't
You Please Come Home," 84, 149;
"The Ballad of Pearly Sue," 172;
"Basin Street Blues," 107; "Billie's
Blues," 105, 183; "Blue Moon," 73,
74; "Blues in the Night," 174; "Bye
Bye Blues," 235; "By the Time I
Get to Phoenix," 99, 159, 160, 172,
174; "Caminos Cruzados," 196,
228; "Can't Take You Nowhere,"
172; "Careless Love," 84, 86; "Cen-
sorship Medley," 207; "Chega de
Saudade," 172; "The Christmas
Song," 162; "Come On, Get
Happy," 148; "Come Rain or
Come Shine," 84; "The Computer
Age," 243; "Da Man Ai Love"
(The Man I Love), 73; "The Day
We Said Goodbye," 186;
"Desafinado," 224; "Do Nothing
Till You Hear From Me," 220;
"Don't Fence Me In," 197; "Don't
Look at Me That Way," 106; "Don't
Smoke in Bed," 109; "Down," 243; "Do You Miss New

York?," 243; "Easy Come, Easy
Go," 111; "Easy to Love," 206;
"Estate," 187; "Everything's Been
Done Before," 172, 197; "Evolu-
tion," 243; "Exactly Like You," 93;
"Faint Music," 228; "Fascinating
Rhythm," 73; "Feet Do Your
Stuff," 243; "The Folks Who Live
on the Hill," 167; "Fools Rush In,"
175; "For All We Know," 158,
243; "42nd Street," 174; "A Friend
Like Me," 194; "From This
Moment On," 205; "Goodbye Lit-
tle Dream," 206; "Happiness," 186;
"Haunted Heart," 243; "He Loves
Me," 197; "The Hungry Years,"
144; "I Ain't Gonna Play No Sec-
ond Fiddle," 229; "I Can Dream,
Can't I?," 243; "I Can't Give You
Anything but Love," 213; "I Don't
Want to Set the World on Fire,"
243; "I'd Rather Lead a Band,"
194; "If I Only Had a Heart," 134;
"If Someday Comes Ever Again,"
139; "I Got Rhythm," 224; "I
Gotta Right to Sing the Blues,"
197; "I Got What It Takes," 197;
"I'll Be Around," 111; "I Love a
Film Cliché," 109, 116; "I Love
My Man," 93; "I Loves You,
Porky," 224; "I'm in Love Again,"
106; "Intuition," 107; "I Remem-
ber Bill," 200; "Is It an Earth-
quake?," 197; "I Thought About
You," 220; It's Anybody's Spring,"
158 ; "It's a Pity to Say Good-
night," 158; "It's So Peaceful in the
Country," 140; "I've Grown
Accustomed to Her Face," 134; "I
Wanna Be a Sideman," 235; "I
Want to Be Loved by You," 104;
"I Wish I Were in Love Again,"
228; "Just One of Those Things,"
206; "The Lady Is a Tramp," 149,